AF841222

SPATIAL COGNITION

UNIVERSITY OF SUNDERLAND
WITHDRAWN

UNIVERSITY OF SUNDERLAND
UNIVERSITY LIBRARY

ADVANCES IN CONSCIOUSNESS RESEARCH

ADVANCES IN CONSCIOUSNESS RESEARCH provides a forum for scholars from different scientific disciplines and fields of knowledge who study consciousness in its multifaceted aspects. Thus the Series will include (but not be limited to) the various areas of cognitive science, including cognitive psychology, linguistics, brain science and philosophy. The orientation of the Series is toward developing new interdisciplinary and integrative approaches for the investigation, description and theory of consciousness, as well as the practical consequences of this research for the individual and society.

Series B: Research in Progress. Experimental, descriptive and clinical research in consciousness.

EDITOR

Maxim I. Stamenov
(*Bulgarian Academy of Sciences*)

EDITORIAL BOARD

David Chalmers (*University of Arizona*)
Gordon G. Globus (*University of California at Irvine*)
Ray Jackendoff (*Brandeis University*)
Christof Koch (*California Institute of Technology*)
Stephen Kosslyn (*Harvard University*)
Earl Mac Cormac (*Duke University*)
George Mandler (*University of California at San Diego*)
John R. Searle (*University of California at Berkeley*)
Petra Stoerig (*Universität Düsseldorf*)
Francisco Varela (*C.R.E.A., Ecole Polytechnique, Paris*)

Volume 26

Seán Ó Nualláin (ed.)

Spatial Cognition: Foundations and applications

Selected papers from Mind III,
Annual Conference of the Cognitive Science Society of Ireland, 1998.

SPATIAL COGNITION

FOUNDATIONS AND APPLICATIONS

SELECTED PAPERS FROM MIND III,
ANNUAL CONFERENCE OF THE
COGNITIVE SCIENCE SOCIETY OF IRELAND, 1998

Edited by

SEÁN Ó NUALLÁIN
Nous Research and Dublin City University

JOHN BENJAMINS PUBLISHING COMPANY
AMSTERDAM/PHILADELPHIA

The paper used in this publication meets the minimum requirements of American National Standard for Information Sciences — Permanence of Paper for Printed Library Materials, ANSI Z39.48–1984.

UNIVERSITY OF SUNDERLAND
SP LIBRARY
Class No.
153.152 OS8
Access No.
111118098 3
Order No.
ND03002897
UNIVERSITY OF SUNDERLAND
WITHDRAWN

Library of Congress Cataloging-in-Publication Data

Mind (Conference) (3rd : Dublin City University)
Spatial cognition: Foundations and applications: selected papers from Mind III, Annual Conference of the Cognitive Science Society of Ireland, 1998 / edited by Seán Ó Nualláin.
p. cm. -- (Advances in consciousness research, ISSN 1381-589X ; v. 26)
Includes bibliographical references and indexes.
1. Spatial behavior--Congresses. 2. Space perception--Congresses. 3. Personal space--Congresses. I. Ó Nualláin, Seán. II. Title. II. Series.
BF469.M56 2000
153.7'52--dc21 00-044499
ISBN 90 272 5146 0 (Eur.) / 1 55619 842 6 (US) (Pb)

© 2000 - John Benjamins B.V.
No part of this book may be reproduced in any form, by print, photoprint, microfilm, or any other means, without written permission from the publisher.

John Benjamins Publishing Co. • P.O.Box 75577 • 1070 AN Amsterdam • The Netherlands
John Benjamins North America • P.O.Box 27519 • Philadelphia PA 19118-0519 • USA

Table of Contents

Introduction: Spatial Cognition – Foundations and Applications ix
Seán Ó Nualláin

Part I
Epistemological Issues

Men and Women, Maps and Minds: Cognitive bases of sex-related differences in reading and interpreting maps 3
Gary L. Allen

A Theoretical Framework for the Study of Spatial Cognition 19
Maurizio Tirassa, Antonella Carassa and Giuliano Geminiani

Describers and Explorers: A method for investigating cognitive maps 33
Antonella Carassa, Alessia Aprigliano and Giuliano Geminiani

The Functional Separability of Self-Reference and Object-to-Object Systems in Spatial Memory 45
M. Jeanne Sholl

In Search for an Overall Organizing Principle in Spatial Mental Models: A question of inference 69
Robin Hörnig, Berry Claus and Klaus Eyferth

Describing the Topology of Spherical Regions using the 'RCC' Formalism 83
Nicholas Mark Gotts

Cognitive Mapping in Rats and Humans: The tent-maze, a place learning task in visually disconnected environments 105
Marie-Claude Grobéty, Muriel Morand and Françoise Schenk

Spatial Cognition Without Spatial Concepts 127
Arnold Smith

Space Under Stress: Spatial understanding and new media technologies 137
Chris Speed and Deborah García-Tobin

PART II
Software Applications: Multimedia, GIS, diagrammatic reasoning and beyond

CHAMELEON Meets Spatial Cognition 149
Paul Mc Kevitt

SONAS: Multimodal, Multi-User Interaction with a Modelled Environment 171
John Kelleher, Tom Doris, Qamir Hussain, DCU, and Seán Ó Nualláin

Designing Real-Time Software Advisors for 3D Spatial Operations 185
Mike and Ann Eisenberg

Using Spatial Semantics to Discover and Verify Diagrammatic Demonstrations of Geometric Propositions 199
Robert K. Lindsay

Formal Specifications of Image Schemata for Interoperability in Geographic Information Systems 213
Andrew U. Frank and Martin Raubal

Using a Spatial Display to Represent the Temporal Structure of Multimedia Documents 233
Mireille Bétrancourt, Anne Pellegrin and Laurent Tardif

PART III
Language and Space

A Computational Multi-layered Model for the Interpretation of Locative Expressions 249
Luca Anibaldi and Seán Ó Nualláin

The Composition of Conceptual Structure for Spatial Motion Imperatives 267
John Gurney and Elizabeth Klipple

Modelling Spatial Inferences in Text Understanding 285
Ute Schmid, Sylvia Wiebrock and Fritz Wysotzki

Linguistic and Graphical Representations and the Characterisation of Individual Differences 299
Keith Stenning and Padraic Monaghan

PART IV
Memory, Consciousness and Space

Given-New Versus New-Given? An analysis of reading times for spatial descriptions 317
Thom Baguley and Stephen J. Payne

A Connectionist Model of the Processes Involved in Generating and Exploring Visual Mental Images 329
Mathias Bollaert

Working Memory and Mental Synthesis: A dual-task approach 347
David G. Pearson and Robert H. Logie.

Name Index 361

Subject Index 363

Acknowledgement

I wish to thank Velibor Korolija, Mary Hegarty, and John Kelleher for their help in organising the event. Dedicated to the people of Omagh, and all other victims of arbitrary borders.

Introduction

Spatial Cognition – Foundations and applications

Seán Ó Nualláin

Mind III, the third annual conference of the Cognitive Science Society of Ireland (CSSI), took place in DCU from August 17 to August 19, 1998. It was sponsored by Nous Research (nous@dna.ie). The Mind conferences focus on a different theme every year; in 1998, 55 researchers from 10 different countries representing the disciplines of Psychology, Computer Science, Linguistics and Geography convened, to discuss how people think and communicate about space. With respect to consciousness studies, several of the papers here discuss the detailed structure of the representation of space in short term memory (STM).

Cognitive scientists study many different phenomena within the general topic of spatial cognition. Those concerned with environmental cognition study people's internal "cognitive maps" of their environment, and how they learn the layout of new places they visit. Other cognitive scientists are concerned with how we communicate about space, e.g. in giving route directions. Some others study the power of spatial metaphors, both in language and graphics, for communicating and reasoning about non-spatial information.

Apart from the obvious human interest of this research, there are massive technological consequences. We are moving fast into the age of intelligent multimedia, an age in which computers will show an ability to process multimodal inputs in real time. These advances have highlighted the need to better understand how people think about space, so that we can design "user-friendly" computer and information systems. For example, cognitive science is informing the development of computer interfaces, multimedia, virtual reality and in-car navigation systems.

This collection is divided into four thematic sections. The first is epistemological issues, where the topics range from a formalization of the topology of spherical regions to descriptions of gender differences in spatial cognition and the way in which usual mass media disrupt normal spatial intuitions. We then venture into the area of software applications. We find here an intriguing range of applications, from intelligent multimedia (intellimedia) products which process multimodal signals (indeed, in the case of the Sonas system, multi-user multimodal signals) in real time, to geographical information systems (GIS) and tools for diagrammatic reasoning. The third section's analysis of space and language emerges from questions like how symbols like cognitive maps arise from sensory stimulation. The critical issues — for example the semantics of prepositions like "at" and "across" — merge here with questions about how to represent sentences involving them in modelled environments. Finally we come to the section most relevant to this Advances in Consciousness Research series; memory, consciousness, and space. We are concerned here in particular with the issue of unpacking the old coarse-grained STM versus LTM dichotomy, and in particular articulating the detailed structure of the former.

Section I. Epistemological issues

Gary Allen, with whose contribution we open this book, must be lauded for his courage! On the one hand, he is exploring the politically sensitive area of cognitive sex differences; on the other, he is concerned with the development of a conceptual taxonomy for spatial abilities in which these differences will emerge in some principled fashion. His conclusions, which focus, inter alia, on sex differences with respect to the use of working memory, make interesting reading indeed. (In section four, we shall note a paper by Pearson and Logie that re-addresses this issue of working memory).

The following three contributions all focus on a theme central to this area; the world considered in terms of the set of possible actions one can perform on it (egocentric cognition) or as some kind of shared map (intersubjective cognition) — Ó Nualláin (1995, 2000), contains an analysis of this distinction. Tirassa's counterpoint to this distinction is "coupled" versus "decoupled" architectures. Only the latter can truly be termed representational. The former can be further divided into pure reflex actions, and information pickup in a Gibsonian manner based on affordances. Representational architectures, on the other hand, begin with the deictic, where organisms represent only what they can perceive. Once object permanence (in the Piagetian sense) is achieved, we enter the realm of base-level representations. The formal, "meta" level, accessible only to higher primates, involves the ability to represent one's own representations. Tiarassa's work is very influenced by the situated cognition view that interaction is key. Carassa et al.'s work, which follows, analyses the shift that occurs from egocentric to intersubjective cognition as familiarity with a scene grows.

Sholl's superb paper, which follows, is concerned about finding experimental evidence for the operational distinction between self-reference (egocentric/coupled) and allocentric (intersubjective/decoupled) systems. She points out that this distinction has a neuroscience basis; experimental work on the hippocampus has indicated that it acts as a locus for egocentric knowledge in rats as in humans. The ingenious experiments described in this paper indicate independent access to the two systems. Hörnig et al.'s work on the same general theme considers Franklin and Tversky's schema as they search for an overall organising principle for mental models. Paradoxically, they find that one may have an allocentric reference frame in an egocentric mental model. Gott's work continues this subsection. With many examples, he shows how his RCC formalism can handle 2–D regions forming part of a spherical surface like Earth's. He is honest about the limitations of these formalisms; there are constraints even on these surfaces, let alone the surfaces defined by Riemann and other geometries, that RCC cannot handle.

Following is a precipitous decline from these theoretical heights to an engaging empirical paper. Again referencing O'Keefe's and Nadel's work on the hippocampus as a cognitive map, Grobéty et al. address the issue of whether cognitive maps are route-like or more flexible. Both rats and humans, they argue, can orient in a visually homogeneous environment.

It is time to introduce at least one non-believer. Smith points out the ambiguity of "on" in such sentences as

Stand on the sidewalk.
The house is on the lake.

We who are working on the Sonas system (which bears mine and Arnold's initials and is Gaelic for "happiness") believe that such sentences can fully be analysed in a large percentage of cases by combining information from the reference and the theme objects, verb and preposition. And no, it's not easy, nor is there a guarantee of success. However, Smith's paper is going for bigger game; the western worldview itself, and its drive to reduction and analysis.

Such a worldview, he argues, must be learned. Continuing on the "worldview" theme, Speed et al. show how new media technologies produce counterintuitive results with respect to the use of spatial expressions. A feed taken from a helicopter concerning traffic can end in much user confusion with the use of "behind", "below", etc. Speed et al.'s conclusion is that Cartesian 3-D space is as inadequate for this type of description as Cartesian dualism is bruited to be for the description of the mind.

Section II. Software applications, multimedia, GIS, diagrammatic reasoning and beyond

In this section, we detect a range of new techniques, at least through a glass darkly. Intellimedia products designed to achieve the age-old goal of "making computers invisible" by making the products so small, and their use so natural, that nobody notices their being used, will begin this section. We then move on to aids to diagrammatic reasoning that will perhaps help us all improve our reasoning abilities. It is too much obviously, to expect that we will all be capable of the insights of a Kékulé, Faraday or Einstein as a result of such products.

At a time when he was groping toward the cyclic model of Benzene which made him famous, Kékulé had a dream involving the archetypal image of a snake swallowing its own tail (though it has to be said that Kékulé gave several different versions of this story). Faraday's insight, followed up by Maxwell, conceived of the electromagnetic medium as fluid under stress, and the electromagnetic field as vortices in the fluid. Lastly, Einstein's investigation of special relativity began with a thought experiment in which he imagined riding astride a light beam.

Paul McKevitt's paper gives an introduction to the general topic of intellimedia, as exemplified by Aalborg's "Chameleon" system. He describes other systems such as those emerging from the Saarbrucken Vitra (visual translator) environment: Soccer (which is self explanatory!) and Moses, which shows how a user generates step — by-step route information. Situated artificial communicators are exemplified by Richert's system, which shows how a model airplane can be constructed from wooden bits by human instructions. Okada's Aesopworld, McKevitt would agree, is hamstrung by a pre-Kantian (and perhaps pre-pre-Socratic) view of mind. Chameleon itself is an exciting system which accepts multimodal input, with a dialogue manager to handle the natural language element, a gesture recogniser to track 2D pointing gestures, a laser system to act as a system pointer as the system explains directions, and customised speech and syntax/semantics modules. The frame-based knowledge representation and the blackboard model to integrate the different modalities are relatively undeveloped, but the system's "Topsy" learning capacity adds some valuable functionality.

The SONAS system, still in its infancy, is introduced by John Kelleher, Tom Doris and Qamir Hussain. Its multimodal and multiuser environment we have previously mentioned; we are currently experimenting with the basic architecture across a range of different graphics environments, including VRML, and OPENGL.

The limitations of this print medium prevent proper appreciation of the next paper by the Eisenbergs. Hypergami is an educational application for the creation of polyhedra; there exist advisors that suggest how to operate on these. The charm of these structures eludes the written word or two-dimensional diagram. Bob Lindsay's paper for this volume "Using spatial semantics to discover and verify diagrammatic demonstrations of geometric propositions" differs from and is considerably more informative than the original conference title "Discovering diagrammatic representations". As he points out, diagrams and maps help preserve spatial representations; language-like representations don't do so. We are, in a sense, back to the killing fields of the mental imagery debate about whether the representations and processes underlying expression of mental images are analog or propositional. Lindsay would probably agree with Shephard's conclusion that mental imagery and its associated cognitive processes are functionally similar to vision processing. Diagrams must be reflected on, with respect to reasoning, vis à vis their comprehension, generation and use. Lindsay's work, which dates back thirty years, must be considered in the context of complementary work by Iwaski, Barwise, MacDougal, and others.

Lindsay emphasises that what geometric rules are about is constraints. These can be expressed in forms as simple as spreadsheets. He goes on to detail the Archimedes system. Andrew Frank, who was one of our keynote speakers, emphasises that a formal specifications of spatial objects and relations is critical for geographical information systems (GIS). He speculates that image schemata (in the Lakoff-Johnson sense) for geographic space are different from those for table-top space. With many references, he gives a thorough description of image schemata in general, passing on to an exemplification before reaching his conclusions.

Betrancourt et al. attack the problem of conveying the temporal structure of multimedia documents. After reviewing spatial mulitimedia authoring problems and the cognition literature, they indicate how their system "Madeus" conveys temoral organisation by a spatial description. With a schorlarly thoroughness, they analyse some experimental results. Finally, on http://www.compapp.dcu.ie/~tdoris/mind3.html, the reader can view a set of papers that didn't make it into this book.

Section III. Language and Space

We begin this section with two papers on the intrinsically difficult topic of lexical semantics of spatial expressions. Smith's paper in section I has given us a basic insight into how complicated this area is; simply put, the use of the preposition "in" in these two (three!) sentences;

Put the bun in the oven
Bloomsday first took place in Dublin

is vastly different. How is a computer meant to process sentences involving such expressions, with the inherent possibility of nightmarish ambiguity ?

One solution, advocated by Landau and Jackendoff (see Anibaldi's paper) is that there exists only one spatial representation for the geometric properties of objects and the spatial relationships between them. If only life were so simple!

For a start, prepositions can be divided between location ("at"), motion ("across") and various misfits like "over". "At" can be said to give the coincidence of a point-object with a point-place in a cognitive map. "Across", in common with other motion prepositions, defines a field of directed lines with respect to the ground, not the orientation of a path. Specifically, "across" involves mapping of ground to volume, volume to area, then the motion is specified. A preposition, then, can either locate the end of a trajectory with respect to the ground, or describe the location of a figure with respect to a reference object. Briefly, a figure, which can be any shape or dimensionality, is the object whose disposition is at issue, and the ground (which can be any shape) is the object conceived of as stationary. However figure/ground information does not yield anything like as much information as we need; *pace* Landau - Jackendoff.

We can also safely deny that the structure of space as encoded by language is given by vision. With that basic discussion which, as Anibaldi's paper makes clear, owes much to the work of Annette Herskovits, let's get to the matter at hand. Gurney and Klipple's paper is concerned with the composition of conceptual structure for spatial motion imperatives. Their work focuses on a 3D geographical information system used, perhaps unfortunately, for military purposes. They focus on such expressions as "Crawl straight ahead" and "Look to the South East". They conclude that language and motion must concern itself with coordinate systems, axes, and both motion and direction vectors. As for the problems pointed out by Smith, they propose with touching American optimism that vagueness can be handled by pragmatics and world knowledge. The parser itself implements principles and parameters syntax.

Anibaldi's and my paper proposes a rich solution to the problem of spatial prepositions. The paper will repay careful reading; briefly, we propose that spatial expressions admit of conceptual, semantic, and geometric levels of analysis. The conceptual level reflects information elicited from the object's place in an ontology and thus can inform us about selectional restrictions. The semantic level involves the mappings to point, area, and volume that the Herskovits approach requires. Finally, the pragmatic level caters for the semantic shift evidenced in the use of "on" here:

The house is on the lake.
The cup is on the saucer.

Tensors are one of the most interesting recent mathematical approaches to modelling mental processes. (See Hoffman's paper in Volume 9 of this series.) The essential inspiration is that many cognitive acts involve mapping entities between spaces of different dimensionalities. For example, the bone-joints (shoulder, wrist, elbow, etc.) we use as we perform an act like catching an object together define a very high dimensional space. Yet the target is a single point in four-dimensional space (I include time). The tensorial theory of mind insists that such transfer of invariants is the core of cognition; in fact, the principles of invariance themselves are analogous to Kantian categories. Schmid et al.'s paper is concerned with the problem of modelling spatial inferences in text understanding. They argue that a tensorial approach works better for spatial relation modelling than usual qualitative approaches. We conclude this section with Stenning and Monaghan's comprehensive review of experimental work focussed on linguistic and graphical representations. Stenning and Monaghan themselves focus eventually on a study that established that diagrammatic teaching using Hyperprof extended students' competence. On the way they cite evidence that mental models, and Euler's circles are manifestations of the same abstract algorithm. Consequently, we should all have massive spatial reasoning abilities; however, performance-competence issue analogous to that in linguistics intervenes. Stenning et al.'s engagement with the area is most impressive.

Section IV. Memory Consciousness and Space

Part of the educational experience of Mind-3 was the precision of the analyses of the structure of memory. Baguley's neat demonstration opens this section for us. He argues that episodic construction trace is a fundamental concept in the analysis of short term memory. There is a considerable computational cost for introducing new objects with respect to old objects. Analysis of processing costs during reading are done in the context of mental models theory, and the experiments make interesting reading.

We end with two enthralling experimental and computational contributions to this, the topic most relevant to consciousness studies. Bollaert first performed experiments on mental manipulation, and then ran a simulation compatible with his and other experimental results. His hypotheses included an expectation that response times would be longer with larger inter-object paths, and that stated spatial relations should result in a shorter response time than unstated such. This eventual model proposes three separate modules; an object memory for higher visual areas, a feature memory for intermediate visual areas, and a shape memory for retinotopically organised areas. His neural network simulation shows patterns compatible with the results of the experiments. Finally, we come to the article closest to the expectations that might be hatched by the writer of this book's blurb. Pearson and Logie's paper is mainly a review proposing a framework in which specialist components act as temporary storage buffers for visual-spatial and verbal material, while a central executive generates and maintains visual images.

I hope these pages convey some of the excitement of the event.

Reference

Ó Nualláin, Sean (1995, 2000) *The Search for Mind.* Exeter: Intellect.

Part I

Epistemological Issues

Men and Women, Maps and Minds

Cognitive bases of sex-related differences in reading and interpreting maps

Gary L. Allen
University of South Carolina

The study of sex-related differences in spatial cognition is motivated in large part by natural curiosity about the evolution of mind. Currently, psychologists, philosophers, and biologists appear to be rather distant from a mutually satisfactory account of how co-actions between genetic and environmental influences have resulted in cognitive differences so pervasive that often they can be detected statistically in modest-sized samples differentiated only on the basis of sex. Of course, a satisfactory account of how sex-related differences in spatial abilities may have evolved must be based on a solid empirical accounting of what differences actually exist, an undertaking that has proven challenging (Montello, Lovelace, Golledge & Self in press; Voyer, Voyer & Bryden 1995). Part of the difficulty in providing this empirical accounting is the lack of a conceptual taxonomy for spatial abilities.

The spatial domain is multifaceted (Lohman 1988), and a male advantage is not uniform across the domain. The most reliable differences have been found on tests requiring the speeded rotation of abstract figures (e.g., Mumaw, Pellegrino, Carter & Kail 1984), judgments of horizontality or verticality in the presence of competing frames of reference (e.g., Witkin, Dyk, Patterson, Goodenough & Karp 1962), learning or tracing mazes (e.g., Porteus 1965), and designation of left and right turns (e.g., Money, Alexander & Walker 1965). In large-scale spatial tasks, differences have been reported for navigational strategies, with men tending to rely on metric distance and direction information more frequently than women, whose behavior reflects a tendency to use proximal landmarks (Baker 1981; Bever 1992; Lawton 1994).

Clearly, these differences do not reflect a unitary domain. Instead, these and other findings suggest the existence of several different functional families of spatial abilities (see Allen 1999). Speeded rotation of figures, along with other abilities involving small figural stimuli, may be thought of as comprising a group of abilities dedicated to the function of object identification, a "What is it?" family of abilities. Such a family may have evolved in the service of identifying and recognizing small objects from a stationary perspective when the objects are viewed from various perspectives, partially obscured, embedded within another object, or fragmented. In contrast, the abilities to determine horizontal and vertical axes, to identify left and right turns, and to negotiate routes may be thought of as constituents of a group of abilities dedicated to maintenance of orientation, a "Where am I?" family of abilities. Such a family may have evolved for the purpose of keeping a mobile traveler oriented with respect to familiar locations.

What would these functional families of abilities have to do with map reading and interpretation? Traditional maps involve arrays of small objects viewed from a fixed perspective, not unlike the stimulus conditions pertinent to the family of abilities dedicated to object identification. Yet, the purpose of object arrays in maps is to facilitate oriented navigation, a purpose pertinent to the family of abilities dedicated to maintaining orientation. Thus, map reading could be construed as involving cognitive translations back and forth between families of abilities. In view of the fact that sex-related differences have been found within each of these two functional families, it is not surprising that such differences have also been found on aspects of map reading and interpretation (e.g., Beatty & Troster 1987; Chang & Antes 1987). However, these differences have been described as specific rather than general. Women have been found to be at a disadvantage compared to men on map reading tasks that require labeling relations among locations and on map drawing tasks that involve no pre-determined frame of reference. Otherwise, sex-related differences have not been reliably documented (see Gilmartin 1986; Gilmartin & Patton 1984).

On the one hand, it is noteworthy that sex-related differences in map reading and interpretation may be confined to problems involving the use of directional terms and the application of spatial frames of reference in general. On the other hand, these problems are not trivial. From a theoretical perspective, they may provide a fuller understanding of the cognitive basis for sex-related differences in spatial cognition, thus providing a very small but useful step towards the goal of eventually understanding the larger picture of the differential evolution of cognitive abilities. From a practical point of view, these difficulties with maps could have profound consequences for wayfinding success and, by extension, have important implications for the design of electronic navigational aids. Thus, further research into sex-related differences in map reading and interpretation is motivated by theoretical and practical concerns.

The aforementioned considerations provide a reasonable rationale for the empirical study of map reading and interpretation skills aimed at identifying and examining specific aspects of these skills that yield performance differences between men and women. Based on this rationale, four different topics are addressed in the sections that follow. The first of these topics is concerned with establishing correspondence between two multi-object spatial arrays, a fundamental skill in map interpretation. The second topic deals with relating a spatial array to a map of that array when both are viewed from a stationary viewpoint. The third topic deals with the challenging situation in which correspondence is established between a traveler's view of a route through a real-world neighborhood and a simple sketch map of that route. The fourth topic involves translating one symbolic representation of space into another; specifically, the focus in on the ability to trace a route on a sketch map after hearing a verbal description of that route. These topics represent a broad range of phenomena involved in map reading and interpretation. This breadth provides the means for identifying limits to sex-related differences, while also affording sufficient opportunity to infer generalizations across tasks.

From one object array to another

Three translations that are fundamental to many map interpretation tasks were examined in this study, specifically, (a) translation of vertical viewing angle from a same-plane three-dimensional view to an overhead two-dimensional view; (b) translation of scale; and (c) translation of orientation so that the configuration of objects in the environment is congruent with the configuration of objects on the map. Previous research suggested that the most likely problem to be encountered by women would be the third type of translation, which involves recognition of a consistent configuration of objects despite array rotation (Evans 1980).

Method

A simple configuration consisting of a box, a cylinder, and a pyramid was used for the study. The configuration was photographed from a variety of viewpoints so as to represent seven different manipulations: vertical viewing angle only (30 versus 90 degrees — overhead — from surface), scale only (2:1 ratio), rotation only (views differing in 165 degree rotation), the two-way combination of vertical viewing angle and scale, the two-way combination of vertical viewing angle and rotation, the two-way combination of scale and rotation, and the three-way combination of vertical angle, scale, and rotation. Foils showing mismatches of configurations were also photographed. From all of these photographs, a test set of 140 pairs of color slides was prepared. Participants in the study were instructed to look at the first slide in a pair very carefully because they subsequently were to compare the arrangement of objects shown in the first picture to that of objects shown in a second picture. Appropriate illustrations of experimental manipulations were included in practice trials. Participants responded “yes” as soon as they determined that the two pictures portrayed the same array of objects (accommodating vertical viewing angle, scale, and array orientation) or “no” as soon as they determined that the arrays in the two pictures could not be the same. Data were collected from 12 men and 12 women who were undergraduates in psychology courses.

Results

A signal detection analysis revealed that men were generally more sensitive than women to the differences between correct pairings and mismatches, collapsing across all three manipulations. Yet, the data showed no difference between the sexes with regard to bias for responding either “yes” or “no.” An analysis of hits, that is, correct “yes” responses when the two pictures showed the same array, also showed no difference between men (79% accuracy) and women (75% accuracy) across the different manipulations. Correct identification of identical arrays was at an above-chance level of performance by both sexes on all problem types. In contrast, an analysis of correct rejections, that is, correct “no” responses when the two pictures showed different arrays, revealed a significant main effect, with men (90% accuracy) performing more accurately than women (70% accuracy). Women showed two instances in which their performance was basically at chance level, correct rejections involving manipulation of both vertical viewing angle and scale (58% accuracy) and correct rejections involving manipulation of both scale and array rotation (58% accuracy). An analysis of response times revealed no differences between the sexes.

Discussion

These results reflected a specific difficulty encountered by women when they must determine whether two configurations of objects are the same while accommodating for vertical viewing angle, scale, and array orientation. When the configurations were indeed the same, women’s responses were as accurate as men’s. However, when the configurations were different, women’s responses were less accurate than men’s across the board and were essentially no better than random when problems required multiple translations (scale and rotation, for example). The implications of these findings for map reading and interpretation are quite interesting. It appears that women may be at risk for a particular type

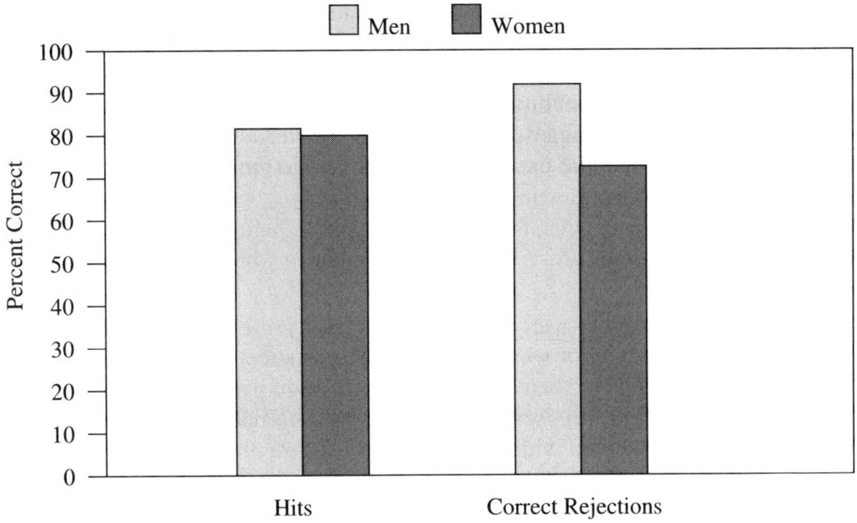

Figure 1. Mean accuracy for men and women in matching arrays consisting of three objects requiring one, two, or three transformations typical of map interpretation

of map-reading error, namely, incorrectly accepting a configuration of map features as properly identifying their location in the environment. Such errors could have a profound impact on orientation and wayfinding success.

In terms of understanding the cognitive basis for these findings, it may be useful to invoke the concept of visual-spatial working memory (Baddeley 1986; Logie 1995), a construct that refers to the simultaneous storage and processing of visually coded spatial information. In problems involving a match between spatial configurations, the correct answer may be obtained without demanding too much of working memory. A particular spatial relationship between two objects could be remembered in one configuration and then subsequently compared to that between the same two objects in a second configuration. If a match occurs, a correct "yes" response would be forthcoming, regardless of the fact that an exhaustive representation of inter-object relationships had not been constructed or examined. However, in problems involving a mismatch between spatial configurations, more demands are placed on working memory. To insure accuracy, multiple inter-object relationships must be encoded in memory initially and then compared with those present in the second configuration. A single match or even two matches between configurations does not preclude the possibility of a mismatch on some relationship. In this study, women may have relied on more limited sampling of spatial relationships when comparing successive object arrays. Consequently, a match on one relationship may have led to a "yes" response when the configurations were actually different. A working memory load hypothesis gains additional credence in view of the fact that problems involving multiple translations tended to take a greater toll on women's performance, suggesting a trade-off between temporary storage of spatial relationships and the execution of spatial transformations.

From pathways to maps

One of the most frequent uses of maps in everyday life involves referring to street maps or road maps for wayfinding purposes. A street map requires the user to establish correspondence between the arrangement of pathways in the environment on the map. The purposes of this study were to determine the impact of map orientation on the ease with which this correspondence is established and to examine the relationship between spatial abilities as assessed using traditional psychometric tests and the ability to establish correspondence between environment and map. Previous research has demonstrated clearly that misalignment of environment and map leads to errors in orientation and wayfinding (Levine 1982). Misalignment results in precisely the kind of conflict between spatial frames of reference that, according to prior research on sex-related differences (Evans 1980; Witkin et al. 1962), should lead to difficulties for women on map interpretation tasks.

Method

This study involved a unique apparatus, a model town (1 : 87 scale) constructed on a 4.5 × 9 ft surface that stood 2.5 ft off the floor. The town included 35 separate buildings, including residential housing, commercial areas, a school, and a factory, all linked by a network of streets lined with street lamps that could be illuminated. The map verification task used in the procedure required participants first to examine a pattern of street lamps illuminated along a particular route through the streets of the town, and then to compare this pattern to a route depicted on a two-dimensional map of the town projected on a large screen just beyond the model. Participants were presented 28 trials. On 16 of these, each of the four routes was matched with an accurate map, one aligned with the viewer's perspective and three misaligned. The 12 remaining trials involved foils, one aligned and two misaligned for each route.

Additionally, each participant was administered a battery of six psychometric tests of spatial abilities, all selected from the Educational Testing Service's *Factor-Referenced Kit of Cognitive Tests* (Ekstrom, French & Harman 1976). The battery included the Surface Development Test to assess visualization ability, the Cube Comparison Test to assess spatial relations ability, the Hidden Figures Test to assess flexibility of closure, and Gestalt Completion Test to assess speed of closure, the Map Memory Test to assess visual memory ability, and the Map Planning Task to assess visual scanning ability. Scores from these tests were expected to be highly intercorrelated. Data were collected from 34 men and 69 women who were undergraduates in psychology courses.

Results

The results showed that men performed more accurately than women on the map verification task when the map to be verified was misaligned with the model town (83% versus 74% accuracy) but not when the map and town were aligned (89% versus 87%). As in the case of Experiment 1, separate analyses were done on hits and correct rejections. The difference between men and women was significant in both analyses, but the performance advantage for males in the case of hits (85% versus 82%) was only a third of that observed in the case of correct rejections (87% versus 78%). An analysis of response times in the map verification task showed a significant effect of alignment but no sex-related effects or interactions. Mean response time for trials when map and town were aligned was 4.4 seconds, as compared to 6.7 seconds when they were misaligned.

Results from the battery of psychometric tests showed sex-related differences in favor of men on all except the test of visual memory, in which no difference was found. As expected, spatial ability test scores correlated significantly with each other, with the single exception of Map Memory (visual memory) and Map Planning (visual scanning). Scores from tests of visualization, spatial relations, speed of closure, flexibility of closure, visual memory, and visual scanning were all positively correlated with performance on the map verification task, and these correlations were equal to or larger than the correlation between sex of participant and map verification performance. Thus, statistically removing the influence of these abilities individually eliminated the significant correlation between sex of participant and performance on the map verification tasks, except in the case of visual memory. Because the statistical relationship between sex of participant and visual memory scores was not significant, removing its influence obviously would not effect the relationship between sex of participant and map verification performance.

Discussion

The results of this study indicated that women were at no disadvantage vis-a-vis men in establishing correspondence between environment and map when their

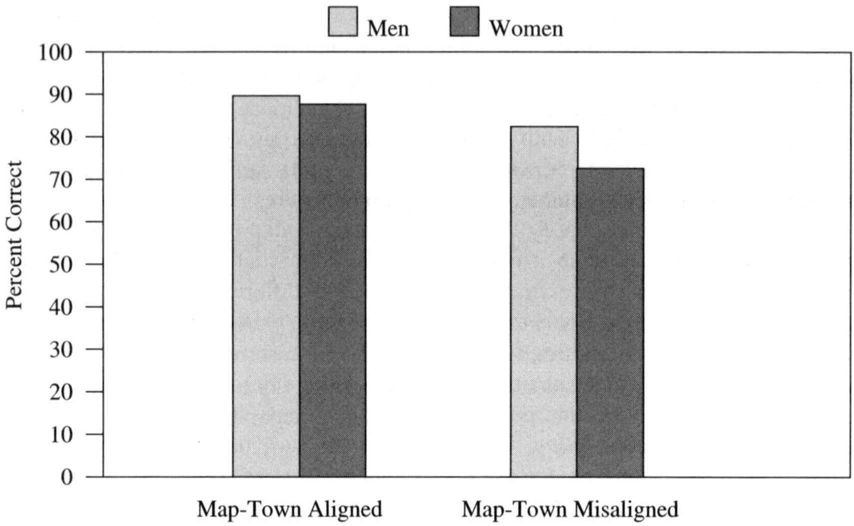

Figure 2. Effect of map-to-town alignment and misalignment on men's and women's accuracy in verifying maps of routes from a model town

Table 1. Correlations among sex of participant, scores on six psychometric tests, and performance on the map verification task

	1	2	3	4	5	6	7
1. Sex	–						
2. Map Verification	.29	–					
3. Surface Development	.36	.41	–				
4. Cube Comparison	.24	.31	.71	–			
5. Hidden Figures	.25	.25	.53	.49	–		
6. Gestalt Completion	.20	.29	.46	.35	.28	–	
7. Map Memory	.09	.29	.32	.27	.30	.25	–
8. Map Planning	.20	.26	.59	.49	.45	.25	.19

Note: Correlations .20 or larger are statistically reliable at $p < .05$.

perspective of the environment was aligned with their perspective of the map. When the map was misaligned, however, their performance level was significantly below that of men, although still above chance. As in Experiment 1, women were less reliable than men in correctly rejecting inaccurate maps. But in this study, they also had less success in accurately identifying correct maps. Thus, women appear to be more at general risk than men for orientation errors in instances in which maps used as wayfinding aids are misaligned with the environment they represent.

Women's difficulties with certain map-reading situations were related to their lower performance on tests assessing complex spatial abilities, such as visualization, spatial relations, flexibility of closure, and spatial scanning. Although basic visual memory ability was related to map reading skill, it did not differentiate men from women in this regard. The fact that complex abilities, but not visual memory per se, mediated sex-related differences in map reading performance provides support for the working memory load hypothesis. Specifically, it implicates difficulties with the simultaneous storage and processing of spatial information rather than with storage alone. Performance on the map verification task can be interpreted in a manner consistent with this view, as well. Establishing correspondence between route and map requires additional processing when misalignment must be accommodated as compared to instances in which the two are viewed from a compatible perspective. In short, the load of working memory is greater with misalignment.

From environmental experience to maps

Maps in the service of wayfinding provide a symbolic representation of a path of observation through the environment. This study was designed to examine the ability of men and women to verify a map as an accurate representation of a specific route after they experienced a visual simulation of travel through an actual neighborhood. This task is a formidable one because visual simulation limits perspective information and excludes proprioceptive and vestibular sources of perceptual information that typically accompany locomotor activity. Also, maps necessarily include a selective representation of environmental objects. Such circumstances pose major challenges to spatial information-processing capabilities. Consistent with prior research, it was expected that men's performance would be more accurate than that of women in this task. The issue of map orientation was examined in this study, as well. However, the concept of alignment between environment and map is not straightforward in this case. During simulated travel, the traveler is always facing forward, so it could be argued that the only map orientation that is congruent was one in which the point of origin is depicted at the base of the map, with the direction of travel upward. However, given the current state of knowledge, the influence of this type of alignment of initial starting perspective and orientation on a map is largely conjectural.

Method

A sequential presentation of color slides depicting standpoints 10 to 20 meters apart along a 1 km. walk was used as a visual simulation of route experience in a real-world environment. The walk began in a park, continued through a university campus and a residential area, and then ended at a large church. None of the participants had ever visited the neighborhood shown in the slide presentation. After viewing it twice, participants were then shown a series of 20 maps showing a route through the neighborhood. In each case, the layout of the neighborhood as depicted on the map was accurate. However, only eight of the maps showed the correct path of travel: two each with the direction of travel left-to-right, right-to-left, bottom-to-top, and top-to-bottom across the map with reference to the participant's point of view. The remaining 12 were foils, which included a wrong turn at one of three possible points along the route, specifically, near the beginning, in the middle, or near the end. These incorrect maps were represented in the same four orientations as the correct maps with respect to direction of travel from the participant's point of view. Data were collected from 24 men and 24 women who were enrolled in undergraduate psychology courses.

Results

An analysis of overall accuracy on the map verification task in this experiment revealed no effect of sex of participant, although accuracy was significantly above chance level for men (70%) but not for women (62%). As in Experiments 1 and 2, separate analyses were then performed on hits and correct rejections. The analysis of hits showed that for three of four direction-of-travel depictions men were better able than women to identify accurate maps of the route through the neighborhood (76% versus 50% accuracy). The exception was when travel on the map was depicted in a left-to-right direction, in which case the two sexes did not differ from each other (60% versus 58% accuracy) or from chance-level performance. The analysis of false alarms showed no main effect or interactions involving sex of participant. However, there was a robust interaction between location of error on the map and direction of travel depicted on the map. Errors at the beginning of the route were uniformly easy to detect, regardless of direction of travel (84% accuracy). In contrast, errors in the middle of the route could not be identified reliably by participants regardless of the direction of travel (58% accuracy). Errors at the end of the route were detected reliably only if the travel depicted on the map was left-to-right or right-to-left (73% accuracy); top-to-bottom or bottom-to-top depictions yielded poor performance (43% accuracy). Response times showed no significant main effect or interactions involving sex of participant.

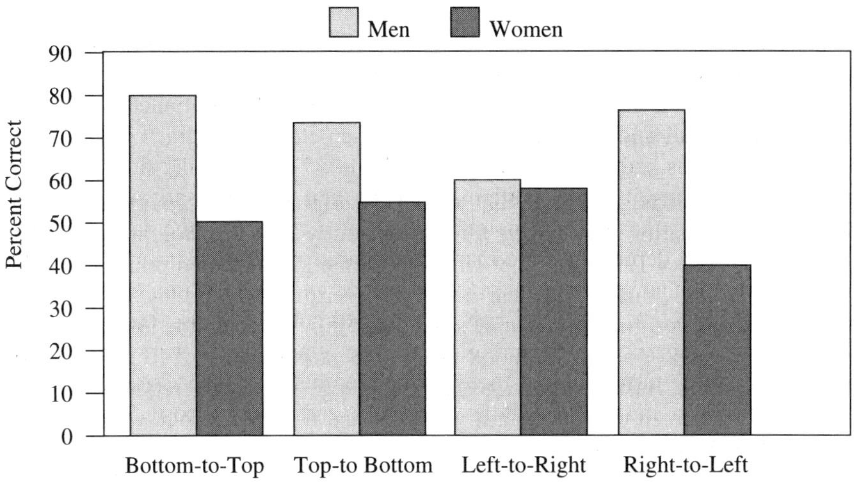

Figure 3. Effect of direction of depicted travel on men's and women's ability to identify accurate maps after viewing a slide presentation simulating travel along a route

Discussion

The results from this study showed that women generally had difficulty with this task; they were unable to identify correct maps reliably under any conditions and unable to detect errors in maps unless the errors appeared early in the route (for all directions of travel depicted on the map) or late in the route (for horizontally depicted directions of travel). Men's performance differed in that they were much more accurate in identifying correct maps.

At this point, it is difficult to suggest the cognitive basis for the sex-related difference found in this study. Clearly, the idea of alignment, interpreted as correspondence between straight-ahead movement through the environment and bottom-to-top directional travel on a map, cannot account for the findings. This alignment did not facilitate performance. One factor that does stand out is that the middle portion of the route posed a major challenge for accuracy. If participants were reduced to chance-level performance with respect to the middle portion of the route, then their reliability in judging the accuracy of correct maps and the inaccuracy of incorrect maps with errors in the middle of the route would be low. This pattern fits the data from women participants, but the results concerning correct rejections also show that men were unreliable in identifying incorrect maps with errors in the middle portion. Thus, a definitive explanation is elusive.

From route descriptions to maps

Recent studies have indicated that verbal descriptions can provide a flexible spatial representation that can be translated readily into a cartographic product (Taylor & Tversky 1992). In other words, accurate maps of environments can be sketched by individuals who hear a verbal description of the layout involved. This study was designed to examine sex-related differences in the ability to draw a route on a map of a neighborhood using information obtained from a description of that route. Based on previous research suggesting more frequent left-right confusion in women than in men, it was expected that men's routes sketched on maps would be more accurate than would women's routes.

Method

A verbal description of a 1.7 km. route was prepared to conform with suggested conventions for effective route directions, including the veridical temporal-spatial sequencing of features encountered along the route, the inclusion of more descriptive information at choice points than a other places along the route, and the inclusion of more descriptive information at the conclusion of the route than at other places (Allen 1997). The description included 63 communicative statement organized into 21 units. Each unit either described a place or described movement from one place to the next. The description far exceeded the amount of information that an individual would normally be expected to retain temporarily in memory. After hearing the description, participants were provided a map of the neighborhood through which the route proceeded and were instructed to mark with a pencil the course of movement described in the route directions. A point of origin was designated on the map. The accuracy of route maps was determined by dividing them into 21 units that corresponded to the 21 units in the route directions. The accuracy of each unit was scored by two judges, and composite accuracy was then computed for the initial one-third, middle one-third, and final one-third of the route. Data were collected from 25 men and 25 women who were undergraduates in psychology courses. All participants reported being unfamiliar with the route involved in the study.

Results

The accuracy scores revealed that men were more accurate than women in their sketching the initial one-third (80% versus 66%) and middle one-third (55% versus 42%) of the route on the map. There was no difference between men and women on the final one-third of the route (44% versus 52%).

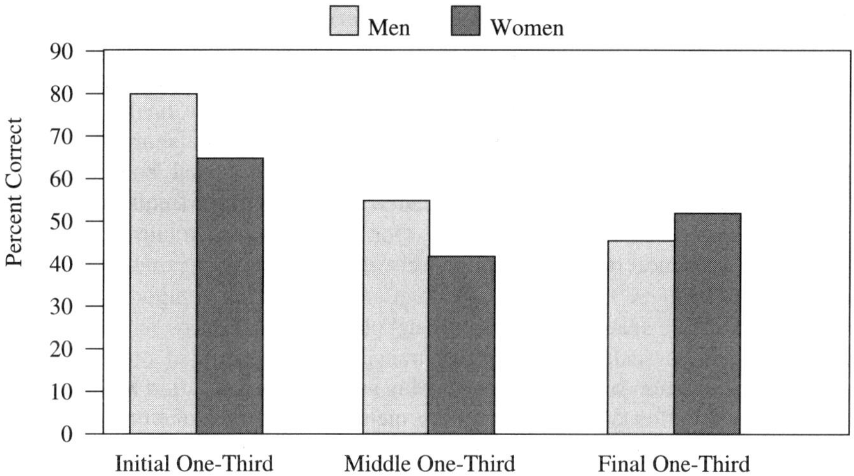

Figure 4. Accuracy of men's and women's routes sketched on a map after hearing route directions

Discussion

The data indicated that men were generally more accurate than women in sketching the course of a route on a map while relying on information obtained from a verbal description of that route. The performance of both men and women showed clear evidence of a primacy effect, which is common in memory tasks in which a list must be recalled in serial order. Interestingly, the pattern of performance by women showed some indication of a recency effect, as well. Because the order or sketching was constrained — it always began at the designated point of origin — it is not the case that the final portion of map was drawn first in such cases. Instead, a recency effect would suggest a somewhat different strategy based on a linear-order representation built from the end-anchors inward rather than from start to finish. More research is needed to develop this hypothesis and test it adequately.

Maps and minds

Taken together, the empirical studies addressing the four topics provided substantial evidence that, in the population sampled, certain aspects of women's map reading and interpretation skills were less reliable than those of men. The differences were significant but not overwhelming, wide-spread but not all-encompassing. The evidence hints at the cognitive bases for observed differences in performance, but additional research is required before more definitive statements are possible. No findings suggested deficits that would be impervious to remediation based on widely recognized principles of skill acquisition.

With regard to the cognitive bases for the performance differences observed, the evidence points to two aspects of spatial working memory. First, women appear to be at greater risk than men of losing temporarily stored information about spatial relations among objects, particularly if a cognitive operation such as scale or perspective translation is performed on the stored information or while the information is being stored. This risk could be attributed to a simplistic notion of reduced working memory capacity, but it could also be tied to the differential efficiency of various formats for storing spatial relations (specifically, proposition lists versus images). Future studies designed to differentiated between more efficient images and less efficient proposition lists would be crucial for exploring this possibility.

The second aspect of working memory that is implicated involves the inspection of spatial relations. While attempting to match object configurations in the absence of a defining frame of reference, women may respond on the basis of limited sampling of spatial relations because of the problem with temporary storage mentioned above. Such a state of affairs would yield reliable success in the event of environment-to-map matches but less reliable rejection of environment-to-map mismatches.

This problem with limited sampling need not necessarily extend to correspondence between routes and maps, however. When attempting to match route patterns, the sequential format of the information may make it much easier to detect route-to-map mismatches than is the case with object configurations. Specifically, limited sampling of the beginning or end portions of the route would yield quick detection of errors. As is frequently the case with sequentially organized information, the middle portion provides the greatest challenge to memory, especially with limited learning opportunities. Studies focusing specifically on the effect of limited sampling of spatial relations in array-to-map or route-to-map matching tasks are needed to explore the hypothesis emerging from these studies.

These findings are not without practical implications. The use of maps as wayfinding and orientation aids may be differentially problematic for women under certain circumstances. There is a need to compare the results from experiments such as these with findings from research comparing the effectiveness for men and women of map-based automated wayfinding aids, such as those available in some automobiles. Available evidence would lead to the prediction that such aids would be ineffective for many women, especially under the conditions of divided attention (i.e., navigation while driving) that is typical of their use.

Results from the experimental studies described in this presentation do not address the larger issue of how sex-related differences in cognition emerged. However, they may provide a measure of progress toward a necessary milestone on the way to that goal, the milestone of a better understanding of the differences that require explanation. Men appear to be somewhat less affected than women by visuo-spatial working memory demands in the context of tasks requiring that a correspondence be established between a spatial array and a symbolic representation of that array.

What questions should be asked about the origins of this difference? Speculative accounts frequently suggest a link between sex-related differences in spatial abilities and differences in travel behavior during human evolution. However, perhaps even more extensive speculation is needed to account for differences involving maps and minds. Because they are artifacts, maps must reflect certain aspects of the modes of thought underlying their creation. Is it possible that map reading as an activity taps the vestiges of male-characteristic cognitive tendencies expressed in the historic conventions associated with map design and use? Answering this question requires interdisciplinary inquiry far beyond experimental studies of map reading and interpretation, but this is the type of question that can attract scholarly attention from a variety of disciplines to the study of spatial cognition.

References

Allen, Gary L. (1997). From knowledge to words to wayfinding: Issues in the production and comprehension of route directions. In S. Hirtle & A. Frank (Eds.), *Spatial Information Theory: A theoretical basis for GIS* (pp. 363–372). Berlin: Springer.

Allen, Gary L. (1999). Spatial abilities, cognitive maps, and wayfinding. In R. G. Golledge (Ed.), *Wayfinding Behavior: Cognitive mapping and other spatial processes* (pp. 46–80). Baltimore: Johns Hopkins University Press.

Baddeley, Alan D. (1986). *Working Memory*. New York: Oxford University Press.

Baker, R. Robin. (1981). *Human Navigation and the Sixth Sense*. New York: Simon and Schuster.

Beatty, William W. & Alexander I. Troster (1987). Gender differences in geographic knowledge. *Sex Roles, 16* 565–589.

Bever, Thomas G. (1992). The logical and extrinsic sources of modularity. In M. Gunnar & M. Maratsos (Eds.), *Modularity and Constraints in Language and Cognition* (pp. 179–212). Hillsdale, NJ: Lawrence Erlbaum Associates

Chang, Kang-tsung & James R. Antes (1987). Sex and cultural differences in map reading. *American Cartographer, 14*, 29–42.

Ekstrom, Ruth. B., John W. French & Harry H. Harman (1976). *Kit of Factor-referenced Cognitive Tests*. Princeton, NJ: Educational Testing Service.

Evans, Gary W. (1980). Environmental cognition. *Psychological Bulletin, 88*, 259–287.

Gilmartin, Patricia P. (1986). Maps, mental imagery, and gender in the recall of geographic information. *American Cartographer, 13*, 335–344.

Gilmartin, Patricia P. & Jeffrey C. Patton (1984). Comparing the sexes on spatial abilities: Map-use skills. *Annals of the Association of American Geographers, 74*, 605–619.

Lawton, Carol A. (1994). Gender differences in way-finding strategies: Relationship to spatial ability and spatial anxiety. *Sex Roles, 30*, 765–779.

Levine, Marvin (1982). You-are-here maps: Psychological considerations. *Environment and Behavior, 14*, 202–237.

Logie, Robert H. (1995). *Visuo-Spatial Working Memory*. Hillsdale, NJ: Erlbaum.

Lohman, David F. (1988). Spatial abilities as traits, processes, and knowledge. In R. Sternberg (Ed.), *Advances in the Psychology of Human Intelligence* (Vol. 4; pp. 181–248). Hillsdale, NJ: Erlbaum.

Money, John, Duane Alexander & H. T. Walker, Jr. (1965). *A Standardized Road-Map Test of Direction Sense*. Baltimore: Johns Hopkins University Press.

Montello, Daniel R., Kristin L. Lovelace, Reginald G. Golledge & Carole M. Self (1999). Sex-related differences and similarities in spatial and geographic abilities. *Annals of the Association of American Geographers, 89*, 515–534

Mumaw, Randy J., James W. Pellegrino, Robert V. Kail & Phillip Carter (1984). Different slopes for different folks: Process analysis of spatial aptitude. *Memory and Cognition, 12*, 515–521.

Porteus, Stanley D. (1965). *Porteus maze test: Fifty years' application*. Pal Alto, CA: Pacific Books.

Taylor, Holly A. & Barbara Tversky (1992). Descriptions and depictions of environments. *Memory and Cognition, 20*, 483–496.

Voyer, Daniel, Susan Voyer & M. Phillip Bryden (1995). Magnitude of sex differences in spatial abilities: A meta-analysis and consideration of critical values. *Psychological Bulletin, 117*, 250–270.

Witkin, H. A., R. B. Dyk, H. F. Patterson, D. R. Goodenough & S. A. Karp (1962). *Psychological Differentiation: Studies of development*. New York: John Wiley and Sons.

A Theoretical Framework for the Study of Spatial Cognition

Maurizio Tirassa
Università di Torino

Antonella Carassa
Università di Padova

Giuliano Geminiani
Università di Torino

1. Introduction

The ultimate goal of this research is to contribute to the understanding of spatial cognition and its consequences on locomotion (that is, on the organization of the whole organism's movements in space). An organism's locomotion depends on what structure it superimposes on space itself and can therefore be understood as a form of interaction with a subjective environment, understandable in turn in terms of the organism's cognitive architecture.

As a first step, we will propose here a large-scale classification of the cognitive architectures possible, outlining the subjective structure that each of them superimposes on space and the relevant consequences on locomotion. Our classification differs from others that have been proposed for spatial cognition (e.g., Papi 1990) in that it does not build on the idea of *spatial behaviors*. We will argue, first, that cognition is better understood as interaction rather than behavior; and, second, that an organism's interactions can only be understood as generated and controlled by its cognitive architecture. This corresponds, in a sense, to the adoption of the organism's (rather than the observer's) subjective point of view.

The main division we will draw is between those architectures whose internal dynamics are entirely coupled to the dynamics in the world, and those that have at least some capability of decoupling. The latter correspond to representational architectures. Each class will be further decomposed according to a criterion of complexity. Our view of representation will not build upon a computationalist account of cognition.

2. Adaptivity and interaction

Adaptivity is a living organism's capability of creating and maintaining a dynamic compatibility with its environment. The notion of adaptivity is circular, in that it involves neither the organism alone nor the world alone, but the interaction between the two. Each (type of) organism thus entertains specific (types of) interactions with a specific environmental niche.

The world has dynamics of its own which a living organism has to cope with if it is to survive and reproduce. From this point of view, adaptivity is an organism's capability of maintaining its own structure in the face of perturbing environmental dynamics. On the other hand, what is to be considered as environmental dynamics depends on what specific organism is considered. From this point of view, adaptivity is an organism's capability of "creating", or "viewing", a subjectively relevant set of environmental dynamics to cope with.

Adaptivity builds upon compatibility rather than correctness or optimality. In the case of a representational organism, for example, the point is not whether its representations faithfully mirror the objective reality of the outside world; nor has it any means to find out whether they do. What matters is instead whether its representations are *compatible* with reality, that is, if their dynamics result in the maintenance of the organism's capability of coping with the world. Chimpanzees are incapable of representing abstract causal links between objects or events and therefore of formulating theories of the world (Premack, Premack & Sperber 1995); nonetheless, their mind is adapted to the subjective environment they live in. Humans are capable of theorizing (Geminiani, Carassa & Bara 1996), but not of representing the sonar profile of a moth like bats do, and so on. And, as we will argue, many species do not entertain representations at all and have simpler ways to maintain their compatibility with their environment.

Thus, while, in a sense, all species share the same "objective" world, each of them may also be said to live in a subjective one of its own, which, of course, may more or less resemble that of phylogenetically related species. Compatibility may then be viewed as a species' capability of capturing those variants and invariants in the world that are relevant for that species' interactions with it; and adaptivity may be viewed as the species' capability of maintaining compatibility.

Many different forms of adaptivity may be conceived of. Therefore, on the one hand, when describing nonhuman species, we should avoid the anthropocentric fallacy of conceiving of them as simply representing a greater or smaller subset of what our species is able to represent. On the other hand, just because, say, insects are unlikely to entertain representations doesn't mean that representations do not exist in more sophisticated species.

It is a consequence of this picture that it may be misleading to study adaptivity in terms of *behaviors*, if the term is taken to refer to factual descriptions of what organisms objectively do in an objectively defined world. Behavior is in the (representational) observer's eye only, not in the organism observed: what organisms do is not to behave, but to interact with their subjectively defined environment. It is more appropriate to study interaction in terms of the structure that generates and controls it. We call this structure the species' *cognitive architecture*.

3. Cognitive architectures and neurobiology

The cognitive architecture of an organism is the functional architecture of its nervous system, that is, a high-level description of the properties and of the aspects of the functioning of its nervous system that are relevant for and causally generate its interactions with the world. In the case of a representational species, by definition, these coincide with its mind.[1]

There are two reasons why we focus on cognitive architecture rather than on neurobiology alone. The first is that the study of the nervous centers that deal with, say, landmarks in a certain species needs a parallel study of what a landmark is to that species, which is in turn part of the study of that species' cognitive architecture. The second is that, in an evolutionary perspective, what is selected for or against is not a nervous system as such (except, of course, for what concerns susceptibility to pathological events like diseases or traumata), but the adaptivity of the interaction that it is able to generate; and this regards again the cognitive, rather than the strictly neurological, architecture of a species.

In the next sections we will sketch some types of cognitive architectures, that is, some different types of solutions to the problem, faced by every active species, of how to adaptively generate and control the interaction with the environment. For the moment, let us consider one property of cognitive architectures, namely, their innateness.

An organism should not be viewed as just cast into the world, a stranger in a strange land: it has instead to be born prepared for the interaction with the niche it will find itself in. In lower organisms, whose life mnespan is too brief and nervous system too simple to allow for individual differentiation or learning, this may mean that each architectural component has to be completely developed from start. In general terms, however, it means rather that the possible modifications that an architecture may physiologically undergo are implicitly defined in the architecture itself (Barkow, Cosmides & Tooby 1992; Cosmides & Tooby 1994; Lorenz 1965). Some architectures may be more rigid and some more flexible, so to let each individual follow its own developmental trajectory, according to the particular interactions it has with the environment; but, in any case, the space of possible developmental trajectories is intrinsic to the initial state of the architecture and is therefore a species-level property, and an adaptive one.

The innate endowment of a species thus determines not the specific interactions that each of its members will entertain with the world, but the whole space of that species' possible interactions with its subjective environment; the complexity of such space varies in accordance with the complexity of the species' architecture. *Learning* is not a natural kind, but the innate capability of a cognitive architecture of undergoing specific types of modifications, possibly triggered in part by specific types of interactions with the subjectively defined environment.

To say that cognitive architectures are innate also means that they, like most biological traits, are the product of evolution. Although adaptivity may be viewed as the property of a whole species as well as of each of its members, natural selection ultimately operates upon the slight individual variations existing between the latter. The phylogeny of cognitive architectures is therefore a side effect of the differences in the innate endowments of the individuals that make up a species (due to statistical differences in the species' genetic pool as well as to mutation, recombination, etc.), plus the differences in their respective reproductive success.

To resume: the living organisms we are interested in are those that engage in active interactions with their subjectively construed environment by way of self-organization (Maturana & Varela 1980; Varela, Thompson & Rosch 1991). The structure which governs an organism's interaction with the environment, thus maintaining that organism's adaptivity, is its innate cognitive architecture. The cognitive architecture of a species defines the subjective structure that its members will superimpose on the world. Our position so far may therefore be described as a Kantian version of constructivism.

In the next sections, we will sketch some types of cognitive architectures, that is, some ways in which an organism's internal dynamics may co-evolve with the subjectively relevant dynamics in the environment so to generate an adaptive interaction. Each type will superimpose a specific type of subjective structure on space, which will have relevant consequences on locomotion. The main division we will draw is between those architectures whose internal dynamics are entirely coupled to the dynamics in the world, and those that have at least some capability of decoupling their internal dynamics from the external ones. The latter correspond to representational architectures. From a neurobiological point of view, we expect this division to mirror the division between species whose nervous system has no proencephalic differentiation and those whose nervous system has at least some. These two main classes will be further decomposed into subclasses according to a criterion of complexity.

4. Coupled architectures

The internal dynamics of these cognitive architectures are entirely coupled to the external ones. These organisms have no internal model of their environment and are therefore only capable of external cognition: to them, the world is the only possible model of itself.

Since concepts are the active constructions of a representational mind which superimposes its own a priori categories on the world, coupled architectures have no concepts of any sort. This implies that their subjective environment does not build upon the existence of *objects*. To say that coupled architectures have no object-based construction of space refers to something far more primitive than object permanence. As we will argue later, the latter term refers to an organism's capability of realizing that objects exist even when they are out of immediate perception, and therefore of recognizing them as being the same in different presentations. The level logically antecedent to object permanence is object impermanence: the difference, however, relates to the type of representation entertained by an organism, rather than to whether that organism entertains representations of any sort. Coupled architectures, instead, have no representations at all, so that the point here is not whether objects are or are not permanent, but simply whether they exist.

Reflex-based architectures

The simplest types of coupled architectures are only composed of reflexes. The internal dynamics of a reflex-based architecture depend exclusively on the external ones. Its interactions may be viewed as a set of fixed stimulus/response patterns, and are therefore completely driven by the environment: there are no internal states relevant to the interaction, except for local modulation of reflexes via activation, habituation, or crossed inhibition.

Since the coexistence of more than a (comparatively) small number of stimulus/response patterns would create inextricable problems of coordination and integration, the overall architecture of a reflex-based organism will necessarily be simple. The subjectively relevant environmental dynamics, and therefore the organism's interactions, will be correspondingly simple.

The subjective space of a reflex-based organism will also be correspondingly limited, consisting of the small set of stimuli that it is sensitive to. These may include taxis and other simple forms of trail following, and the avoidance of aversive stimuli. In practice, therefore, space has no proper *structure*, in the literal sense of the term, to these organisms.

Affordance-based architectures

The organisms that belong to this second class of coupled architectures have internal states that play a role in their interactions with the environment; we borrow the term *affordance* from Gibson (1977) to refer to them.

Although the internal dynamics of an affordance-based architecture are still entirely coupled to the environmental ones, the picture becomes far more complex than was with reflex-based organisms. The coupling here is flexible, in that the internal states contribute in determining what environmental dynamics are currently the most relevant, among the several available at each moment. Thus, an individual who is looking for prey and one who is looking for mate will react to different affordances; and both will have to be able to adjust their internal dynamics if required by the external ones (e.g., if a predator is detected). These architectures may thus be described as dynamically ascribing a comparative weight to each affordance available, according to the current internal state, and then reacting to the balance of weights that has thus been created. Of course, the criterion with which these weights are allocated is part of the architecture itself.

The subjective space of these organisms is composed of all the affordances that are available at each moment. It has therefore a proper structure, although a non-objectual one, because the various affordances are spatially oriented with respect to the organism's egocentric positioning and because they vary in attractiveness or aversiveness.

The interactions of these types of organisms with their subjective environment may therefore be conceived of as a complex and continuously changing balance between the affordances available. The complexity of this balance may vary greatly from species to species. Some species can stabilize specific types of affordance, so to let them govern the interaction over a certain interval of time; this interval may be longer or shorter, thus making the stabilization more or less permanent. The honeybee, for example, is capable of permanently fixing the flight trajectory that leads from the hive to an interesting source of food; the desert ant impermanently keeps track of the direction that will lead it back to the nest at the end of the current cycle of exploration; and the housefly is incapable of stabilizing its affordances at all.

What is interesting, in describing the interactions of all these different species in terms of a dynamic balance between affordances, is that there is no need to ascribe special representational or quasi-representational capabilities to honeybees or to desert ants with respect to houseflies; it suffices for an explanation of the differences between these species that the former be capable of assigning a permanent or impermanent relative weight to certain environmental affordances. Since the nervous systems of all these insects are roughly similar, any other solution would be implausible from a neurobiological point of view.

5. Decoupled architectures

The architectures that belong to this second main class are those whose internal dynamics are decoupled from the external ones; that is, those that entertain representations. These should correspond roughly to the species whose nervous system includes proencephalic structures.

The concept of representation lies at the very heart of cognitive science, but it comes in different acceptances; it is therefore necessary to explain briefly what we mean by it.

We reject the computationalist framework, according to which mental representations are pieces of information internally stored in some predefined formal code (Newell & Simon 1976). This position is nowadays philosophically and psychologically unacceptable (Bruner 1990; Edelman 1992; Harnad 1990; Nagel 1986; Putnam 1988; Searle 1980, 1992), if only because of its rather controvertible consequence that whatever physical object undergoes internal changes due to world events could then be considered representational — including autonomous robots à la Brooks (Vera & Simon 1993) as well as thermostats and computers. On the other hand, the perceived failure of symbolic accounts of cognition has lately led many researchers to completely reject the very idea of representation (e.g., Brooks 1991) while, at the same time, keeping a view of cognition based on computational functionalism. We view these positions as the two horns of one dilemma (Tirassa, 1999a), and want to avoid both.

To entertain a representation is instead to be in a certain semantic, or *intentional* (Searle 1983), relationship with the world (including one's own body and, for a few species, even one's own representations). This is the (largely unexplained systems) material property of certain types of physical objects, namely, certain highly sophisticated types of nervous system. Like all the material properties of a physical object, representations will have a causal role in some of the interactions that that object has with the world: they are thus at the same time (part of the) causes and effects of the organism's interactions with the world (Tirassa, 1999b). It is therefore more correct to talk of mind/body rather than of mind (or body) alone. (For further discussion of the problem of representations in cognitive ethology, see Allen & Bekoff 1997; Griffin 1978; Prato Previde, Colombetti, Poli & Cenami Spada 1992).

Representational architectures are, by definition, decoupled from the external world. *Decoupled* here does neither mean that representational organisms have internal dynamics that are abstract entities independent on the world, as is typical of classical artificial intelligence, nor that they live in a world of Platonic symbols or that environmental contingencies and opportunities are not crucial to them, a position that would simply be solipsistic. The point is instead that representational architectures have internal models of their subjective environment. These models are based on concepts, that is, on subjective ontologies resulting from largely innate categories superimposed on the world.

As regards the structure of space, the subjective environments of representational architectures will build upon the existence of *objects*. In this section we will discuss the three possible main subclasses of these architectures.

Deictic architectures

Deictic architectures are the simplest representational architectures. A deictic architecture (the term is borrowed from Agre & Chapman 1990) only represents what it can currently perceive. Objects are thus impermanent to it: they only exist insofar as they can be perceived. This means that it can have no token/type distinction: each object represented is at the same time a prototype of the whole class which it belongs to and a specific instance thereof. An object to these architectures is therefore represented as the whole set of interactions that it is (subjectively) possible to entertain with it.

This may resemble the case of affordance-based architectures. The difference is that an affordance (in our acceptation of the term) is not an object proper, but simply the potential for a certain action. The action that an affordance calls for will possibly be executed according to its relative weight as compared with the other affordances available. To entertain a deictic representation means instead to view an object as the experience of the possible interactions that concern that particular world entity. Thus, it is not that the concept of affordance applies to nonrepresentational architectures and not to representational ones; it is only that it means something very different in the two cases (which is why we have restricted our use of the term to the former case).

The idea of a deictic representation may also seem to apply to any representational architecture, at least under a certain acceptance of the concept (e.g., Glenberg 1997; Millikan 1998). From this point of view, the main difference between a deictic architecture and a more sophisticated one is that the former has no object permanence, that is, that it is incapable of singling an object out and possibly labeling it as an individual entity, and thereby of realizing that it exists even when it is out of immediate perception. This makes a great difference in the subjective structure of the environment.

As regards the subjective structure of space, a deictic organism will only interact with the space it can currently perceive; but, differently from what happens in a coupled architecture, it will represent that space as a region wherein proper objects exist (which is also why we have started to use the term *perception* only here). It will therefore be able to plan a trajectory in this region, deciding in advance what path to follow (according to criteria such as distance or dangerousness), what obstacles to avoid and how, and so on. This capability, although confined to the space that is currently perceived, allows nonetheless highly sophisticated interactions, at least as compared to those that are possible to lower-level architectures.

In principle, two particularly simple forms of learning are possible in a deictic architecture, one consisting in the acquisition of a novel way to cope with a deictic object, and the other in the addition of a new deictic object to the architecture's subjective ontology, possibly as a specialization of a previously existing one. Thus, if an animal is capable of creating a new deictic object (say, *my mate* in a monogamous species), it may be able to interact with it in ways that would be specific to that particular individual, while at the same time never being able to realize that it is an individual object (because there is no such thing as an individual object in the animal's subjective ontology).

The capability of forming a deictic object which happens to be "objectively" composed of only one instance also allows for the creation of a nest. Although, in order to go back to it, the organism has either to perceive it or to resort to simple modalities of orientation like trail following, it is however a (deictic) object or place, and therefore something very different from the nest of an affordance-based organism.

Base-level representational architectures

The logically successive step is an architecture capable of object permanence. This corresponds to the possess of concepts in the proper sense of the term, that is, as types of entities to which different tokens, or individuals, may belong.

This makes true learning possible, whereby a novel individual may be added to an existing class or a new class may be created, possibly as a specialization of one that already exists. The new class, differently from what happens in deictic architectures, would be a true class in its own respect, that is, it would comprise a proper token/type distinction, a set of individual entities that belong to it to a possibly variable degree, and so on. In any type of architecture, of course, learning can only take place within the space of possibilities generated by the innate endowment of the architecture.

As regards the subjective structure of space, base-level representational organisms are the first to possess a map of the territory they inhabit. A region to them may be divided into subregions, or zones; each region or zone comprises individual paths and individual objects that may be used as landmarks. A landmark (or, in general, an object) to these organisms needs not be a physical piece of matter in the material sense of the term; it may also be a landscape, a skyline, a socially shared mark like an odor, and so on.

To a base-level representational architecture, the nest is therefore an individual place, reachable via a network of individual paths that are characterized in their turn by landmarks. Other individual places may include sources of food or water, dangerous zones, and so on.

Metarepresentational architectures

The final step is metacognition, that is, an organism's capability of representing its own representations. As far as we know, the human species is likely to be the only one on this planet to have such capabilities, that could be shared, in the best case, by a few other primates (see Premack, Premack & Sperber 1995).

Metacognition dramatically changes a species' interactions with its subjective environment. It makes it possible to attach abstract labels (that is, symbols) to existing entities, to imagine non-existing entities and to treat them as if they were real, to use symbols for referential purposes or as place-markers, and so on.[2] This makes it possible in turn to formulate theories about the world, to reason formally, to reuse in a certain type of interaction the features of the world that were relevant to a different type of interaction, and to communicate in a mentalist way with conspecifics.

As regards the subjective structure of space, a metarepresentational species is capable of creating abstract regions or zones with abstract borders and landmarks and, most important, of entertaining survey maps. We do not conceive of survey maps as allocentric: since a representation is, by definition, someone's subjective point of view, they can only be egocentric. Survey maps result instead from the pretense to be dislocated in a different position (say, one kilometer above the city) and watching the world from that perspective. This allows to draw spatial inferences and therefore to plan in advance a path in a known as well as in a partially unknown region. It must be remembered, however, that these plans are always, by necessity, partial: they are not recipes for action to be followed blindly, but guides for action to be further specified in the interaction with the real world (Tirassa 1997).

Metacognitive organisms have two further capabilities. First, given the appropriate cognitive tools, they can externalize their representations by means of drawings or language. Second, given the ability to understand the representations entertained by a conspecific and to affect them in a desired way, they may communicate spatial information to one another with the aid of these externalized tools.

6. Future developments

The classification we have proposed here has a very high level of abstraction and currently relies fundamentally on analytical considerations. The next step of our research will be to derive, for each class of architectures described, a description of the types of interaction that it may generate with regard to the control of space and locomotion. Subsequently, we will check the empirical validity of our analysis by looking for confirming or disconfirming evidence from neurobiology, ethology and autonomous robotics. This is also likely to lead to a refinement of the classification.

The ultimate goal of this research is to build a taxonomy of active organisms based on three columns, namely, *cognitive architecture*, *neurobiology and embodiment*, and *interaction*, that be analytically and empirically consistent on each level.

Acknowledgments

We are grateful to Alessandra Valpiani for her participation in different phases of the research. Maurizio Tirassa has been supported by the Italian Ministry of University and Scientific and Technological Research (MURST), 40% Program *Nuovi paradigmi per l'interazione e nuovi ambienti di comunicazione*, 1995–1997. Antonella Carassa and Giuliano Geminiani have also been separately supported by the MURST, 60% for the years 1996 and 1997.

Notes

1. In this perspective, the term *cognition* and its derivatives should have been kept for the species that possess a mind, that is, those that entertain representations. On the other hand, the term is widely used in the relevant literature (e.g., Maturana & Varela 1980) and most alternatives are not less ambiguous from a philosophical point of view (*control architecture*, for instance, is typically used in autonomous robotics and would have therefore been inappropriate to the discussion of biological entities, let alone representational ones).
2. Let us remark that *to be capable of using symbols* is not the same thing as *being a symbol system* as postulated in classical cognitivism (see also the discussion at the beginning of this section).

References

Agre, Philip E. & David Chapman (1990). What are plans for? *Robotics and Autonomous Systems*, *6*, 17–34.

Allen, Colin & Marc Bekoff (1997). *Species of mind.* Cambridge, MA: MIT Press.

Barkow, John H., Leda Cosmides & John Tooby (Eds.) (1992). *The adapted mind. Evolutionary psychology and the generation of culture.* Oxford: Oxford University Press.

Brooks, Rodney A. (1991). Intelligence without representation. *Artificial Intelligence*, *47*, 139–159.

Bruner, Jerome S. (1990). *Acts of meaning*. Cambridge: Cambridge University Press.

Cosmides, Leda & John Tooby (1994). Beyond intuition and instinct blindness: Toward an evolutionarily rigorous cognitive science. *Cognition*, *50*, 41–77.

Edelman, Gerald M. (1992). *Bright air, brilliant fire: On the matter of the mind.* New York: Basic Books.

Geminiani, Giuliano, Antonella Carassa & Bruno G. Bara (1996). Causality by contact. In J. Oakhill & A. Garnham (Eds.), *Mental models in cognitive science. Essays in honor of Phil Johnson-Laird*. Hove, UK: Erlbaum/Taylor & Francis.

Gibson, J. J. (1977). The theory of affordances. In R. E. Shaw & J. Bransford (Eds.), *Perceiving, acting, and knowing*. Hillsdale, NJ: Erlbaum.

Glenberg, Arthur M. (1997). What memory is for. *Behavioral and Brain Sciences*, *20*, 1–55.

Griffin, David R. (1978). Prospects for a cognitive ethology. *Behavioral and Brain Sciences*, *4*, 527–538.

Harnad, Stevan (1990). The symbol grounding problem. *Physica D*, *42*, 335–346.

Lorenz, Konrad (1965). *Evolution and modification of behavior*. Chicago & London: The University of Chicago Press.

Maturana, Humberto D. & Francisco J. Varela (1980). *Autopoiesis and cognition. The realization of the living*. Dordrecht: Reidel.

Millikan, Ruth G. (1998). A common structure for concepts of individuals, stuffs, and real kinds: More Mama, more milk, and more mouse. *Behavioral and Brain Sciences*, *21*, 55–100.

Nagel, Thomas (1986). *The view from nowhere*. Oxford: Oxford University Press.

Newell, Allen & Herbert A. Simon (1976). Computer science as empirical enquiry: Symbols and search. *Communications of the Association for Computing Machinery*, *19*, 113–126.

Papi, Floriano (1990). Homing phenomena: Mechanisms and classification. *Ethology Ecology & Evolution*, 2, 3–10.

Prato Previde, Emanuela, Marco Colombetti, Marco Poli & Emanuela Cenami Spada (1992). The mind of organisms: Some issues about animal cognition. *International Journal of Comparative Psychology*, *6*, 79–119.

Premack, Ann J., David Premack & Dan Sperber (Eds.) (1995). *Causal cognition: A multidisciplinary debate*. Oxford: Clarendon.

Putnam, Hilary (1988). *Representation and reality*. Cambridge, MA: MIT Press.

Searle, John R. (1980). Minds, brains, and programs. *Behavioral and Brain Sciences*, *3*, 417–424.

Searle, John R. (1983). *Intentionality: An essay in the philosophy of mind*. Cambridge: Cambridge University Press.

Searle, John R. (1992). *The rediscovery of the mind*. Cambridge, MA: MIT Press.

Tirassa, Maurizio (1997). Mental states in communication. In *Proceedings of the 2nd European Conference on Cognitive Science*, Manchester, UK.

Tirassa, Maurizio (1999a). Taking the trivial doctrine seriously: Functionalism, eliminativism, and materialism. *Behavioral and Brain Sciences, 22*, 851–852.

Tirassa, Maurizio (1999b). Communicative competence and the architecture of the mind/brain. *Brain and Language, 68,* 419–441.

Varela, Francisco J., Evan Thompson & Eleanor Rosch (1991). *The embodied mind. Cognitive science and human experience*. Cambridge, MA: MIT Press.

Vera, Alonzo H. & Herbert A. Simon (1993). Situated action: A symbolic interpretation. *Cognitive Science*, *17*, 7–133.

Describers and Explorers

A method for investigating cognitive maps

Antonella Carassa, Alessia Aprigliano
Università di Padova

Giuliano Geminiani
Università di Torino

1. Introduction

Empirical and theoretical research on human spatial cognition supports the hypothesis that spatial knowledge of large-scale environments is elaborated in specialized mental structures called cognitive maps (Golledge 1987, 1990). There is evidence that when interacting with a novel environment, individuals go through several phases in the construction of their spatial knowledge (Golledge 1978; Evans 1985) involving a shift from an initial egocentric frame of reference (where the environment is represented in terms of a sequence of landmarks) to a bird's eye perspective in which distant places are linked together to form a coherent whole. Studies on the acquisition of spatial knowledge have shown that active exploration is critical to the generation of the more complex bird's eye stage of spatial knowledge.

When discussing the elaboration of spatial representations, most authors have made a distinction between "landmark", "route" and "survey" representations, but complete agreement as to nature of the concepts to which these three terms refer is lacking (Lynch 1960; Shemyakin 1962; Hart & Moore 1973; Siegel & White 1975). In 1995, Chown, Kaplan and Kortenkamp proposed a theory of cognitive mapping that describes how maps of increasing complexity are built up using the previous map as a basis for constructing the successive. This theory, which emphasizes adaptiveness and aims to relate spatial cognition to the way humans perceive the environment and interact with it, encompasses a wider spectrum of issues in spatial cognition than most other theories, particularly in relation to way-finding. Furthermore it is consistent with developmental constraints, and results from several other disciplines are taken into account.

According to this theory, the first phase of mapping consists of learning a basic topological structure built out from landmarks through experience. This kind of *route map*, or topological network of landmarks is used to find one's way from the starting point to a given target point. This representation contains local information only in that a landmark is connected only with the landmarks that can be seen from it. As experience grows, a second kind of *route map* is acquired, a local directional map, that provides information about where to find the next location when standing at given place.

This map is useful when a person has to select a new direction in response to environmental triggers, such as choice points. Its function is to give qualitative information about the change of orientation necessary to find a nearby target landmark. Both these kinds of *route maps* are rich in information about places close to the current location but do not connect landmarks separated by great distances. As experience grows further, a *survey map* is created; this is a compact representation of the large-scale environment, that allows to take multiple perspectives (the one from above included). Unlike *route maps,* which rely heavily on the situated interaction with the environment and require to find part of information in the world, *survey maps* are global overviews that allow a completely internal form of planning and reasoning, so that abstract (never experienced) paths such as *shortcuts* can be planned.

We carried out the present study in the context of the above-outlined theoretical framework. Our first aim was to test experimentally the hypothesis that there are two distinctive levels of spatial representations, viz, *route maps* and *survey maps* (we were not interested in distinguishing between the two types of *route maps*), and that these representations, and the elaboration of the first kind into the second, depend on a person's direct experience of an area. To this purpose, we investigated two groups of subjects with very different levels of familiarity with a given area. The second aim, arising out of the first, was to create a method for investigating spatial cognition, which we expect will be useful in our continuing research in this area.

As is the case with all mental representations, it is problematic to find a suitable method for investigating spatial representations. Commonly used methods involve the use of sketch maps, drawings, verbal reports and model building, each of which has its drawbacks and limitations (Torell 1990).

The main assumptions in setting up our method were as follows:

a. It is possible to identify different types of *descriptions* of complex routes, by analyzing the verbal characteristics of the descriptions themselves (Taylor & Tversky 1996).
b. There are different types of mental *representations* of complex routes,

depending on varying levels of familiarity the individual has with the environment in which the routes are located (Golledge 1978; Evans 1985; Chown, Kaplan & Kortenkamp 1995).

In seeking to develop a way of inferring mental representations from verbal descriptions, we took account of the fact that the nature of a description will depend on other factors in addition to the type of spatial representation possessed by a person. One such factor would be the aim of the description: an example germane to the present context would be whether or not the aim of the *describer* was to enable the other to find his way to a certain point. If we consider the possible relations between representation and description (with a view to inferring the former form the latter), the most important property of a survey-type representation is that it may be described as a route if the type of task renders this necessary (i.e., if the aim is to tell the other how to reach a specific point). This implies that in order to reveal a survey-type representation, we have to give a task to the *describer* which induces him to produce a description of his survey map. Such would be the case when the aim of the description is induce in the other optimized exploratory behavior, in which case it would be important to provide an overview of the environment to the *explorer* so that the latter may plan alternative routes and *shortcuts*.

A second factor influencing the description would be the *describer*'s opinion as to how familiar the other was with the environment being described. In the paper by Taylor & Tversky (1995), this variable was controlled for by instructing the subject to describe the environment as if the other knew nothing whatever about it.

Other problems arise from the procedures used to analyze the content of descriptions. In this study we codified descriptions following the criteria of Taylor & Tversky (1996); that is we sought to identify systematic differences in the use of language which indicate whether a description was from a route or a survey perspective. It is important to realize, however, that a subject's representation is unlikely to be expressed, in his description, as either a pure route or a pure survey. As shown by Taylor & Tversky (1996), many descriptions are mixed and sometimes mixed descriptions are more numerous than pure ones.

Furthermore, the verbal characteristics used to classify descriptions are not always unambiguously interpretable in terms of either route or survey, since their meaning may change according to the context. For these reasons, in addition to analysis of semantic indicators of route or survey type, we also analyzed the exploration behavior that these descriptions induced in other.

The experimental setup we devised was that one subject communicated with another with the aim of directing him to a target point. The task was therefore a cooperative one, and the investigator observed how the participants communicated maps to each other in order to reach their common goal. This differs from the normal setup of experiments in which participants present verbal reports to an investigator. Another feature was that half the participants had no prior acquaintance with the environment in which the experiment takes place, and everyone was informed of this fact. In our hypothesis, this condition forces one participant, the *describer*, to tune his description to the knowledge of the environment he attributes to the partner, the *explorer*.

The general aim of this research is to show how it is possible, by following the experimental method hereby presented, to infer the type of spatial representation of the *describer* by analyzing his/her verbal descriptions of complex routes and relating them to the explorative behaviors those descriptions induce in the *explorer.*

2. Methods

Subjects

We recruited 40 children in their last year of primary school. At this age (age range 9.3–10.2 years) spatial ability is comparable to that of adults (Cornell, Heth, Alberts 1994; Heth, Cornell, Alberts 1997). Furthermore, although both types of map are possessed at this age we believe that cultural influences, above all educational influences, in the use of survey descriptions are not yet overriding.

Twenty participants (11 girls, 9 boys) attended the school that was the setting for the way-finding experiment, and were therefore familiar with the environment. The other twenty participants (11 girls, 9 boys) came from a different school and had no prior knowledge of that environment.

Procedure

The experiment was carried out in a primary school which was of two stories and had a cross-shaped ground plan. Two itineraries were designated, each ranged over the two floors and each required exploration of four target locations (labeled with colored cards) along the trail before arriving at destination locations, where a goal object was placed.

The subjects were divided into pairs (see later) and each member of the pair was assigned a specific role. One subject (the *describer*) accompanied the investigator on first one and then the other trail. The investigator then gave the *describer* the following instructions: "The game starts now. You have to explain to your teammate the route he has to take in order to collect all the cards and the two final objects I have shown you. The winning team will be the one that collects most cards and most final objects in the shortest time. If you think you know a better way to reach all these items, than the route you followed with me, then you can describe that to your teammate".

The investigator then took the *describer* to a room and introduced him to his *explorer* teammate.

The *describer*'s task was now to explain to the *explorer* how to reach the intermediate and *final targets*. Previously the *explorer* had been motivated by the investigator and the competitive nature of the game made clear. The entire conversation between *describer* and *explorer* was recorded for subsequent analysis. After receiving what he/she considered enough information to find the objects, the *explorer* went off to find them followed by the investigator who noted the trail followed on a plan of the building.

Thus the task of the *describer* was to give information to the *explorer* teammate that would enable to latter reach the greatest number of target locations in the shortest possible time, without any restriction as to the route taken. In fact the shortest route was not that followed initially with the investigator. This task is such, therefore, that if the *describer* has a survey-type representation, he would tend to give a description having a survey-type perspective in order to allow his/her teammate to find *shortcuts* which are a characteristic of a survey as opposed to a landmark representation. Since the description is given to a real *explorer* whose subsequent behavior is observed, we can overcome the limitations of an analysis that only considers descriptions in terms of indicators: the *explorer* therefore functions as an external judge of the description furnished, since his/her behavior will reflect the type of information received.

The subjects were paired off in order to form four relations between *describer* and *explorer* with respect to familiarity with the environment:

A. Both *describer* and *explorer* know the environment.
B. The *describer* is familiar with the environment, the *explorer* not.
C. The *describer* is not familiar with the environment, the *explorer* is.
D. Neither *describer* nor *explorer* are familiar with the environment.

These four pairs of subjects allow us to investigate the two methodological hypotheses which are:

a. The description given depends on how familiar the *describer* is with the environment.

b. The *explorer* is an unknowing judge of the descriptions, which can be analysed through his/her exploration behavior.

Data analysis

Because there were only five pairs of subjects for each experimental situation, we carried out non-statistical analysis of the data. *Describers*' verbal reports were analyzed in terms of indicators route and survey, which according to Taylor & Tversky (1996) characterize *route* and *survey maps* (Table 1).

Table 1. Characteristic of route and survey maps

Dimension	Route Map		Survey map	
	criterion	example of indicator	criterion	example of indicator
Point of view of describer	many	active verbs (e.g. "go..", "start..", "turn round..")	only one	stative verbs (e.g. "it is..", "there is..")
Indicator of spatial organisation	route (sequential)	spatial or temporal adverbs (e.g. "after..", "before..")	map (hierarchical organization)	configurational indicator (e.g. "it's shaped like this..", "here is..", subject draws a map)
Co-ordinates	right/left, front/back	egocentric coordinates (e.g. "on your right/left..") signs (e.g. "on this that side..")	cardinal points (or substitutes)	allocentric indicators coordinates (e.g. "on the right/left of..")

To analyze the explorative behavior we distinguished between path and neighborhood behavior components: the former related to the path (defined by the investigator when showing the *describer* the route) from the starting point to the final target; the latter related to exploration of places off the path. We used three factors to quantify each of these components of the explorative behavior.

a. The *quantity* of path and neighborhood exploration. For path exploration we assessed quantity as the number of repeated passages through a single target point on the path (backtracks). For neighborhood exploration quantity was the number of times the subject left the path and returned to it, without reaching a target location (*detours*).

b. The *efficacy* of path and neighborhood exploration. We assessed the number of final and target locations reached, calculating efficacy as the number of explored target locations divided by the number of described locations.

c. The *flexibility* of path and neighborhood exploration. Flexibility was assessed in terms of variations from routes indicated by the describer, that led to better exploration. For path exploration, we defined flexibility as the number of variations in the path that allowed the *explorer* to avoid retracing his/her steps (*backtracking* avoidance). For neighborhood exploration, we assessed flexibility as the number of *shortcuts* found. We only counted *backtracking* avoidance and *shortcuts* discovered by *explorer*s, not those indicated by *describer*s; thus the differences between instances of *backtracking* avoidance and *shortcuts* explored and described were calculated for each pair.

3. Results

Analysis of describers' verbal reports

The number of route and survey indicators used in the descriptions is given in Table 2 for the four experimental situations.

Table 2. Number of route and survey indicators used in the descriptions

Experimental Situation	Total No. of survey indicators	Total No. of route indicators	Mean of S/S+R
A	83	120	0.504
B	150	164	0.490
C	57	57	0.488
D	70	154	0.380

The mean indicator (No of survey indicators/No of survey indicators + No of route indicators) in situation D differs from that in the other three situations. The mean indicator is greatest in the two situations in which the *describer* is highly familiar with the environment (A and B). Situation B (where only the *explorer* is highly familiar with the environment) is characterized by a high number of both survey and route indicators.

In situations C and D (*describer* not very familiar with the environment) the number of survey indicators is less than in the other two situations; in situation C the total number of indicators is low compared to the other situations, while in situation D the route indicators dominate the scene.

Table 3 shows the results of the analyses of the *quantity*, *efficacy* and *flexibility* of path and neighbourhood exploration.

Table 3. Results of the analyses of the quantity, efficacy and flexibility of path and neighbourhood exploration. Describers and Explorers

Experimental Situation	Quantity		Efficacy (explored/ described locations		Flexibility	
	backtracking	detours	final targets	intermediate targets	avoidance of backtracking	shortcuts
A	9	20	6 (0.67)	26 (1.08)	2	3
B	12	22	5 (0.62)	24 (1.04)	3	7
C	11	25	8 (1.33)	20 (1.43)	2	10
D	4	15	9 (1.5)	18 (1.06)	3	3

The results in the Table concerning the *quantity* of path and neighborhood exploration show that the poorest performance is in situation D (both, *describer* and *explorer* have low familiarity). The number of backtracks in situation B was high, where *explorers* with low familiarity obtained comparable results to those familiar with the environment (A and C) as a result of their interaction with *describers* familiar with the environment. *Explorers* familiar with the environment achieved similar performance irrespective of the familiarity of the decribers familiar with the environment.

With regard to *efficacy* of exploration, it is surprising that *explorers* familiar with the environment were successful even when they interacted with *describers* not familiar with the environment. This cannot be due to the information communicated to them by their *describers* as shown by the high value for the explored/described ratio. Conversely, the targets were explored with more *efficacy* by the *explorers* with high familiarity and by those who interacted with highly familiar *describers*. As regards *flexibility* the most interesting finding was that *explorers* who interacted with both highly familiar and poorly familiar *describers* (situations B and C) used a high number of new *shortcuts*.

4. Discussion

Various types of spatial descriptions were produced by the *describers* to communicate the same routes. We found that these descriptions were related to the familiarity of the *describers* with the environment. *Describers* familiar with the environment give descriptions containing more survey indicators, not only absolutely but also in proportion to the number of route indicators (survey/route). This supports the hypothesis that the type of verbal description, analyzed in terms of survey and route, is related to the type of underlying spatial representation (spatial map). A second finding was that spatial descriptions also depended on the *explorers*' familiarity with the environment.

One would expect that survey maps would be able provide all the possibilities offered by the simpler route maps in terms of spatial behavior (to find a route between two given points), as well as providing more information enabling routes to be found by planning on the basis of varying contextual criteria (shortest, safest, etc.). Conversely *route maps* would be useful for communicating spatial knowledge: a subject trying to explain how to traverse a route to an individual with no prior knowledge of a given environment would try to communicate routes as sequences of easily recoverable landmarks.

Our findings support the hypothesis that in an interaction between individuals of different familiarity with the environment, a description consisting mainly of survey components is used. Thus although the survey/route ratio was highest when both partners were familiar with the environment, even when only one of the partners was familiar this ratio was high, and greater than when both partners hardly knew the environment. This seems to support the interpretation that survey representations are more flexible and informative than route representations.

This conclusion is further supported by our finding that that it was not possible to distinguish between the two types of descriptions/representations, since a high number of route indicators was present in the descriptions in which the high survey/route ratio was high. This further suggests that typical route aspects are contained in survey descriptions/representations. Obviously, route indicators in these survey descriptions do not have the same meaning as route indicators in more route-oriented descriptions. Thus, in situations B and situation D, *explorers* are not very familiar with the environment and receive a large number of route indicators in their descriptions; but in situation B, these route indicators are set in a rich survey context, while in situation D they are not.

In further support of our conclusion that route indicators have different meanings in the two cases, we note that exploration behavior related to route differed greatly for *final targets* compared to *backtracking*. This illustrates the importance of relating the description to the exploration behavior the description induces and helps us better understand the meaning of the descriptions. By analyzing the exploration behavior it is possible to reveal the real survey-type meaning of the descriptions used in situation B. In this situation, the low familiarity *explorer* in fact uses a survey type description and this is shown by the high number of backtracks used and target-locations found, and also by the large number of *shortcuts* used that were not mentioned by the *describer*. Analysis of the behavior thus allows us to distinguish between the descriptions in situations A and C: the larger number of route indicators used in situation C is understandable if we consider the number of explored target-locations.

In conclusion, we have devised a useful methodology for studying spatial representations, in which subjects with differing familiarity with an environment interact, and the descriptions communicated are analyzed and related to the exploration behavior induced. Although the method is complicated, it overcomes some of the limits of other experimental methodologies, one of which is that analysis of descriptions in terms of route and survey only does not allow unequivocal interpretation of results since a given verbal description contains both survey and route indicators, and route indicators can assume survey significance in a survey context. The analysis of drawings, maps and diagrams produced by a *describer* also presents a number of difficulties: analysis criteria are still not well defined; graphic abilities and visuo-motor coordination vary considerably between of individuals especially those in developmental age confounding the analysis, and cultural factors may also influence expertise in using street plans, maps and building plans.

The most interesting aspect of the method we propose is that it allows experiments to be designed in which individuals with differing familiarities to a given environment are compared. Since familiarity determines the type of the spatial representation (as shown by Golledge 1978 and Evans 1985, for example) it becomes possible to relate different behaviors to underlying spatial representations.

Acknowledgments

We are grateful to A. Schweitzer and A. Modigliani school children (in Segrate, Milano) who participated in this study and to Erminielda Peron for helpful suggestions. Antonella Carassa and Giuliano Geminiani were both supported MURST grants (60%) for the years 1996 and 1997.

References

Biel, Anders & Gunilla Torell (1979). The mapped environment: Cognitive aspects of children's drawings. *Man-Environment Systems*, *9*, 187–194.

Chown, Eric, Stephen Kaplan & David Kortenkamp (1995). Prototypes, Location and Associative Networks (PLAN): Towards a unified theory of cognitive mapping. *Cognitive Science*, *19*, 1–51.

Cornell, Edward H., Donald C. Heth & Denise M. Alberts (1994). Place recognition and way finding by children and adults. *Memory and Cognition*, *22*, 633–643.

Evans, Gary W. (1980). Environmental cognition. *Psychological Bullettin*, *88*, 259–287.

Evans, Gary W. (1985). Review of Lindberg E.: Acquisition of cognitive maps of large scale environments. *Scandinavian Journal of Psychology*, *26*, 95–96.

Golledge, Reginald G. (1978). Learning about urban environments. In T. Carlstein, D. & N. Thrift (Eds.), *Timing Space and Spacing Time*. London: Edward Arnold.

Golledge, Reginald G. (1987). Environmental cognition. In D. Stokols & I. Altman (Eds.), *Handbook of Environmental Psychology*. New York: John Wiley and Sons.

Golledge, Reginald G. (1990). Cognition of physical and built environments. In T. Garling, G. Evans (Eds.), *Environment, Cognition and Action: A Multidisciplinary Integrative Approach*. New York: Oxford University Press.

Hart, Roger A., Gary T. Moore (1973). The development of spatial cognition: A review. In R.M. Downs, Stea (Eds.), *Image and Environment: Cognitive Mapping and Spatial Behavior*. Chicago: Aldline.

Heth, Donald C., Edward H. Cornell, Denise M. Alberts (1997). Differential use of landmarks by 8- and 12-year-old children during route reversal navigation. *Journal of Environmental Psychology*, *17*, 199–213.

Lynch, Kevin (1960). *The Image of the City*. Cambridge, MA: MIT Press.

Shemyakin, F.N. (1962). General problems of orientation in space and space representations. In B.G. Anayev (Eds.), *Psychological Science in the USSR* (vol 1.). Washington, DC: US Joint Publications Research Service.

Siegel, Alexander W. & Sheldon H. White, (1975). The development of spatial representations of large scale environments. In H.W. Reese (Eds.), *Advances in Child Development and Behavior*. New York: Academic Press.

Taylor, Holly A. & Barbara Tversky (1996). Perspective in spatial description. *Journal of Memory and Language*, *35*, 371–391.

Torell, Gunilla (1990). Children conceptions of large-scale environments. *Goteborg Psychological Reports*, *20*, II.

The Functional Separability of Self-Reference and Object-to-Object Systems in Spatial Memory

M. Jeanne Sholl
Boston College

When people learn the layout of large-scale space by walking around within it, their ability to orient, either in imagination or in actuality, to surrounding landmarks that are hidden from view is generally accurate and highly flexible (Presson & Hazelrigg 1984; Thorndyke & Hayes-Roth 1982; Sholl 1987). This facility likely requires using locally available spatial cues to establish one's location and facing direction, and then retrieving the location of nonvisible landmarks within that frame of reference. Sholl (Easton & Sholl 1995; Sholl & Nolin 1997) has proposed a coordinate-system model of retrieval to account for the seeming ease with which people retrieve the direction of unseen landmarks from a variety of actual and imagined locations and facing directions in a known environment (e.g., Easton & Sholl 1995; Sholl 1987). The model's scope is limited to the representation and retrieval of spatial knowledge learned by navigating an environment on foot. It distinguishes between the storage of metric object-to-object relations in an allocentrically organized long-term spatial memory system and the retrieval of object-to-object relations within a body-centered coordinate system. In its conceptualization, the model draws heavily from animal models of navigation (Gallistel 1990; O'Keefe 1991), because the components of a model of spatial retrieval need ultimately to fit within a general model of human spatial navigation.

It should be acknowledged at the outset that metric models of spatial representation can not account for all human spatial behavior. A metric model of large-scale space that conforms to the axioms of Euclidean geometry codes the straight-line distances and angles inter-connecting the landmarks contained within the space. A mental representation that preserves the metric properties of Euclidean space should produce spatial judgments that uphold Euclidean axioms (see Montello 1992, for a more in-depth discussion of this point). That is, inter-landmark distance judgments should be symmetrical (i.e., the distance of Landmark A from Landmark B should be estimated to be the same as the distance from Landmark B to Landmark A) and judgments of relative direction should be consistent with the triangle inequality axiom (i.e., estimates of the spatial angles at the vertices of a triangle formed by three landmarks [e.g., Landmarks 2, 3 & 4 in Figure 1A] should not sum to more than 180°). However, it is not uncommon for people to make systematically distorted and non-commutative judgments of inter-landmark distance and angle in violation of Euclidean axioms (e.g., Moar & Bower 1983; Sadalla, Burroughs & Staplin 1980; Tversky 1981; etc.). In spite of that, animals, including humans, skillfully navigate complex trajectories through cluttered environments to destinations which cannot be seen from the starting point, behavior which is consistent with an underlying representation that preserves the metric properties of space.

Current theories of spatial memory resolve the dilemma of routine non-metric spatial judgments coupled with highly evolved navigation skills by proposing a metric level of representation, plus another level of representation to account for non-metric behavior. For example, Huttenlocher, Hedges & Duncan (1991) propose a categorical level of representation which when combined with imprecise metric knowledge produces systematically biased judgments of spatial location. Similarly, Poucet (1993) suggests that both topological and metric representational systems are needed to account for contradictory spatial behaviors observed in animals. The present model focuses on a metric level of representation and retrieval, while acknowledging that other types of representation are needed to account for the full range of human spatial behavior.

The coordinate system model of retrieval

Key terms

Before describing the model, a few key terms will be defined. An *allocentric* representation is an environment-centered representation which stores inter-landmark Euclidean relations independently of any momentary perspective of the viewer. *Large-scale space* refers to a scale of space which is large enough to walk around and contain landmarks which cannot be simultaneously apprehended. The immobile, behaviorally relevant landmarks that structure large-scale space are the *objects* represented in the object-to-object system. The *coordinate system* is an orthogonal set of reference axes used to compute the Euclidean coordinates of objects represented in the cognitive vector space, when retrieved in working memory.

Cognitive vector space

In the model, object-to-object relations are stored allocentrically in a representation which functions as if it were an orientation-free vector space. An orientation-free representation is one which can be accessed equally easily from any facing direction. Current evidence suggests that an orientation-free representation is formed when a person moves freely through space, but that an orientation-specific representation is formed when a large-scale space is observed from a single, static observation point (Shelton & McNamara 1997; Sholl & Nolin 1997). The latter finding is consistent with the idea that an orientation-free representation is built up from multiple orientation specific representations. According to this view, an unspecified number of discrete visual samples are taken along the person's movement trajectory, each sample producing an orientation-specific representation of the inter-object relations observed in the forward field of view. Orientation invariance then arises in one of two ways: either functionally from the collective activity of multiple orientation-specific representations or structurally as a single, higher-level orientation-free representation constructed from multiple, lower-level orientation-specific representations.

The present model assumes a single, higher-level orientation-free representation of object-to-object relations. If indeed a unitary representation of inter-object relations is formed as a result of navigating a large-scale space by foot, an additional possibility should be considered regarding its formation. Instead, of being built up from multiple orientation-specific representations, a unitary orientation-free representation of inter-object relations may be formed directly from the higher order structural invariances which emerge in the optical flow generated by the act of walking (Gibson 1979). However, irrespective of how the representation is formed, the model proposes that it functions like a cognitive vector space. As illustrated in Figure 1A, the circular nodes symbolize the objects represented in the metric network and the vectors connecting the nodes code the distances and angles which physically separate objects in the real world. The vector space contains no global system of reference, and, as a consequence, vector angles are underdetermined and a minimum of three objects are needed to create a spatial angle.

Self-reference system

Consistent with findings showing that people organize their knowledge of surrounding space within a frame-of-reference centered on the body (e.g., Franklin & Tversky 1990; Franklin, Henkel & Zangas 1995; Shepard & Hurwitz 1984), a central premise of the model is that a representation of the anatomical axes of the body forms the coordinate system which mediates the retrieval of metric inter-landmark relations (see also Presson & Montello 1994). The coordinate system, illustrated in Figure 1B, consists of an orthogonal set of front-back and right-left reference axes, which when superposed on the vector space, as illustrated in Figure 1C, provides a set of basis vectors for computing metric distance and direction. The origin of the reference system is located in the vector space at the place corresponding to the person's actual or imagined location in the physical world. In addition, the reference axes are oriented so that the front pole of the front-back axis is pointed in the direction of the person's actual or imagined facing direction in the physical world. At a computational level, the vectors coding inter-object relations could be referred to the reference axes in either polar or Cartesian coordinates, and the model takes no position regarding how the vector angles coding the relative direction of objects are calculated geometrically.

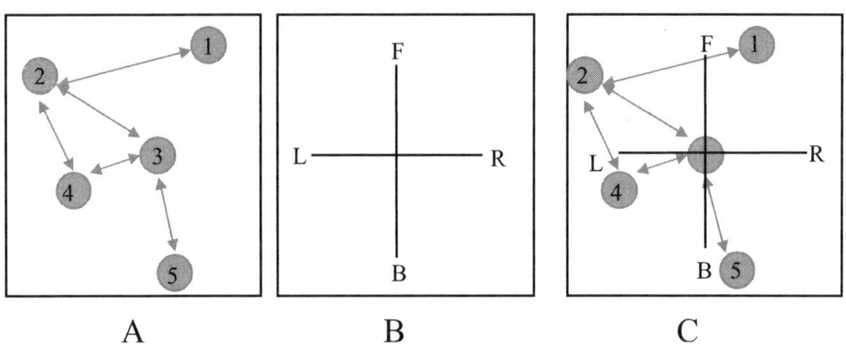

Figure 1. 1A is a schematic illustration of a cognitive vector space, 1B illustrates a self-reference system consisting of a representation of the front-back/right-left axes of the body, and 1C illustrates superposition of a self-reference system on the cognitive vector space. The metric coordinates of the objects represented in the vector space are computed by the self-reference system.

Separability of the object-to-object and self-reference systems

If the model is correct in its premise that the cognitive vector system and the self-reference system are functionally separable, then it ought to be possible to influence the accessibility of spatial relations within one system independently of the other. For example, a variable which influences the accessibility of a landmark's relative direction within the self-reference system should have no influence on its accessibility in the cognitive vector space, and complementarily, a variable which influences the accessibility of relative direction within the cognitive vector space should not influence its accessibility within the self reference system. The experiments reported here tease apart accessibility in the self-reference system from accessibility in the cognitive vector space.

Accessibility within the self-reference system

Prior research has shown that pointing responses to non-visible landmarks located in the anterior part of body space are faster than pointing responses to non-visible landmarks located in the posterior part of body space (Sholl 1987). This front-back effect is observed when people point to landmarks as they imagine them to be from either their actual or imagined position in space. That the effect is attributable to the landmark's location in body space and not to a characteristic property of the landmark itself is demonstrated by duplicating the effect from two diametrically opposite facing directions. That is, a single landmark which is more accessible when it is located in the anterior half of body space from one facing direction becomes less accessible when located in the posterior half of body space following a 180° turn in place. Independent verification of an anterior/posterior asymmetry in the accessibility of ego-centrically referenced spatial relations has been reported by Franklin et al. (1995). It is of particular importance to the present argument that Franklin et al. (1995) found a front-back effect when using a task which eliminated any reliance on object-to-object spatial relations, thereby isolating memory for the location of a target event in body-centered space.

The coordinate system model attributes the front-back effect to faster computation of spatial coordinates in the anterior than posterior half of the self-reference system, thereby mirroring at a representational level, asymmetries in response readiness at the sensory-motor level. Thus, one variable that influences accessibility of a landmark's relative direction in the self reference system is its anterior/posterior location in body space, and the model predicts that the effect of this variable should be independent of the accessibility of the landmark's relative direction at the level of the cognitive vector space.

Accessibility within the cognitive vector space

Consider an example to help clarify the distinction being made between accessibility in the self-reference system and the cognitive vector space. Figure 1C illustrates the arrangement of the self-reference system in the cognitive vector space if a person were to imagine herself at Landmark 3, facing in the direction indicated by the front pole of the front/back axis. Assume that the person is then asked to point in the direction of Landmark 2 from her imagined location in the environment. Retrieval of the relative direction of Landmark 2 takes place at two levels. At the level of the cognitive vector space, the retrieval of the direction of Landmark 2 relative to Landmark 3 can be thought of as corresponding to the activation of the vector connecting them. There are various potential variables that could affect the speed of vector activation. One obvious possibility is vector strength, which could vary as a function of the frequency of travel between two landmarks, with stronger vectors being more quickly activated than weaker vectors. Inter-landmark distance is another possibility: longer vectors may take longer to activate than shorter vectors. Yet a third possibility is the directness of the connection between two landmarks. Landmarks which are directly connected by a vector should be more accessible than landmarks connected indirectly through one or more other landmarks (e.g., in Figure 1A, Landmarks 4 and 5 are indirectly connected through their connections to Landmark 3). Once the target vector is activated, then its Euclidean coordinates are calculated within the self-reference system. In this example, the direction of Landmark 2 relative to the body is computed. As previously discussed, the location of Landmark 2 in the anterior half of the self-reference system (body space) means that the coordinates of the vector connecting Landmark 2 to Landmark 3 (Vector_{3-2}) will be computed more quickly than the coordinates of vectors in posterior body space (e.g., Vector_{3-4}, Vector_{3-5}).

Earlier accounts of the accessibility of inter-object relations in object-to-object representations did not allow for the possibility of differential accessibility of inter-object relations (Levine, Jankovic & Palij 1982). In their proposal that cognitive maps have picture-like properties, Levine et al. proposed that sequentially experienced inter-object relations are read into a representational system which makes all inter-object relations, even those not directly experienced, simultaneously and equally available. The principle of the equi-availability of inter-object relations has been confirmed by earlier findings (Levine et al. 1982;

Sholl 1987); however, in these instances, either the test spaces were very simple or care was taken to ensure that variables which might affect inter-object accessibility were controlled. Thus, given the complexity of the large-scale environments along with prior findings suggesting functional differences between environmental landmarks differing in familiarity, geographic prominence, and cultural importance (Sadella, Borroughs & Staplin 1980), inter-object relations are likely to be differentially accessible in an object-to-object system representing natural environments.

The experimental task and predicted outcomes

The extent to which the accessibility of relative direction within the self-to-object system is independent of its accessibility within the object-to-object system should be demonstrable with a point-to-unseen-targets task developed by Sholl (1987). The task manipulates facing direction, landmark set, and egocentric target location in a Latin square design. In the task, a central location in a known environment (or test space) serves as a reference location, and people's knowledge of the direction of landmarks relative to the reference location is tested from two facing directions diametrically opposed. The test space is bisected at the reference location along an imaginary axis orthogonal to the facing direction axis. For example in the schematic illustration below, east and west facing directions are tested, and a north-south axis divides the test space into an eastern and western half. An equal number of landmarks from each side of the test space are selected as targets.

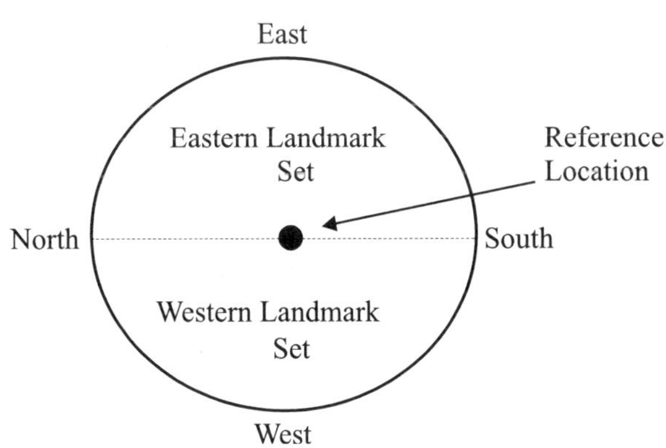

Figure 2. Schematic of experimental design for point to unseen targets task

1 11 1180985 3

The participants' task is to imagine themselves at the reference location and to use a joystick to point to the center of the target landmark from their position in space. According to the model, retrieval involves centering the self-reference system over the place in the vector space corresponding to the reference location and aligning the front pole of the front/back reference axis in the facing direction. In the task there are two blocks of trials: in one, participants imagine themselves facing east and, in the other, they imagine themselves facing west. The same set of landmarks serve as targets in both blocks of trials.

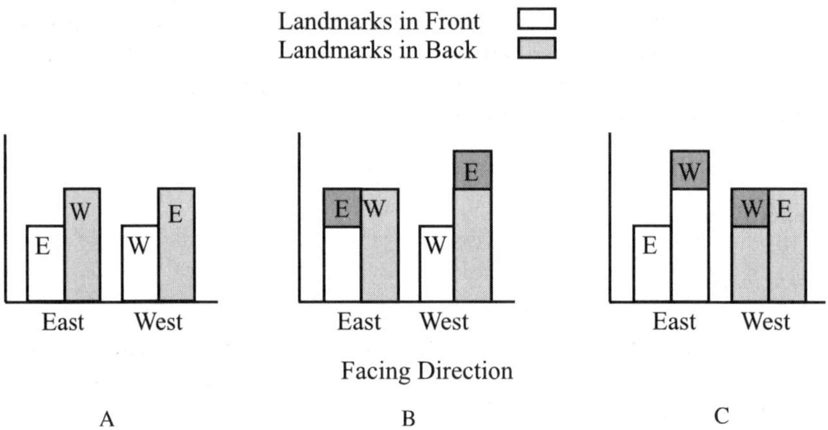

Figure 3. *Performance plotted as a function of egocentric target location (front, back), facing direction (east, west), and landmark set (eastern [E], western [W]), with the landmark set condition indicated by the letter located at the top of each bar. Panel A illustrates a front-back effect of egocentric target location. Panels B and C illustrate the expected latency pattern for additive effects of egocentric target location and landmark set.*

Figure 3A illustrates the typical front-back effect. In both the east and west facing-direction conditions, landmarks located in front of the body are pointed to faster than landmarks behind the body, regardless of whether the landmarks are from the eastern or western landmark sets. This finding illustrates the differential accessibility of spatial relations in the self-reference system, in the special case in which there is no effect of landmark set. An effect of landmark set is expected if on average the relative directions of the members of one landmark set are more easily accessible in the cognitive vector space than the members of the other landmark set. Figures 3B and 3C illustrate the more complex pattern of results expected if a front-back effect is combined with an effect of landmark set. An advantage of western over eastern landmarks is illustrated in Figure 3B and an advantage of eastern over western landmarks in Figure 3C. The darker gray area of the bars in Figures 3B and C depict the additional time required to point to the less accessible landmark set.[1]

The experiments reported in this paper show that accessibility within a body-centered reference system is indeed separable from accessibility in the object-to-object system. Experiment 1 produced the latency profile illustrated in Figure 3C, a finding consistent with an effect of landmark set combined with a front-back effect. However, because the latency profile was produced by a Latin square design, a main effect of landmark set is indistinguishable from an interaction between facing direction and egocentric target location. Experiments 2 and 3 ruled out the possibility that an interaction accounted for the latency profile observed in Experiment 1 and demonstrated that landmark size accounted for the observed effect of landmark set.

General method

Participants

Participants were Boston College undergraduates of at least sophomore status to insure familiarity with campus landmarks. Students participated either for pay or to fulfill a course requirement. Twelve students participated in Experiment 1, 12 in Experiment 2, and 16 in Experiment 3

Test space and target landmarks

Figure 4 shows a map of the Chestnut Hill Campus of Boston College, which served as the test space in the present study. The reference location in Experiments 1 and 3 is depicted on the map by the dot to the left of the letter *B*, and Experiment 2's reference location is depicted by the dot below the letter *D*.[2] A line drawn parallel to the vertical edges of the map through the reference location divided the test space into eastern and western halves.[3] The east/west facing directions were orthogonal to the line bisecting the test space. Target landmarks were selected from the two halves of the test space and will be described separately for each experiment. To the extent possible, target landmarks were evenly distributed across the eastern and western halves of the test space.

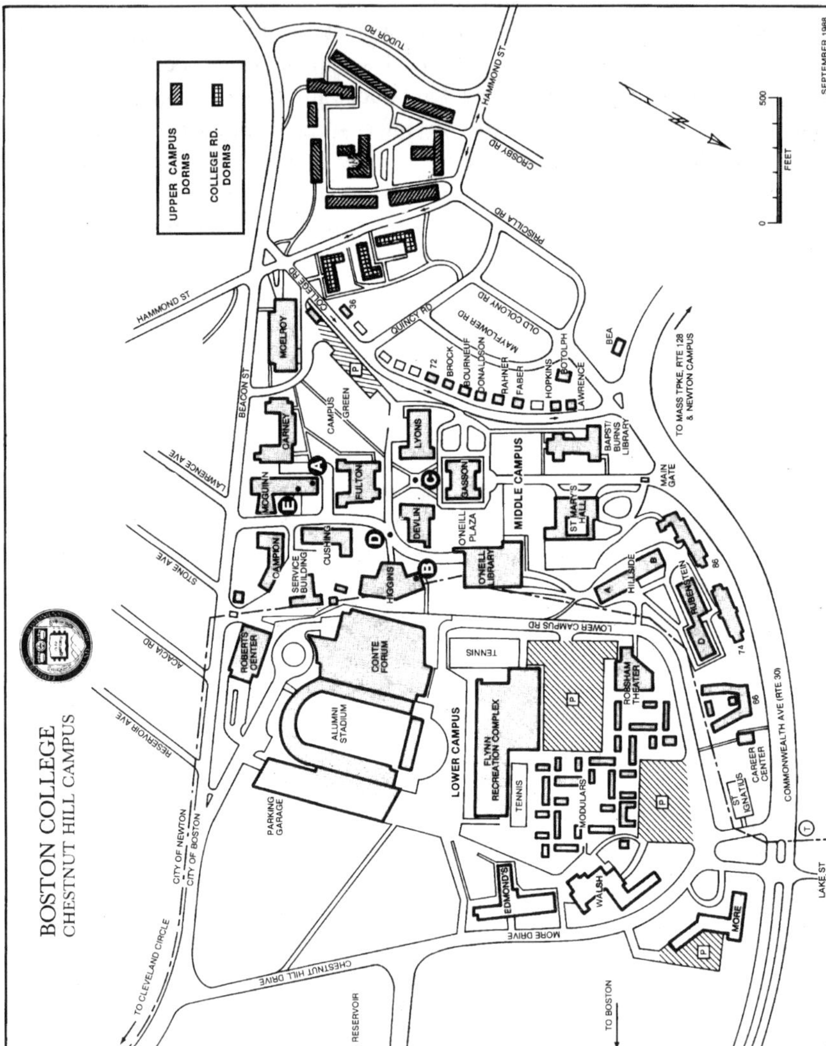

Figure 4. Map of the Chestnut Hill Campus of Boston College

Apparatus

The point-to-unseen targets task was controlled on line by an Apple IIe microcomputer with Z80 microprocessor and equipped with a Mountain Computer Clock. Participants made their pointing responses with a modified Apple II joystick, connected to the computer via an analog/digital interface card. A detailed description of the apparatus and the supporting software routines is given by Sholl (1987).

Procedure

All testing was done in a room located at the dot to the left of the letter *A* in Figure 4. The testing room provided no outside view of the campus. In order to ensure that each participant was familiar with the target landmarks, the experimenter read a list of landmarks to the participant, and participants indicated whether they knew each landmark's location. If a participant did not know a landmark's location, the experimenter gave a brief verbal description of its whereabouts. The list contained all the target landmarks as well as some foils that were not targets. After landmark familiarization, the experiment proceeded under computer control. First, the participant was instructed how to use the joystick to make pointing responses. These instructions were followed by a set of 12 practice trials in which participants pointed to the randomly ordered numbers 1 to 12 as they imagined them to be on the clockface and were provided accuracy feedback to help them fine-tune their responses.

Each practice and experimental trial had an identical sequence. First, there was a joystick centering routine, in which the joystick was physically placed at the origin of its coordinate system. Once the joystick was centered, the participant initiated the trial, and the name of the target was presented at the center of the CRT screen. Participants made their pointing response by moving the joystick radially in the direction they imagined the target to be. When the joystick movement exceeded a radius of 120 units in the "joystick" space, the computer recorded both the response latency from the onset of the target name and the angle of the response to the nearest degree space (see Sholl 1987, for a more detailed description).

The experimental trials followed directly after the practice trials. Participants were told to take as much time as they needed to imagine the campus from the specified position, to move the joystick in the direction they imagined each landmark to be in relation to their body, and to point to the center of each target. The reference location and facing direction were described using local visual cues, which never served as target landmarks. The order of the two within-subjects facing-direction conditions was counter-balanced across subjects. Order was included in analyses of variance as a control variable and is not reported.[4] Target landmarks were presented in a different random order for each participant and in each facing-direction condition. After the experimental trials were completed, there were twelve more clock trials with no accuracy feedback. These trials served as a control check for the relative speed of forward and rearward joystick movements.

Data analysis

Although three variables are manipulated in a Latin Square design, only two variables are entered into the analysis of variance (ANOVA). In the experiments reported here, egocentric target location and facing direction were entered in the ANOVA, and the results are reported as a function of these two variables.

Experiment 1

Method

Target Landmarks. The eastern landmark set consisted of the Recreation Complex, Alumni Stadium, Robsham Theater, Roberts Center, Parking Garage, and More Hall. The western landmark set included Cushing Hall, Gasson Hall, Carney Hall, Main Gate, Lyons Hall, and O'Connell Hall. Mean familiarity rating, collected from a separate group of Boston College undergraduates ($n = 22$) on a 5-point scale, were 4.07 and 4.02 for the eastern and western landmark sets, respectively, $t\ (10) < 1.0$. High ratings indicate high familiarity. On average, the distance of eastern and western landmarks from Reference Location B was 293.1 *m* and 245.4 *m*, respectively, $t\ (10) < 1.0$.

Results

Landmark targets. Mean response latencies are shown in Figure 5A. There was a main effect of egocentric target location, $F\ (1, 10) = 6.15$, $p = .03$, $MS_e = .56$, qualified by an interaction between egocentric target location and imagined facing direction, $F\ (1, 10) = 7.89$, $p = .02$, $MS_e = .43$. The interaction reflected a significant 1.23 s front-back effect for the east facing-direction condition and no front-back effect for the west facing-direction condition. As shown in Figure 5B, pointing error did not mimic pointing latencies. For pointing error, there was a front-back effect, $F\ (1, 10) = 13.68$, $p = .004$, $MS_e = 141.70$, which did not interact with facing direction condition, $F\ (1, 10) < 1.0$.

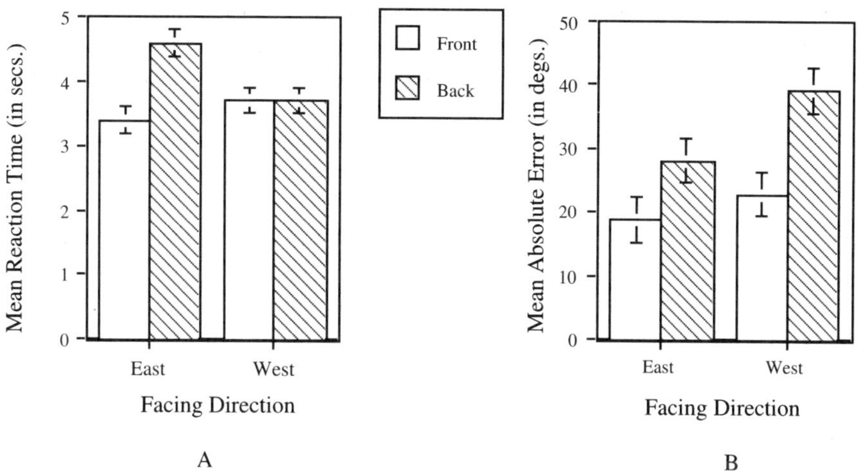

Figure 5. Mean pointing latency (in Panel A) and error (in Panel B) as a function of facing direction and front/back target location in Experiment 1. Error bars are standard errors of the mean

Clock numeral targets. Pointing responses on the second set of clock trials (excluding the clock numerals 3 and 9) were analyzed to test whether forward and rearward movements of the joystick were equivalent in speed and accuracy. For forward and rearward joystick movement, mean latency was 1.603 s and 1.634 s, respectively, and mean error was 9.17° and 8.75°, respectively. Neither difference was significant, *ts* (11) < 1.0.

Discussion

The latency profile observed in Experiment 1 is consistent with additive front-back and landmark set effects, with the latter reflecting an advantage of eastern over western landmarks. For pointing error there was a front-back effect only, suggesting that an advantage of eastern over western targets is restricted to pointing latency and does not generalize to pointing accuracy. However, before concluding that the latency profile reflects the main effects of landmark set and egocentric target location, the possibility that the profile is actually attributable to an interaction between egocentric target location and facing direction needs to be considered.

While additive main effects of landmark set and egocentric target location are consistent with the present model's premise of separate levels of accessibility when retrieving spatial relations, the alternative of an egocentric target location by facing direction interaction is consistent with a different view of how spatial memory is organized and retrieved. In Zipser's (1987) distributed field view model of place knowledge, a representation of large-scale space is not stored as an integrated network of metric spatial relations, but instead consists of multiple individual representations, each storing a local view encoded from a different vantage point. The different viewpoint-specific representations are connected together with motor programs for how to get from one represented scene to another. The idea that knowledge of large scale space is made up of a collection of viewpoint-specific representations has more recently been espoused by McNamara and his colleagues to account for their findings of viewpoint specificity in spatial representations formed from static viewing points (e.g., Roskos-Ewoldsen, McNamara, Shelton & Carr 1998; Shelton & McNamara 1997).

It seems reasonable to assume that a local-view model of spatial memory would predict that the accessibility of relative landmark direction is, at least in part, a function of whether the target landmark is represented in the local view activated by the facing direction instruction used in the present task. Certainly different viewpoints in a cluttered environment have differentially expansive vistas which, dependent upon the number of landmarks visible in the vista, are more or less revealing of inter-object relations. For example, a view of an expansive vista in which numerous landmarks are simultaneously visible provides more direct information about inter-object relations than a view of a limited vista containing few visible landmarks. In this regard, it is notable that Reference Location B is at the top of a steep flight of 116 stairs connecting the "lower" and "middle"[5] parts of campus.

When facing east at Reference Location B, the stairs extend downward in front of you, and the local view is an aerial view revealing a large portion of the lower campus, especially in the winter when the trees have lost their leaves. In contrast when facing west, the local view is a ground-level view of middle campus, with a single building (Devlin Hall) at its center and limited vistas to either side. Accordingly, a viewpoint-specific representation of the more expansive eastern vista may code more interobject relations directly, and hence more accessibly, than a viewpoint-specific representation of the less expansive western vista. If it is further assumed that any advantage accorded by a local view is mitigated when it is "behind the head", the latency profile observed in Experiment 1 could be accounted for by an advantage of the eastern local view over the western local view in the east facing direction condition, which is mitigated in the west facing direction condition when the eastern local view is behind the head.

In order to test whether the latency profile observed in Experiment 1 is attributable to differential accessibility of spatial relations in the different local views afforded by the east and west facing directions, the experiment was replicated at a different reference location. Experiment 2 tested people's ability to point to essentially the same set of landmarks as tested in Experiment 1, but now from Reference Location D (see Figure 4). Reference Location D affords a ground-level perspective of the middle campus. When facing east, the central visual field is occupied by a large academic building (Higgens Hall) and when facing west the central visual field is occupied by a narrow road running between several academic buildings. If the same latency profile is observed in Experiment 2 as in Experiment 1, then it is unlikely attributable to the local aerial view of lower campus afforded when facing east at Reference Location B.

Experiment 2

Method

Target landmarks. The eastern and western landmark sets were identical to those in Experiment 1, except McElroy Commons was substituted for Cushing Hall, which could not be used because it switches into the eastern landmark set at Reference Location D. With this change, the mean familiarity of the western landmark set was 4.10. The mean distance of the eastern and western landmarks from Reference Location D was 334.3 m and 243.8 m, respectively, $t(10) = 1.10$, $p > .10$.

Results

Landmark Targets. As shown in Figure 6A, a latency profile similar to the one observed in Experiment 1 was observed in Experiment 2. There was main effect of egocentric target location, $F\ (1,\ 10) = 10.74$, $MS_e = .45$, $p = .008$, and a marginally significant interaction between egocentric target location and facing direction, $F\ (1,\ 10) = 4.03$, $MS_e = 1.20$, $p = .07$. As shown in Figure 6B, there was an effect of egocentric target location on pointing errors, $F\ (1,\ 10) = 5.35$,

$MS_e = 251.5$, $p = .04$. Targets located in the front part of body space ($M = 24.6°$) were pointed to more accurately than targets located in the back part of body space ($M = 35.2°$). There were no other main or interaction effects.

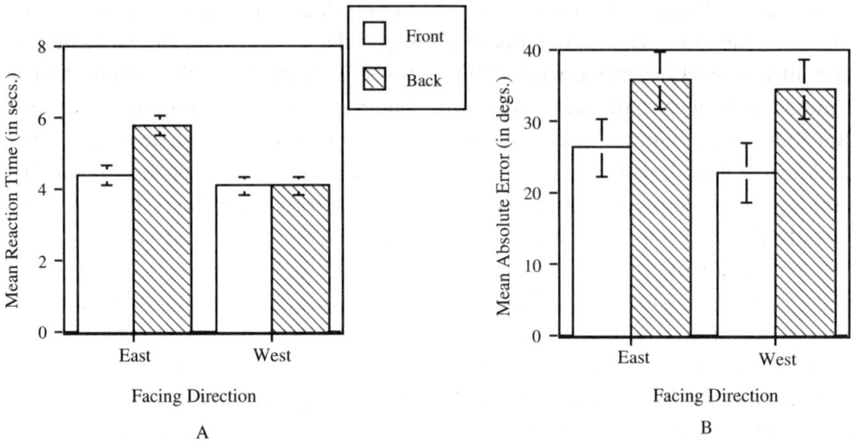

Figure 6. Mean pointing latency (in Panel A) and error (in Panel B) as a function of facing direction and front/back target location in Experiment 2. Error bars are standard errors of the mean.

Clock numeral targets. For forward and rearward joystick movements, mean latency was 1.655 *s* and 1.681 *s*, respectively, and mean error was 9.75° and 11.67°, respectively. Neither difference was significant, *ts* $(11) < 1.0$.

Discussion

When participants imagined themselves at Reference Location D, they showed the same latency profile as when they imagined themselves at Reference Location B. Therefore, it is unlikely that the aerial local view afforded when facing east at Reference Location B accounted for the interaction between facing direction and egocentric target location in Experiment 1. If we return to the idea that the interaction represents additive effects of egocentric target location and landmark set, the question then becomes why can people point to targets in the eastern landmark set more quickly than to targets in the western landmark set? This question is considered by exploring two variables that might differentiate the two landmark sets: One variable is an attitudinal variable, landmark pleasantness, and the other is a physical variable, landmark size.

With respect to student's attitudes about landmarks, it is important to consider that the campus is divided up functionally as well as geographically. In Experiments 1 and 2, all the landmarks in the eastern landmark set were located on lower campus, which contains residential, leisure, and recreational facilities, and all landmarks in the western landmark set, with the exception of one upper-campus residence hall, were academic buildings located on middle campus. Because lower campus buildings serve primarily nonacademic functions and middle campus landmarks serve primarily academic functions, lower campus buildings may be perceived as more pleasant, and hence may be more accessible cognitively, than the middle campus buildings. Places perceived to be pleasant are both more likely to be physically approached (Mehrabian & Russel 1974) and to elicit an attitude of approach and exploration (Russel & Mehrabian 1978).

To determine whether middle campus landmarks were perceived as less pleasant than lower campus landmarks, a group of 37 Boston College students were asked to rate the pleasantness of 28 landmarks on a 7-point scale (1 = very unpleasant, 7 = very pleasant). Pleasantness was defined as how much participants would enjoy themselves and/or how comfortable they would feel when visiting the landmark. As expected, academic buildings were perceived as less pleasant ($M = 3.55$) then nonacademic structures ($M = 4.80$), $t\ (26) = 2.26$. However, the pleasantness ratings for the lower and middle/upper target landmarks used in Experiments 1 ($Ms = 4.57$ & 4.16, respectively) and 2 ($Ms = 4.57$ & 4.08, respectively) were not significantly different, and therefore pleasantness cannot account for an effect of landmark set.

Another variable that might differentiate the landmarks comprising the eastern and western landmark sets is their size. As can be seen in Figure 4, two eastern landmarks, the Recreation Complex and Alumni Stadium, cover a particularly large area. There are no western landmarks of comparable size. Pointing latencies may be faster for eastern than western landmarks because on average the former cover a larger area than the latter. In the coordinate-system model of retrieval, information about landmark size would be stored directly in the object-to-object system. While speculative, one possible mechanism underlying an effect of landmark size is that nodes coding larger landmarks are more quickly activated in the network than nodes coding smaller landmarks. Another possible mechanism is that the self-reference system computes a range of polar angles for each target, with the size of the range positively related to the size of the landmark. If so, pointing responses to large landmarks could be executed with less precision than pointing responses to small landmarks. This latter account implicates the response execution stage of processing, with pointing responses to large landmarks executed more quickly but with greater variability than those to small landmarks (e.g., Fitts 1954; Hardwick, McIntyre & Pick 1976).

Landmark area, measured on the map shown in Figure 4, provided a measure of landmark size. Other measures of size (visual angle, perimeter) are equally valid, and area was used primarily because it was easy to measure, not because of any underlying assumptions about its psychological relevance. The average area covered by the eastern targets in Experiments 1 and 2 was 6269 sq m. Average area covered by western targets in Experiment 1 was 1492 sq m, $t(10) = 1.89$, $p < .05$, and in Experiment 2, it was 1833 sq m, $t(10) = 1.75$, $p < .10$. With landmark as the unit of analysis, correlations between area and pointing latency (averaged over front/back location in body space) were computed: $rs = -.46$, $p < .06$, and $-.64$, $p < .01$, in Experiments 1 and 2, respectively. In order to test experimentally whether landmark size contributed to an effect of landmark set in Experiments 1 and 2, the Reference Location B condition was again tested in Experiment 3, but this time controlling the size of targets in addition to their familiarity and distance. Controlling for size should eliminate any effect of landmark set, so that Experiment 3 should exhibit only a front-back effect.

Experiment 3

Method

Target Landmarks. Four matched pairs, each pair consisting of one eastern and one western landmark, were created for this experiment. Pairs were matched on distance, area, and familiarity as well as being directional mirror images. The target pairs (listed as eastern landmark/western landmark) were Robsham Theater/Bapst Library; Tennis Courts/O'Neill Plaza; Stadium-Forum/Upper Campus Dorms; Roberts Center/Carney Hall. Matching produced eastern and western landmark sets equated on distance (205 m vs. 273 m), $t(6) < 1.0$, familiarity (4.24 vs. 3.93), $t(6) < 1.0$, and area (7650 sq m vs. 7608 sq m), $t(6) < 1.0$.

Procedure. The procedure in Experiment 3 differed from the general procedure in two ways. First there were 4 instead of 6 landmarks in each of the landmark sets. Second, unbeknownst to the participant there were two practice trials directly preceding the experimental trials. In the practice trials, the first target was always Devlin Hall and the second was Higgens Hall. Data collected on these trials was excluded from further analysis.

Results

Landmark targets. Mean response latencies are shown in Figure 7A. There was a 1.0 s front-back effect, $F\ (1, 14) = 4.14$, $MS_e = 3.84$, $p < .06$. There were no other main or interaction effects. As in Experiments 1 and 2, there was a front-back effect for pointing accuracy, $F\ (1, 14) = 10.04$, $MS_e = 84.21$.

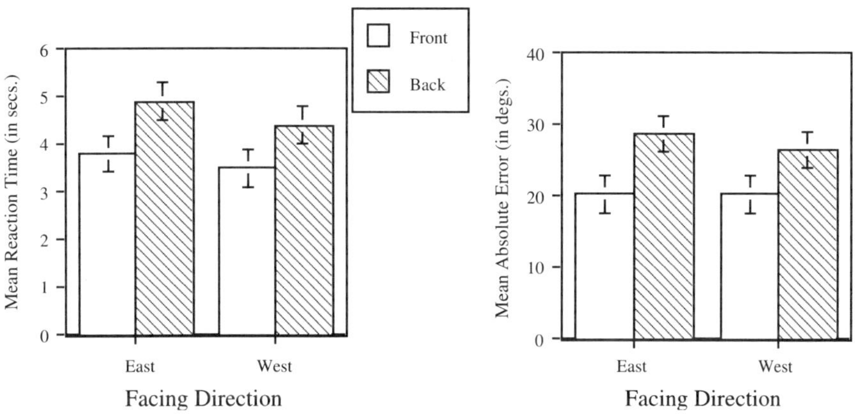

Figure 7. Mean pointing latency (in Panel A) and error (in Panel B) as a function of facing direction and front/back target location in Experiment 3. Error bars are standard errors of the mean.

Clock numeral targets. Mean latencies for forward ($M = 1.785\ s$) and rearward ($M = 1.75\ s$) joystick movements did not differ significantly, $t\ (15) < 1.0$. Furthermore, there was no statistically significant difference in the accuracy with which forward ($M = 7.25°$) and rearward ($M = 8.5°$) movements were executed, $t\ (15) < 1.0$.

Discussion

The facing direction by egocentric target location interaction was eliminated in Experiment 3 by controlling for landmark size. This result in addition to the negative correlations between landmark size and reaction time in Experiments 1 and 2 suggests that landmarks with a larger "footprint" on the ground are pointed to more quickly than landmarks with a smaller footprint. In order to determine whether this effect is attributable to less precise pointing responses for large targets, the variability of pointing responses was computed with landmark as the unit of analysis. For each experiment, variability in pointing response angles was averaged across the landmark's front/back location in body space and then correlated with landmark size. The correlations are listed in Table 1.

Table 1. Correlations between landmark size and response variability in Experiments 1 to 3 with landmark as the unit of analysis

Experiment	Number of Landmarks	Correlation
1	12	–.07
2	12	–.05
3	8	–.55

None of the correlations reported in Table 1 were statistically significance and two of them were close to 0 in magnitude. Thus there is no hint in the data that landmark size and response variability are positively related. This result is inconsistent with the idea that the locus of the effect of landmark set is in the response execution stage of processing. Instead it appears more likely that the effect can be attributed to how quickly information about relative location can be retrieved from long-term memory. The underlying mechanism is undetermined at this time and needs further study.

General discussion

To summarize the findings reported in this study. Experiment 1 produced the latency profile introduced in Figure 3C, which is consistent with additive effects for egocentric target location and landmark set. Experiment 2 experimentally ruled out the possibility that the latency profile observed in Experiment 1 was produced by an interaction effect involving facing direction and egocentric target location, and a closer analysis of the data from Experiments 1 and 2 suggested that an effect of landmark set may have emerged because of the larger average size of eastern than western landmarks. Experiment 3 showed that if landmark size is controlled, the effect of landmark set disappears, leaving a main effect of front-back target location. Additionally in Experiments 1 through 3, there was a consistent front-back effect for pointing error.

Together, the results show that the front/back location of the target in body space affects both the speed and accuracy of pointing responses, which in the

Sholl, M. J. & Nolin, T. L. (1997). Orientation specificity in place representations. *Journal of Experimental Psychology: Learning, Memory & Cognition, 23*, 1494–1507.

Thorndyke, P. W. & Hayes-Roth, B. (1982). Differences in spatial knowledge acquired from maps and navigation. *Cognitive Psychology, 14,* 560–589.

Tversky, B. (1981). Distortions in memory for maps. *Cognitive Psychology, 13*, 407–433.

Zipser, D. (1987). Biologically plausible models of place recognition and goal location. In J.L. McCelland & D.E. Rumelhart (Eds.), *Parallel Distributed Processing, Volume 2: Psychological and biological models* (pgs. 432–470). Cambridge, MA: MIT Press.

In Search for an Overall Organizing Principle in Spatial Mental Models

A question of inference

Robin Hörnig, Berry Claus and Klaus Eyferth
Technical University of Berlin

Translating Descriptions into Mental Models

Our cognitive modelling approach to spatial mental models in text understanding relies on a representation formalism originally developed in the area of robotics (Ambler and Popplestone 1975). It is outlined in more detail in Schmid, Wiebrock, and Wysotzki (this volume; see also Claus, Gips, Eyferth, Hörnig, Schmid, Wiebrock, and Wysotzki 1998). Within this approach a spatial object configuration is represented as a graph whose nodes denote objects. Every object is provided with a three-dimensional coordinate-system (reference frame) that allows for an intrinsic interpretation if the object bears intrinsic properties (e.g., humans). Two nodes in the graph may be connected by a directed arc labelled by a transformation matrix that codes the spatial relation between the represented objects by specifying constraints upon the position (as well as the orientation) of one of the objects relative to the coordinate system of the other object. The matrix indicates how to transform the coordinate-system of one of the objects onto the one of the other object in terms of translation and rotation.

(1) The refrigerator [= *referent*] is standing on the left of Torsten [= *relatum*].
Der Kühlschrank steht links von Torsten.

Given the intrinsic reading of a relational expression such as *left of* in sentence (1), the construction of the mental model, i.e. the corresponding graph, is straightforward. The node representing the referent *refrigerator* is connected with the node for the relatum *Torsten* by an arc that is annotated by a transformation matrix specifying the relative position of the referent within the intrinsic reference frame of the relatum. In our example, the possible position of the refrigerator is constrained to the negative region on the left/right-axis of the reference frame of Torsten.

(2) The bowl [= *referent*] is standing on the refrigerator [= *relatum*].
Die Schüssel steht auf dem Kühlschrank.

If sentence (1) is followed by the second input sentence (2), the mental model is extended by a third node denoting the new referent *bowl*. This node is then connected with the node for the relatum of the second sentence, the refrigerator. Again, the corresponding matrix specifies the position of the referent (*bowl*) with respect to the reference frame of the relatum (*refrigerator*). We want to emphasize that in this case, the positions of the referents of the two sentences are not specified with respect to a unique reference frame, because they are linguistically related to different relata. As the example illustrates, the mental model specifies object positions with respect to as many different reference frames as there are relata used in the text. This turns out to be a specific characteristic of the intrinsic reading of spatial relational expressions.

Given the deictic reading of *left of* in (1), the sentence linguistically localizes the referent *refrigerator* relative to the relatum *Torsten* with respect to a deictic reference frame. The deictic reference frame, which is linguistically not explicitly indicated, is commonly assumed to be the egocentric reference frame of the speaker or the hearer (see Miller and Johnson-Laird 1976; Levelt 1996). The position of the referent is linguistically given relative to the relatum but has to be determined within the deictic reference frame. Reading sentence (2) deictically as well, the position of the bowl must also be determined within the deictic reference frame. Obviously, the deictic reading leads to a mental model that specifies the position of every object mentioned in the text within one unique reference frame: the deictic reference frame. The mental model will include an Ego-node for the speaker or hearer providing the deictic reference frame, which will be connected with every object node in the graph. Since the deictic reference frame is the unique reference frame relative to which every object position has to be determined, it sets up an *overall organizing principle* of the mental model. On the other hand, given an intrinsic reading, the mental model seems not to be governed by an overall organizing principle. That the "intrinsic perspective system", as Levelt calls it, is less coherent than the deictic one in terms of their inferential potential, was demonstrated by Levelt (1996 1986): Converseness and transitivity hold in the deictic perspective system but not in the intrinsic one. From the point of view of the psychology of text comprehension, lack of coherence raises the question, if recipients establish coherence by means of inferences during comprehension. By reading the two example sentences above intrinsically, the mental model would become coherent if the recipient infers the position of the bowl with respect to the reference frame of Torsten, i.e., that the bowl is on the left of Torsten. The reference frame of Torsten then would set up an overall organizing principle as defined above for the mental model of the two sentences.

An overall organizing principle for egocentric mental models

Given a text about a single protagonist who is surrounded by several objects, a recipient may be expected to take the *protagonist's perspective*: he imagines his own position and orientation relative to the described object configuration in accordance with the protagonist (see Bryant, Tversky, and Franklin 1992; Franklin, Tversky, and Coon 1992; a summary is given by Tversky, Franklin, Taylor, and Bryant 1994). By virtue of the protagonist's perspective, the recipient may interpret every sentence expressing a spatial relation between an object and the protagonist as expressing a spatial relation between the object and the recipient himself. The recipient may then interpret (1) in the sense of (3):

(3) The refrigerator is standing on my left.
Der Kühlschrank steht links von mir.

If he takes the protagonist's perspective, the recipient will construct an egocentric mental model. An egocentric mental model will always include an Ego-node representing the recipient himself. If the recipient is interpreting sentence (1) egocentrically in the sense of (3), the *refrigerator*-node will be connected with the Ego-node by an arc that is annotated with the matrix corresponding to *left of*.

To claim for egocentricity does not imply that the egocentric reference frame sets up an overall organizing principle. The mental model may already be called "egocentric" if some — i.e. at least one — of the object-nodes is connected with the Ego-node, i.e. if the Ego-node is part of the configuration at all. But in our view, it is sensible to assume that the egocentric reference frame might set up an overall organizing principle, as in the case of a deictic reading. The recipient taking the protagonist's perspective could aim at constructing a coherent mental model with all objects localized within the egocentric reference frame. But then every sentence introducing a referent relative to a relatum different from the protagonist will require an inference to determine the position of the new referent within the egocentric reference frame. For example, a recipient, who has interpreted sentence (1) egocentrically and is now receiving sentence (2), would have to infer that the bowl is on his left in order to establish coherence.

Primarily for intuitive reasons, we think it is plausible that the egocentric reference frame may set up an overall organizing principle. But our modelling approach predicts higher cognitive effort for such a principle if the text continues by mentioning a movement of the protagonist, e.g., a reorientation. If the text is continued with sentence (4), the object configuration changes relative to Ego.

(4) Torsten turns to his left.
Torsten wendet sich nach links.

Since the mental model does not represent the description but the situation described, the representation has to be updated according to the mentioned reorientation. For example, the refrigerator is now to be located behind Ego. As is predicted by our modelling approach, an update of the egocentric mental model in the case of a reorientation of the protagonist requires to update all, but only those, arcs that connect the Ego-node with an object-node, i.e. every object position specified relative to the egocentric reference frame. Consequently, if the egocentric reference frame sets up an overall organizing principle, the update of the mental model in case of a reorientation is predicted to be maximally expensive in terms of required inferences.

In maintaining that a coherent egocentric mental model has to be governed by an overall organizing principle, the cognitive effort for an update of the mental model could be diminished by using a unique reference frame that is invariant against a reorientation of Ego. For example, Klatzky (1998) acknowledges the possibility, that a reorientation of Ego may be represented by means of an allocentric reference frame (sometimes called "absolute reference frame", e.g. Levelt 1996). As Klatzky further points out, the reference direction of an allocentric reference frame, i.e. its orientation, might be derived from the geometry of a room. The texts we investigate introduce the protagonist standing in a room, as in (5).

(5) Torsten is standing in the middle of the kitchen.
Torsten steht inmitten der Küche.

Thus, the egocentric mental model must include a node for the room (here: *kitchen*), which, as any other node in the graph, provides a three-dimensional reference frame. The room reference frame might then set up an allocentric overall organizing principle: Every object mentioned in the text is to be located within the allocentric reference frame provided by the room-node. Contrary to the egocentric reference frame, the allocentric reference frame captures the intuition, that the object configuration does not change if Ego does reorient. There is no need for an update of object positions that are specified with respect to the allocentric reference frame. Therefore, we suggest that in addition to the egocentric reference frame the egocentric mental model might be supplied with an allocentric reference frame. Hörnig, Claus, and Eyferth (1997) present further arguments in favor of an allocentric reference frame for an egocentric mental model, that allows for a representational distinction between movements of Ego and objects. Especially if the cognitive demand of the task at hand is high, egocentric object localizations might be abandoned in favour of allocentric localizations.

Those objects that are linguistically related to the protagonist constitute a special class of objects, in that they are localized within the egocentric reference frame (because of the protagonist's perspective) as well as within the allocentric reference frame (because of the suggested allocentric overall organizing principle). We call this special class of objects *anchoring objects* because they anchor the egocentric reference frame within the allocentric one. In our view, anchoring objects establish egocentric orientation within the allocentrically defined surrounding environment. Objects not classified as anchoring objects will be called *critical objects*. While anchoring objects are always localized egocentrically, critical objects might be localized either egocentrically or allocentrically. A third possiblity would be that a critical object is localized only within the reference frame of the relatum, e.g., an anchoring object. In this case, it would be accessible in the mental model only after the corresponding anchoring object has already been accessed.

Evidence reported by Levinson (1996) may cast doubt on our suggestion, that recipients will construct their egocentric mental models using an allocentric reference frame. Levinson compared native speakers of Dutch and Tzeltal. Whereas Dutch, as well as English and German, makes extensive use of egocentrically defined localizations (deixis), spatial descriptions in Tzeltal are made with respect to an allocentric or absolute reference frame. As Levinson could demonstrate in a variety of investigations, this difference of the languages is reflected in the behaviour of the native speakers even in nonverbal tasks. For example, if subjects had to judge the identity of two arrays of five cards *A*, *B*, *C*, *D*, *E* in a recognition task, after they had been reoriented by 180°, native speakers of Dutch exhibited an egocentrically defined identity criterion. Neglecting the intervening reorientation, two arrays were judged as identical if the arrangement from left to right was kept identical. In contrast, native speakers of Tzeltal took the reorientation into account, judging the array as identical if the arrangement was now reversed: *E*, *D*, *C*, *B*, *A*. These findings clearly indicate that native speakers of Dutch, and presumably those of English and German too, code object arrangements egocentrically, while native speakers of Tzeltal code them allocentrically. This preference for egocentric coding should show up in constructing egocentric mental models as well. On the other hand, as we argued above, an exclusively egocentric coding is cognitively very demanding in case of an update. Thus, even if people prefer to code object positions egocentrically, the cognitive demand of the task at hand might prevent them from doing so.

If people prefer to code object positions egocentrically as long as the cognitive demand allows them to do so, one might expect an influence of the modality of text presentation. As compared with aural text presentation, visual presentation can be shown to interfere with constructing and maintaining spatial mental models (e.g., Kaup, Kelter, Habel, and Clauser 1997). The reading process does by itself reduce the cognitive capacities available for other spatial tasks. While a listener might be able to cope with the high cognitive demand of constructing and updating a mental model governed by an egocentric overall organizing principle, a reader might have to abandon his preference for egocentric coding. Instead, he or she might code positions of critical objects allocentrically in order to reduce the cognitive demand required for updating the mental model in case of a reorientation.

Empirical evaluation

Franklin and Tversky (1990) discuss two alternative conceptions of egocentric mental models that are related to our present problem: the *mental transformation model* and the *spatial framework model*. The mental transformation model basically relies on the idea that object access (i.e. retrieval) in egocentric mental models proceeds much in the way of a visual search in surrounding space. Because only objects in front of Ego are directly accessible, access to an object located elsewhere requires Ego to mentally reorient until the object lies in front and therefore becomes accessible. As is stipulated, the cognitive effort for a reorientation increases with the angle of the needed reorientation, leading to slowest access to objects behind Ego (180°) and fastest access to objects in front (no reorientation needed). Latencies for the retrieval of objects on either side should be intermediate (90°). In contrast, the spatial framework model emphasizes the properties of the egocentric reference frame, in which objects in every direction are immediately accessible without any need for an intervening transformation. In the first place, the model argues for dominance relations between the three axes of the egocentric reference frame. The above/below-axis is taken as the most dominating one because canonically (i.e. upright posture) it is in accordance with gravity. The left/right-axis is dominated by the front/back-axis, from which it is derived. Object access in egocentric mental models is claimed to proceed according to the dominance relations of the axes. Within the horizontal plane, objects located on the front/back-axis should be accessed faster than those on the left/right-axis. A second principle rests on the asymmetry of the front/back-axis and states that front is perceptually as well as functionally more salient than back. Therefore, objects in front of Ego are predicted to be accessed faster than objects behind. Since the mental transformation model and the spatial framework model make contradicting predictions for access latencies for objects behind and beside Ego, the adequacy of the models can be evaluated empirically. As a third alternative, Franklin and Tversky (1990) consider the equiavailability model, i.e. that objects in either direction are equally well accessible. In a series of experiments on egocentric mental models, Franklin and Tversky (1990; see also Bryant and Franklin 1992) report access latency patterns that agree with the spatial framework model, but contradict the mental transformation model as well as the equiavailability model. Thus, we may conclude that these egocentric mental models are organized in a way that reflects the properties of the egocentric reference frame.

Hypotheses. As Bryant and Tversky (1992: 29) put it: “A spatial framework is a mental model that specifies the spatial relations among objects with respect to an observer in the environment.” We take this as a statement about objects localized within the egocentric reference frame, e.g., anchoring objects. Because these objects are represented immediatcly within the egocentric reference frame they are directly accessible without any need for a mental transformation. On the other hand, the mental transformation model makes sense only by modelling the access to objects that are not immediately represented within the egocentric reference frame, but whose locations are solely defined with respect to the environment, i.e. — in our terms — with respect to an allocentric reference frame. To put it the other way round: Since Barbara Tversky and her co-workers could demonstrate that access to objects linguistically located within the egocentric reference frame, i.e. anchoring objects, exhibits the spatial framework pattern, the question of an overall organizing principle can be evaluated empirically. If the egocentric reference frame sets up an overall organizing principle, the position of every object mentioned in a text has to be specified with respect to the egocentric reference frame, eventually by an inference. As a consequence, object access latencies should exhibit the spatial framework pattern for anchoring objects in the same way as for critical objects. On the other hand, if an allocentric reference frame sets up an overall organizing principle, the spatial framework pattern should be observable for anchoring objects, whereas for critical objects we would expect deviant access latencies. Moreover, if the mental transformation model adequately characterizes access to objects that are localized only within the allocentric reference frame, access latencies should deviate in the way that the mental transformation model predicts: critical objects on either side of Ego should be accessed faster than objects behind. Access latencies for critical objects would also deviate from the spatial framework pattern, if they are equally well accessible in either direction. If recipients do infer neither egocentric nor allocentric positions, accessing a critical object would at first require to retrieve the corresponding anchoring object relative to which it was linguistically located. In this case, access latencies for anchoring and critical objects should both correspond to the spatial framework pattern, but critical objects should always take longer to retrieve than anchoring objects.

Finally, people might prefer to code objects positions always egocentrically, as long as they may cope with the cognitive demand of the task at hand. We therefore regard the possibility, that the egocentric reference frame will show to set up an overall organizing principle only if people listen to the texts but not when reading them, because listening is cognitively less demanding than reading.

Material and procedure. As experimental material we constructed eight (German) texts, each beginning by introducing a protagonist standing in the middle of a room. Thereafter, the four walls of the room were described one after another. Each wall was described as being occupied by an anchoring object and a critical object with the latter being linguistically localized relative to the anchoring object. For each text we created four variants in which the placement of the four object combinations (front, right, behind or left of the protagonist) was systematically varied. The order of mentioning object combinations (anchoring object and critical object) was held constant across variants. The description of the object arrangement was followed by the testing phase. For each text, subjects were probed three times with three object terms (held constant across variants) and had to respond with the direction in which the probed object was located. The second and the third object probe were preceded by a reorientation sentence, respectively, that mentioned a reorientation of the protagonist either to his right, to his back, or to his left. Subjects were instructed to respond with the direction dependent on the current orientation of the protagonist. They were told that the task was easier if they would take the protagonist's perspective. Response times were collected in two successive steps: subjects were instructed to press the space-bar as soon as they knew the correct answer (RT1). Afterwards they had to indicate the remembered direction by pressing the corresponding key on the numerical key pad (RT2). No feedback was given about the correctness of the response.

Every subject was probed 24 times (three probes for each of the eight stories). One half of the probes involved anchoring objects, the other half involved critical objects. The three object probes for each text as well as the order in which they were presented were held constant for each text. The correct direction differed dependent on the variant of the story that a subject had received, i.e. each test object was probed for every direction (varied between subjects). The variants of the eight different texts were combined in a way that every subject had to respond to three object probes for each object type (anchoring and critical object) in each direction (front, right, back, left).

In the first experiment (*reading*), subjects read the description of the object arrangement on a single display on a PC screen. Reading times were self paced. In the testing phase, reorientation sentences and object probes were also presented visually on the PC screen. In the second experiment (*listening*), subjects heard the description of the object arrangement via earphones. To mimic self paced reading, subjects could call for the description of any one of the four walls by pressing a corresponding key without restriction for order and frequency. In the testing phase, reorientation sentences and object probes were also presented aurally via earphones. During listening, nothing was displayed on the screen. The material was exactly the same in both experiments.

Results. Analyses of response times are based on the correct responses of 23 and 26 subjects in experiment 1 (21% errors) and 2 (11% errors), respectively. Since there were no effects on RT2, analyses were limited to RT1 (see Table 1). In experiment 1 (*reading*), responses to anchoring objects were significantly faster (3838 ms) than to critical objects (4200 ms): $F(1,22) = 15.24$; $p < .01$. But there was no overall main effect for direction: $F(3,66) = 1.61$; $p > .10$. Since object type tended to interact with direction, $F(3,66) = 2.69$; $p = .10$, response times for anchoring objects and critical objects were analysed separately. The separate analysis for anchoring objects revealed a significant effect of direction: $F(3,66) = 4.68$, $p = .01$. Pairwise comparisons showed that anchoring objects located in front or behind were responded to significantly faster than objects located on the left or right: front = back < left = right. For critical objects, response times did not differ significantly for the four directions: $F(3,66) < 1$.

In experiment 2 (*listening*), there was a significant overall main effect of direction, $F(3,75) = 6.29$; $p < .01$, that did not interact with object type: $F(3,75) < 1$. The main effect is due to shorter response times for objects located

Table 1. Mean response times for determining directions for object probes (RT1 in ms) dependent on object type and direction for experiment 1 (reading) and experiment 2 (listening).

	Experiment 1: Reading				*Experiment 2: Listening*			
	front	*right*	*behind*	*left*	*front*	*right*	*behind*	*left*
anchoring objects	2773	3665	2994	4161	3059	4094	3593	3980
critical objects	4206	4081	4304	4150	3476	4080	3357	4261

in front or behind as compared with objects located on the left or right: front = back < left = right. There was no difference for object type: $F(1,25) < 1$.

Discussion

As expected, the response time pattern for anchoring objects corresponded to the spatial framework pattern in both experiments. Objects located on the front/back-axis are responded to faster than objects located on the left/right-axis in the reading condition as well as in the listening condition. Because anchoring objects are always represented immediatly within the egocentric reference frame, and therefore are directly accessible, response times agree with the spatial framework model. We regard this claim not discarded by the fact that the asymmetry of the front/back-axis was not confirmed.

For critical objects, the spatial framework pattern was obtained in the listening condition but not in the reading condition. When subjects had to read the texts, direction of critical objects did yield no influence at all. Critical objects were expected to exhibit the spatial framework pattern in the same way as anchoring objects only if they were immediately located within the egocentric reference frame, i.e. if egocentric object positions would have been inferred. This was the case with listeners but not with readers. We take this to indicate that people prefer to code all object positions egocentrically if possible: the egocentric reference frame sets up an overall organizing principle in egocentric mental models. Even if a referent is linguistically localized to a relatum different from the protagonist, a reader taking the protagonist's perspective tries to infer the object position relative to Ego already during comprehension. These online inferences establish coherence.

As the finding for critical objects in the reading condition indicates, objects not linguistically related to the protagonist are not always located within the egocentric reference frame. We explain the fact, that readers do not code the positions of critical objects egocentrically by the high cognitive demand of an update of the mental model when Ego has to reorient. Because the reading process reduces the cognitive ressources available to construct and maintain the spatial mental model, the expense of an update is diminished by abandoning egocentric localizations of critical objects. That reading is more difficult than listening is confirmed by the higher error rates with visual presentation (21%) than with aural presentation (11%). Since response times for critical objects in the reading condition do not correspond to the predictions of the mental transformation model, we lack explicit evidence that critical objects instead are localized within an allocentric reference frame. But on the one hand, the mental transformation model stipulates that a mental reorientation of Ego takes more time if it is towards the back than towards the side. One would expect that reading times for reorientation sentences reflect this difference, because the egocentric mental model requires an according update: a mental rotation. Actually, reading times for reorientation sentences did not differ significantly whether the protagonist was described as turning to his back (6423 ms), to his right (7313 ms), or to his left (6801 ms). If these reading time data elucidate the concept of a mental reorientation as addressed by the mental transformation model, they are apt to doubt that a reorientation of Ego to the back takes more time than to either side. On the other hand, critical objects seem not to be accessed within the reference frames of anchoring objects in the reading condition, because in this case, access latencies should also reflect access latencies for anchoring objects. That critical objects in the reading condition were equally well accessible in either direction at least indirectly speaks in favour of an allocentric localization. More direct evidence for an allocentric reference frame in an egocentric mental model has to be addressed to future work.

In the light of the findings of Levinson (1996), the observed preference for an egocentric overall organizing principle should not be taken as a universal principle, but has to be restricted to native speakers of languages that express object locations egocentrically, as does for example German, English, and Dutch. It should not be generalized for speakers of languages like Tzeltal.

Acknowledgments

This research was supported by the Deutsche Forschungsgemeinschaft (DFG) in the project "Modelling Inferences in Mental Models" (Wy 20/2–1) within the priority program on spatial cognition ("Raumkognition").

Correspondence should be addressed to Robin Hörnig, Sekr. FR 5–8, Department of Computer

Science, Technical University of Berlin, Franklinstr. 28/29, D-10587 Berlin; email: rhoernig@cs.tu-berlin.de

References

Ambler, A.P. & Robin J. Popplestone (1975). Inferring the positions of bodies from specified spatial relationships. *Artificial Intelligence*, *6*, 157–174.

Bryant, David J. & Barbara Tversky (1992). Assessing spatial frameworks with object and direction probes. *Bulletin of the Psychonomic Society*, *30*, 29–32.

Bryant, David J., Barbara Tversky & Nancy Franklin (1992). Internal and external spatial frameworks for representing described scenes. *Journal of Memory & Language, 31*, 74–98.

Claus, Berry, Klaus Eyferth, Carsten Gips, Robin Hörnig, Ute Schmid, Sylvia Wiebrock & Fritz Wysotzki (1998). Reference frames for spatial inferences in text comprehension. In C. Freksa, C. Habel & K.F. Wender (Eds.), *Spatial Cognition. An interdisciplinary approach to representing and processing spatial knowledge* (241–266). Berlin: Springer.

Franklin, Nancy & Barbara Tversky (1990). Searching imagined environments. *Journal of Experimental Psychology: General*, *119*, 63–76.

Franklin, Nancy, Barbara Tversky & Vicky Coon (1992). Switching points of view in spatial mental models. *Memory & Cognition, 20*, 507–518.

Hörnig, Robin, Berry Claus & Klaus Eyferth (1997). Objektzugriff in Mentalen Modellen: Eine Frage der Perspektive. In C. Umbach, M. Grabski & R. Hörnig (Eds.), *Perspektive in Sprache und Raum* (81–104). Wiesbaden: Deutscher Universitätsverlag.

Kaup, Barbara, Stephanie Kelter, Christopher Habel & Constanze Clauser (1997). Zur Wahl des repräsentierten Bildausschnitts beim Aufbau mentaler Modelle während der Textrezeption. In C. Umbach, M. Grabski & R. Hörnig (Eds.), *Perspektive in Sprache und Raum* (61–79). Wiesbaden: Deutscher Universitätsverlag.

Klatzky, Roberta L. (1998). Allocentric and egocentric spatial representations: definitions, distinctions, and interconnections. In C. Freksa, C. Habel & K.F. Wender (Eds.), *Spatial cognition. An interdisciplinary approach to representing and processing spatial knowledge* (1–17). Berlin: Springer.

Levelt, Willem J.M. (1986) Zur sprachlichen Abbildung des Raumes: Deiktische und intrinsische Perspektive. In H.-G. Bosshardt (Ed.) *Perspektive auf Sprache. Interdisziplinäre Beiträge zum Gedenken an Hans Hörmann* (187–211). Berlin: de Gruyter.

Levelt, Willem J.M. (1996). Perspective taking and ellipsis in spatial description. In P. Bloom, M.A. Peterson, L. Nadel & M.F. Garrett (Eds.), *Language and Space* (77–108). Cambridge, MA: MIT Press.

Levinson, S.C. (1996). Frames of reference and Molyneux's question: Crosslinguistic evidence. In P. Bloom, M.A. Peterson, L. Nadel & M.F. Garrett (Eds.), *Language and Space* (109–169). Cambridge, MA: MIT Press.

Miller, George A. & Philip N. Johnson-Laird (1976). *Language and Perception*. Cambridge, MA: Cambridge University Press.

Schmid, Ute, Sylvia Wiebrock & Fritz Wysotzki (1999). Modelling spatial inferences in text understanding. *This volume*.

Tversky, B., Franklin, N., Taylor, H.A. & Bryant, D.J. (1994). Spatial mental models from descriptions. *Journal of the American Society for Information Science, 45*, 656–668.

Describing the Topology of Spherical Regions using the 'RCC' Formalism

Nicholas Mark Gotts
Macaulay Land Use Research Institute

Introduction

Formal representations of "commonsense" or "intuitive" spatial concepts are potentially useful both in computational modelling of human spatial reasoning, and in the design of user-friendly GIS (geographical information systems) and similar kinds of software system. This paper explores the possible use of the topological part of the "RCC Calculus", a first-order logic spatial formalism described in Randell, Cui and Cohn (1992) and in Gotts, Gooday and Cohn (1996), as the basis for human like reasoning in a specific domain: the topology of sharply delimited regions of the Earth's surface (as defined in legal and diplomatic documents, for example). The domain is highly relevant to geographical information systems; related work includes Worboys and Bofakos (1993), and Egenhofer and Franzosa (1995). Much of the analysis transfers to planar regions.

Human spatial competence includes the ability to acquire novel systems of spatial representation and reasoning for particular purposes. This occurs both on an individual level, and collectively as groups of specialists (e.g. anatomists, geographers, engineers) devise and modify ways to store and manipulate spatial information. Both the spatial reasoning we all perform in everyday life, and specialist systems of spatial representation and reasoning other than formal mathematical approaches, are referred to here as "non-mathematical" spatial reasoning; our central concern is with geographical reasoning. Simulation of non-mathematical spatial reasoning, and automation of human-like spatial reasoning in interactive computer programs, are likely to require a family of related formalisms for different types of spatial information (topological, orientational or metric, precise or vague, etc.) and different kinds of space (atomistic or not, one-, two-, or three-dimensional). This paper bears on whether RCC would be a suitable foundation for such a family, and if not, why not.

It has been claimed for RCC (Randell, Cui and Cohn 1992) that its use of extended *regions* — rather than points — as basic spatial entities, makes it a more suitable formalism for non-mathematical qualitative spatial reasoning than topology as developed by mathematicians, avoiding many complexities and counterintuitive results while remaining rich enough for everyday reasoning. The analysis in this paper leads to a topological taxonomy of spherical regions, confirming RCC's usefulness in clarifying and sharpening intuitive spatial concepts. However, RCC turns out to be insufficiently expressive to capture some desirable limitations on the properties of geographical regions, or to express some significant constraints between properties of regions that can themselves be formulated within it. Because of these limitations, it is concluded that RCC will probably not be an adequate basis for formalizing "non-mathematical" topological reasoning.

Capturing intuitions about geographical regions

It is hard to formulate exactly what we mean by a "geographical region". Intuitively, we want to be able to draw a line around any part of the Earth's surface that we have a geographical reason to single out, and call it a region. It seems reasonable to allow a region to consist of disconnected pieces (e.g, Indonesia consists of a large number of islands), but not that it should include an *infinite* number of them. Similarly, it seems reasonable to allow regions with a finite but not an infinite number of internal "holes", and regions which meet at a finite but not an infinite number of separate boundary lines and/or points. We cannot, however, express precisely these requirements within a first-order logic theory such as RCC. Instead, we have to express them as a limitation on the range of intended models of our theory. This follows from the compactness theorem (Boolos and Jeffrey 1980: 131), which states that if any set of first-order sentences is inconsistent, some finite subset of that set is inconsistent. As we will see, RCC allows us to express the assertions:

Region x consists of at least two separate pieces.
Region x consists of at least three separate pieces.
Region x consists of at least four separate pieces…

and so on indefinitely. If the RCC axioms were inconsistent with the infinite set of assertions implied by the dots, it would follow that those axioms must be inconsistent with some finite subset of them, implying some finite limit on the number of separate pieces a region may have.

There is a second problem, which undermines the idea that we can define each geographical region independently of any other: it is quite possible to have two regions that meet the restrictions suggested above, while the union of the two does not. This is easier to describe for two planar than two spherical regions. Let A and B be equal-sized squares sharing a side, each having an infinite sequence of semicircular "bites" removed from the shared side: the first with the middle third of the side as its diameter, the second the middle third of the upper third, the next the middle third of the uppermost ninth, etc. A and B both meet the restrictions suggested above, but the union of the two is a "region" with an infinite number of holes.

This paper restricts the range of intended models of RCC to those in which the variables standing for regions range over parts of a *locally Euclidean space* (Armstrong 1979). Such a space is of uniform dimensionality (ruling out a disc with a one-dimensional "spike" protruding from it, for example). For any two non-boundary points, sufficiently small neighbourhoods of the two points will be topologically indistinguishable; in the case of a two-dimensional space, such neighbourhoods will be topological discs. If a locally Euclidean space has boundaries, sufficiently small neighbourhoods of any two boundary points will again be topologically indistinguishable; in the two-dimensional case, these neighbourhoods will be half-discs, and the boundaries themselves will be simple closed curves. Regions will be assumed to consist of one or more separate components, each of which is *regular closed* (Requicha and Tilove 1978), is *path-connected* (Armstrong 1979), and is such that every boundary point is the boundary point of at least one maximal connected component of the region's interior. These further restrictions serve to rule out unacceptable regions of various kinds. When the space containing the regions is the sphere S^2 (or the plane E^2), a region obeying them is uniformly two-dimensional, includes all the points on its own boundary, and has no isolated lines or points removed. In S^2 it will also have a finite number of components. These restrictions may not exclude all we would like to exclude, but avoid excluding anything we want to permit. Notice that we do *not* insist that all regions should themselves be locally Euclidean spaces, only that the space containing all the regions should be one.

RCC: Regions, relations and functions

RCC has two parts, concerning topology and convexity. The topological part, to which attention is confined here, uses a single primitive: $C(x,y)$, read: "region x is connected to region y". Given the interpretation of "region" given above, it means that x and y share at least one point. The current version of RCC's topological part was first presented in Randell, Cui and Cohn (1992). The presentation here is similar to that in Gotts (1994).

The first two axioms ensure that C is reflexive and symmetric:

Axiom (1) $\forall\, x\ C(x,x)$
Axiom (2) $\forall\, x,y\ [C(x,y) \rightarrow C(y,x)]$.

Additional relations are defined in terms of C. Those used here are:

$DC(x,y) \equiv_{def} \neg C(x,y)$ (x is disconnected from y),
$P(x,y) \equiv_{def} \forall\, z\ [C(z,x) \rightarrow C(z,y)]$ (x is part of y),
$PP(x,y) \equiv_{def} P(x,y) \wedge \neg P(y,x)$ (x is a proper part of y),
$EQ(x,y) \equiv_{def} P(x,y) \wedge P(y,x)$ (x coincides with y),
$O(x,y) \equiv_{def} \exists\, z\ [P(z,x) \wedge P(z,y)]$ (x overlaps with y),
$DR(x,y) \equiv_{def} \neg O(x,y)$ (x is discrete from y),
$PO(x,y) \equiv_{def} O(x,y) \wedge \neg P(x,y) \wedge \neg P(y,x)$ (x partially overlaps with y),
$EC(x,y) \equiv_{def} C(x,y) \wedge \neg O(x,y)$ (x is externally connected with y),
$TPP(x,y) \equiv_{def} PP(x,y) \wedge \exists z\ [EC(z,x) \wedge EC(z,y)]$ (x is a tangential proper part of y),
$NTPP(x,y) \equiv_{def} PP(x,y) \wedge \neg\exists z[EC(z,x) \wedge EC(z,y)]$ (x is a non-tangential proper part of y).

Any pair of RCC regions must be related by one of a set of eight binary relations, shown in Figure 1 (TPPi and NTPPi are inverses of TPP and NTPP respectively).

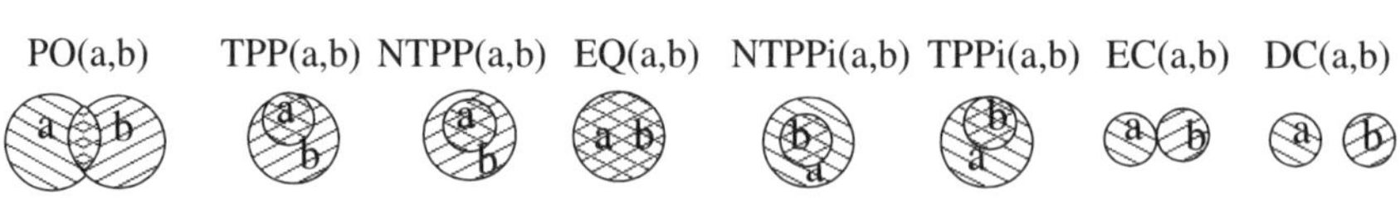

Figure 1. The RCC-8 relation set

Further axioms guarantee the existence of a universal region (U) (which will always be a locally Euclidean space for the purposes of this paper), and some "quasi-Boolean" functions (these functions are quasi-Boolean rather than Boolean because there is no null region). These are COMPL(x) (the region-complement of x in U); SUM(x,y) (the region-sum of x and y); PROD(x,y) (the region-product or intersection of x and y); and DIFF(x,y) (the region-difference of x and y). The complement, difference and product functions can produce the "NULL" object as a result — meaning that there is no such region. Cohn (1992) explains the technicalities involved in dealing with this possibility using the "sorted logic" LLAMA.

Axiom (3) $\forall x[\mathrm{C}(x,\mathrm{U})]$
Axiom (4) $\forall x,y\ [[\mathrm{C}(y,\mathrm{COMPL}(x)) \equiv \neg\mathrm{NTPP}(y,x)] \wedge [\mathrm{O}(y,\mathrm{COMPL}(x)) \equiv \neg\mathrm{P}(y,x)]]$
Axiom (5) $\forall\ x,y,z[\mathrm{C}(z,\mathrm{SUM}(x,y)) \equiv \mathrm{C}(z,x) \vee \mathrm{C}(z,y)]$
Axiom (6) $\forall\ x,y,z[\mathrm{C}(z,\mathrm{PROD}(x,y)) \equiv \exists w[\mathrm{P}(w,x) \wedge \mathrm{P}(w,y) \wedge \mathrm{C}(z,w)]]$
Axiom (7) $\forall\ x,y\ [\mathrm{NULL}(\mathrm{PROD}(x,y)) \equiv \mathrm{DR}(x,y)]$.

We can define the other quasi-Boolean function, DIFF, as follows:

$\mathrm{DIFF}(x,y) =_{def} \mathrm{PROD}(x,\mathrm{COMPL}(y))$.

The final axiom serves to rule out "atomic" regions (those without proper parts):

Axiom (8) $\forall x \exists y[\mathrm{NTPP}(y,x)]$.

Nothing in the eight RCC axioms specifies the dimensionality of regions, and many of their other topological properties are also left undefined. The axioms do establish that the universal region U is self-connected (all one piece) (Gotts 1996a). It has usually been envisaged as a two- or three-dimensional Euclidean space (E^2 or E^3). Here, though, we concentrate on a model in which U is a spherical surface, S^2.

Levels of structure in RCC regions

As we consider the range of possible topologies for spherical regions, three levels of structure become evident. These emerge from the RCC axioms themselves, and would apply whatever space RCC was applied to, yet they are clearly important in reasoning about spatial relations, distributions and processes in a wide range of geographical contexts.

A region may be composed of any finite number of separate self-connected (in RCC terminology, CON) parts. The number of these maximal self-connected parts, and the way they are embedded in the sphere relative to each other, form the first structural level. Next, a connected region may itself be composed of any finite number of parts which share only boundary points of the region, like the three parts of the dark region in the lower left subfigure of Figure 3. A connected region of the sphere *not* so divided, like each of these three parts, is referred to here as interior-connected (INTCON). The number and arrangement of maximal interior-connected parts in each maximal connected part forms the second level of structure. The topology of the maximal interior-connected parts forms the third.

CON(x) can be defined thus ("x cannot be divided into two DC parts"):

$$\text{CON}(x) \equiv_{def} \forall y \forall z[\text{EQ}(x,\text{SUM}(y,z)) \rightarrow \text{C}(y,z)].$$

For disconnected regions, we might define a "separation-number": the number of maximal connected parts it divides into (upper-case italics here stand for variables ranging over the natural numbers):

$$\text{SEPNUM}(x,1) \equiv_{def} \text{CON}(x),$$
$$\text{SEPNUM}(x,N{+}1) \equiv_{def}$$
$$\exists y,z[\text{EQ}(x,\text{SUM}(y,z)) \wedge \text{DC}(y,z) \wedge \text{CON}(y) \wedge \text{SEPNUM}(z,N)]$$

However, this definition requires at least part of arithmetic (addition of the natural numbers) to be added to RCC-theory. We do not need arithmetic axioms sufficient to support multiplication; axioms for addition only, so-called "Presburger arithmetic" (Harel 1987: 179–180) suffice. These also allow us to state that one number is at least as large as another. Alternatively, and staying within RCC, we could avoid the need for any arithmetic axioms, defining a succession of as many predicates as we require, as follows:

$$\text{SEPNUM2}(x) \equiv_{def} \exists\, y,z[\text{EQ}(x,\text{SUM}(y,z)) \wedge \text{DC}(y,z) \wedge \text{CON(y)} \wedge \text{CON}(z)],$$
$$\text{SEPNUM3}(x) \equiv_{def} \exists\, y,z[\text{EQ}(x,\text{SUM}(y,z)) \wedge \text{DC}(y,z) \wedge \text{CON(y)} \wedge \text{SEPNUM2}(z)]$$

... concluding with a predicate SEPMANY, which applies to all regions with more than some fixed number of separate parts. However, we will see that avoiding explicit arithmetic has drawbacks.

If the universal region U is the one-dimensional counterpart of the sphere (the circle, S^1), regions other than U can *only* differ topologically in their number of MAX-Ps (maximal CON components), as illustrated in Figure 2.

If U is more than one-dimensional, however, this is only the first stage in a topological taxonomy of regions. Figure 3 shows CON, SEPNUM2, and SEPNUM3 spherical regions: the simplest possible example of each at the top, a more complicated example of each below. This figure uses a representational format which is re-used several times: a spherical region is shown as a distinc-

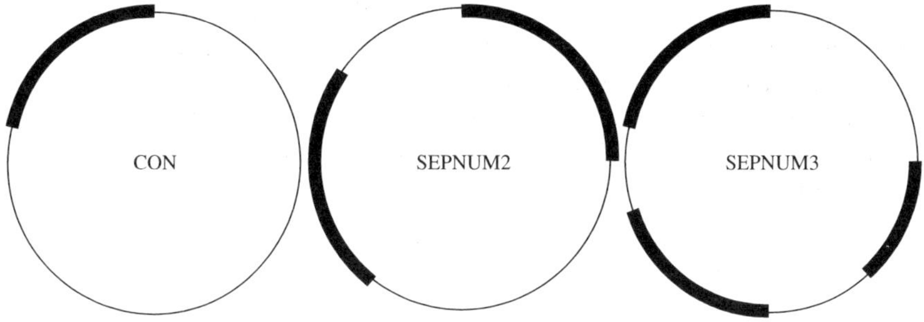

Figure 2. One-dimensional CON, SEPNUM2 and SEPNUM3 regions

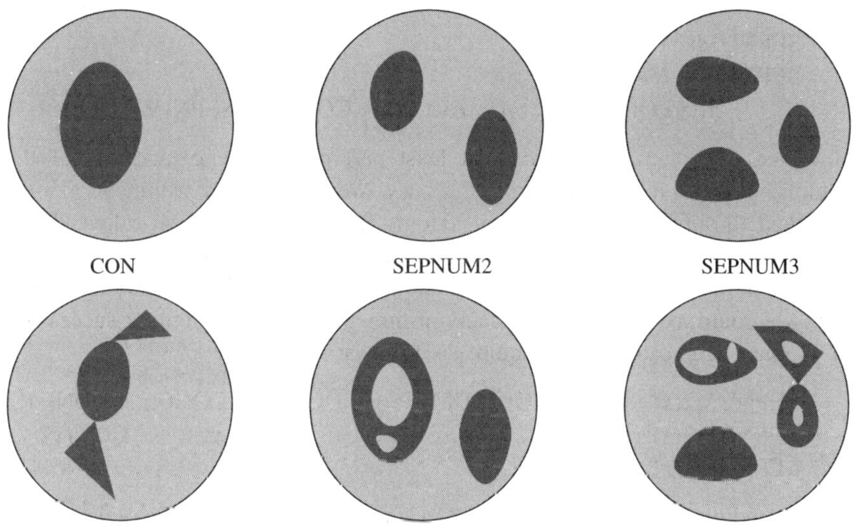

Figure 3. CON, SEPNUM2 and SEPNUM3 regions

tively shaded part of a disc, which represents the visible hemisphere of a spherical surface.

Assuming the universal region U to be a spherical surface, we can capture the intuitive concept of interior-connectedness in two different ways. The simpler approach in terms of the complexity of RCC definitions is to say that any non-tangential proper part of an interior-connected region is part of a *connected* non-tangential proper part of that region:

$$\mathrm{INTCON}(x) \equiv_{def} \forall y[\mathrm{NTPP}(y,x) \rightarrow \exists z[\mathrm{CON}(z) \wedge \mathrm{P}(y,z) \wedge \mathrm{NTPP}(z,x)]].$$

Just as SEPNUM was defined from CON, we can define INTSEPNUM, associating a region with the number of its maximal interior-connected parts. INTSEPNUM can be applied to both connected and disconnected regions: the INTSEPNUM of the latter being the sum of the INTSEPNUMs of its maximal connected parts. The left part of Figure 4 shows a connected region with three interior-connected subregions: pairs of these meet at different numbers of points. The right shows a region with three connected subregions, themselves composed of one, two and three interior-connected parts.

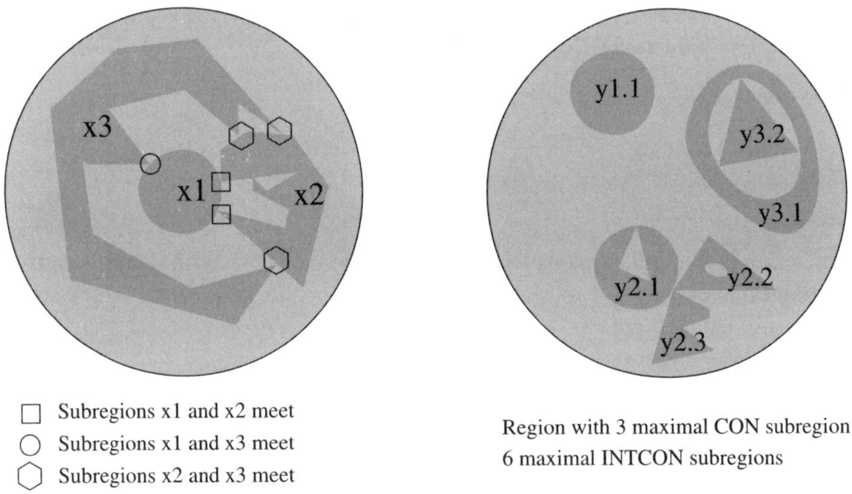

Figure 4. Spherical CON and INTCON subregions

In the spherical case, INTCON regions will coincide with those we will call "line-connected" (LINECON): these are connected, and cannot be divided into two parts linked only at isolated points. Defining line-connectedness in RCC terms is more complicated than defining INTCON: we first need some intermediate terms. MAX-P(x,y) means that x is a *maximal* connected part (we will sometimes say simply "component") of y:

$$\text{MAX-P}(x,y) \equiv_{def} \text{CON}(x) \wedge \text{P}(x,y) \wedge \neg\exists z[\text{PP}(x,z) \wedge \text{P}(z,y) \wedge \text{CON}(z)].$$

Next, we define the predicate SBNUM1(x,y) ("Regions x and y do not overlap, and share exactly one boundary"):

$$\text{SBNUM1}(x,y) \equiv_{def} \text{EC}(x,y) \wedge \exists z[\text{PP}(z,x) \wedge \text{DC}(\text{DIFF}(x,z),y) \wedge \text{CON}(z)] \wedge \neg\exists z[\text{PP}(z,x) \wedge \text{DC}(\text{DIFF}(x,z),y) \wedge \text{SEPNUM2}(z) \wedge \forall w[\text{MAX-P}(w,z) \rightarrow \text{EC}(w,y)]].$$

The relation SBNUM2(x,y) ("Regions x and y do not overlap, and share exactly two boundaries") will also be needed, and so is defined here:

$$\text{SBNUM2}(x,y) \equiv_{def} \text{EC}(x,y) \wedge \exists z[\text{PP}(z,x) \wedge \text{DC}(\text{DIFF}(x,z),y) \wedge \text{SEPNUM2}(z) \wedge \forall w[\text{MAX-P}(w,z) \rightarrow \text{EC}(w,y)]] \wedge \neg\exists z[\text{PP}(z,x) \wedge \text{DC}(\text{DIFF}(x,z),y) \wedge \text{SEPNUM3}(z) \wedge \forall w[\text{MAX-P}(w,z) \rightarrow \text{EC}(w,y)]].$$

Line-connectedness can now be defined:

$$\text{LINECON}(x) \equiv_{def} \text{CON}(x) \wedge \forall y,z[\text{EQ}(x,\text{SUM}(y,z)) \wedge \text{EC}(y,z) \rightarrow \exists u,v,w[\text{P}(w,y) \wedge \text{SBNUM1}(w,z) \wedge \text{P}(u,w) \wedge \text{P}(v,w) \wedge \text{DC}(u,v) \wedge \text{C}(u,z) \wedge \text{C}(v,z)]].$$

This ensures that w is a part of y having a single boundary with z, but with two disconnected subparts of its own that both touch z: this is impossible if y and z share only isolated points.

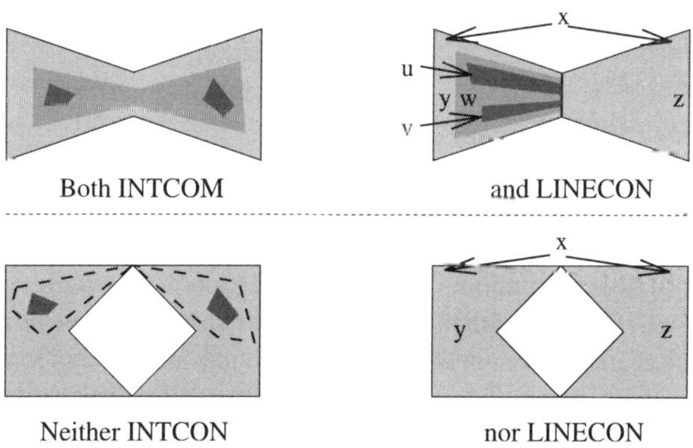

Figure 5. INTCON and LINECON in two dimensions

On the left of Figure 5, it is clear that the upper region meets the INTCON definition, while the lower picture shows a choice of NTPP which is not part of a CON NTPP. On the right, the same pair of regions are used to illustrate the LINECON definition; it should be clear that no choice of a part w of y in the lower region would allow subparts u and v to be chosen to meet the conditions required.

Note that in one dimensional models of RCC no region is line-connected. In three dimensions, some but not all line-connected regions are also surface-connected: i.e., the parts of any two-part division share at least one *surface*, as illustrated in Figure 6. Only these would be INTCON.

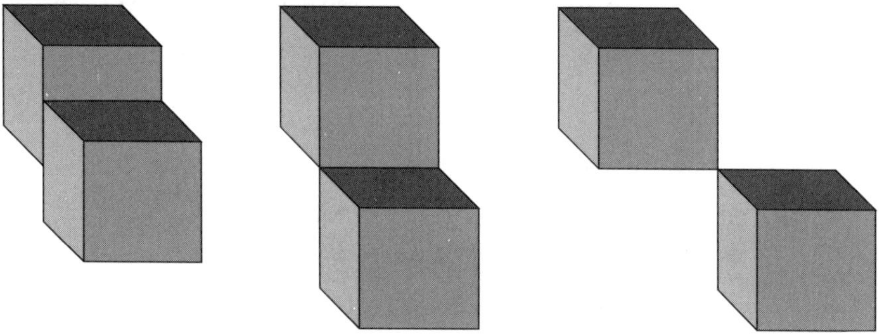

Figure 6. Three kinds of CON three-dimensional regions

Taxonomy of spherical regions

We can distinguish two kinds of topological property which a region may have: *extrinsic*, and *intrinsic*. The former, but not the latter, depend on how the region is embedded in some containing space — in the current context, generally the sphere. INTCON is an extrinsic property, while LINECON is an intrinsic one (however, since interior-connected and line-connected regions coincide on a sphere, we can use them interchangeably in our classification). In point-set topological terms, two regions are intrinsically different if there is no *homeomorphism* (one-to-one continuous function with a continuous inverse) between the points of the two. The distinction is illustrated in Figure 7. The region at the top left is intrinsically different from the other three, which are homeomorphic. (In all but the upper left subfigure, the two maximal INTCON subregions that touch each other both have an interior "hole"; in the upper left subfigure, only one of the pair does.) Note that the regions in the two lower subfigures can be continuously transformed into each other on the surface of a sphere, but not into the somewhat lighter-shaded region at top right, even though they are homeomorphic to it. There is thus no topological difference between the regions shown in the two lower subfigures, an extrinsic topological difference between these and the region in the top right subfigure, and an intrinsic topological difference between the region in the top left subfigure and the other three.

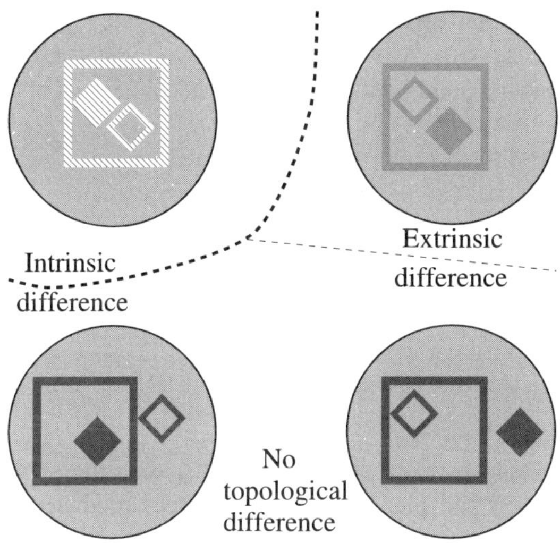

Figure 7. Spherical regions: Intrinsic and extrinsic differences

Classifying spherical regions first by their intrinsic topology, and only using differences in the extrinsic topology to distinguish regions with the same intrinsic topology, has the advantage that the intrinsic classification used in the spherical case can be used almost without change for finite regions of the plane: the only difference being that the entire sphere has no corresponding finite planar region.

What do we need to add to the existing RCC axioms to specify that the universal region U is a topological sphere, given the assumption that it is a locally Euclidean space? We can actually go a long way towards this using the identity between interior-connected and line-connected spherical regions. If we assert that:

Axiom (9) $\forall x[\mathrm{INTCON}(x) \equiv \mathrm{LINECON}(x)]$,

we rule out all possible Us of one dimension (where any line-segment is interior-connected but no region is line-connected), or of more than two dimensions (where there will be line-connected regions that are not interior-connected).

Having ruled out all but two-dimensional Us, we can then specify that U is simply-connected. The usual definition of "simply-connected" is that any simple closed curve embedded in a simply-connected region of any dimensionality can be continuously shrunk to a point within that region without any part of it at any time crossing the region's boundaries. We shall make informal use of this below. Another characterisation of a simply-connected region (applicable only to the two-dimensional case) stipulates that a cut through it which forms a closed curve or joins two boundary points will necessarily disconnect it. RCC does not allow us to refer explicitly to entities of lower dimensionality than regions, so we have to adopt a slightly different approach: a connected region is simply-connected if and only if there is no way of dividing it into two connected parts sharing two separate boundaries:

$$\mathrm{SCON}(x) \equiv_{def} \mathrm{CON}(x) \wedge \forall\ y,z[\mathrm{EQ}(\mathrm{SUM}(y,z),x) \wedge \mathrm{SBNUM2}(y,z) \rightarrow \neg(\mathrm{CON}(y) \wedge \mathrm{CON}(z))].$$

If we now added:

$$\mathrm{SCON}(\mathrm{U})$$

as an axiom, it would rule out all surfaces other than the sphere, the disc, the plane, the topological half-plane, and some surfaces produced by attaching two or more such half-planes to a disc. However, we can rule out *all* the two-dimensional alternatives to the sphere by insisting that the complement of any simply-connected and interior-connected region is itself always a simply-connected and interior-connected region:

Axiom (10) $\forall\ x[\mathrm{SCON}(x) \wedge \mathrm{INTCON}(x) \wedge \mathrm{PP}(x,\mathrm{U}) \rightarrow \mathrm{SCON}(\mathrm{COMPL}(x)) \wedge \mathrm{INTCON}(\mathrm{COMPL}(x))]$.

The only such region in the spherical case (other than the sphere itself) is the disc, the complement of which is again a disc. In all the other two-dimensional cases, removing a disc can be done in such a way that the complement is non-SCON. (Note that axiom (10) would not rule out, for example, the circle, or the three-dimensional and higher analogues of the circle and sphere, so axiom (9) is still required.)

To take the classification of spherical regions forward, a further distinction between two types of spherical interior-connected regions is needed. Figure 8 illustrates this distinction, and the way it cuts across the distinction between SCON and non-SCON regions. The two regions at the right are not interior-connected: each consists of two parts which are joined only at a point. The regions at the left and centre are all interior-connected but that in the centre is not what we will call *well-connected*, or WELLCON: its boundary includes an anomalous point, where two otherwise locally disconnected parts of the region touch. (Note that this region, like that on its right, has only one boundary, as one can get from any boundary-point to any other without going through the interior; but this boundary is not a simple closed curve.)

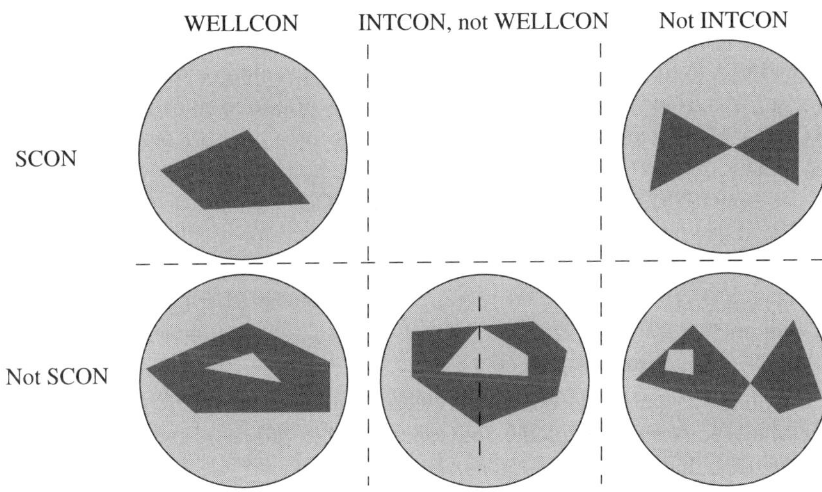

Figure 8. Five types of CON spherical regions

In the two-dimensional case we can define well-connectedness thus:

$$\mathrm{WELLCON}(x) \equiv_{def} \forall y[\mathrm{P}(y,x) \wedge \mathrm{SCON}(y) \wedge \neg\mathrm{INTCON}(y) \rightarrow \exists z[\mathrm{P}(y,z) \wedge \mathrm{P}(z,x) \wedge \mathrm{SCON}(z) \wedge \mathrm{INTCON}(z)]]$$

(a region is well-connected if every simply-connected but not interior-connected part of it is also part of some simply-connected *and* interior-connected part of it). If a finite two-dimensional region is well-connected, all its boundaries (if any) will be simple closed curves, and the region will be a locally Euclidean space. The definition would not do for a three-dimensional model, if we wanted all a three-dimensional well-connected region's boundaries to be two-dimensional *manifolds*, without anomalous points where sheets of surface meet.

We now appear to have six categories into which connected spherical regions can fall: a connected region can be simply-connected or not, and it can be well-connected, interior-connected but not well-connected, or not interior-connected. However, one of the six is empty: a two-dimensional simply-connected region that is interior-connected must also be well-connected. The central region of Figure 8 shows why. A spherical (or planar) region which is interior-connected but not well-connected must be divisible into two CON parts which share at least two separate boundaries (at least one of which will be a point), as shown by the line through the dark region. Such a region cannot therefore be simply-connected.

The classification of CON spherical regions implicit in Figure 8 can be extended in a useful way to disconnected regions. A region of which all components are SCON will be called ALLSCON, one of which all components are INTCON will be called ALLINTCON, and one of which all components are WELLCON, ALLWELLCON. Notice that since a connected region is its own sole component, SCON regions are also ALLSCON, etc.

The only simply-connected and well-connected spherical regions are the disc, and the sphere itself. A spherical simply-connected region other than these must be a collection of discs, each pair either disjoint or sharing a single point, and with no "cycles" such that disc 1 touches disc 2, disc 2 touches disc 3... disc *n-1* touches disc *n*, and disc *n* touches disc 1.

Spherical and finite planar well-connected regions can be classified simply by the number of (simple closed curve) boundaries they have. Classification of spherical and finite planar regions which are interior-connected but not necessarily well-connected is considerably more complicated.

We can begin classifying *all* spherical interior-connected regions in the same way as those that are well-connected, by their number of separate boundaries. However, the three interior-connected regions shown in black in Figure 9 have the same number of boundaries (two in each case), but are intrinsically distinct. We need to be able to characterise the individual boundaries.

Classification of interior-connected spherical regions is easier if we realize that the complement of a INTCON region is always an ALLSCON region, and vice versa. Consider the first characterisation of a simply-connected region given above: that any circle embedded in it can be continuously shrunk to a point within it without any part of it leaving the region. This applies to any ALLSCON region, since a circle can only lie within a single part. If we consider a non-ALLSCON region embedded in the sphere, there must be a circle embedded in it which cannot be so shrunk. Imagine that the non-ALLSCON region covers the equator, and that the equator itself is such a circle (this can always be ensured by stretching the region in the right way — a circle embedded in a sphere divides

Figure 9. Three intrinsically different INTCON regions

it into two discs, and these can be made into hemispheres by appropriate stretching). For the circle to be unshrinkable, part of the COMPL of the non-ALLSCON region must lie in each hemisphere, and at most, these parts of the COMPL will connect at a finite number of points (if they connected along a segment of the equator, the unshrinkable circle would not, as supposed, be embedded in the non-ALLSCON region). Thus the spherical COMPL of a non-ALLSCON region must be non-INTCON. Conversely, the complement of an ALLSCON region in a sphere must be INTCON, as there will be no circle within the ALLSCON region separating the complement into two parts touching only at a finite set of points. We can subtract as many disjoint SCON regions as we please from the sphere, and the remainder will always be INTCON, but as soon as we subtract a non-SCON region, the remainder will no longer be INTCON. The constraints of this paragraph are specific to the sphere: they do not apply to the plane (where the complement of the INTCON but non WELLCON region of Figure 8 includes all of the plane outside the region's outer rim, and is thus non-SCON); nor to compact surfaces which are non-simply-connected, such as the torus.

This analysis suggest several ways of classifying spherical interior-connected regions.

1. Divide such regions into classes according to the number of separate boundaries they have (their CBNUM, for "complement boundary number": the SBNUM of a region and its COMPL).
2. Divide into classes according to their total number of boundary *lobes* (LOBENUM), summed over all boundaries. A "boundary lobe" is a simple closed curve making up part or all of a boundary. The inner boundaries of the three regions in Figure 9 have 2, 4 and 4 lobes.
3. Combine (1) and (2), defining a class by both CBNUM and LOBENUM.

4. Define a class by a CBNUM, a LOBENUM, and a partition of the LOBENUM into CBNUM parts. (So a region with two boundaries each of two lobes is distinguished from one with one three-lobe and one one-lobe boundary. This still fails to distinguish two of the regions of Figure 9.
5. Classifying as finely as possible, put INTCON spherical regions in different classes if they have a different collection of boundaries or, equivalently, a different complement.

As Figure 9 shows, two boundaries of INTCON regions may be different even if they have the same number of lobes. An interior-connected spherical region can be given a full description by specifying how many boundaries it has, how many simple closed curves ("lobes") make up each boundary, and how these are joined to each other: the different types of boundary with n lobes correspond to the different embedded trees with n nodes. With embedded trees, we might or might not classify asymmetric mirror-image pairs as distinct; we need to do so for boundaries, however, in order to produce a complete topological taxonomy of spherical regions.

Each of the systems for classifying interior-connected spherical regions listed above gives rise to a classification of connected regions, in which each class has a specified number of maximal interior-connected regions belonging to each of the classes of interior-connected regions. Even if the collection of interior-connected parts making up a connected region is fully specified, however, a connected but not interior-connected region has not been fully described. For example, if the maximal interior-connected sub-regions of a connected region are simply two discs, the two may have 1, 2, 3... points of contact. With more complex interior-connected sub-regions, there will also be distinct ways of sharing a given number of points. Figure 10 shows two regions, each of which has two interior-connected parts, one with a single, one-lobe boundary, the other with one one-lobe and one three-lobe boundary (each boundary is traced in a distinctive way). The two can only be distinguished by considering the order of points of inter-lobe contact around each boundary lobe. RCC could be used to make this distinction, but only with difficulty, as it cannot refer directly to boundary lobes and meeting points. A full description of *any* connected spherical region can be produced by listing all the boundary lobes of every interior-connected sub-region, numbering all the points around each lobe at which it meets other lobes, and noting which lobe-number pairs refer to the same points. This taxonomic scheme cannot be expressed directly within RCC.

There may be a number of ways of embedding a given collection of connected sub-regions into a sphere, producing regions that are *extrinsically* distinct. This is not so if all the components are simply-connected. In this case,

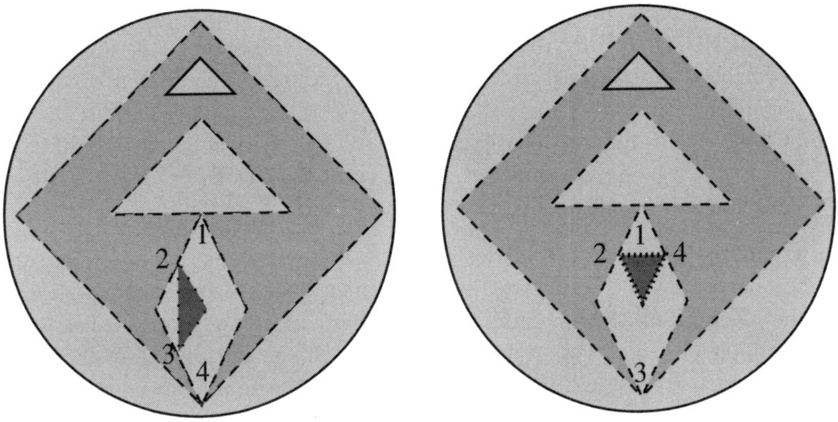

Figure 10. Two regions difficult to distinguish

or if there are no more than two components, and all the boundary-lobes of each component are topologically equivalent, there will be only one possible embedding. In all other cases, there are distinct ways to embed a given collection of components. There are, however, generally fewer (and never more) such embeddings in the sphere than in the plane: given a spherical embedding of an intrinsically-defined region, a distinct planar embedding can be produced from every topologically distinct class of points in the spherical complement of the region: simply pierce the sphere at such a point, expand this hole so its edge surrounds the surface and flatten the surface into the plane. As illustrated in Figure 11, this may produce obviously different results, as shown in Figure 11 (b), or may simply interchange topologically indistinguishable components, as in the upper pair of possibilities in 11(c).

Constraints between integer-valued properties

Some integer-valued properties of interior-connected spherical regions have already been defined. There are also useful integer-valued properties of connected and general spherical regions (SEPNUM and INTSEPNUM have already been mentioned). Constraints between integer-valued properties cannot be expressed within RCC.

We can define the "excess connectivity" or EXCONNUM, as the number of self-connected parts of a region, disconnected from each other and each sharing

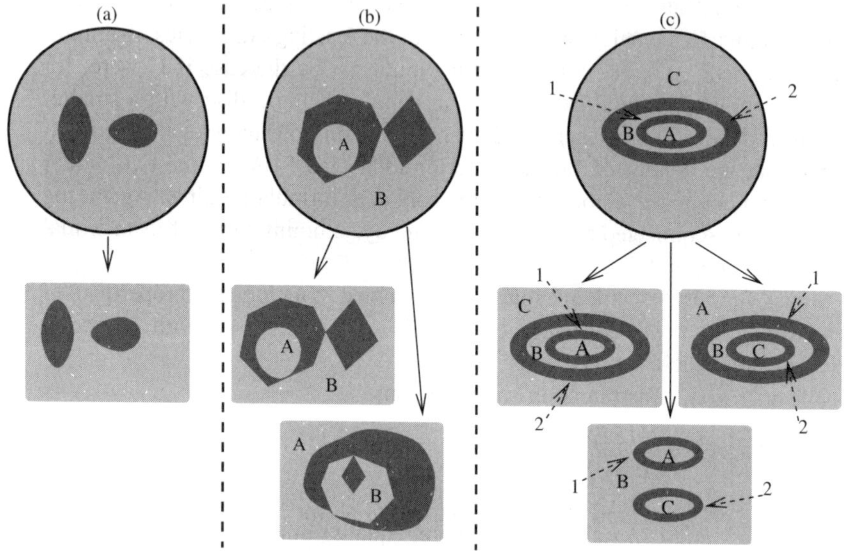

Figure 11. Mapping spherical regions into the plane

two boundaries with the remainder of the region, that can be removed without increasing the region's number of components. For a spherical interior-connected region (other than the entire sphere, for which both LOBENUM and EXCONNUM are 0), this will be one less than the LOBENUM. One can also calculate EXCONNUM for connected but not interior-connected regions. This is equal to the sum of the EXCONNUMs of the maximal interior-connected subregions, *plus* a contribution from the way in which these components are connected to each other. This contribution can be calculated by constructing a "multigraph" in which each interior-connected component is represented by a vertex, and each connecting point between two such components as an edge. The contribution from this level of the region's structure is then the number of edges that can be removed from this multigraph without disconnecting the remainder. Finally, the EXCONNUM of a disconnected region is just the arithmetic sum of the EXCONNUMs of its maximal connected components.

The number of boundaries (CBNUM) of a connected region is equal to the sum of the numbers of boundaries of its interior-connected sub-regions, minus the number of such components, plus one. Clearly, this is so for a connected region that is also interior-connected. If we consider adding further maximal interior-connected sub-regions one at a time, each when added must have exactly one of its boundaries amalgamated with one of the existing boundaries, maintaining the arithmetic relation. Note that this would *not* be the case if U were, for example, a torus, on which two annuli (an annulus being a disc with a smaller disc removed from its interior) could share points on both pairs of their boundaries, so that the connected but not interior-connected SUM of the two would have just two boundaries, not three as the spherical formula requires. Again, the CBNUM of a disconnected region is calculated by summing those of its maximal connected components.

Some further constraints on integer-valued topological properties of spherical regions are listed below. Some hold only for regions with particular properties, others across all regions.

Consider first, constraints on single regions.

1. SEPNUM(*x*) ≤ INTSEPNUM(*x*)
2. SEPNUM(*x*) ≤ CBNUM(*x*)
3. LOBENUM(*x*) ≤ INTSEPNUM(*x*) + EXCONNUM(*x*) (If the region is well-connected, and is *not* the whole sphere, equality holds.)
4. CBNUM(*x*) – SEPNUM(*x*) ≤ EXCONNUM(*x*) (Again, equality holds if the region is WELLCON, and is not the whole of the sphere.)

Next, consider constraints on regions related by the COMPL function.

5. CBNUM(*x*) = CBNUM(COMPL(*x*))
6. INTSEPNUM(*x*) = EXCONNUM(COMPL(*x*))+1
7. If *x* is CON, then CBNUM(*x*) = SEPNUM(COMPL(*x*)).

Note that these could be considered to hold even when *x* is the entire sphere, if we allowed for the existence of a null region, but constraint (6) would not then hold if *x* were the null region. Constraint (6) is illustrated in Figure 12, in which the eight maximal INTCON subregions of the dark-shaded region are numbered. Subtracting the seven white regions from its complement leaves that complement unaffected, but no further regions could be subtracted from it in the same way without disconnecting it.

Next, constraints on regions related by the SUM function.

8. For SEPNUM, INTSEPNUM, CBNUM and LOBENUM, an upper limit for SUM(*x*,*y*) is the arithmetic sum of the values for *x* and *y*. If *x* and *y* are DC, these maxima will be achieved. If C(*x*,*y*), then the SEPNUM and CBNUM maxima will *not* be achieved, while if *x* and *y* have some stretch of common boundary, none of them will be achieved.
9. For EXCONNUM, the same maximum will hold if the boundaries of the

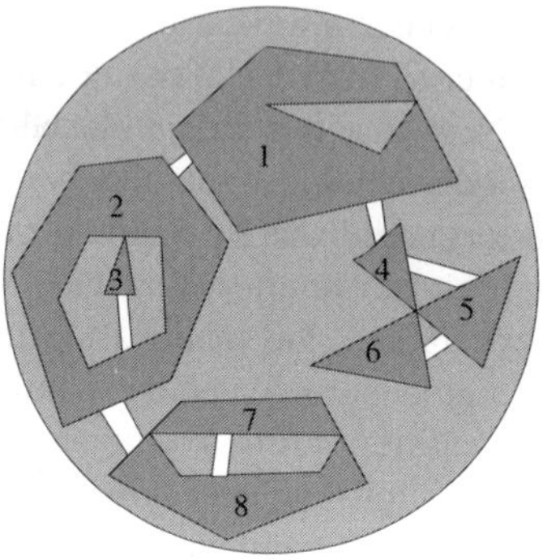

Figure 12. A connectivity constraint

two regions have no points of contact, and will be achieved if the regions are DC.

Finally, constraints on regions related by the PROD function.

10. An upper limit on the EXCONNUM of PROD(x,y) is set by the sum of the values for x and y.
11. If the boundaries of the two regions have no points of contact, the same maximum applies for SEPNUM, INTSEPNUM, CBNUM and LOBENUM.

Constraints of these kinds have potential uses in the kinds of topological reasoning we might expect a human problem-solver to perform: for example, calculating how many separate parcels of land or boundaries an amalgamation of two estates might have. They are also of potential use in checking the *consistency* of spatial databases. RCC's inability to express them is thus a serious drawback.

Conclusions

This paper has discussed an attempt to develop a specialized version of the RCC calculus, to deal with the particular domain of "well-behaved" two-dimensional parts of a spherical surface such as that of the Earth. The three-level hierarchical structure of RCC regions (the whole region and its maximal connected and interior-connected subregions), and some of the numerical relations listed above, arise as consequences of the basic RCC axioms. Other features of the classification of spherical regions arise from these basic axioms, plus the additional constraints imposed by taking the universal region to be a sphere. In describing the topology of spherical regions, however, it is natural to talk in terms of numerical constraints, and in terms of the relationships between regions and their boundary lines and points. Neither is possible within the language of RCC. We can conclude — see also (Gotts 1996b) — that the topological aspect of RCC is insufficiently expressive to form the basis of a formalization of non-mathematical topological reasoning, despite the fact that RCC is undecidable (this is deducible from (Grzegorczyk 1951)). Given this, it is not clear that we would lose anything by using a more expressive theory, able to refer explicitly to numerical constraints, and to entities of different dimensionalities. An alternative is to seek subsets or simplifications of RCC which are decidable, sacrificing expressivity in favour of an effective computational procedure. This alternative is pursued in Cohn et al (1997: 19–24), and in Bennett (1997). In this context, and given the potential usefulness of constraints between integer-valued properties of regions, it is worth noting that Presburger arithmetic, which would make it possible to talk about constraints involving equality, inequality and addition, is decidable. However, the computational resources required to guarantee proving the truth or falsity of an arbitrary Presburger arithmetic formula increases extremely fast as the size of the formula grows (Harel 1987: 179–180).

Acknowledgments

The support of the EPSRC under grant no. GR/H 78955, and helpful comments from Tony Cohn and three anonymous referees, are gratefully acknowledged. This paper was written while the author was employed successively in the School of Computer Studies, University of Leeds, UK and the Department of Computer Science, University of Wales Aberystwyth, UK. An earlier and considerably shorter version of the paper appeared as University of Leeds School of Computer Studies Research Report 96.24.

References

Armstrong, M.A. (1979). *Basic Topology*. London: McGraw-Hill.

Bennett, Brandon (1997). Determining consistency of topological relations, *Constraints, 3*, 213–225.

Boolos, George & Richard C. Jeffrey (1980). *Computability and Logic*, 2nd edn. Cambridge University Press.

Cohn, Anthony (1992). Completing sort hierarchies. *Computers and Mathematics with Applications, 23*, 477–491.

Cohn, Anthony, Brandon Bennett, John Gooday & Nicholas Gotts (1997). Qualitative spatial representation and reasoning with the region connection calculus. *Geoinformatica, 1*, 275–316.

Egenhofer, Max & Robert Franzosa (1995). On the equivalence of topological relations. *International Journal of Geographical Information Systems, 9(2)*, 133–152.

Gotts, Nicholas (1994). How far can we "C"? Defining a "doughnut" through connection alone. In Jon Doyle, Erik Sandewall and Pietro Torasso (Eds.) *Principles of Knowledge Representation and Reasoning: Proceedings of the fourth international conference (KR'94)*, 246–257. San Francisco: Morgan Kaufmann.

Gotts, Nicholas (1996a). An axiomatic approach to topology for spatial information systems [School of Computer Studies Research Report, 96.25]. University of Leeds.

Gotts, Nicholas (1996b). Formalizing commonsense topology: The INCH calculus. In *Proceedings, fourth international symposium on artificial intelligence and mathematics, AI/MATH-96*, 72–75.

Gotts, Nicholas, John Gooday & Anthony Cohn (1996). A connection based approach to commonsense topological description and reasoning. *The Monist, 79(1)*, 51–75.

Grzegorczyk, Andrzej (1951). Undecidability of some topological theories. *Fundamenta Mathematicae, 38*, 137–152.

Harel, David (1987). *Algorithmics: the spirit of computing*. Addison-Wesley.

Randell, David, Zhan Cui & Anthony Cohn (1992). A spatial logic based on regions and connection. In Bernhard Nebel, Charles Rich & William Swartout (Eds.) *Principles of Knowledge Representation and Reasoning: Proceedings of the third international conference (KR'92)*, 165–176. San Mateo: Morgan Kaufmann.

Requicha, Aristides & Robert Tilove (1978). Mathematical foundations of constructive solid geometry: General topology of closed regular sets [Technical Report, TM-27a]. University of Rochester.

Worboys, Michael and Petros Bofakos (1993). A canonical model for a class of areal spatial objects. In D. Abel and B.C. Ooi (Eds.), *Avances in Spatial Databases: Third international symposium, SSD'93* [Lecture Notes in Computer Science, 692]. Springer-Verlag.

Cognitive Mapping in Rats and Humans

The tent-maze, a place learning task in visually disconnected environments

Marie-Claude Grobéty, Muriel Morand and Françoise Schenk
University of Lausanne

Introduction

The term cognitive map is generally used to describe the mental representations that people or animals built of their spatial environment and reflect their spatial knowledge. Although many questions stay opened regarding the formation, the nature and the substrate of these representations, the concept of cognitive map is largely used by cognitive psychologist and neuroethologist, because the cognitive mapping abilities of a subject can be approach through his spatial behaviour and his ability to solve spatial problems. In the human literature, at minimum a distinction between three elements of spatial knowledge has been made (Chase & Chi 1981; Siegel & White 1975): landmarks, route knowledge and survey or configurational knowledge. This last level is thought to include relational information about elements that can not be seen simultancously and allow to localise places that are not perceptually available. Such places or references points can then serve in determining one's position in the environment (Gärling et al. 1986). Whether and how rats and humans can reach this configurational knowledge of an environment, will be tested here in a place learning task, taking place in visually disconnected environments.

Coping with visually disconnected environments is part of our everyday experience. Imagine viewing the arrangement of objects in a room, then walk into an adjacent room and note how easily you can point at the first room's features, which are then out of view. Upon moving from one bounded region to the next, we will usually notice the spatial arrangement of the features. As more of the first region will be occluded from view, a reciprocal amount of the following area is revealed allowing extracting the relationships between features. In the case of abrupt or blind transitions, spatial arrangement of the features detected within different regions can be linked through path integration processes i.e., the analyses of the proprioceptive information generated by the movements of the observer (Rieser et al. 1986; Etienne et al. 1995; Gallistel 1990; Kayton 1990). This co-ordination of piecemeal information leads to configurational representations of the environment which is regarded as the end product of the processes involved in environmental learning (Downs and Stea 1973; Siegel and White 1975). Configurational knowledge provides the opportunity to infer spatial relationships among previously unrelated locations and is therefore important for negotiating new routes and detours (Tolman 1948; Lockman 1984; Siegel et al. 1978).

In humans, configurational knowledge is usually tested by examining the performances of the subjects in complex direction or distance estimation tasks, or by the evaluation of their map drawing production (Kirasic et al. 1984; Moeser 1988; Herman et al. 1986). Pointing procedures can be even used at an early age (Herman 1980; Herman et al. 1987; Rider & Rieser 1988; Pick & Rieser 1982) but the use of map drawing studies and complex direction or distance estimation tasks is limited, particularly with children. Of course, human paradigms do not suit animals; however, some animal paradigms can be adapted to humans allowing us interesting comparisons. The main advantage of such transposition is that animal paradigms are independent of verbal instruction, verbal production, drawing production etc. Therefore they can be used undistinctively with young or old subjects, normal or deficient.

In animals, the discovery of hippocampal place cells by O'Keefe and Dostrovsky (1971) and the idea that a place cell, firing in a specific region of a familiar environment, participates in the neural substrate of cognitive mapping (O'Keefe & Nadel 1978), burst out the interest for spatial cognitive mapping tasks. Since then, spatial tasks and in particular place learning tasks have taken a major place in neurocognitive sciences as they create an extremely fruitful approach to the study of the biological substrate of cognition. As the number of anatomical structures and neurochemical systems known to be involved in place navigation multiplies, it becomes increasingly important that we understand the exact nature of the competencies exhibited by animals (including humans). Therefore, more sophisticated place learning tests or better controlled testing procedures should be used.

Spatial knowledge in animals is often assessed through the expression of spatial searching behaviour in place learning tasks such as the Morris water maze, the Homing board task, etc. (Morris 1984; Schenk 1989). However, classically, these experimental situations do not imply necessarily the use of a cognitive mapping strategy. In these classical tasks, animals move in open arenas from which a complete view of the environment is permanently available. Like humans, animals can often solved spatial tasks with one or a combination of simpler strategies, e.g. taxis strategies (moving along a specific cue gradient), route strategies (following a specific learned sequence of movements or taxis) snapshot memory (memorised view of the surrounding of a place) etc. Because the use of different strategies could lead to apparently similar searching behaviour or same level of spatial efficiency in raw place learning tests confusing or contradictory results are often found in the literature (see a discussion in Schenk et al. 1997)

In the search of an experimental test that would necessarily require the use of a high level of spatial cognition (i.e. a configurational representation of space), we developed a new place learning task in visually disconnected environments, adaptable for both rats and humans: the tent-maze.

For rats, the principle of this task was to locate a specific goal place (escape hole) in a white homogenous circular arena surrounded by curtains. No local cues (visual, auditory or olfactory) were available inside this arena, apart from the shape of the enclosure itself. Access to a surrounding visually rich environment was possible through small doors. Subjects were allowed to move freely from the outside environment to the inside one and vice versa, to connect the two environments and to develop a configurational knowledge of them. The goal could not simply be identified on the basis of a specific view (snapshot) or taxis due to the visually homogenous aspect of the arena. Selecting new entrance directions for probe trials allowed eliminating the use of route strategies. These conditions ensured the use of cognitive mapping to solve the task.

Curtains have often been used by several authors to enclose a test arena, but they were used to create a so-called "cue-controlled environment" inside the curtains and to dissociate it from the surrounding laboratory (see for ex. O'Keefe and Speakman 1987). Most often, the orientation of the cue-controlled environment relative to the experimental room was unpredictable due to inter-trial rotations. In some experiments, subjects were even disoriented before being placed in to the controlled environment, to insure a more complete dependency upon the controlled environment. In our experiments, on the contrary, curtains could be crossed freely by the subjects to link the external visually rich world with the cueless test enclosure. Therefore, the rats could theoretically orient themselves in the blind enclosure on the basis of an association of the memorised room features (no longer visible once inside the arena) and the integration of their own movements.

A similar design was developed for human subjects. A circular arena, circumscribed by curtains and deprived of cues, apart from its own geometry, was used. The arena was located in a building hall. The subjects had to enter the homogenous enclosure through blind doors from different directions to locate a goal card (fixed position in space) among hundred of others.

As rats and humans are confronted in their natural habitat with such disconnected environments we can assume that both species could solved a task like our tent-maze. The experiments presented here will focus on the following questions: How rapidly and spontaneously does a spatial search hypothesis appear in the tent-maze? How does the number, the stability and the shape of the paths between the inside arena and the surrounding environment (all factors influencing the complexity of path integration information) affect the acquisition of the task?

Rats in visually disconnected environments

All experiments were based on the following principles. Rats had to find a goal (escape hole or baited box) whose location was fixed in space. The environment was divided into two concentric areas. (1) A central circular or square area was delimited by curtains, and was visually homogeneous. Four possible escape holes, covered by lids, were distributed regularly on the arena surface. Only one of them was connected to the animal cage. Olfactory cues in the inside arena were controlled by rotation of the substrate of the inside arena between trials. The correct hole was only identifiable by its fixed spatial position. The enclosed area was accessible only through doors or barriers of thick fringe curtains. (2) Surrounding this central arena was a circular platform giving access to the rich and well-differentiated visuospatial cues of the experimental room. It was assumed that free exploration of this environment from the platform around the enclosed arena would provide sufficient orientation information to allow rats to orient themselves in the inside enclosure. Number of trials and special probe tests are detailed in each of the following sections (for more details see also Schenk et al. 1995; and Schenk et al. 1997).

Several variations of the general design were tested with rats. Design variations focused on the importance of the type of connections permitted between the inside arena and the outside environment and on the role that they may play in facilitating the elaboration of configurational relationships between the two environments. The following specific questions were addressed: (1) is place learning facilitated when only a few predetermined entrances are available? (2) Does a fixed entrance position assist in structuring the inside environment? (3) Will the shape of the entrance paths influence the path integration efficiency of the studied subjects?

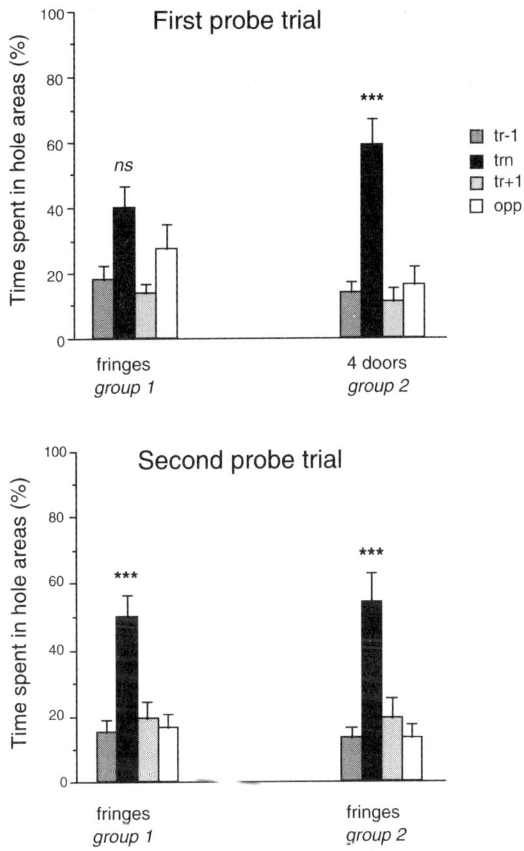

*Figure 1. Mean of the relative time spent in each hole sector during the probe trials. The discrimination of the training sector (trn) in the different groups is based on separate one-way ANOVAs (n.s.= non significant; $p<.01$ **; $p<.001$ ***). For the second probe trial, the group "4 doors" was tested with a mere fringe curtain*

Random access paths versus structured, predetermined entrances

Access into the internal arena was either restricted through 4 orthogonally placed doors (**4-door condition**), or it was not predetermined (*free access through "fringes"*). In the latter case, a circular curtain extended by tight fringes (10 cm) touching the ground circumscribed the internal arena. Rats could not see through the fringes but could pass through and make their way in and out at any point.

Training consisted of trials during which the rats learned how to leave the central arena through one hole out of four, allowing escape into the subject's home cage. After several training sessions (3 days, 4 trials per day), knowledge regarding the goal position was assessed during a first probe trial. For the probe test, all holes were equivalent and none were connected to the home cage. The subjects' knowledge of the spatial position of the goal place was evaluated as a function of the time spent searching in the four hole areas. Further training trials and a second probe tests were then run.

The discrimination of the goal was optimal in the *4-door condition*, indicating that rats can learn a place on the basis of the interaction between the collection of piecemeal information memorised from the outside arena and path integration information. In the *free access through "fringes"* condition, the discrimination of the goal was less clearly marked in the first probe test (Figure 1). However, rats in the *free access through "fringes"* condition required only more time to learn the task and demonstrated good place learning performance in the second probe trial (1 day later). In addition, rats originally trained with four doors were not affected when having to locate the hole in the free access condition (second probe trial, group 2, Figure 1). The *4-door condition* implies repeated use of the same entrances and a lower variability in the paths leading to the goal, facilitating route learning. Therefore, this design inherently simplifies the collection and the integration of path integration and visual information. The repeated use of only four orthogonal entrances helped anchor the inner arena into a representation of the room environment but these predetermined entrances were no longer necessary after this learning phase. The experimental condition minimising the complexity of the path integration information was the least difficult for the rats. This underlines the importance of the path integration process in these tasks and more generally its essential role in successful place learning. By constantly keeping track of one's own movements through space, path integration allows one first to integrate directions and distances between features and to build configurational knowledge of the environment. But it is also essential to orient and guide one's path to a memorised goal location.

New versus familiar entrance direction, zigzag versus direct doors

In the above two designs, rats could have implemented a simplified strategy to locate the goal. They could have defined a preferred entrance point and memorised only the relative position of the goal from this access point (route learning). Although we did not observe such stereotyped behaviour, a testing procedure that would exclude the use of such a strategy was utilised in a second series of experiments. In a squared four-door arena, 3 of the doors served as frequent access doors during training ("*familiar doors*"). The fourth door was only accessible twice during training ("*new door*"). Two types of access doors were used: (1) "*Direct doors*" were simple fringed openings in the arena wall, allowing straight entrance in the enclosed arena. (2) "*Zigzag doors*" allowed access via Z shaped alleys with a section parallel to the arena walls (Figure 2).

Surprisingly, in the "*direct door*" condition, probe trials with access through any of the familiar doors indicated a weak discrimination of the training position, whereas probe trials via the new door indicated a more significant discrimination of the training position. In the "*Zigzag door*" condition, rats demonstrated a significant spatial discrimination in probe trials when access into the homogenous arena took place through one of the three familiar doors. In this condition, however, a transfer probe trial with access via the "*new door*" indicated a poor discrimination of the training position. Rats indeed demonstrated a strange search pattern focus around the new entrance door.

Therefore, rats in the easiest test situation ("*direct and familiar*" door) and in the most complex one ("*zigzag and unfamiliar*") performed less efficiently than in the intermediate conditions ("*direct and unfamiliar*" or "*zigzag and familiar*"). This may suggest that an aspecific and of course non-controlled arousal level affect the expression of a spatial bias during probe trials. The novelty of the access path for the probe test seemed to influence positively the level of arousal in the direct doors condition focusing activity around the correct goal position. A novel entrance door in the zigzag condition either make the task too difficult or the new door too attractive in itself that it disrupted searching behaviour. Unfortunately we can not eliminate at this point a disorientation of the subjects. However, the strange search pattern of the animals, focused around the entrance area instead of the escape holes, suggest more a strong attractiveness of the new entrance alley than pure disorientation. Novelty is known to induce re-exploration (see Thinus-Blanc et al. 1998 for a review) This re-exploration burst may be more apparent when the subjects clearly have some objects or points to focus on with their re-exploratory behaviour. More often however, novelty increases the general level of activity due to a shift in the priority between the achievement of the task and curiosity or fear. Negative results of several experiments on cognitive mapping may be partially due to this shifting factor (Sutherland et al. 1987; Benhamou 1996). As we will see in the following experiments, human subjects will also react strongly to the novelty of an entrance.

This series of experiments, however, clearly indicate that at least in the direct entrance condition, rats do not need to rely upon familiar access and that therefore they are able to identify a place in the visually homogeneous arena of the tent-maze without relying on route strategies. According to our hypothesis, this suggests that they were able to build and use a configurational knowledge of the visually disconnected environments.

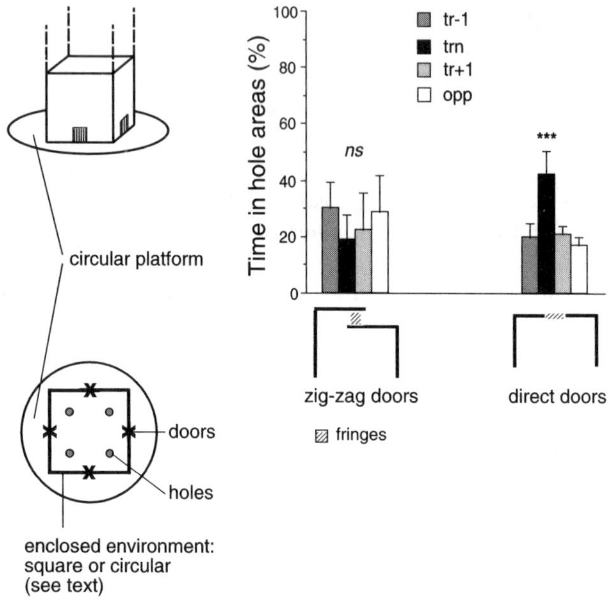

Figure 2. Experimental set-up and time spent by the rats in the four sectors following access to the arena via a new door

Human subjects in a visually disconnected arena

Standardised spatial tests in cue controlled environments are not very often encountered in the spatial literature concerning human adults. Neuropsychologists and neurologists working with patients suffering from spatial disorientation mainly use visuospatial psychometric tests (Beaumont 1998) or tests of general culturo-spatial knowledge. However, the demand for the development of standardised procedures for testing spatial orientation and place learning capacities in a real space of movement is evident (see for example Van der Linden & Meuleman 1998).

We have already seen that the tent maze test we developed for rats is ecologically relevant for humans, as building complex representations of disconnected environments is a common problem of everyday life. But would such laboratory procedure really be adequate for humans? Would human subjects develop configurational knowledge in such environment? If so, how quickly?

Without or with verbal instructions? Would new entrance directions and complex entrance paths affect human performance? Is this task relevant to distinguish between subjects favouring spatial or non-spatial strategies?

Familiar versus new access conditions

Our first human version of the test consisted of an enclosed octagonal arena (3.5m diam.) with eight possible blind entrance doors. The arena, completely homogenous from the inside, was situated in the main hall of a building, an external environment rich in visuospatial information. The assigned task was to find a goal, a textual "well done" sign written under a white plastic disc or card. The goal disc was placed on the arena floor among other identical ones. It could be discriminated from other discs only by its position in space.

Forty-nine adult subjects (from both sexes, ranging from 16–50 years old), divided into four groups, were tested according to the following procedure (see Figure 3). During the first two training trials only four white discs (the goal and 3 others in symmetrical positions) were present in the arena. Subjects were first conducted to a blind entrance door (E1). Once there, they were instructed to enter the arena, to explore it and to look at the objects within it and when they would be finished, to get out throughout any door. This was the only verbal instruction for the all experiment, excepted for the A+ and B+ group (see below). A second training trial was allowed, this time using E2 entrance. Subsequent to this learning phase, an initial test was run with 60 identical discs on the floor of the arena. The goal disc was of course located at the same position as during the learning phase. The entrance door for this test was either an already used one ("*familiar*" (door E1, group A)) or a new one ("*new*" door (group B)). Prior to entering the arena, some of the subjects of each group were given the instruction: "the object is at the same place as before" (A+ and B+ instruction Group). Training was prolonged by two trials using the first two entrance doors (E1 and E2). A second test was then conducted with 120 discs on the arena floor. For all groups, a new entrance door and no verbal instructions were used. This time, in order to assess to what extent subjects would focus their search around the correct baited place, no "well done" card was present (similar to the rats procedure in the probe trials, when no escape hole was connected to the cage).

Searching strategies are not necessarily spatial

Interestingly, a group of 7 subjects (6 males and 1 female) among those tested without verbal instruction (Groups A and B) developed no spatial hypothesis at

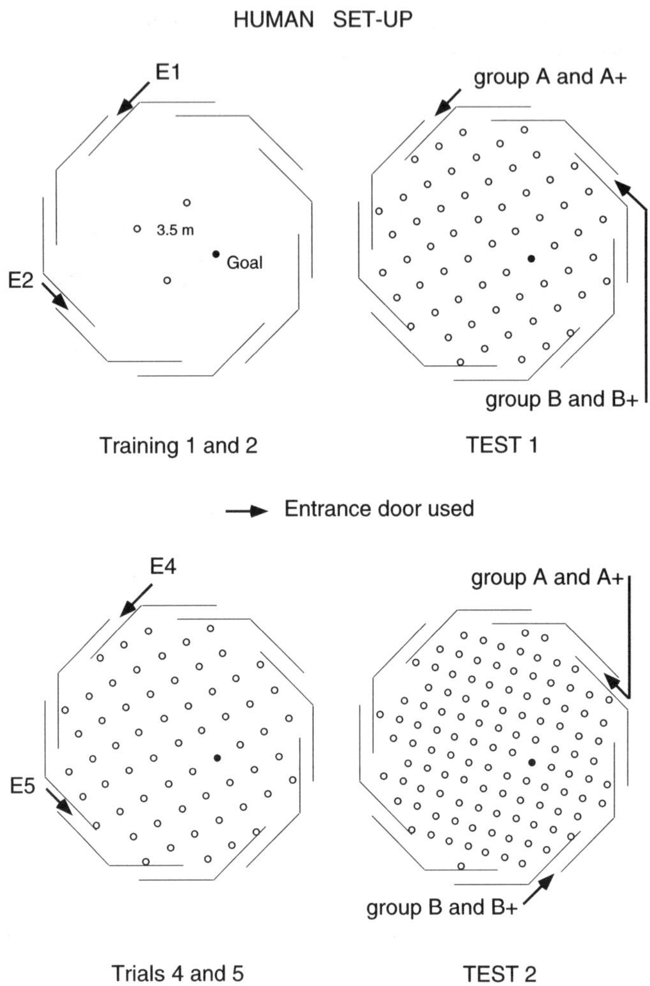

Figure 3. Human set-up and testing procedure (see text)

all. Through the course of the 6 tests, this group of subjects were not aware that the goal was always at the same place (and were even surprised when informed so). They behaved in a systematic manner in each trial; opening the discs one after another, row after row. Were these systematic subjects unable to build a cognitive map of the environment or did they enter in the test with an *a priori* non-spatial search hypothesis? Unfortunately these first series of subjects were not further tested. The subjects with a systematic search pattern were removed from their respective groups for the following analyses.

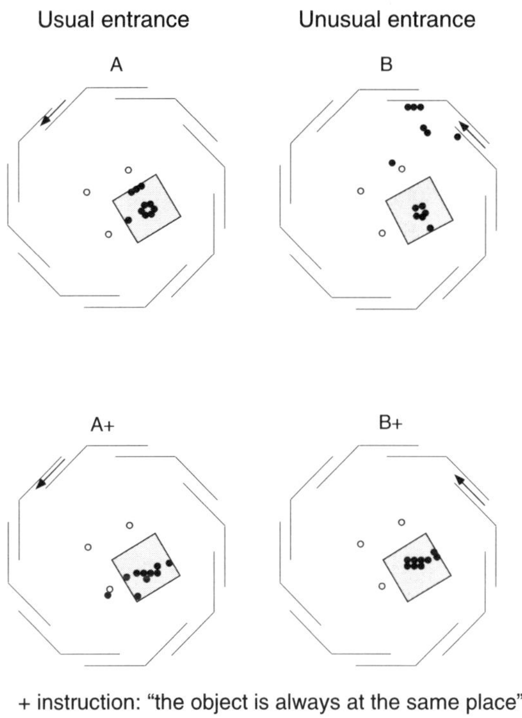

Figure 4. Position of the first disc returned by the subjects during test 1 (group A, N= 10; group B, N=13; group A+, N=10; group B+ N= 9). The grey square represents the position of the goal (centre) and the 8 discs around it. The choice of a first disc located inside this squared area was considered as a hit. The positions of the 3 other initial discs are also represented.

The increased number of discs present during the test (60 instead of 4 discs) had no influence on the search strategy and the spatial precision of the subjects of the group A, A+ and B+. Subjects entering through a familiar door (groups A and A+) overturned their first disc right in the goal area. In contrast, seven out of the 13 subjects entering through a new door (Group B) were disoriented. The first discs overturned by these subjects were situated in the proximity of the entrance point. On the other hand, subjects of the B + instruction Group, also entering via a new door, were well oriented toward the goal spot, as shown in Figure 4.

None of the B+ instruction subjects were disoriented by the use of a new entrance door. However, the verbal instruction given to the B+ group subjects right before the test contained in itself no spatial information (i.e., no information was imparted regarding location and/or where to seek) but rather underlined the search strategy to apply (i.e., a spatial strategy). The behaviour of the B+ subjects revealed that they relied on a configurational type of representation of the arena. Their efficiency in re-orienting and locating the goal via a new entrance was almost immediate, although prior experience of the arena was brief (Figure 5a).

Entering through a new door was not disorienting in itself. But for half of the subjects of the group B, this novel direction of entrance combined with the absence of instruction was sufficient to invalidate spatial search strategy. Instead, they focused their attention on the entrance area, beginning their search sequences as in a new task or as in an unknown environment. The higher number of discs in this test could also have contributed to the impression of novelty however in itself it was not sufficient to disturb the subjects of the other groups.

During Test 2, wherein no "well done" sign could be found, subjects in Group B demonstrated a weakly focused search around the goal. It appeared that having doubted, at one point during test 1, that the bait was always at the same place, they became more prone to start searching in a spatially dispersed manner (Figure 5b).

In summary, half of the subjects entering through a new access door, without any clear verbal instructions that they could rely on a spatial search strategy, developed a non-spatial search hypothesis. Like the subjects of the B+ group, they were certainly able to memorise the spatial representation of the set up and the different door positions but they did not use it spontaneously to locate the goal, because of the apparent novelty of the test situation. One can only observe with interest the similarities between the results of the human subjects in groups A and B and the rats in the familiar or new zigzag doors conditions. The verbal instructions used with the human subjects of the B+ group were fortunately able to disentangle the influence of novelty (on arousal level and on search strategy) from real spatial disorientation.

Influence of direct versus zigzag entrance doors

A second series of experiments was run with human subjects. This design was chosen to replicate the zigzag alley entrances used with the rats. A double wall of curtains that created a blind circular alley of 80cm wide surrounded a hexagonal enclosed arena. The subjects, guided by the experimenter, would enter from one direction in the blind alley, then turn around the arena between the

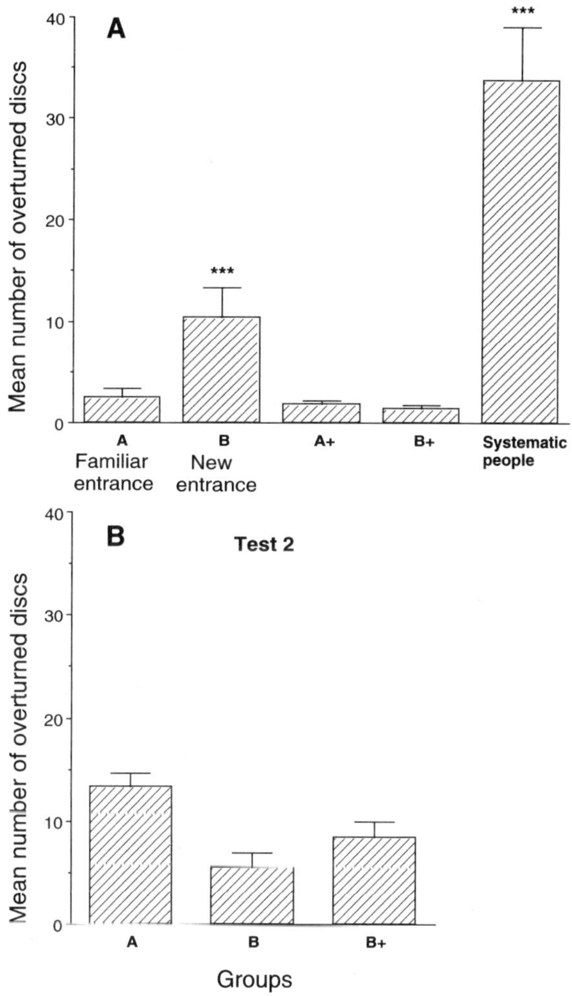

Figure 5. (A) Mean number of discs opened to find the baited one. (B) Number of discs overturned in an area around the goal in Test 2.

curtained walls, to finally enter into the arena from another direction. Of course for humans the amplitude of the deviation from straight entrance direction was higher than for rats. Two turn conditions were chosen, subjects could turn around the peripheric arena with full access to visual cues all along the way, or turn inside the blind alley with no vision of the visually rich environment during the turn. Amplitude of the turns were varied from 120° around the peripheral arena ("*120° around*") to 240° around ("*240° around*") or 240° in the blind alley ("*240° blind alley*").

Forty-two subjects were tested. The general set-up was similar to the previous one with 3 exceptions: the shape of the arena (hexagonal instead of octagonal), the presence of the surrounding blind alley and the number of white discs used during the test (n = 120). After two training trials, the subjects were divided into 3 groups according to the type of entrance used ("*120 around*", "*240° around*" or "*240° blind alley*"). All subjects, whatever their turn amplitude in the blind alley, entered in the arena through the same new door.

As in the first experiments, one subject with a systematic search pattern was removed from the following results.

This test was more difficult than the previous one. The percentage of the subject overturning a disc in the hit zone (one discs around the goal) was respectively: 69% ("*120° around*"), 46% ("*240° around*") and 71% ("*240° blind alley*"). Fifty percent of all the subjects did not find the goal in the first 10 overturned discs. To take into account the performance of these subjects, we calculated for all groups the mean proportion of the first ten overturned discs per sector (4 sectors). If a subject had found the goal in less than ten discs, then its mean proportion of discs overturned by sectors was calculated on all its opened discs. Subjects of the groups "*120° around*" and "*240° blind alley*" entrance significantly focused their search behaviour on the correct sector (Figure 6). Subjects from the third group ("*240° around*") did not significantly identify the correct sector and showed the least success of goal retrieval. Theoretically, the 240° path around the arena, allowing full access to the visually rich environment during the rotation, should have been less disorienting than the 240° blind one. However, the results showed the reverse tendency.

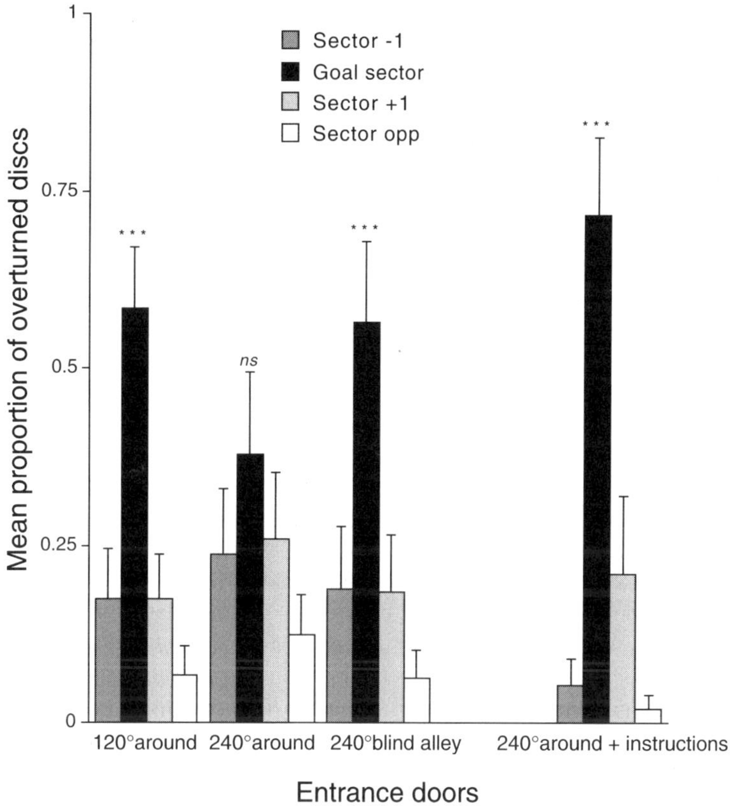

Figure 6. Mean proportion of white discs overturned per subject in each sector for the first ten discs. This proportion reflects how much subjects focused on the goal sector during their search.

A fourth group of subjects using the same procedure as the "*240° around*" with the exception of verbal instruction "the goal is at the same place as before" ("*240° around + instructions*") was run. Here again, similar to the first series of experiments, this simple instruction, given prior to the start of the test, was sufficient to improve the results of the subjects and 70% of them hit the goal zone during their first choice. These subjects were not disoriented by the 240° turn and focused their search in the correct sector.

Verbal instructions and arousal level

Similar to the results of the rats' experiments, arousal level appeared to interfere with the production of the correct spatial behaviour. When the task condition was simple, the search was spatially oriented. When the difficulty of the task slightly increased but not enough to arouse the attention level, path integration information was not taken fully into account and the spatial efficiency reverted to a random search. However, if the task became clearly difficult, attention was increased and spatial performance was good again. An assumption could be made that a further increase of the task difficulty would eventually cause the spatial performance to deteriorate. The 240° turn in the blind alley is of a sufficient length to challenge the subjects but not enough to disorient them. Subjects reported feeling progressively stressed and disoriented when moving in the blind alley and therefore tried to be more attentive to their movements. This factor was sufficient to improve their performances. It is however important to note that in this "*240° blind alley*" group both the best performance (the highest number of goals found at the first opened discs) and the worst (the highest number of goals not found in a 90-sec. search) were found. This may reflect the variability of individual spatial competencies and strategies, each subject being challenged by the difficulty of the task.

Self-evaluated spatial capabilities in everyday life and spatial efficiency in the tent-maze

Was the performance of the subjects in the tent-maze related to their spatial capabilities in everyday life? To approach this question, we regrouped the results of 51 subjects of the last experiment (across different testing procedures) and compared their performance in the maze with their self-evaluation of their spatial capabilities. The subject's spatial capabilities in everyday life were self-evaluated in a questionnaire filled out before the test of the tent maze. Questions are summarised in Figure 7. Subjects could answer on a 4-point scale. Their performances in the tent-maze were expressed in terms of distance of the first overturned discs to the position of the goal and were regrouped in three classes according to their spatial precision (1 = 0 to 1 disc away from the goal, 2 = 2 discs away, 3 = 3 and more discs away). The Anova with repeated factors ran on this measure of performances and the scores of each question per subject showed a significant difference between groups ($F(2,49) = 3.625$; $p = 0.035$). The most efficient subjects in the tent-maze self-evaluated their orientation capabilities as higher than did the less spatially efficient group (distance of the first overturned discs 3 or more).

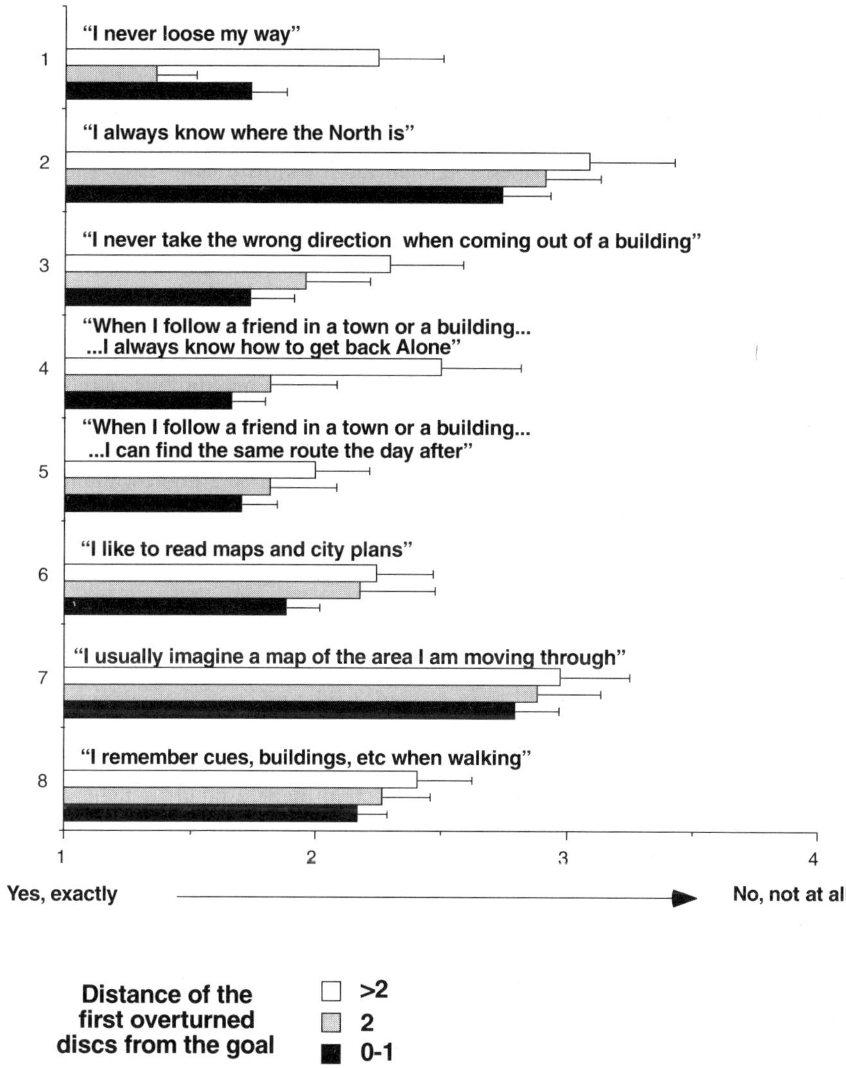

Figure 7. Self evaluation of wayfinding performances (4 point scale)

Interestingly, in terms of performance, we did not observe any difference between men and women in the tent-maze. However, women in self-evaluating their spatial capabilities in everyday life rated their spatial orientation capabilities lower than the men did (Anova: $F(1,47) = 7.108$, $p = 0.01$). These results are consistent with previous studies showing gender differences in spatial anxiety and self-confidence (Schmitz 1997), but do not confirm gender differences in spatial efficiency (see for ex: Lawton 1994; Lawton 1996; Linn & Petersen 1985; etc.).

In general, the tests developed in the tent-maze were not at all trivial for the human subjects and challenged most of them, creating stimulating experimental conditions. The results showed that most of the human subjects do not require extended training to obtain and use a configurational knowledge of the environment, even in such controlled laboratory settings. Our results in these two series of tests demonstrated the validity of such a testing procedure for human and its possible use for descriptions of individual spatial competencies and strategy preferences. The fact that efficiency in the tent-maze and self-evaluation of spatial orientation capacities tend to correlate, reinforced the validity of this test for spatial orientation studies and encourage us to continue to further develop it.

Conclusion

The experiments presented here shed some light on the controversy about the existence of cognitive maps in animals (Bennet 1996; Poucet & Benhamou 1997). The place learning tests in the tent-maze presented here meet the operationally defined conditions for the demonstration of a configurational representation of the environment (no specific snapshot memory, capacity for detours and new routes). Rats, like human subjects demonstrated their capability to orient in a homogenous arena through interconnections with a surrounding varied environment. More specifically, they were able to identify a specific location on the basis of the collection of path integration information and piecemeal visual information obtained from the surrounding environment. The use of a new entrance door not yet experienced and hypothetically not yet coded on the representation of the environment disrupted the rats'accuracy in the most complex tested designs only, but also affected human performance in some conditions. Rats, as well as humans, were however able to develop new routes to the goal when tested in appropriate conditions (respectively "*Direct doors*" new entrance for rats and new entrance + *instruction* for human). In the first experiment, when human subjects were tested without verbal instructions, a new entrance direction seemed to reset the searching hypothesis, leading to what is classically interpreted as a misoriented or random search pattern. However, as demonstrated by the groups + instruction, the indication that space was the reference to follow ("the goal is at the same place as before"), was sufficient to orient human subjects to the correct goal position despite the new entrance direction. The emergence of a spatial search hypothesis appeared to be affected in a similar manner in both rats and humans by non-specific factors such as the degree of novelty of the experimental situation and the general arousal level of the subjects. It underlines the importance of control trials in which these factors are varied, particularly when negative results are found in animal studies.

For rats, the multiplicity, variability and shape complexity of the entrance points, all factors increasing the complexity of the path integration information, delayed the acquisition of the spatial representation of the inner area. The observed correlation between the complexity of the path integration information and the delayed acquisition of optimal orientation performances underlines the importance of the path integration information to successfully build a configurational type of representation.

For humans too, the complexity of the entrance route influences the orientation performances of the subjects. But motivation and arousal level also strongly influence their efficiency in the task. These last factors can however indirectly be influenced by different verbal instructions given before or during the test. Comparing the subject's performances with or without different types of instructions in the tent-maze could really help to classify subjects as to the nature of their spatial strategies and competencies. Such studies would also be useful to evaluate the exact nature of the spatial deficit of disoriented patients, completing the classical visuospatial and psychometric test battery. Developing standardised laboratory spatial tests for humans such as the tent-maze appears to us as absolutely necessary. Visuospatial tests, test of culturo-spatial knowledge, or even spatial tests realised in virtual environments or based on slides presentation, will never be sufficient to study navigation and acquisition of spatial configurational knowledge as they do not take into account the important role of path integration information. Path integration information are essential for the elaboration of a configurational representation of an environment as they allow to extract direction and distance information between places (Klatzky et al. 1995; Loomis et al. 1993; Gallistel 1990). Previous spatial studies have already pointed out not only the importance of path integration information but also the importance of active movements for top spatial performance (Gibson 1979; Foreman et al. 1990; McComas et al. 1997). The nature of the deficit of disoriented patients, the influence of ageing on spatial orientation, etc., should be studied with appropriate tools that can also report for possible deficits in movement perception and in the integration of path integration information.

Finally, spatial tests, like the tent-maze, that do not necessitate any verbal or drawing ability also have the advantage of being adequate for humans at any age as well as for animals. They allow comparative approaches, which can only be beneficial to the understanding of brain mechanisms underlying spatial cognition of species which, however different they are, live in the same environments and solve similar spatial problems.

References

Beaumont J. G. (1998). Visual-spatial skill and standard psychometric tests. In N. Foreman & R. Gillet (ed). *Handbook of Spatial Research paradigms and Methodologies*. Vol 2, 11–32. Clinical and comparative Studies. Psychology Press.

Benhamou, S. (1996). No evidence for cognitive mapping in rats. *Animal Behaviour*, 52,: 201–212.

Bennett, A. T. (1996). Do animals have cognitive maps? *Journal of Experimental Biology*. 199, 219–224.

Chase, W. G. & Chi, M. T. H. (1981). Cognitive skill: Implications for spatial skills in large environments. In J. H. Harvey (Ed.), *Cognition, social behavior, and the environment* (pp. 111–136). Hillsdale, NJ: Lawrence Erlbaum.

Downs, R. & Stea, D. (1973). *Image and Environment*. Chicago: AVC

Etienne, A. S., Maurer, R. & Seguinot, V. (1995). Path integration in mammals and its interaction with visual landmarks. *Journal of Experimental Biology*, 199, 201–209.

Foreman, N., Foreman, D., Cummings, A., Owens, S. (1990). Locomotion, active choice, and spatial memory in children. *Journal of General Psychology*. Vol 117(2) 215–233.

Gallistel, C. R. (1990). *The organization of learning*. Cambridge, MA: MIT Press.

Gärling, T., Lindberg, E., Carreiras, M. & Böök, A. (1986). Reference systems in cognitive maps. *Journal of Experimental Psychology*, 6, 1–8.

Gibson, J. J. (1979). *The Ecological Approach to Visual Perception*. Boston: Houghton-Mifflin.

Herman, J. F. (1980). Children's cognitive maps of large scale spaces: Effects of exploration, direction and repeated experiences. *Journal of Experimental Child psychology*, 29, 126–143.

Herman, J. F., Heins, J. A. & Cohen, D. S. (1987). Children's spatial knowledge of their neighborhood environment. *Journal of Applied Psychology*, 8, 1–15.

Herman, J. F., Klein, C. A. & Blomquist, S. L. (1986). Developmental differences in the use of an abstract reference frame to infer spatial relationship. *Developmental Psychology*, 22, 468–476.

Kayton, M. (1990). *Navigation: Land, sea, air and space*. New York: IEEE Press.

Kirasic, K. C., Allen, G. L & Siegel, A. W. (1984). Expression of configurational knowledge of large-scale environments. Students' performance of cognitive tasks. *Environment and Behavior*, 16, 687–712.

Klatzky, R. L; Colledge, R. G; Loomis, J. M; Cicinelli, J. G; et al. (1995). Performance of blind and sighted persons on spatial tasks. *Journal of Visual Impairment & Blindness*. Vol 89(1), 70–82.

Lockman, J. J. (1984). The development of detour ability during infancy. *Child Development*. Vol 55(2) 482–491.

Loomis, J. M; Klatzky, R. L; Golledge, R. G; Cicinelli, J. G; et al. (1993). Nonvisual navigation by blind and sighted: Assessment of path integration ability. *Journal of Experimental Psychology*: General. Vol 122(1), 73–91.

McComas, J., Dulberg, C., Latter, J. (1997). Children's memory for locations visited: Importance of movement and choice. *Journal of Motor Behavior*. Vol 29(3) 223–229.

Moeser, S. D. (1988). Cognitive mapping in complex building. *Environment and Behavior*, 20, 21–49.

Morris, R. G. M. (1984). Developments of a water maze procedure for studying spatial leearning in the rat. *Journal of Neurosciences Methods*. 11, 47–60.

O'Keefe J. Dostrovsky J. (1971). The hippocampus as a spatial map. Preliminary evidence from unit activity in the freely-moving rat. *Brain Research*. 34(1):171–5.

O'Keefe, J. & Nadel, L. (1978). *The Hippocampus as a Cognitive Map*. Oxford: Oxford University Press.

Pick, H. L. & Rieser, J. J. (1982). Children's cognitive mapping. In M. Potegal (ed.), *Spatial Orientation: Development and physiological bases*. Academic Press NY.

Poucet, B. & Benhamou, S. (1997). The neuropsychology of spatial cognition in the rat. *Critical reviews in Neurobiology*. 11: 101–120.

Rider, E. A. & Rieser, J. J. (1988). Pointing at objects in other rooms, young children's sensitivity to perspective after walking with and without vision. *Child Development*, 59, 480–494.

Rieser, J. J., Guth, D. A. & Hill, E. W. (1986). Sensitivity to perspective structure while walking without vision. *Perception*, 15, 173–188.

Rossier J., Grobéty M.-C., Schenk F. (1996). Place learning under discontinuous access to a limited number of visual cues, *European Journal of Neuroscience Suppl.* n° 9, p. 119.

Schenk, F. (1989). A homing procedure for studying spatial memory in immature and adult rodents. *Journal of Neurosciences Methods*, 26, 249–258.

Schenk, F., Grobéty, M.-C. & Gafner, M. (1997). Spatial learning by rats across visually disconnected environments. *Quarterly Journal of Experimental Psychology* 50B, 54–78.

Schenk, F., Grobéty, M.-C., Lavenex, P. & Lipp, H.-P. (1995). Dissociation between basic components of spatial memory in rats. In E. Alleva, A. Fasolo, H-P. Lipp, L. Nadel & L. Ricceri (Eds) *Behavioral Brain Research In Naturalistic And Semi-Naturalistic Settings: Possibilities And Perspectives*, pp. 277–300. Kluwer Press.

Schmitz, S. (1997). Gender-related strategies in environmental development: Effects of anxiety on wayfinding in and representation of a three-dimensional maze. *Journal of Environmental Psychology*. Vol 17(3), 215–228.

Siegel, A. W. & White, S. H. (1975). The development of spatial representations of large scale environments. In H. W. Reese (ed.) *Advances in Child Development and Behaviour*. New York: Academic.

Siegel, A. W., Kirasic, K. C. & Kail, R. V. Stalking the elusive cognitive map. The development of children's representations of geographic space. In Wohlwill and I Altman (eds) *Human behavior and the Environment*. New York: Plenum.

Sutherland, R. J., Chew, G. L., Baker, J. C. & Linggard, R. C. (1987). Some limitations on the use of distal cues in place navigation by rats. *Psychobiology*, 15, 48–57.

Thinus-Blanc C. , Save E. & Poucet B. (1998). Animal spatial cognition and exploration. In N. Foreman & R. Gillet (ed). *Handbook of Spatial Research Paradigms and Methodologies*. Vol 2, 59–86. *Clinical and Comparative Studies*. Psychology Press.

Tolman E. C. (1948). Cognitive maps in rats and men. *Psychological Review*, 55, 189–208.

Van der Linden M. & Meulemans T. (1998). A cognitive neuropsychological approach to spatial memory deficits in brain-damaged patients. In N. Foreman & R. Gillet (ed). *Handbook of spatial research paradigms and methodologies*. Vol 2, 33–58 *Clinical and Comparative Studies*. Psychology Press

Spatial Cognition Without Spatial Concepts

Arnold Smith
National Research Council, Canada

1. Introduction

The intent of this chapter is to suggest that all of the ways of thinking about human spatial cognition that loosely adhere to an information-processing paradigm, whether these are quantitative or qualitative, are based on a set of assumptions about the nature of language and mind that is incomplete and can be no more than partially correct. When we examine these assumptions carefully, we find that they are quite inadequate to explain what is going on. This lack of adequacy, in turn, is related to the very slow progress (one might even say 'failure') of computational language understanding and artificial intelligence more generally. Spatial cognition is far from being the only domain in which one can begin to see this, but it is perhaps as good a vantage point as any from which to develop a sense for the problems.

The core of the argument is that language and conceptual thinking, which we of course use all the time, constitute a faculty that in humans is superimposed on a quite different mode of knowing and awareness, and that it is the latter, far more than the former, that we rely on in order to act in and reason about our physical environment. I will argue that language and its associated concepts are much too abstract to mediate our direct interaction with the world, and that language would not work at all, even for communication, without the rich non-conceptual substrate on which it depends. The implication is that we cannot directly model the world and its relationships, nor can we mimic human cognition and its achievements, using concepts rooted in language as a basis for model construction. What should we be doing instead? Well, that is a long story … a story we are still learning to tell.

This chapter represents work in progress. When the author began this investigation (into the "visual" interpretation of spatial expressions), he little expected to find himself exploring a vast unfamiliar terrain. But gradually he became convinced that if we really want to understand the phenomena at stake, we have to be prepared to leave familiar assumptions behind.

2. A representational perspective

In the early nineties, a small group of us started working on a project called Spoken Image (see, e.g. Ó Nualláin and Smith 1994). In the system we developed, a user could interact via typed, and later spoken, natural language with a dynamically-represented three-dimensional world shown visually on the screen. The user could move around in this simulated world, and make changes to the world, by speaking English utterances. The goal was to use the 3D world model to ground the linguistic interpretations, neatly solving a number of traditional problems in natural language interpretation. I half thought that this might be a step towards the really intuitive interfaces that the HCI and AI communities have always dreamed of. On the other hand, this optimism was shadowed by a pretty strong hunch that this was not really going to be the route to the intuitive naturalistic speech-understanding computer. Nevertheless, I felt that we needed a first-hand feel for the problems to help us translate that hunch into something more articulate.

Sure enough, as we got a certain distance along the way to building such a system (we got it working pretty well, by some criteria), we began to run into really hard problems, some of which are enumerated below. From my perspective, this was the real payoff of the research — not the system itself, but the view it provided of some underlying issues.

Before getting to the unsolved problems, it is worth paying some attention to the problems that *were* solved. Because of the nature of the system, in which language interpretation always took place in the context of a view of the world which was the subject of the discourse, some issues could be handled far more elegantly than any system based on propositional representation alone could possibly have done. For example, the so-called "frame problem" did not arise, for essentially the same reason as it does not arise in the real world: the model to which linguistic expressions made reference was identical with the actual (in this case virtual) world being viewed and talked about, so there was no possibility of model and world getting out of synch. As another example, a user could say "Put the mailbox in front of the house with the green roof", and later, having walked around to the other side of the house, could refer to "the mailbox behind the house". In addition, the continual presence of a viewpoint onto the scene meant that there was automatically a context that could be used to aid the interpretation of deixis and other forms of reference. And there were further benefits.

Nevertheless there were problems that were not so easily solved. Confining our attention to the interpretation of spatial referring expressions, we can see at least the following hard problems:

"Put the mailbox (car) *in front of* the house."

The interpretation of this kind of sentence requires the system to find a suitable place to position the mailbox or car. But cars typically go on roads or driveways — mailboxes typically don't. Almost all objects should be placed on a supporting surface, and objects should never be placed in such a way that they interpenetrate each other. A system that pays no attention to such issues looks ridiculous, and arguably does not successfully understand English. So we see that the interpretation of *'in front of'* seems to depend on complex social conventions about object type, as well as on many issues of physical simulation. It is possible of course to wriggle out of this kind of problem by saying that such considerations are not part of the *meaning* of the phrase, but instead are part of the felicity conditions for interpretation of the utterance. From a system design perspective, however, this is not a way out. Unless we can address such problems, we can't design a usable system.

Similar considerations lead us to realize that collision detection and path planning are relevant to spatial expressions involving action verbs, and that many issues of friction and complex object geometry, for example, are relevant to prepositions dealing with placement.

Or take an expression such as "Go and stand *on the sidewalk*", and consider the problem of the system choosing a suitable reference location. In this sentence, we appear to have a generic reference to the category sidewalk, rather than a reference to a unique or salient sidewalk object (it isn't even clear if 'sidewalk' is a count noun or a mass noun in this kind of usage). Now in an urban model there may be many stretches of sidewalk. Yet in a particular context of utterance such as this, it is not the case that any point on any sidewalk in the city is as good as any other. A new special kind of felicity condition applies here. The reader is invited to propose a general rule that governs this case, and to think about how many other similar rules might be needed for a realistic application.

It is issues such as these that explain why we have been making so little progress in artificial intelligence generally. We like to think that we are making incremental progress, and are gradually understanding how to solve the myriad problems that arise. But is it not possible that we are deeply on the wrong track? Are we perhaps missing something crucial?

3. Spatial 'reasoning' in the real world

Let us return to spatial reasoning in particular. Think about our real interaction with physical environments. Imagine what it feels like to find your way through an unfamiliar forest, to run across a rock-strewn landscape, to pilot a white-water canoe down a swiftly-running river, to figure out a way to climb up a steep mountainside. These are the essential tasks of navigation through the environment, the essence of spatial reasoning and cognition. Most of the mental work is inarticulate, best carried out in a state of relaxed but intense concentration — with a mind that is mostly quiet, where logical analysis, if carried out at all, is secondary to intuitive appraisal and the experience of the body. If you're trying to step across a rushing stream on a series of rocks that look as if they span it, your decision about whether you can safely leap to that next boulder depends on many things — the length of leap you're capable of, the difference in height of the surfaces of the rock you're leaping from and the one you'll land on, the texture and wetness of the surfaces, the kind of shoes you're wearing, your fitness, your fatigue, the consequences of a slip... But all of this is assessed in a gut-feel decision that takes perhaps a second or two, and pretty clearly does not involve analytical modelling.

Or consider the white-water canoeist. He or she is in an environment in which there are very few objects and only a few important boundaries. Alertness is high, and visual assessment is constant and skilled, but navigation is dependent on the "feel" of the water. This is skilled performance. This is the way we used to interact with the world before we acquired language, before we began to build abstractions to analyse our experience.

For a third example consider a pair of dancers, engaged in an interpretive modern dance. In some sense everything in the dance is about spatial relationships — relationships between the dancers, the positions and movements of their limbs and bodies. In this case we can take the role of an observer, perhaps a dance critic. He or she could find words to describe what the dancers are doing, but the description would fall far short of the dance itself, no matter how eloquent or how detailed it might be. And in the description, metaphors would abound — a literal description would be particularly pointless.

Now think about spatial concepts and terms: adjacency, superposition, connectedness, "on", "next to", "behind", "above", "in", "at". And think of some relevant nouns, adjectives, etc.: "rock", "water", "swiftly flowing", "deep",... If we go back to the scenes we have been imagining, there are plenty of resources for creating a description (after all, I myself have been using nothing but words in this article), but astonishing inadequacy for action — for deciding whether to leap to the next stone, for example. To make a decision, which we can often do in a split second, we need a far more detailed assessment than language can give us, not to mention integrating all kinds of non-spatial contextual factors. And we may make several such decisions each second.

Nor does resort to quantitative analysis seem to account for what is going on. The numerical complexity involved in adequately modelling the surfaces, positions, textures, stability and wetness of all the rocks in the river, the flexions, accelerations and momenta of all the limbs and body masses, not to mention the fatigue, danger, urgency and exuberance of the situation would be vast. Forty years of research in robotics has brought us nowhere close to replicating what humans do, or even to understanding how they do it.

Neural nets don't throw much light on the problem either. What does one use as inputs? If we supply extracted 'features' of the situation, we are pre-judging what it is that people attend to, probably missing the boat from the beginning, and begging the question of how the features are derived. If we supply raw retinal pixel data as inputs, the problem is far too unconstrained to be solved.

4. Evolution of language

In evolutionary terms, language is a remarkable development. As well as allowing us to communicate with others about experiences which are perceptually remote, it has given us tools with which to reflect on our experience in the world, to abstract and generalize from the particular to the typical. The tokens of language — its names and symbols — are the ingredients of much of modern consciousness. We learn to think conceptually, and the concepts that we use have much in common with the elements of language. The whole of science, and the scientific description of the world, relies exquisitely on the kinds abstraction and conceptual thinking that language has given us.

But since at least the time of Kant and Blake in the west, and in Taoist, Zen, and some aspects of Mahayana Buddhist philosophy, there has been a suspicion that conceptual thinking is inherently problematic as a way of understanding the true nature of reality. I believe those of us in the computer and cognitive sciences should worry about the same issue, and for essentially the same reasons. As we can begin to see from the examples above, the categories and delineations that language gives us are rich enough by now that we can always stitch together a description of what we are experiencing. But we shouldn't be fooled into thinking that when we do this, we have captured the essence of it. It isn't even easy to say how comprehensive our conceptual models of the world are — because consciousness appears to be normally focussed on our conceptual thinking, it is hard to be aware of what is not conceptually mapped.

From an evolutionary point of view, language is recent, and we can come to see it as still light-weight and fragile. When we abstract from our interaction with the world, and build structures and representations on a basis of language and its concepts, we are already pulling back from our direct experience. Conceptual abstraction is powerful — all the more so now that we have computers to help us build and maintain more elaborate structures than we can keep in our heads — but it is dangerous precisely because of its disconnection from its subject-matter. To a far greater degree than we usually realize, we let our conceptual models of reality, which are fashioned as much by our culture and our media as by our own visceral experience, determine what and how we perceive.

5. What terms of analysis?

There are several points to note here. One is that the mapping of linguistic concepts to the richness of the world is extremely sparse, far too sparse to form a basis for action or systematic reconstruction. Another is that despite the apparent richness of detail, we have no difficulty acting, or even imagining ourselves acting, in such situations. On the contrary, there is often an exhilarating sense of absorption in the fluid handling of this kind of complexity. It is pretty clear that have a way of apprehending the world, and even "reasoning" about it, that is very different from language. Not only do we have such a way, it is presumably the basis for much of our behaviour (cf. Polanyi 1962).

Of course, when we *talk* about what we do, when we want to describe what is happening, we superimpose rational categories, categories of classification, dimension, shape, quantity, quality, etc. When we tell a story, or describe a scene, we have in mind (in some sense) the kind of visually-rich imagined world that serves us well in action, and we use the short brush-strokes of language to lightly sketch what we "see". Our hearers draw on their own experience to imaginatively reconstruct their own rich images of what may have been. It is a wonderful process.

But to imagine that the world is really captured in those brief brush-strokes, and that we can use them as foundations for valid models, is to dangerously misinterpret what is going on. Because we talk to each other and to ourselves so much, we tend to take the categories as primary, and to project them back out into the world as if they were elemental and 'given'. We assume that in our analysis of what the world is like, we can start from clean, clear, discrete elements, and can elaborate towards the complexity of the world from that. It is a compositional view, a view that lends itself well to structuring and manipulation, to symbolic reasoning, and to computation. We are so used to thinking in this kind of way that it is hard to imagine any other.

Unfortunately, or interestingly anyway, the world doesn't seem to be like that. Even the independent existence of objects, which we take absolutely for granted, is far more problematic than it appears (Smith 1996). One aspect of the problem is that the world is more fluid, messier, more continuous, than our conceptual models of it. And the fluidity and the messiness are not simply at the periphery — they involve breakdown, unexpected change, and underlying continuity across sharp consequential boundaries.

At some level, it is not even obvious that a scenario such as fording a river on rocks is complex. Any three-year-old child can easily understand what is happening, and many six- and seven-year-olds can do it with skill and grace. Do we bring extrinsic complexity with us into the situation because of our unexamined habits of scientific thought?

Another pervasive source of trouble for our models is the apparently inescapable context-dependence of every situation, every interpretation. The "Y2K" problem is one of the current big examples — all those programmers, comfortably ensconced in the 20th century, failed to notice the contextual dependence of their assumptions. All symbolic modelling involves abstraction, and all abstraction involves ignoring details and particulars, in an attempt to say something whose value will transcend its original context. But something about the fabric of the world never quite lets us get away with this attempt to tear out a patch of cloth from the whole. The ideal of context-independence is always something of an illusion.

6. What do we do?

In fact, as we have noted above, we as humans have wonderful skills for dealing with all of this at the level of the intuitive, or of direct apprehension. But as individuals and as a society we want the world to be under our control, and so we are constantly trying to neaten things up so that our analytical categories *do* apply. By neatly arranging the furniture in a room, and choosing manufactured items that match each other well, concepts like "above", "beside", and "in front of" can be descriptively pretty adequate. It is not entirely accidental that some of the most convincing examples of the inadequacy of conceptual analysis come from the wilderness, from the untamed world. As Smith notes, we are constantly trying to push the world into place so that objects maintain their identity and conform to our abstract models. (This is why we have bureaucracies — and why they can be so stifling).

But it is never enough. Things are always breaking, or missing, or there isn't enough room, or other considerations are applicable. And because, as humans, we have constant recourse to this other, richer, more flexible mode of dealing with the world, we can cope pretty well. The way we cope best is not by exhaustive analysis, not by building huge, finely-structured symbolic models of the world in our heads. Our understanding and our acting involve a constant interplay between a language-compliant, model-based ideal, and a pre-conceptual direct awareness that can deal with an extraordinary range of circumstance. What seems to happen is that when our rough conceptual models break, we briefly revert to pre-conceptual mode, assess what is really happening, and then leap back to repair and elaborate our conceptual models as needed. We hardly notice it happening, but this interplay between the two modes is essential for our survival and success. Without our pre-conceptual fall-back, we would crash as often as our computer systems. And as we depend more and more on computer systems that have no such fall-back, we risk crashes on a larger scale.

The most surprising thing about all this is that the non-conceptual substrate has not been more obvious all along. We actually have remarkably little idea of how it works, or what its boundaries and limitations are. (The psychologist Mihaly Csikszentmihalyi (1991) has made a study of the 'flow' experience, which is closely related). Part of the problem is that to talk about it, to analyse and understand it, we need to use just those conceptual tools that are its antithesis. It is a question of using language and analysis to understand what is intrinsically non-linguistic and non-analytical. This however cannot be the whole problem — if we can describe a world that is not intrinsically conceptual, we should be able to talk about a way of knowing that is not conceptual.

I suspect that the reasons for this ignorance on our part are deep and fascinating. On the one hand, it is partly that this direct sense of the world is so intimate, so innate, that it has been hard for us to notice. And because it is tacit, unlike language, it doesn't call out for analysis in quite the same way. Consciousness seems to be much more associated with our conceptual, discursive mind than with the quiet, intuitive side, so that it is more difficult (though far from impossible) to direct our attention to the deeper modes of awareness.

Unconscious fears may even play a role. This intuitive, inarticulate awareness is probably continuous with the unconscious, with a knowledge of aspects of the world that are not under our control but which we are dimly aware of and may want to keep from our conscious gaze. The anthropologist Morris Berman (Berman 1981) points to some of the consequences that may flow from taking this kind of awareness seriously. And the historian Richard Tarnas (1993) brilliantly traces the evolution of our current strongly science-based worldview, suggesting that further deep changes are probably in store.

7. Conclusion

Despite the richness of language and vocabulary, the relationship of linguistic expression to the richness of the world itself is sparse and partial. We like to imagine that we can create a conceptual model of the world via which we can map its salient features to conceptual correlates in our model. Unfortunately, our conceptual structures are impressive enough to fool us into thinking that we can do quite a good job. These days we can, and do, build elaborate structures (knowledge bases, engineering design models, virtual environments) that seem to include many details of the world outside. But this attempt begins to blind us to what the world is really like. We model what we can, and then we pay attention to what we can talk about, forgetting that there is much more that we intuitively know, but have missed in our analysis.

To correct this lack, we need to figure out what goes on in our minds when we are interacting with the world directly and intuitively, without concepts. We need a conceptual analysis of non-conceptual understanding. Only when we have made some progress in this direction will we have a chance of building systems that can fluently interact with the world. Until then we have little chance of really making sense of either the world or ourselves.

References

Berman, Morris (1981) *The Re-enchantment of the World*. Ithaca, New York: Cornell University Press.

Csikszentmihalyi, Mihaly (1991) *Flow: The Psychology of Optimal Experience*. New York: HarperCollins.

Hernández, D. (1994) *Qualitative Representation of Spatial Knowledge*, Berlin: Springer-Verlag.

Herskovits, Annette (1986) *Language and Spatial Cognition*. Cambridge, England: Cambridge University Press.

Monk, Ray (1990) *Ludwig Wittgenstein: The Duty of Genius*. London: Jonathan Cape.

Ó Nualláin, Seán and Arnold G. Smith (1994). "An Investigation into the Common Semantics of Language and Vision", *Artificial Intelligence Review* 8: 113–122.

Polanyi, Michael (1962) *Personal Knowledge: Towards a Post-Critical Philosophy*, Chicago: University of Chicago Press.

Smith, Brian Cantwell (1996) *On the Origin of Objects*, Cambridge, Massachussetts: MIT Press.

Tarnas, Richard (1993) *The Passion of the Western Mind: Understanding the Ideas That Have Shaped Our Worldview*. New York: Ballantine.

Space Under Stress

Spatial understanding and new media technologies

Chris Speed and Deborah García-Tobin
University of Plymouth

Introduction

The aim of the work reported here is to promote the exploration of spatial understanding and identity in a time when our abilities for spatial perception are under constant duress from the influx of new media technologies. These technologies demand a perceptual shift between different ideas and representations of spaces — local, global, networked, real, and virtual. Given the complexity and subtleties of these shifts, it is unsurprising that the Cartesian model of space proves unable to provide a satisfactory framework for understanding these new media spaces. In order to illustrate the nature of these shifts and 'slips', presented below are three examples of our perception of time and space under the stress of new media as it breaks conventional forms and structures. These shifts are then discussed in relation to previous attempts by late twentieth century theorists to reconcile mental space and real space (Bourdieu 1977; Lefebvre 1991). It is then argued that the problems created by new media technologies for these spatial models require a new approach, consolidating the break away from the Cartesians, reuniting the spatial and temporal aspects of information and representation, whilst providing a flexibility capable of embracing non-linearity.

New media spaces

Establishing 'where we are' is becoming an increasingly common task in our everyday existence. We are required to work out where we want to go and how we wish to get there; Via path, road, rail, air, phone line, radio frequency,

Television channel, our expectations for travel, movement and speed, demanding we orientate ourselves in anticipation of the next move. It is not so much the new technologies of immersive virtual reality environments, or the stunning sensory effects now routinely found in films or theme parks. Rather, what is focused on here, are the seemingly insignificant events which infiltrate our daily life.

Example one

Virgin Radio's traffic information during its breakfast show is unusual because of the way in which it asks us to comprehend the traffic problems across the country. In a dynamic, noisy minute and a half, a loud male voice asks us to join him in contacting his colleagues who, as he speaks, are hovering over 'Britain's worst hit traffic spots'. One by one, from helicopter or some other high vantage point, voices describe how slowly cars appear to be moving on roads below: 'I'm circling over junction 8 of the M6, and as I look under my wing, I can see a long tail back stretching way back to junction 7, all queuing to get past a jack-knifed lorry that has shed its load'. This continues whilst another three or four flying traffic specialists recount the sights from their cockpits.

The problems of this particular case may by unclear from the point of view of the reader, but from the point of view of a driver and listener to the report, it requires some consideration in order to establish if their particular route will be hampered that morning. When we make a journey we concentrate on the combination of roads that make up our route from the perspective of being behind the steering wheel, and that any news regarding road status is expected to be introduced from an announcer located somewhere in the nowhere land behind your car stereo; a geographical model that is bound by conventions of a 'face on' environment and point of view. Thus, when a voice from above you proclaims that a road 'below' is experiencing problems, it introduces an additional interface causing some initial confusion to the driver, one that involves a different model of geography; the birds eye view. This clash of geographic models is only made possible by the use of technologies and the aspirations of a radio station, attempting to make a dull aspect of their service more spectacular, more filmic. It is doubtful that this situation produces more than momentary confusion for the driver before they are able to make sense of the information. However, the 'slip' caused by the collision of two models for geographic space and the absorption of one model into the other appears to be an interesting and complex phenomenon worthy of further consideration.

Example two

BBC Television Breakfast News often attempt to carry out debates around current affairs in the twenty minute slots between hourly and half hourly news bulletins. Ambitious not only because it's early in the morning for most viewers to take seriously, but because the discussions often feature up to four participants. Traditionally, the group is made up of three people in 'the studio' and one other contributor who is located in some 'far off' place, joining the debate via telematics, appearing framed on a screen behind the breakfast presenter. Once the debate begins, the programme controllers are able to cut between cameras to construct a coherent 'in-studio' discussion chaired by the presenter using well established cinema technique, the 180° rule. Confusion sets in when the virtual participant is introduced, switching from studio camera to the live feed coming from another location. Announcing the introduction of the new member to the group, gives the viewers just time to observe the mystification on the faces of the other participants as to where to look for their adversary. Since the new member of the debate is superimposed on to the stage via 'blue screen' technology the 180° camera rule is rendered useless since he cannot be seen to exist in the studio. Hence, the only space to which the panel can look, is into the camera, or from the point of view of the viewer, into the screen where our virtual guest will appear. Unfortunately, such a complex conceptual conclusion is not always made in time by all members of the group, some of whom recognise the new guest on an off set monitor and can be seen to look off screen, left and down, to where the virtual participant can be seen.

The complex conundrum that has to be thought out carefully by each participant, if a consistent spatial geography is communicated to the viewers, breaks so many spatial and geographical rules that it is inevitable that people are quickly confused and disorientated.

Further to the complex mixing of spatial models, the broadcast team appear to make things worse by attempting to locate some people and not others; The backdrop behind the virtual guest is clearly superimposed, and goes some way to help locate him, a digitally blurred and colour saturated still of the former BBC Television headquarters (to those who can make it out), with the words 'Central London' supposedly clarifying the point across the top of the screen. The debate continues and our man from Central London is performing well, in fact, his lengthy answers provide an opportunity to introduce another framing device to enable us to see the presenter and his virtual guest at the same time. Composed within a saturated blue background, hover the two moving images of presenter and guest, clearly in different frames and labelled accordingly: 'Studio' and 'Central London'.

If the presenter is in the 'Studio', our virtual guest in 'Central London' where is the frame located? Where is home to ourselves, if home is where we locate our own point of view on the proceedings? Typically, we place ourselves in the studio audience, but then we are alienated from that warm, well lit space and located somewhere with over saturated blue walls, and Helvetica type that labels the windows through which we see anything. The naming of the 'Studio' and 'Central London' seem to suggest a break down in spatial conventions. By introducing Central London as a means of locating the virtual guest, the production team are forced to locate the studio, but without a geographical context for it, it must remain as the 'Studio', an ambiguous term, but one that the audience have taken on board because of the introduction of such new media.

Example three

In contrast to the above case, the televisual space offered by the BBC's Match of the Day soccer program, represents the synthesis of new models for geography in a new media age. For years television audiences have absorbed the idea of what television studios look like and where they are because they have grown out of the theatre with a stage, backdrop, audience, and left and right wings. They were even given addresses: Wood Lane, Pebble Mill, Camden Lock, etc. New media technology over the past few years has introduced a different kind of television studio. The BBC Nine o'clock News is a well known example of a hyper-studio. Its introductory sequence, although computer generated imagery, looks like a traditional TV studio, with a backdrop and lighting rig overhead. Although simulated graphics are employed they still adhere to the spatial convention that is a 'Television Studio'.

Since this time we have seen many virtual sets employed, and the distinct nature of computer graphic imagery enables an audience to recognise when a set is not a set, rather an example of the blue screen technique. Whilst much of the imagery aspires to remove the presenters from the 'TV studio', as an audience, we are still able to deconstruct a scene and establish the somewhere behind all the special effects, a TV studio in the traditional sense.

In contrast to this illusion, BBC's Match of the Day adopts a spatial metaphor that aspires not to remove the set from the TV studio, but to assertively re-locate it in a different space. A strategy that once again confuses another model of geography. The superimposed imagery behind the presenters is simply a window, a window overlooking a football pitch late at night. As the camera pans left to right to complete an idea of the space, the viewers see a West stand to the left with its floodlight, a central stand with its pediment inferring the halfway line of the pitch that is directly below, and an East stand, with its flood light, to complete the composition. For an audience who are used to live games from stadia around the world, the composition demands we locate the presentation team in a press booth above such a stadium, and no longer in a TV Studio at all. Whilst representing a successful synthesis of subject and metaphor, it suggests that once again new media is eroding the conventions of space that we use to locate ourselves in our relationship with television.

Models for space

Over the past twenty years the social and psychological sciences have provided the most thorough work in attempting to model and make sense of our dealings with space. In particular, significant contributions have been made by Bourdieu (1977), Lefebvre (1991), and Foucault (1980). Coming from quite different directions, they represent the consolidation of Social Spatialisation as a field of study that addresses the relationship between objects and their environments. Prior to their work, post-enlightenment aspirations described 'mental images' of our environment that we carried around, to enable our successful navigation through geographies. However, whilst revealing many aspects of human spatial interaction, much of the work struggles to account for the effects of new media technologies, as highlighted in the examples given above. Bourdieu's work looks to a structural approach to establishing key methods for making sense of space and time, constructing his *habitus,* a system using different class patterns and activities to represent a vocabulary for our actions in time and space. It is described thus:

> Experience is a system and consequently the objective world is constructed through the imposition of cultural categories on reality. Perception thus takes place through a mediating value-framework which differentiates the facticity of the environment in which one lives (Shields 1991: 32).

The vocabulary of *habitus* consists of aspects of routine, and as Bourdieu would have us believe habits, the characteristics by which we identify many jobs and tasks:

> All the actions performed in a space constructed in this way are immediately qualified symbolically and function as so many structural exercises through which is built up practical mastery of the fundamental schemes, which organise…practiced and representations: going in and coming out, filling and emptying, opening and shutting, going leftwards and going eastwards (Bourdieu 1977: 91).

In this way *habitus* becomes his proposal for the system that motivates the human to interact with a world and in turn, allows them to make sense of a world. Treating the mind as a metaphor of a world that is made up of objects, that in turn consist of metaphors embodied in tasks. Systems within systems that can be identified as resulting from class oriented childhood experiences. However, whilst Bourdieu successfully deconstructs a Kabyle village and house using his metaphors and 'time-geography' (Hagerstrand 1973, 1974, 1975), it has been criticised due to his over structuring. Before long the reader is left wondering which structure came first, the Kabyle Village or Bourdieu's *habitus*. Although Bourdieu embraces the complexity of fourth dimensional space, his preoccupation with the use of aspects of task, makes it very difficult to take account of the impact new technology has upon lifestyles as they adapt to take on board new representations of space. Leisure space, such as watching television, can be happily absorbed into Bourdieu's work, but what happens to our models for the world as we watch telematic news events is disregarded. In addition, he provides no proposals for the stresses his 'habits' come under as our lifestyles change as a result of the technologies.

Foucault represents a move away from Bourdieu's causal proposals, the result of a social situation, and instead looks to identify where the motivation comes from. Not discounting Bourdieu's social effects, Foucault tries to identify how they become embroiled with other aspirations that inform how we discover space. Foucault set out to readdress a conceptual model for space, not that dissimilar to the aspirations of the enlightenment, but instead of proposing a mental map that mirrors the world, he explores the idea of a spatial impression of reality. A framework for space that embraces aspects of a Cartesian means of sorting space, whilst placing them in a social and psychological context.

> *Territory* is no doubt a geographical notion, but it's first of all a juridico-political one: the area controlled by a certain kind of power. *Field* is an economico-juridical notion. *Displacement:* what displaces itself is an army, a squadron, a population. *Domain* is a juridico-political notion. *Soil* is a historico-geological notion. *Region* is a fiscal, administrative, military notion. *Horizon* is a pictorial, but also a strategic notion. (Foucault 1980: 68).

Through his *dispositif* Foucault outlines the complexity that our position or state is founded on by identifying three parts: i. from formative acts that are the result of a response to a new situation ('emergency') comes a strategy for action, ii. a 'jurisdiction' is developed as the action becomes stable and ordered, and iii. the actions become heterogeneous as we struggle and succeed to fit new events into the initial strategy. In this way, Foucault finds we interpret space through strategies that form order and in turn, procedures.

> There is an administration of knowledge, a politics of knowledge, relations of power which pass via knowledge and which, if one tries to transcribe them, lead one to consider forms of domination designated by such notions as field, region and territory. (Foucault 1980: 69).

Whilst providing a thorough and rewarding means of understanding how we survive and maintain order through actions, much of the rhetoric of *dispositif* relies upon strategy, and the Cartesian models for order, to the extent that one senses the work is almost militarian in its conception.

The work is enjoyable because it recognises a procedural manner in which we navigate through space, but its sense of rigour fails to explore the dilemmas we face as we become caught in the spatial dichotomies that new media generates. Certainly, whilst aspiring to escape Cartesian time and space, in the end, Foucault's work is effective because it utilises a linear and objective relationship with time and space, and thus becomes problematic when it takes on board the non-linear and hyper directional nature of new media.

Lefebvre attempted to avoid the problem of adopting systems loaded with time and space properties (Foucault), or social positions (Bourdieu), by identifying a problem in the Cartesian semantics that describe space. Suggesting that in order to fulfil the enlightenment panacea, space was split and separated into an abstraction of space, identifiable through experience, and phenomenon of space that is how it manifests itself in systems and form. In particular the development and application of perspective within paintings represented for him the conquest and embodiment of space, and one that inevitably empowered the bourgeois component of society.

> What interests Lefebvre is less the techniques than the politics of modernism, which he treats as a politics of space by virtue of its involvement in the production of a spatial imaginary whose assumptions and entailments extended far beyond the canvas. (Gregory 1994: 393)

Consequently, any attempts to suppose how we understand space must readdress this split and attempt to reconcile them through a dialectic of three parts: (i) spatial practices, (ii) representations of space, and (iii) spaces of representation. The first, spatial practices being the ownership of spaces that become named spaces; parks, fields, museums, walks etc. Representing our absorption of space, our fetishisation of it, so they become embedded with clear semiotic code and recognised in this way. Second, representations of space becomes the abstract and conceptual depiction's of space; plans, maps, and in particular, the methods of recording location through co-ordinates. These become 'truth' base structures that are utilised to enforce power structures of meaning and force. The third and most complex is space of representation, this being the most discursive aspect, representing the sum of the two previous parts in conflict. It is particularly useful to describe spaces that are modern and post-modern, such as the shopping mall, with all its leisure activities and facades, neither is it simply a shopping space, or an easy to conceive of planned space. 'It constructs in a literal sense a 'space of representation', a privatised public space in which the social imaginary is opened to new visions' (Shields 1991: 55).

Criticism of Lefebvre's Dialectic of Space from his contemporaries is directed at its assertions, whilst retaining an ambiguity toward the role of 'space of representation', there is a concern over its ease of use as a 'get out clause' for the new. However, this 'get out clause' represents a prime opportunity to place the fallout (McLuhan 1964) from new media, and whilst it fails to predict its effects upon the two remaining axioms, it provides the opportunity for new developments in our models of space. The key attributes of the inquiry into space that Bourdieu, Foucault and Lefebvre were able to identify was i. the linear series of events that made up our experience of a space, and ii. the classification of spaces and events into tasks or named spaces. Clearly the nature of the digital age with its technologies that transfer information at the speed of light was destined to bend time and space. Since the first transatlantic telephone cable was connected to the West Coast of Ireland to Newfoundland, allowing verbal communication to transcend local space, enabling participants in conversations to construct relationships without ever seeing each other, our geo-spatial models for the world were never going to be as simple as the Enlightenment's 'mental map'.

However, the close relationship that social and cultural theorists would suggest occurs between time and space is under a great deal of stress as our classifications for spaces are becoming detached from time. Media technologies, as the examples hopefully show, illustrate that the classifications that occurred as linear tasks in Bourdieu's work, and as emergent strategies in Foucault's work begin to fail us as hyper media forces us to break a linear experience of time.

Conclusions

It has been shown that Bourdieu's task based assumptions become inadequate as he fails to take on board the consequences of multi-tasking on behalf of the human in order to fit together the opposing spatial models and develop a new task. Foucault's work is more hopeful, since it addresses our struggle to make sense of emergencies. Unfortunately, his adoption of the Cartesian framework of space and time, makes it hard to see how his three part sequence of events that describes our struggle, can operate so deftly in a non-linear context. Inevitably, because Lefebvre opens his writings up with his third concept of 'spaces of representation' we can more readily see how the condensation of a digital culture can be absorbed and reconciled within our spatial concepts. Indeed, his foresight to dissolve the Cartesian relationship between abstract space and physical space, helps his model adopt non linear events. However, his 'spatial practices', used to term and categorise spaces, comes under stress because it requires a consistency that is derived from social activity. But if social activity is being transformed and indeed simulated (as is the case with the Match of the Day set) through new technologies it is questionable how well this model fits.

The primary problem in much of this inquiry is the temporal aspect of the relationships. If the Organising Action of Bourdieu, the Strategies of Foucault, and the Representation of Space coupled with Daily Practice of Lefebvre did not represent small linear time based tasks or procedures that had to be acted out, then the conflict with time would not occur. Instead, if they were replaced with more flexible time based elements that anticipate a change of events, and non-linear occurrences, it may be possible to construct models to embrace new media technologies. Whilst not providing answers, it is hoped that this and other such discussions will provide a greater understanding of the problems of understanding new media spaces, but also prove a catalyst for work in this area to encourage the production of appropriate models to improve our understanding of the perception of new media technologies and consequently inform our design practice, enabling more intuitive and effective interfaces.

References

Bourdieu, P. (1977). *Outline of a Theory of Practice.* Cambridge: Cambridge University Press.

Foucault, M. (1980). *Power-Knowledge: Selected Interviews and Other Writings, 1972–1977.* Gordon, C. (Ed). Brighton: Harvester Press.

Hagerstrand, T. (1973). The domain of human geography. In R. J. Chorley (Ed), *Directions in Geography* (67–87). London: Methuen,

Hagerstrand, T. (1975). Space, time and human conditions. In A. Karlqvist, L. Lundqvist, and F. Snickars (Eds). *Dynamic Allocation of Urban Space* (3–12). Farnborough: Saxon House.

Levebvre, H. (1991). *The Production of Space.* Oxford: Blackwell Publishers.

McLuhan, M. (1964). *Understanding Media: The Extensions of Man.* New York: McGraw-Hill.

Shields, R. (1991). *Places on the Margin.* London: Routledge.

Part II

Software Applications: Multimedia, GIS, diagrammatic reasoning and beyond

CHAMELEON Meets Spatial Cognition

Paul Mc Kevitt
Queens's University, Belfast

1. Introduction

IntelliMedia, which involves the computer processing and understanding of perceptual input from at least speech, text and visual images, and then reacting to it, is complex and involves signal and symbol processing techniques from not just engineering and computer science but also artificial intelligence and cognitive science (Mc Kevitt 1994, 1995/1996, 1997a). With IntelliMedia systems, people can interact in spoken dialogues with machines, querying about what is being presented and even their gestures and body language can be interpreted.

People are able to combine the processing of language and vision with apparent ease. In particular, people can use words to describe a picture, and can reproduce a picture from a language description. Moreover, people can exhibit this kind of behaviour over a very wide range of input pictures and language descriptions. Although there are theories of how we process vision and language, there are few theories about how such processing is integrated. There have been large debates in Psychology and Philosophy with respect to the degree to which people store knowledge as propositions or pictures (Kosslyn and Pomerantz 1977; Pylyshyn 1973). Other recent moves towards integration are reported in Denis and Carfantan (1993), Mc Kevitt (1994, 1995/96) and Pentland (1993). It is often the case that when people use language about the visual environment they often need to refer to spatial relationships and they use prepositions to do so (Retz-Schmidt 1988; Zelinsky-Wibbelt 1993). Spatial relations are a central issue in the integration of natural language and vision processing (Maaβ 1996; Olivier 1995, 1996, 1997).

The Institute for Electronic Systems at Aalborg University, Denmark has expertise in the area of IntelliMedia and has already established an initiative on

Multimodal and Multimedia User Interfaces (MMUI) called IntelliMedia 2000+ by the Faculty of Science and Technology. IntelliMedia 2000+ coordinates research on the production of a number of real-time demonstrators exhibiting examples of IntelliMedia applications, established a new Master's degree in IntelliMedia, and coordinates a nation-wide MultiMedia Network (MMN) concerned with technology transfer to industry. IntelliMedia 2000+ involves three departments and is coordinated from the Center for PersonKommunikation (CPK) which has a wealth of experience and expertise in spoken language processing, one of the central components of IntelliMedia, but also radio communications which would be useful for mobile applications. More details on IntelliMedia 2000+ can be found on WWW: http://www.cpk.auc.dk/imm.

2. CHAMELEON and the IntelliMedia WorkBench

IntelliMedia 2000+ has developed the first prototype of an IntelliMedia software and hardware platform called CHAMELEON which is general enough to be used for a number of different applications. CHAMELEON demonstrates that existing software modules for (1) distributed processing and learning, (2) decision taking, (3) image processing, and (4) spoken dialogue processing can be interfaced to a single platform and act as communicating agent modules within it. CHAMELEON is independent of any particular application domain and the various modules can be distributed over different machines. Most of the modules are programmed in C++ and C.

2.1 *IntelliMedia WorkBench*

An initial application of CHAMELEON is the *IntelliMedia WorkBench* which is a hardware and software platform as shown in Figure 1.

One or more cameras and lasers can be mounted in the ceiling, microphone array placed on the wall and there is a table where things (objects, gadgets, people, pictures, 2D/3D models, building plans, or whatever) can be placed. The current domain is a *Campus Information System* which at present gives information on the architectural and functional layout of a building. 2D architectural plans of the building drawn on white paper are laid on the table and the user can ask questions about them. At present the plans represent two floors of the 'A' (A2) building at Fredrik Bajers Vej 7, Aalborg University. The 2D plan is shown in Figure 2.

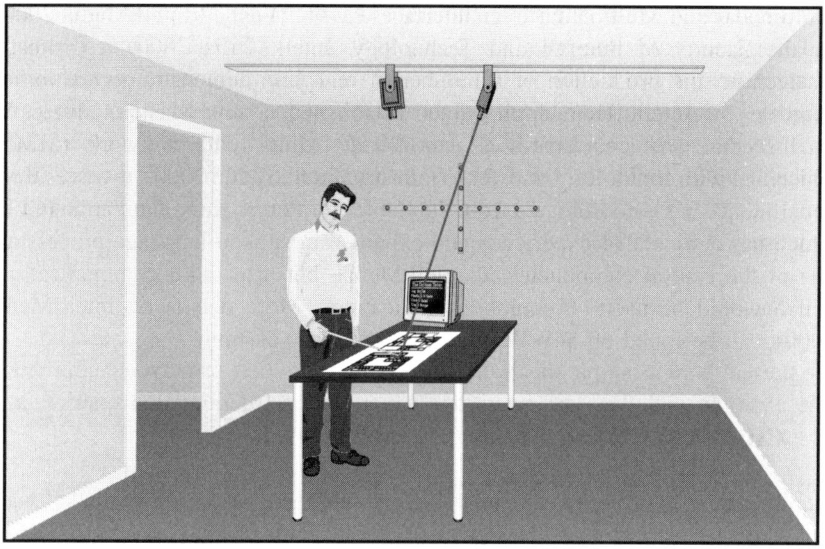

Figure 1. Physical layout of the IntelliMedia WorkBench

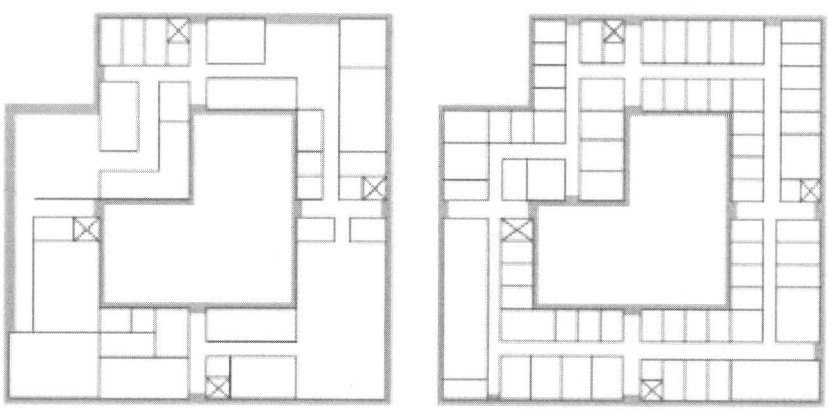

Figure 2. 2D plan of the 'A' building at Fredrik Bajers Vej 7, Aalborg University. Left: ground floor; Right: 1st floor.

Presently, there is one static camera which calibrates the plans on the table and the laser, and interprets the user's pointing while the system points to locations and draws routes with a laser. Inputs are simultaneous speech and/or pointing gestures and outputs are synchronised speech synthesis and pointing. We currently run all of CHAMELEON on a 200 MHz Intel pentium computer (r2d2) which handles input for the Campus Information System in real-time. More details on CHAMELEON and the IntelliMedia WorkBench can be found in Brøndsted et al. (1998).

2.2 *Sample interaction dialogue*

We present here a sample dialogue which the current first prototype can process. The example includes user intentions which are instructions and queries, and exophoric/deictic reference.

USER:	Show me Tom's office.
CHAMELEON:	[points] This is Tom's office.
USER:	Point to Thomas' office.
CHAMELEON:	[points] This is Thomas' office.
USER:	Where is the computer room?
CHAMELEON:	[points] The computer room is here.
USER:	[points to instrument repair] Whose office is this?
CHAMELEON:	[points] This is not an office, this is instrument repair.
USER:	[points] Whose office is this?
CHAMELEON:	[points] This is Paul's office.
USER:	Show me the route from Lars Bo Larsen's office to Hanne Gade's office.
CHAMELEON:	[draws route] This is the route from Lars Bo's office to Hanne's office.
USER:	Show me the route from Paul Mc Kevitt's office to instrument repair.
CHAMELEON:	[draws route] This is the route from Paul's office to instrument repair.
USER:	Show me Paul's office.
CHAMELEON:	[points] This is Paul's office.

Note that CHAMELEON assumes Paul Dalsgaard as default Paul[1] although there are two Pauls. A later prototype of the system should become active here and ask the user a question by first pointing out that there are two Pauls and then asking which does he/she mean. CHAMELEON can process deictic reference ("Whose office is *this*?") which is one of the most frequently occurring phenomena in IntelliMedia. However, spatial relations (e.g. "Who's in the office *beside* him?") are another phenomenon occurring regularly in language and vision integration which are not yet implemented in CHAMELEON. Also, there are other projective spatial relations such as "left", "right", "above", "below", and queries like "Who's in the office two up from him?" which occur regularly.

2.3 *Architecture of CHAMELEON*

CHAMELEON has a distributed architecture of communicating agent modules processing inputs and outputs from different modalities and each of which can be tailored to a number of application domains. The process synchronisation and intercommunication for CHAMELEON modules is performed using the DACS (Distributed Applications Communication System) Inter Process Communication (IPC) software (Fink et al. 1996) which enables CHAMELEON modules to be glued together and distributed across a number of servers. Presently, there are ten software modules in CHAMELEON: blackboard, dialogue manager, domain model, gesture recogniser, laser system, microphone array, speech recogniser, speech synthesiser, natural language processor (NLP), and Topsy as shown in Figure 3. The blackboard and dialogue manager form the kernel of CHAMELEON. We shall now give a brief description of each module.

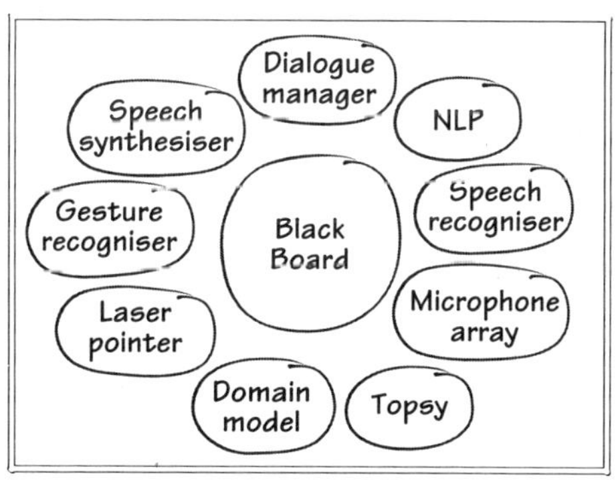

Figure 3. Architecture of CHAMELEON

The *blackboard* stores semantic representations produced by each of the other modules and keeps a history of these over the course of an interaction. All modules communicate through the exchange of semantic representations with each other or the blackboard. Semantic representations are frames in the spirit of Minsky (1975). The intention is that all modules in the system will produce and read frames. The frame semantics was first presented in Mc Kevitt and Dalsgaard (1997) and for the sample dialogue given in Section 2.2 CHAMELEON's actual blackboard history in terms of frames (messages) is shown in Appendix A.

The *dialogue manager* makes decisions about which actions to take and accordingly sends commands to the output modules (laser and speech synthesiser) via the blackboard. At present the functionality of the dialogue manager is to integrate and react to information coming in from the speech/NLP and gesture modules and to sending synchronised commands to the laser system and the speech synthesiser modules.

The *domain model* contains a database of all locations and their functionality, tenants and coordinates. The model is organised in a hierarchical structure: areas, buildings and rooms. Rooms are described by an identifier for the room (room number) and the type of the room (office, corridor, toilet, etc.). The model includes functions that return information about a room or a person. Possible inputs are coordinates or room number for rooms and name for persons, but in principle any attribute can be used as key and any other attribute can be returned. Furthermore, a path planner is provided, calculating the shortest route between two locations.

A design principle of imposing as few physical constraints as possible on the user (e.g. data gloves or touch screens) leads to thc inclusion of a vision based *gesture recogniser*. Currently, it tracks a pointer via a camera mounted in the ceiling. Using one camera, the gesture recogniser is able to track 2D pointing gestures in real time. Only two gestures are recognised at present: pointing and not-pointing. From each digitised image the background is subtracted leaving only the motion (and some noise) within this image. This motion is analysed in order to find the direction of the pointing device and its tip. By temporal segmenting of these two parameters, a clear indication of the position the user is pointing to at a given time is found. The error of the tracker is less than one pixel (through an interpolation process) for the pointer.

A *laser system* acts as a "system pointer". It can be used for pointing to positions, drawing lines and displaying text. The laser beam is controlled in real-time (30 kHz). It can scan frames containing up to 600 points with a refresh rate of 50 Hz thus drawing very steady images on surfaces. It is controlled by a standard Pentium PC host computer. The pointer tracker and the laser pointer have been carefully calibrated so that they can work together. An automatic calibration procedure has been set up involving both the camera and laser where they are tested by asking the laser to follow the pointer.

A *microphone array* (Leth-Espensen and Lindberg 1996) is used to locate sound sources, e.g. a person speaking. Depending upon the placement of a maximum of 12 microphones it calculates sound source positions in 2D or 3D. It is based on measurement of the delays with which a sound wave arrives at the different microphones. From this information the location of the sound source can be identified. Another application of the array is to use it to focus at a specific location thus enhancing any acoustic activity at that location. This module is in the process of being incorporated into CHAMELEON.

Speech recognition is handled by the grapHvite real-time continuous speech recogniser (Power et al. 1997). It is based on HMMs (Hidden Markov Models) of triphones for acoustic decoding of English or Danish. The recognition process focusses on recognition of speech concepts and ignores non content words or phrases. A finite state network describing phrases is created by hand in accordance with the domain model and the grammar for the natural language parser. The latter can also be performed automatically by a grammar converter in the NLP module. The speech recogniser takes speech signals as input and produces text strings as output. Integration of the the latest CPK speech recogniser (Christensen et al. 1998) which is under development is being considered.

We use the Infovox Text-To-Speech (TTS) *speech synthesiser* which at present is capable of synthesising Danish and English (Infovox 1994). It is a rule based formant synthesiser and can simultaneously cope with multiple languages, e.g. pronounce a Danish name within an English utterance. Infovox takes text as input and produces speech as output. Integration of the the CPK speech synthesiser (Nielsen et al. 1997) which is under development for English is being considered.

Natural language processing is based on a compound feature based (so-called unification) grammar formalism for extracting semantics from the one-best utterance text output from the speech recogniser (Brøndsted 1998). The parser carries out a syntactic constituent analysis of input and subsequently maps values into semantic frames. The rules used for syntactic parsing are based on a subset of the EUROTRA formalism, i.e. in terms of lexical rules and structure building rules (Bech 1991). Semantic rules define certain syntactic subtrees and which frames to create if the subtrees are found in the syntactic parse trees. The natural language generator is currently under construction and at present generation is conducted by using canned text.

The basis of the Phase Web paradigm (Manthey 1998), and its incarnation in the form of a program called *Topsy*, is to represent knowledge and behaviour in the form of hierarchical relationships between the mutual exclusion and co-occurrence of events. In AI parlance, Topsy is a distributed, associative, continuous-action, dynamic partial-order planner that learns from experience. Relative to

MultiMedia, integrating independent data from multiple media begins with noticing that what ties otherwise independent inputs together is the fact that they occur simultaneously (more or less). This is also Topsy's basic operating principle, but this is further combined with the notion of mutual exclusion, and thence to hierarchies of such relationships (Manthey 1998).

3. Frame semantics

The meaning of interactions over the course of a MultiModal dialogue is represented using a frame semantics with frames in the spirit of Minsky (1975). The intention is that all modules in the system can produce and read frames. Frames are coded in CHAMELEON with messages built as predicate-argument structures following a BNF definition. Frames represent some crucial elements such as *module*, *input/output*, *intention*, *location*, and *timestamp*. Module is simply the name of the module producing the frame (e.g. NLP). Inputs are the input recognised whether spoken (e.g. "Show me Hanne's office") or gestures (e.g. pointing coordinates) and outputs the intended output whether spoken (e.g. "This is Hanne's office.") or gestures (e.g. pointing coordinates). Timestamps can include the times a given module commenced and terminated processing and the time a frame was written on the blackboard. The frame semantics also includes representations for two key phenomena in language/vision integration: reference and spatial relations.

Frames can be grouped into three categories: (1) *input*, (2) *output* and (3) *integration*. Input frames are those which come from modules processing perceptual input, output frames are those produced by modules generating system output and integration frames are integrated meaning representations constructed over the course of a dialogue (i.e. all other frames). Here, we shall discuss frames with a focus more on frame semantics than on frame syntax and in fact the actual coding of frames as messages within CHAMELEON has a different syntax (see Appendix A).

3.1 *Input frames*

An input frame takes the general form:

[MODULE
 INPUT: input
 INTENTION: intention-type
 TIME: timestamp]

where MODULE is the name of the input module producing the frame, INPUT can be at least UTTERANCE or GESTURE, *input* is the utterance or gesture and *intention-type* includes different types of utterances and gestures. An utterance input frame can at least have intention-type (1) query?, (2) instruction! and (3) declarative. An example of an utterance input frame is:

[SPEECH-RECOGNISER
UTTERANCE: (Point to Hanne's office)
INTENTION: instruction!
TIME: timestamp]

A gesture input frame is where *intention-type* can be at least (1) pointing, (2) mark-area, and (3) indicate-direction. An example of a gesture input frame is:

[GESTURE
GESTURE: coordinates (3, 2)
INTENTION: pointing
TIME: timestamp]

3.2 *Output frames*

An output frame takes the general form:

[MODULE
INTENTION: intention-type
OUTPUT: output
TIME: timestamp]

where MODULE is the name of the output module producing the frame, *intention-type* includes different types of utterances and gestures and OUTPUT is at least UTTERANCE or GESTURE. An utterance output frame can at least have intention-type (1) query? (2) instruction!, and (3) declarative. An example utterance output frame is:

[SPEECH-SYNTHESIZER
INTENTION: declarative
UTTERANCE: (This is Hanne's office)
TIME: timestamp]

A gesture output frame can at least have intention-type (1) description (pointing), (2) description (route), (3) description (mark-area), and (4) description (indicate-direction). An example gesture output frame is:

[LASER
INTENTION: description (pointing)
LOCATION: coordinates (5, 2)
TIME: timestamp]

3.3 *Integration frames*

Integration frames are all those other than input/output frames. An example utterance integration frame is:

[NLP
INTENTION: description (pointing)
LOCATION: office (tenant Hanne) (coordinates (5, 2))
UTTERANCE: (This is Hanne's office)
TIME: timestamp]

Things become even more complex with the occurrence of references and spatial relationships:

[MODULE
INTENTION: intention-type
LOCATION: location
LOCATION: location
LOCATION: location
SPACE-RELATION: beside
REFERENT: person
LOCATION: location
TIME: timestamp]

An example of such an integration frame is:

[DOMAIN-MODEL
INTENTION: query? (who)
LOCATION: office (tenant Hanne) (coordinates (5, 2))
LOCATION: office (tenant Jørgen) (coordinates (4, 2))
LOCATION: office (tenant Børge) (coordinates (3, 1))
SPACE-RELATION: beside
REFERENT: (person Paul-Dalsgaard)
LOCATION: office (tenant Paul-Dalsgaard) (coordinates (4, 1))
TIME: timestamp]

Here we derive all the frames appearing on the blackboard for the example:

"Who's in the office beside him?" We have reported complete blackboard histories for the instruction "Point to Hanne's office" and the query "Whose office is this?" + [pointing] (exophoric/deictic reference) in Brøndsted et al. (1998), Mc Kevitt and Dalsgaard (1997), and Mc Kevitt (1997b).

There are input, output and integration frames (F-in, F-out, F-int), input and output gestures (G-in, G-out) and input and output utterances (U-in, U-out). Input modules are SPEECH-RECOGNISER (U-in) and GESTURE (G-in). Output modules are LASER (G-out) and SPEECH-SYNTHESIZER (U-out). Most modules give and take frames to/from the blackboard database and process them (F-int).

We choose to have modules interacting in a completely distributed manner with no single coordinating module. The actual present implementation of CHAMELEON has a dialogue manager which acts as a central coordinator. Although we show the various modules acting in a given sequence here, module processing and frames may not necessarily run in this order. The frames given are placed on the blackboard as they are produced and processed.

3.4 *Projective relation "beside"*

USER(U-in): Who's in the office beside him?

PROCESSING(1):
SPEECH-RECOGNISER:
(1) wakes up when it detects registering of U-in
(2) maps U-in into F-in
(3) places and registers F-in on blackboard:

FRAME(F-in)(1):
[SPEECH-RECOGNISER
UTTERANCE: (Who is in the office beside him?)
INTENTION: query?
TIME: timestamp]

PROCESSING(2):
NLP:
(1) wakes up when it detects registering of F-in
(2) maps F-in into F-int
(3) places and registers F-int on blackboard:

FRAME(F-int)(1):
[NLP
INTENTION: query? (who)

LOCATION: office (tenant Person) (coordinates (X, Y))
SPACE-RELATION: beside
REFERENT: (person him)
LOCATION: office (tenant Person) (coordinates (X, Y))
TIME: timestamp]

PROCESSING(3):
DIALOGUE-MANAGER:
(1) wakes up when it detects registering of F-int
(2) reads F-int and sees it's got a reference "him"
(3) searches the blackboard history for the referent "him"
(4) finds the last person mentioned: "Paul Dalsgaard"
(5) produces updated F-int (referent)
(6) places and registers updated F-int on blackboard:

FRAME(F-int)(2):
[DIALOGUE-MANAGER
INTENTION: query? (who)
LOCATION: office (tenant Person) (coordinates (X, Y))
SPACE-RELATION: beside
REFERENT: (person Paul-Dalsgaard)
LOCATION: office (tenant Paul-Dalsgaard) (coordinates (X, Y))
TIME: timestamp]

PROCESSING(4):
DOMAIN-MODEL:
(1) wakes up when it detects registering of F-int
(2) reads F-int and sees its from DIALOGUE-MANAGER
(3) produces updated F-int (space-relation + coordinates)
(4) places and registers filled F-int on blackboard:

FRAME(F-int)(3):
[DOMAIN-MODEL
INTENTION: query? (who)
LOCATION: office (tenant Hanne) (coordinates (5, 2))
LOCATION: office (tenant Jørgen) (coordinates (4, 2))
LOCATION: office (tenant Bøerge) (coordinates (3, 1))
SPACE-RELATION: beside
REFERENT: (person Paul-Dalsgaard)
LOCATION: office (tenant Paul-Dalsgaard) (coordinates (4, 1))
TIME: timestamp]

PROCESSING(5):
NLP:
(1) wakes up when it detects registering of F-int
(2) reads F-int and sees it's from DOMAIN-MODEL
(3) produces updated F-int (intention + utterance)
(4) places and registers updated F-int on blackboard:

FRAME(F-int)(4):
[NLP
INTENTION: declarative (who)
LOCATION: office (tenant Hanne) (coordinates (5, 2))
LOCATION: office (tenant Jørgen) (coordinates (4, 2))
LOCATION: office (tenant Bøerge) (coordinates (3, 1))
SPACE-RELATION: beside
REFERENT: (person Paul-Dalsgaard)
LOCATION: office (tenant Paul-Dalsgaard) (coordinates (4, 1))
UTTERANCE: (Bøerge, Jørgen and Hanne's offices are beside Paul Dalsgaard's office)
TIME: timestamp]

PROCESSING(6):
LASER:
(1) wakes up when it detects registering of F-int
(2) reads F-int and sees it's from DOMAIN-MODEL
(3) produces F-out (pruning + registering)
(4) places and registers F-out on blackboard:

FRAME(F-out)(1):
[LASER
INTENTION: description (pointing)
LOCATION: coordinates (5, 2)
LOCATION: coordinates (4, 2)
LOCATION: coordinates (3, 1)
SPACE-RELATION: beside
REFERENT: (person Paul-Dalsgaard)
LOCATION: coordinates (4, 1)
TIME: timestamp]

PROCESSING(7):
SPEECH-SYNTHESIZER:
(1) wakes up when it detects registering of F-int

(2) reads F-int and sees it's from NLP
(3) produces F-out (pruning + registering)
places and registers F-out on blackboard:

FRAME(F-out)(2):
[SPEECH-SYNTHESIZER
 INTENTION: declarative (who)
 UTTERANCE: (Bøerge, Jørgen and Hanne's offices are beside Paul
 Dalsgaard's office)
 TIME: timestamp]

PROCESSING(8):
DIALOGUE-MANAGER:
(1) wakes up when it detects registering of F-out and F-out
(2) reads F-out and F-out and sees they are from
LASER and SPEECH-SYNTHESIZER
(3) dials and fires LASER and SPEECH-SYNTHESIZER
in a rhythmic way (synchronized)
    (1) LASER reads its own F-out and fires G-out
    (2) SPEECH-SYNTHESIZER reads its own F-out and fires U-out

CHAMELEON(G-out): [points (4 times)]
CHAMELEON(U-out): Bøerge, Jørgen and Hanne's offices are beside Paul Dalsgaard's office.

Note that the above dialogue could also be one where CHAMELEON becomes active and says "There are three offices beside Paul Dalsgaard's, do you mean to the left, in front of or to the right of his office?" This would, of course, involve more complex processing, especially for the dialogue manager.

4. Relation to other work

The representation of the spatial relation "beside" as given in the frame semantics above is similar to what Herskovits (1986) termed a spatial proposition,

(⟨relation name⟩ ⟨LO⟩ ⟨sequence of ROs⟩)

where LO is an object to be localised and RO is reference object. In our example above the LO is "Paul Dalsgaard" and the ROs are the other offices beside his.

Blocher and Stopp (1995) give a detailed computational model for representing and generating spatial relations for SOCCER, a system which automatically generates reports of short soccer games. Their focus is more on generating spatial relations rather than processing them as input queries. Maaβ (1994) looks at the area of route descriptions and how a speaker presents step-by-step relevant route information in a 3D environment with an implementation called MOSES. Specifically addressed is the interaction between the spatial relation and the presentation representation used for natural language descriptions. Again, the focus here is generating spatial relations rather than recognising them. SOCCER and MOSES are part of a general project called VITRA (VIsual TRAnslator) concerning the design and construction of integrated knowledge-based systems for translating visual information into natural language descriptions (Herzog and Wazinski 1994).

The L_0 project (Feldman et al. 1996) focusses on combining not only vision and natural language modelling, but also learning. The task is to build a system that can learn the appropriate fragment of any natural language from sentence-picture pairs. Important lessons have been learned in the subtle semantics of spatial language, especially since L_0 is multilingual (English, Mixtec, German, Bengali, and Japanese) and spatial language is something which changes a lot over languages. The L_0 implementation of spatial language modelling is conducted mainly in the connectionist computational framework. Situated Artificial Communicators (SFB-360) (Rickheit and Wachsmuth 1996) is a collaborative research project at the University of Bielefeld, Germany which focusses on modelling that which a person performs when with a partner he cooperatively solves a simple assembly task in a given situation. The object chosen is a model airplane (Baufix) to be constructed by a robot from the components of a wooden building kit with instructions from a human. SFB-360 includes equivalents of the modules in CHAMELEON although there is no learning module competitor to Topsy. What SFB-360 gains in size it may loose in integration, i.e. it is not clear yet that all the technology from the subprojects have been fitted together and in particular what exactly the semantic representations passed between the modules are. The DACS process communication system currently used in CHAMELEON is a useful product from SFB-360.

Gandalf is a communicative humanoid which interacts with users in MultiModal dialogue through using and interpreting gestures, facial expressions, body language and spoken dialogue (Thórisson 1997). Gandalf is an application of an architecture called *Ymir* which includes perceptual integration of multi-modal events, distributed planning and decision making, layered input analysis and motor-control with human-like characteristics and an inherent knowledge of time. Ymir has a blackboard architecture and includes modules equivalent to those in CHAMELEON. However, there is no vision/image processing module since gesture tracking is done with the use of a data glove and body tracking suit and an eye tracker is used for detecting the user's eye gaze. Also, Ymir has no learning module equivalent to Topsy. Ymir's architecture is even more distributed than CHAMELEON's with many more modules interacting with each other. Also, Ymir's semantic representation is much more distributed with smaller chunks of information than our frames being passed between modules.

AESOPWORLD is an integrated comprehension and generation system for integration of vision, language and motion (Okada 1997). It includes a model of mind consisting of nine domains according to the contents of mental activities and five levels along the process of concept formation. The system simulates the protagonist or fox of an AESOP fable, "the Fox and the Grapes", and his mental and physical behaviour are shown by graphic displays, a voice generator, and a music generator which expresses his emotional states. AESOPWORLD has an agent-based distributed architecture and also uses frames as semantic representations. It has many modules in common with CHAMELEON although again there is no vision input to AESOPWORLD which uses computer graphics to depict scenes. AESOPWORLD has an extensive planning module but conducts more traditional planning than CHAMELEON's Topsy.

The INTERACT project (Waibel et al. 1996) involves developing Multi-Modal Human Computer Interfaces including the modalities of speech, gesture and pointing, eye-gaze, lip motion and facial expression, handwriting, face recognition and tracking, and sound localisation. The main concern is with improving recognition accuracies of modality specific component processors as well as developing optimal combinations of multiple input signals to deduce user intent more reliably in cross-modal speech-acts. INTERACT also uses a frame representation for integrated semantics from gesture and speech and partial hypotheses are developed in terms of partially filled frames. The output of the interpreter is obtained by unifying the information contained in the partial frames. Although Waibel et al. present good work on multimodal interfaces it is not clear that they have developed an integrated platform which can be used for developing multimodal applications.

5. Conclusion and future work

We have described the architecture and implementation of CHAMELEON: an open, distributed architecture with ten modules glued into a single platform using the DACS communication system. Also described is the IntelliMedia WorkBench application, a software and physical platform where a user can ask for information about things on a physical table and, in particular, the Campus Information System domain. Next, we discussed the frame semantics representation of CHAMELEON and how the query, "Who's in the office beside him?" is processed through the semantics with all associated frames and module interactions. More details on CHAMELEON and the IntelliMedia WorkBench can be found in Brøndsted et al. (1998).

There are a number of avenues for future work with CHAMELEON. The frame semantics handling of "beside" has yet to be implemented and the next step is to move onto modelling other projective spatial relations. Also, presently CHAMELEON provides route descriptions through laser pointing but also more detailed verbal descriptions could be given hand-in-hand with those drawn by the laser, mentioning "left", "right" and other turns for routes. It is hoped that more complex decision taking can be introduced to operate over semantic representations in the dialogue manager or blackboard using, for example, the HUGIN software tool (Jensen F. 1996) based on Bayesian Networks (Jensen F.V. 1996). The gesture module will be augmented so that it can handle gestures other than pointing. Topsy will be asked to do more complex learning and processing of input/output from frames. The microphone array has to be integrated into CHAMELEON and set to work.

Intelligent MultiMedia will be important in the future of international computing and media development and IntelliMedia 2000+ at Aalborg University, Denmark brings together the necessary ingredients from research, teaching and links to industry to enable its successful implementation. Our CHAMELEON platform and IntelliMedia WorkBench application are ideal for testing integrated processing of language and vision for the future of SuperinformationhighwayS.

Acknowledgments

This opportunity is taken to acknowledge support from the Faculty of Science and Technology, Aalborg University, Denmark and Paul Mc Kevitt would also like to acknowledge the British Engineering and Physical Sciences Research Council (EPSRC) for their generous funded support under grant B/94/AF/1833 for the Integration of Natural Language, Speech and Vision Processing (Advanced Fellow) and LIMSI-CNRS, Orsay, France where he was a Visiting Professor whilst completing this paper. Annelies Braffort, Tom Brøndsted, Paul Dalsgaard, Rachid Gherbi, Lars Bo Larsen, Michael Manthey, Thomas B. Moeslund, and Kristian G. Olesen are acknowledged for useful discussions.

Note

1. This is because Paul Dalsgaard is more senior.

References

Beck, A. (1991). Description of the EUROTRA framework. *The Eurotra Formal Specifications, Studies in Machine Translation and Natural Language Processing*. C. Copeland, J. Durand, S. Krauwer and B. Maegaard (Eds) Vol 2, 7–40. Luxembourg: Office for Official Publications of the Commision of the European Community.

Blocker, A. and E. Stopp (1995). Time-dependent generation of minimal sets of spatial . descriptions. In *Working notes of the Workshop on Representation and Processing of Spatial Descriptions*. Oliver, Patrick Luke (Ed) 1–7, Fourteenth IJCAI, Montréal, Canada.

Brøndsted (1998) *nlparser*. WWW: http://www.kom.auc.dk/~tb/nlparser.

Brøndsted, T., P. Dalsgaard, L. B. Larsen, M. Manthey, P. Mc Kevitt, T. B. Moeslund, K. G. Olesen (1998) *A platform for developing Intelligent MultiMedia applications*. Technical Report R-98–1004, Center for PersonKommunikation (CPK), Institute for Electronic Systems (IES), Aalborg University, Denmark, May.

Christensen, Heidi, Børge Lindberg and Pall Steingrimsson (1998) *Functional specification of the CPK Spoken LANGuage recognition research system (SLANG)*. Center for Personkommunikation, Aalborg University, Denmark, March.

Denis, M. and M. Carfantan (Eds.) (1993) *Images et langages: multimodalitée et modelisation cognitive*. Actes du Colloque Interdisciplinaire du Comitée National de la Recherche Scientifique, Salle des Conférences, Siège du CNRS, Paris, April.

Feldman, Jerome, George Lakoff, David Bailey, Srini Narayanan, Terry Regier and Andreas Stolcke (1996) L_0 — the first five years of an automated language acquisition project. In *Artificial Intelligence Review*, 8, 175–187.

Fink, Gernot A., Nils Jungclaus, Franz Kummert, Helge Ritter and Gerhard Sagerer (1996) A distributed system for integrated speech and image understanding. In *Proceedings of the International Symposium on Artificial Intelligence, Rogelio Soto (Ed.), 117–126*. Cancun, Mexico.

Herskovits (1986) *Language and spatial cognition: an interdisciplinary study of the prepositions in English*. Cambridge, England: Cambridge University Press.

Herzog, Gerd and Peter Wazinski (1994) VIsual TRAnslator: linking perceptions and natural language descriptions. In *Artificial Intelligence Review*, 8, 175–187.

Infovox (1994) *INFOVOX: Text-to-speech converter user's manual (version 3.4)*. Solna, Sweden: Telia Promotor Infovox AB.

Jensen, Finn V. (1996) *An introduction to Bayesian Networks*. London, England: UCL Press.

Jensen, Frank (1996) Bayesian belief network technology and the HUGIN system. In *Proceedings of UNICOM seminar on Intelligent Data Management, Alex Gammerman (Ed.), 240–248*. Chelsea Village, London, England, April.

Kosslyn, S. M. and J. R. Pomerantz (1977) Imagery, propositions and the form of internal representations. In *Cognitive Psychology*, 9, 52–76.

Leth-Espensen, P. and B. Lindberg (1996) Separation of speech signals using eigen-filtering in a dual beamforming system. In *Proc. IEEE Nordic Signal Processing Symposium (NORSIG)*, Espoo, Finland, September, 235–238.

Maaβ, Wolfgang (1994) From vision to multimodal communication: incremental route descriptions. In *Artificial Intelligence Review*, 8, 159–174.

Maaβ, Wolfgang (Ed.) (1996) *Proceedings of the ECAI-96 Workshop on the representations and processes between vision and natural language*. Twelfth European Conference on Artificial Intelligence (ECAI-96), Budapest, Hungary.

Manthey, Michael J. (1998) The Phase Web Paradigm. In *International Journal of General Systems, special issue on General Physical Systems Theories,* K. Bowden (Ed.).

Mc Kevitt, Paul (1994) Visions for language. In *Proceedings of the Workshop on Integration of Natural Language and Vision processing*, Twelfth American National Conference on Artificial Intelligence (AAAI-94), Seattle, Washington, USA, August, 47–57.

Mc Kevitt, Paul (Ed.) (1995/1996) *Integration of Natural Language and Vision Processing (Vols. I-IV)*. Dordrecht, The Netherlands: Kluwer-Academic Publishers.

Mc Kevitt, Paul (1997a) SuperinformationhighwayS. In *"Sprog og Multimedier" (Speech and Multimedia)*, Tom Brøndsted and Inger Lytje (Eds.), 166–183, April 1997. Aalborg, Denmark: Aalborg Universitetsforlag (Aalborg University Press).

Mc Kevitt, Paul (1997b) IntelliMedia TourGuide: understanding reference at the language/vision interface. In Proceedings of the European Science Foundation (ESF) Network on Converging Computing Methodologies in Astronomy (CCMA), *Final Conference on Advanced Techniques and Methods for Astronomical Information Handling, M. C. Maccarone, F. Murtagh, M. Kurtz and A. Bijaoui (Eds.), 93–103*. Sonthofen, Germany, September, Observatoire de la Cote d'Azur — B. P. 4229 06304 Cedex 4, France. (also published on Web; see http://ncwb6.u-strasbg.fr/~ccma).

Mc Kevitt, Paul and Paul Dalsgaard (1997) A frame semantics for an IntelliMedia TourGuide. In *Proceedings of the Eighth Ireland Conference on Artificial Intelligence (AI-97), Volume 1, 104–111*. University of Uster, Magee, Derry, Northern Ireland, September.

Minsky, Marvin (1975) A framework for representing knowledge. In *The Psychology of Computer Vision*, P. H. Winston (Ed.), 211–217. New York: McGraw-Hill.

Nielsen, Claus, Jesper Jensen, Ove Andersen, and Egon Hansen (1997) *Speech synthesis based on diphone concatenation*. Technical Report, No. CPK971120-JJe (in confidence), Center for PersonKommunikation, Aalborg University, Denmark.

Okada, Naoyuki (1997) Integrating vision, motion and language through mind. In *Proceedings of the Eighth Ireland Conference on Artificial Intelligence (AI-97), Volume 1, 7–16.* University of Uster, Magee, Derry, Northern Ireland, September.

Olivier, Patrick Luke (Ed.) (1995) *Working notes of the workshop on Representation and processing of spatial expressions.* Fourteenth International Joint Conference on Artificial Intelligence (IJCAI-95), Montreal, Canada, August.

Olivier, Patrick Luke (Ed.) (1996) *Proceedings of the ECAI-96 workshop on the representations and processing of spatial expressions.* Twelfth European Conference on Artificial Intelligence (ECAI-96), Budapest, Hungary.

Olivier, Patrick Luke (Ed.) (1997) *Proceedings of the AAAI-97 workshop on language and space.* Fourteenth American National Conference on Artificial Intelligence (AAAI-97), Rhode Island, New Jersey.

Pentland, Alex (Ed.) (1993) *Looking at people: recognition and interpretation of human action.* IJCAI-93 Workshop (W28) at The 13th International Conference on Artificial Intelligence (IJCAI-93), Chambery, France, EU, August.

Power, Kevin, Caroline Matheson, Dave Ollason and Rachel Morton (1997) *The grapHvite book (version 1.0).* Cambridge, England: Entropic Cambridge Research Laboratory Ltd.

Pylyshyn, Zenon (1973) What the mind's eye tells the mind's brain: a critique of mental imagery. In *Psychological Bulletin*, 80, 1–24.

Retz-Schmidt, Gudala (1988) Various views on spatial prepositions. In *AI Magazine*, 9:95–105.

Rickheit, Gert and Ipke Wachsmuth (1996) Collaborative Research Centre "Situated Artificial Communicators" at the University of Bielefeld, Germany. In *Integration of Natural Language and Vision Processing, Volume IV, Recent Advances, Mc Kevitt, Paul (ed.), 11–16.* Dordrecht, The Netherlands: Kluwer Academic Publishers.

Thórisson, Kris R. (1997) Layered action control in communicative humanoids. In *Proceedings of Computer Graphics Europe '97*, June 5–7, Geneva, Switzerland.

Waibel, Alex, Minh Tue Vo, Paul Duchnowski and Stefan Manke (1996) Multimodal interfaces. In *Integration of Natural Language and Vision Processing, Volume IV, Recent Advances*, Mc Kevitt, Paul (Ed.), 145–165. Dordrecht, The Netherlands: Kluwer Academic Publishers.

Zelinsky-Wibbelt (Ed.), Cornelia (1993) *The semantics of prepositions: from mental Processing to natural language processing (NLP 3).* Berlin, Germany: Mouton de Gruyter.

Appendix A

Blackboard in practice

Here we show the complete blackboard (with all frames) as produced exactly by CHAMELEON for the example dialogue given in Section 2.

Received: nlp(intention(instruction(pointing)),location(person(tb),type(office)), time(889524794))
which is passed on to dialog_manager
Received: dialog_manager(output(laser(point(coordinates(249,623))), speech_synthesizer(utterance("This is Toms office"))))
Calling laser: laser(point(coordinates(249,623)))
Calling speech_synthesizer: speech_synthesizer(utterance("This is Toms office"))

Received: nlp(intention(instruction(pointing)),location(person(tbm),type(office)), time(889524818))
which is passed on to dialog_manager
Received: dialog_manager(output(laser(point(coordinates(278,623))), speech_synthesizer(utterance("This is Thomass office"))))
Calling laser: laser(point(coordinates(278,623)))
Calling speech_synthesizer: speech_synthesizer(utterance("This is Thomass office"))

Received: nlp(intention(query(where)),location(place(a2_221)), time(889524831))
which is passed on to dialog_manager
Received: dialog_manager(output(laser(point(coordinates(132,500))), speech_synthesizer(utterance("computer room is here"))))
Calling laser: laser(point(coordinates(132,500)))
Calling speech_synthesizer: speech_synthesizer(utterance("computer room is here"))

Received: nlp(intention(query(who)),location(this($Deixis),type(office)), time(889524864))
which is passed on to dialog_manager
Received: dialog_manager(output(laser(point(coordinates(658,546))), speech_synthesizer(utterance("This is not an office, this is instrument repair"))))
Calling laser: laser(point(coordinates(658,546)))
Calling speech_synthesizer:
speech_synthesizer(utterance("This is not an office, this is instrument repair"))

Received: nlp(intention(query(who)),location(this($Deixis),type(office)), time(889524885))
which is passed on to dialog_manager

Received: dialog_manager(output(laser(point(coordinates(223,568))),
speech_synthesizer(utterance("This is Pauls office"))))
Calling laser: laser(point(coordinates(223,568)))
Calling speech_synthesizer: speech_synthesizer(utterance("This is Pauls office"))

Received: nlp(intention(instruction(show_route)),source(location(person(lbl),
type(office))),
destination(location(person(hg),type(office))),time(889524919))
which is passed on to dialog_manager
Received: dialog_manager(output(laser(route(coordinates(278,585,278,603,249,
603,220,603,197,603,197,623))),
speech_synthesizer(utterance("This is the route from Lars Bos office to Hannes OF-
fice"))))
Calling laser:
laser(route(coordinates(278,585,278,603,249,603,220,603,197,603,197,623)))
Calling speech_synthesizer:
speech_synthesizer(utterance("This is the route from Lars Bos office to Hannes office"))

Received: nlp(intention(instruction(show_route)),source(location(person(pmck),
type(office))),destination(location(place(a2_105))),time(889524942))
which is passed on to dialog_manager
Received: dialog_manager(output(laser(route(coordinates(174,453,153,453,153,
481,153,500,153,510,153,540,153,569,153,599,153,603,184,603,197,603,220,603,
249,603,278,603,307,603,330,603,330,655,354,655,911,655,884,655,884,603,810,
603,759,603,717,603,717,570,696,570))),
speech_synthesizer(utterance("This is the route from Pauls office to instrument repair"))))
Calling laser: laser(route(coordinates(174,453,153,453,153,481,153,500,153,
510,153,540,153,569,153,599,153,603,184,603,197,603,220,603,249,603,278,603,
307,603,330,603,330,655,354,655,911,655,884,655,884,603,810,603,759,603,717,
603,717,570,696,570)))
Calling speech_synthesizer:
speech_synthesizer(utterance("This is the route from Pauls office to instrument repair"))

Received: nlp(intention(instruction(pointing)),location(person(pd),type(office)),
time(889524958))
which is passed on to dialog_manager
Received: dialog_manager(output(laser(point(coordinates(220,585))),
speech_synthesizer(utterance("This is Pauls office"))))

SONAS: Multimodal, Multi-User Interaction with a Modelled Environment

John Kelleher, Tom Doris, Qamir Hussain
DCU

Seán Ó Nualláin
NOUS Research

Introduction

This paper describes some of the work being carried out by the IME (Interaction with Modelled Environments) group at NOUS on the SONAS system. We describe the theoretical foundations of the system, and discuss the research being carried out in the area of natural language and vision integration. Finally, we give a description of the general architecture of the current SONAS implementation. The primary aim of this research is to develop a system for navigating and interacting with a 3D environment through spoken natural language, gesture, hand-written characters/icons, and whatever other modes emerge.

Motivation

Over the last 40 years computer systems have developed at a staggering rate in both power and complexity. This development has given modern computer users access to massive amounts of information. Indeed, the modern user has so much information at their fingertips that it is becoming difficult for them to extract the desired information from the deluge that is presented to them.

The primary cause of this is that very little progress has been made in developing machines that are able to interact and present information in a manner that is natural to the user. For this reason the development of simpler and more natural interfaces is becoming increasingly important.

Human perceptual skills are quite remarkable and largely under-utilised in current information and computing systems. Humans are expert at communicating through multiple modalities, switching from one to another or combining several as the situation requires. The future of computer interfaces is systems that allow the user to express queries and interact with the system in such a multimodal manner. Such an interface should allow the user to concentrate on the tasks they are trying to accomplish, as opposed to grappling with the idiosyncrasies of a particular interface. With such designs, it is hoped that the current flood of data can be turned into a productive river of knowledge.

Natural Language Interfaces & 3D environments

Natural Language is a primary communication medium for humans; however, to date, it is a medium that has been ignored by the majority of computer systems interfaces.

This mode of interaction would be particularly useful when navigating and interacting with 3D environments. In most systems that deal with these environments the user navigates through the world using specially designed hardware. Usually these devices are extremely expensive, cumbersome to use, and more often than not the users' ability to directly manipulate objects in the world is extremely restricted.

On the other hand, in such a situation a natural language interface completely avoids these problems. This is due to the ease of use it offers, the lack of need for specialised hardware, and the ability it offers the user to convey information with changing accuracy and on different levels of abstraction.

The relatively primitive state of present day natural language interfaces is no doubt due to the complexity of the problem of formalising language sufficiently to accommodate peoples use of it. We believe that by concentrating on a restricted domain and finding generalised rules within that domain, is the appropriate course of action in the face of the obvious intractability of a totally complete system for natural language processing.

Specifically, this belief is based on analogous characteristics that language and vision share and the advantages that the marriage of these two offer.

While functionally language and vision differ enormously they share the following characteristics (see Ó Nualláin & Smith, 1995):

– A hierarchical organisation,
– A syntax—semantics division,
– Ambiguity.

These similarities have led many researchers to believe that visual images are closely connected to the mental models that underlie the human use of language.

The advantages of a system that links language and vision are manifold. The visual model grounds the language and situates the dialogue in time and space, thus references can almost always be constrained by locality. Also in such a system the model of the world is in some sense closed. This gives us the ability to exhaustively represent certain properties of objects in the world. This exhaustive representation allows a planner to ignore possible effects of the frame problem. In addition, the system has ability to give the user immediate feedback about how it understands what is being said. This is an enormous advantage and addresses a major drawback of more traditional natural language interfaces that was highlighted by Dennett(1991, p57–58):

> Surely a major source of widespread scepticism about "machine understanding" of natural language is that such systems almost never avail themselves of anything like a visual workspace in which to parse of analyse the input. If they did, the sense that they were actually understanding what they processed would be greatly heightened (whether or not it would still be, as some insist, as illusion). As it is, if a computer says, "I see what you mean" in response to input, there is a strong temptation to dismiss the assertion as an obvious fraud.

However, if one wishes to claim that a natural language system has a cognitively plausible understanding of what it is "hearing", the system must do more than consider the relationship between expression of a knowledge representation language and natural language expression, but must also rely on the definition of a referential semantics. To achieve this we associate naive physical attributes with each object in the environment, and use these attributes as selectional restrictions on the applicability of a verb on a object.

HCI: Overview first, zoom and filter, then details on demand

While a major part of our work is directed towards the development of NLP input to the system, we are also extremely interested in utilising and organising input from and feedback to the user through other modalities, especially vision.

The design of the visual front end has be based on Ben Schneiderman's mantra of "overview first, zoom and filter, the details on demand."

There are two visual displays in the user interface: a 2D-overview map of the world and a 3D OpenGL viewer which displays the location in the world where the viewer is currently situated.

The user can position themselves in the world through the 2D overview map, inputting instructions through mouse, language, gesture or a combination of these. The result of this input is displayed as a scene change in the OpenGL 3D environment. If the user wishes to interact directly with any object that they come across in the world, they can do so again through multiple modalities. It is this process of object manipulation that we discuss in the next section.

Background: The Spoken Image System

In the Spoken Image project, the predecessor to the SONAS system, a three-dimensional view of a physical environment is always present on the screen, seen through the eyes of a user agent that moves around and modifies the world in response to the user's utterance's and gestures. The goal of the project was a system that anyone could use without training to quickly build a house or a town scene, modifying almost any of the details until it is exactly as the user has envisioned it.

The original project was developed at the NRC, Canada. This system takes natural language input via the keyboard. The Alvey Natural Language Toolkit is then used for the initial stages of the linguistic analysis. The output of the ANLT parser is a logical form representation of the English input, which forms the basis for further interpretation in the system. The physical model against which linguistic propositions are evaluated, and in which most actions are carried out, is built from the data structures that directly support the three-dimensional graphical display. Elements of any particular scene are instances of classes in an object-oriented system implemented in C++. The way the physical model is linked with the interpretation of the logical form expressions is conceptually simple. Word-senses are defined as instances in another object-oriented hierarchy, whose classes group concepts and grammatical operators. Each class has its own interpretation methods, which can be made as specific as needed. The instances of any model class are the actual objects that appear in a world — none of the model classes have instances until a world is created or loaded.

A world can contain several 'viewers', and the user can ask to look through the eyes of any viewer in the scene. The currently selected viewer is the one that responds to instructions to move and look around, while the 'bodies' of the other viewers appear in the world where they were most recently abandoned. This system was single user, and lacked provision for gestural and spoken input.

The SONAS system

The SONAS system, the successor to Spoken Image, is an Intelligent Multimedia multi-user system that uses a synergistic combination of several input modalities. The system facilitates advanced human computer interaction methodologies such as natural language and gesture interfaces. The environment the user finds themselves in is a model of a town. The project is a feasibility test-bed for several theories ranging from the design of computer interfaces with virtual environments and intelligent agents to theories on the pragmatic interpretation of spatial language.

One goal of the system is the manipulation of objects in a 3D environment using natural language. To achieve this the system must be able to interpret and react to the input of telic action phrases. For example, consider the input,

Put the book on the table.

The user should see "the book" moving onto the table. However, before this can happen several stages of processing must be gone through.

Firstly the phrase must be parsed and broken down into the Figure "the book", the reference object "the table", the action "Put", and the spatial relation "on". This is achieved using a parser and lexicon that was developed for the system (see Anibaldi and O'Nuallain 2000 in this volume).

Next, we search the visual model for the figure and reference objects. Elements in the model are instances of an Object Oriented C++ class hierarchy that have been inserted into a scene graph. The 3D model of world is rendered using OpenGL and the OpenGL Utility Library (GLU/GLUT). During the OpenGL event loop the system traverses through scene graph invoking each object's display function. When searching for an object we step through the graph checking each object's attributes against our search criteria (e.g. Object Name, Colour). During the design of this class hierarchy we distinguished between object physical attributes that remain constant throughout an object's life e.g. Mass, and object states that can change over time, e.g. World Location (Figure 1) A Telic Action when applied to an object changes its temporally dependent state without changing its attributes:

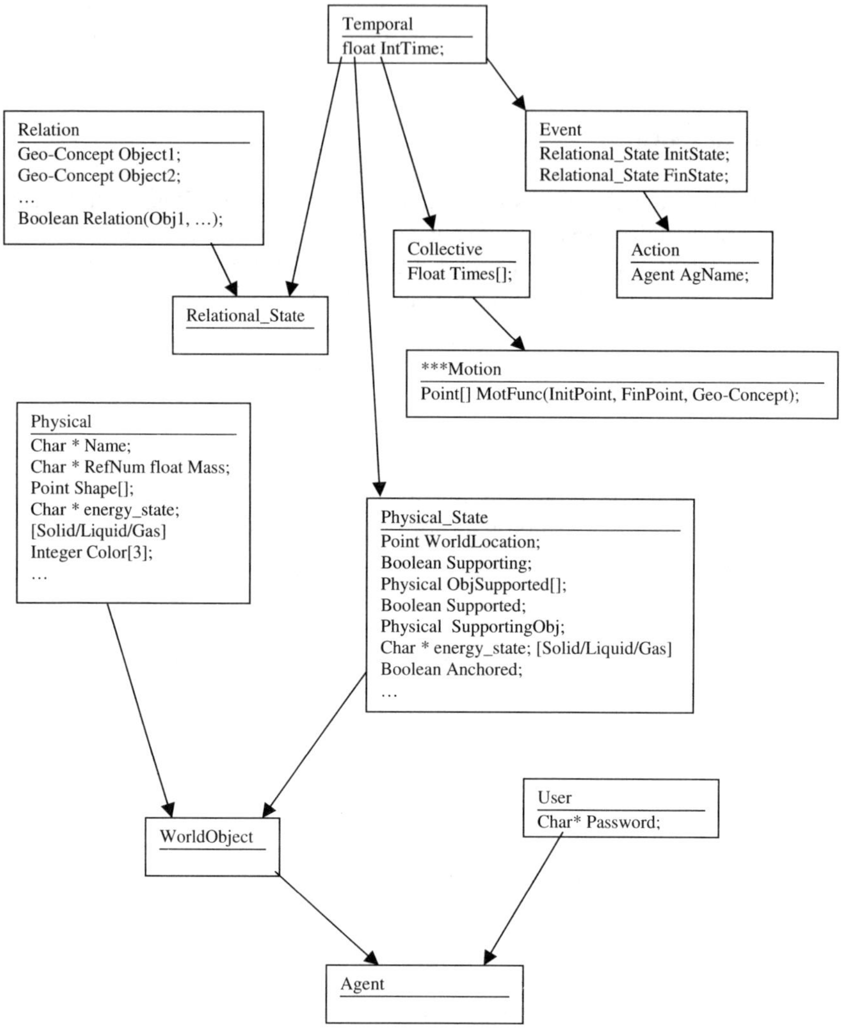

Figure 1. Classes derived from the Temporal Class

TelicAction (Object.Attribute + Object.State) $\Rightarrow$ Object.Attribute + Object.State$'$

Once the Theme and Reference have been identified, an instance of the appropriate telic action class is instantiated.

Due to the incredible gradation in natural language (e.g. push, slide, stack), we must develop a separate motion class to deal with each telic action (Figure 2). These motion classes each have a function that takes a geometrical conceptualisation of the action theme, the initial world location of the theme and the final world location of the theme as parameters and returns an array of points representing the path that the theme must take to mimic the action. Each telic action class inherits from one of these motion classes and uses these functions when calculating the transform to be applied to the action theme (Figure 3). However, not only must the Telic Action classes cause a change in the visual environment which resembles the real world action they mimic, but they must also check that the final state spatial relation between the theme and the reference object is valid with respect to the physical attributes of the objects involved. The Telic Action base class has an instance of the agent class (usually the user's

General form of the Motion class set.

Motion
Point[] MotFunc(InitPoint, FinPoint, Geo-Concept, ...);

Some examples of Motion classes in the hierarchy.

StackMotion
Point[] StackFunc(InitPoint, FinPoint, Point);

SlideMotion
Point[] SlideFunc(InitPoint, FinPoint, Point, Surface);

Figure 2.General Form of the Motion Classes

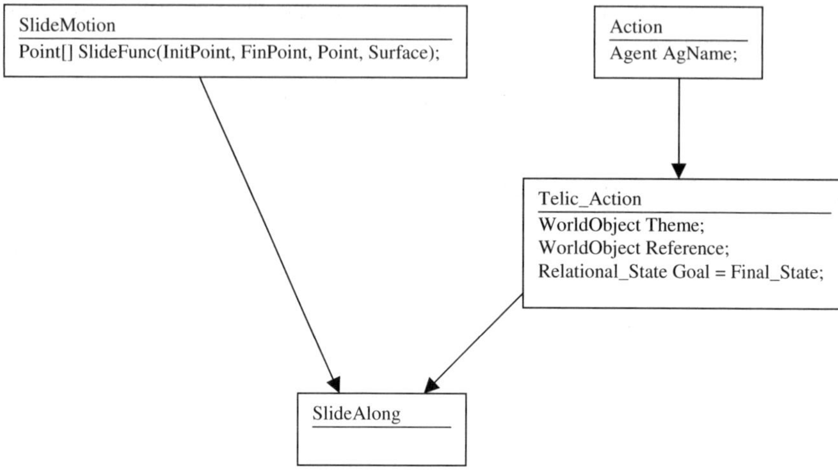

Figure 3. The derivation of a specific Telic Action class

avatar), instances of the Relational State classes, namely Initial State, Final State, and Goal State (which in the case of a Telic Action is equal to the Final State) and instances of the WorldObject classes representing the Reference and Figure of the action as attributes. In our approach to analysing the semantic meaning of a spatial expression we agree with the multiple relations model as proposed in [Herskovits, 1986]. This is a multilayer approach where a spatial relation is considered from a conceptual and semantic level.

At the conceptual level, the objects involved in the action are considered with respect to their position in the physical ontology of objects. Here the physical attributes of the objects are checked against the selectional restrictions associated with the verb. In the SONAS system, this is achieved by checking the Physical Attributes of the WorldObject Attributes representing the Figure and Reference against restrictions associated with the verb. If the Physical Attributes of the Figure and Reference are found to be consistent with the selectional restrictions on the verb, we then proceed with the semantic layer of analysis.

At the semantic level in the Herskovits approach, the Reference and Figure objects are reduced to geometric conceptualisations (Point, Line, Plane etc). Also there is an ideal meaning for each preposition. These ideal meanings are relations between two or more geometric concepts. Examples of these ideal meanings are coincidence of points and contiguity of two surfaces. A set of use types for each preposition is derived from ideal meaning by applying adaptations and shifts which are dependent upon which geometric concepts the Reference and Figure have been reduced to (Figure 4).

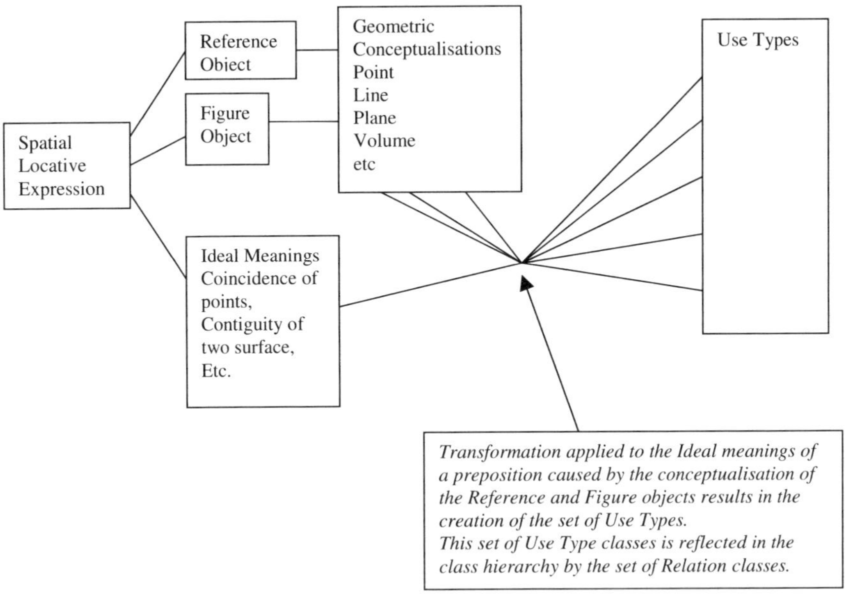

Figure 4. The conceptual composition of a spatial locative expression at the semantic level in the Herskovits ontology

In the SONAS system the Use Types level of abstraction in the Herskovits ontology is reflected in the set of relational classes in the class hierarchy (Figures 5 and 7). The initial state and final state attributes of the telic action are instances of these relational classes; these are used in conjunction with the Motion classes function to compute the Translation required for the action. This is then applied to the Figure object causing values in the Theme Object's Physical State to be altered. The next time through the event loop the changed state values causes the object's display function to update the scene in response to the user input.

The class hierarchy

These classes reflect the geometric forms that the Figure and Reference objects are reduced to at the Semantic layer of analysis.

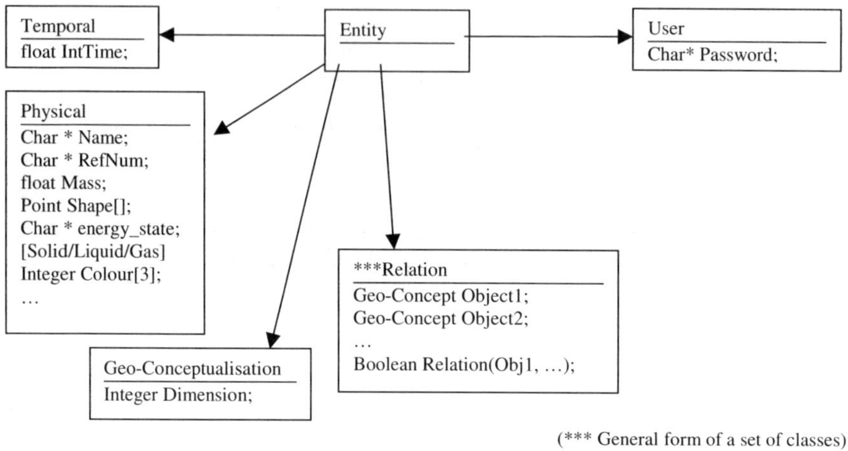

Figure 5. Base classes (Abstract)

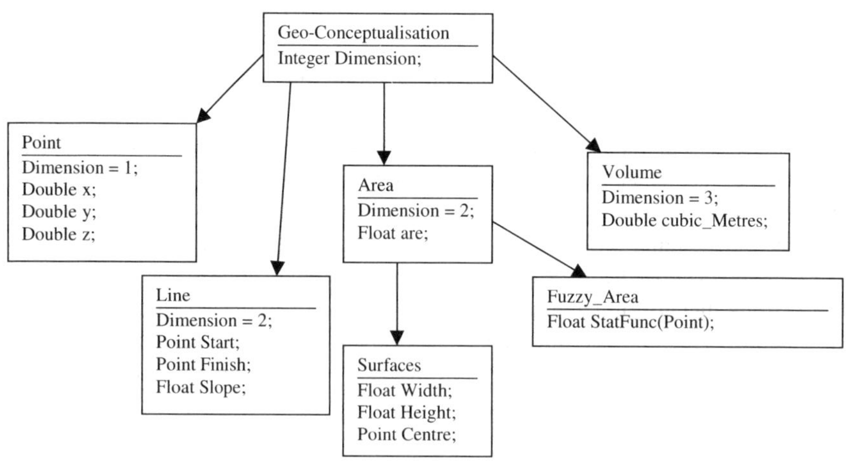

Figure 6. The Geometric Conceptualisation classes

Relation
Geo-Concept Object1; Geo-Concept Object2; ... Boolean Relation(Obj1, ...);

Some examples of Relation classes in the hierarchy.

Coincidence_of_points
Point Reference; Point Figure; Boolean CoinPoints(Ref, Fig);

Contiguity_of_two_surfaces
Surface Reference; Surface Figure; Boolean Cont2Surf(Ref, Fig);

Figure 7. General form of the Relation class set. This set of classes represent the Use Type level of abstraction in the Herskovits ontology

SONAS as a Multimodal System

Much of the impetus for the SONAS has its roots in the prevailing HCI paradigm. For this reason the system has been designed to have multimodal capabilities. The ultimate goal of multimodal user interfaces is the increased transparency of computational devices to end users. While Natural language input represents the most obvious target of exploitation for designers of such systems in the physical world, people often find difficulty expressing complex series of actions in spoken form. Yet we can express such actions with ease through the medium of gesture, or 'actually doing it'. Thus gesture is a useful element to add to multimodal access, and a practically indispensable one when modelling spatial environments.

Either modality on its own has strengths and weaknesses, but the two together should provide a medium rich enough to express most, if not all, of the instructions that a non-technically proficient user would wish to express to an information system. The increase in complexity for the developer of such applications is considerable, however, when we grant the user the ability to arbitrarily combine gesture and speech when interacting.

SONAS General Architecture

The Sonas system is built upon the Open Agent Architecture developed at SRI. The OAA provides a general ontology for the development of distributed agent applications, in addition to the 'Facilitator' software, which as a first cut can be described as the middle-ware that provides inter-agent communication services. The Facilitator also maintains a blackboard, which agents may write data to and read data from. The data on the blackboard is stored in Horn clause form; functor(arg,arg...) e.g. noun([phone_number,'phone number']) encodes that there is a noun whose written form is 'phone number' which refers to the symbol phone_number.

Upon connection to the Facilitator, the agent must declare the services that it provides. Such services are referred to as 'solvables' in keeping with the Prolog-inspired nomenclature. Such solvables also define the interface to the agent, and generally reveal their purpose upon inspection. For instance, say(Text) is a solvable declared by a text to speech agent, and its purpose and effect is immediately obvious from its form.

Agents provide solvables, and may also issue solve requests. To do this an agent formulates the goal that it needs solved (a goal may be the retrieval of information or the performance of a task) and passes it to the facilitator. The facilitator then uses its database of solvables to decide which agent can provide the needed services. It then sends the solve request to that agent, and upon completion of the task, it returns the solution to the original agent.

Typical interactions involve many such exchanges between members of the agent community. Additionally, the facilitator provides a backtracking mechanism similar to Prolog's. The 'language' which agents communicate in is referred to as the Interagent Communication Language (ICL); basically it consists of horn-clauses and has few reserved symbols.

Sonas Architecture

An agent-based system is best viewed as a community of uncoupled software entities capable of communicating with one another. The agents in the Sonas system are:

- World Server — OpenGL 3D VR environment. This entity provides the final context in which users' spatial instructions are executed. Also provides a stream of hand gestures.

- World Client — Manages the rendering of the virtual environment on the user's screen. For performance reasons, this agent handles the rendering of the virtual hand in the world, and also provides a stream of gestures, such as 'grab', 'drop', 'move in direction A', 'pointing in direction B'.
- ViaVoice — Speech recognition services provided by IBM's ViaVoice, integrated into Sonas via an Agent wrapper which automatically updates the vocabulary of recognisable words to match the vocabulary on the blackboard.
- TextToSpeech — Multivoice Speech synthesiser accepts its input from the serial port.
- Handwriting — Neural Network based hand-written character/icon recognition.
- Query Management — Agent which manages the interpretation and solution of user requests.
- WWW DB — Agent which is web-aware and can retrieve information from web pages in response to requests.
- Main Interface — Main on-screen UI.
- Camera Agent: Vision system with digital camera on top of the monitor identifies the user currently sitting at the keyboard.
- User Agent: An agent which maintains a DB of user-specific information, also manages the user's appearance in the 3D worlds (avatar).
- Embodied Agents: Agents which provide services but which also have a physical embodiment in the VR world. (E.g. a calendar agent which tracks a user's appointments would appear as a calendar hanging on the wall of the user's virtual office). Provision is made for such agents so that in future such agents may attach to the world and be represented therein as easily as agents can join the OAA agent community itself.
- Notification Agent: Manages the delivery of messages to users, and the processing of requests such as "When email about hard-drives arrives, notify me immediately".
- Telephony agent: provides the facility of sending text messages to GSM mobile phones, generally at the behest of the notification agent.
- Spatial Expertise Parser: NL parser with detailed ontology regarding spatial prepositions.
- Email Agent: Sends, retrieves and filters email.
- Calendar agent: Stores information on appointments.
- Merge Agent: Combines input streams from the various input modalities and produces a disambiguated stream of horn clauses representing user input.

- FileSystem Agent: Provides an interface to the user's computer account (in the Unix sense), also provides the 3D world with a representation of the directory structure based at the users home directory, with an emphasis on permitting the user to access his/her documents through the medium of the 3D world. The file system agent integrates natural language at a low level in the process of document search and retrieval, so that requests such as "Get me the document about security" are handled with ease.
- Neurologic Agent: This agent is a hybrid system consisting of series of modular neural networks coupled with symbolic logic module. The ANNs have access to the data arriving at the various modalities and may create associations in the traditional Hebbian manner.
- NL generation agent — converts ICL horn clauses to natural language prior to delivery to the user.

References

Anibaldi. L & Ó Nualláin. S. (2000) A computational multilayered model for the interpretation of locative expressions. This volume.

Herskovits. A. (1986) *Language and Spatial Cognition*. Cambridge, England: Cambridge University Press.

Ó Nualláin, S. & Smith, A. (1994) An investigation into the common semantics of language and vision. AAAI Spring Symposium, Stanford, CA. In Mc Kevitt (Ed.), 1995 *Integration of Natural Language and Vision Processing*. Dordrecht: Kluwer, 1, 21–31.

Ó Nualláin S, Farley B, Smith A. G. (1994) The Spoken Image System: On the visual interpretation of verbal scene descriptions. In *AAAI94 Workshop Program: Integration of Natural Language and Vision Processing.*

Smith A, Farley B, Ó Nualláin S. (1996) Visualization of natural language. In *Proceedings of the Third Spoken Dialogue and Discourse Workshop*. Moncton: New Brunswick.

Designing Real-Time Software Advisors for 3D Spatial Operations

Mike and Ann Eisenberg
University of Colorado

Introduction: Educational software to support mathematical visualization

It is a common observation among mathematicians and scientists that the ability to reason "visually" is an important element — perhaps *the* most important element — of their intellectual personality. Hadamard (1949), in a classic study of mathematical thinking, noted of himself that "I insist that words are totally absent from my mind when I really think". (p. 75) He illustrated the point with an account of his understanding of a proof in number theory, accompanied by "strange and cloudy imagery". (p. 77) In a similar vein Fomenko (1994), in a recent book on geometry and topology, writes "It happens rather frequently that the proof of one or another mathematical fact can at first be 'seen', and only after that (and following this visual idea) can we present a logically consistent formulation…." (p. vii); while the renowned mathematical physicist Stanislaw Ulam observed that "It is one thing to know about physics abstractly, and quite another to have a practical encounter with problems directly connected with experimental data… I found out that the main ability to have was a visual, and also an almost tactile, way to imagine the physical situations, rather than a merely logical picture of the problems… Very few mathematicians seem to possess (such an imagination) to any great degree" (quoted in Cooper 1989, p. 15). Such observations are found often among scientists and engineers as well: Miller (1984) devotes a marvelous book to the way in which physicists such as Einstein and Boltzmann employed visual imagery in their thought processes, while Ferguson, in his book *Engineering and the Mind's Eye* (1992), writes "Despite the low academic status of visual thought, it is an intrinsic and inseparable part of engineering." (p. 47) In an especially intriguing interview, the astronomer Margaret Geller recalled of her own childhood:

> My father is a crystallographer.... He had an attraction for any kind of toy that had anything to do with geometry.... (T)here were toys where you could connect flat shapes up with rubber bands to make solid figures. He bought me that, and he'd explain to me the relationship between things that I built and things in the world. For example, I'd make a cube, and he'd explain to me the relationship between that and the structure of table salt. And I'd make an icosahedron, and he'd explain how you see that in the real world.... I would be able to visualize in 3-D. And I realize now — I've talked to lots of people in science — that very few people have that ability. (Lightman and Brawer 1990, p. 361)

While the theme of visual (or more broadly visuospatial) thinking is often struck in the discourse of mathematicians and scientists, trying to pin down just what this notion might mean is difficult. Geometers and topologists may generate a body of introspective folklore about their own mental operations; but cognitive scientists, in attempting to treat the topic rigorously, are faced with a host of puzzles relating to topics such as mental imagery, visual memory, the relationship between the senses of vision and touch, the relationship between visual and linguistic cognition, and many more.

This paper is not the occasion for an attempt to sort out, or even summarize, the myriad questions over what "mathematical visualization" might be, or what role it plays in mathematical cognition and education. Nonetheless, it is worth mentioning that there is some evidence (besides the purely anecdotal) that spatial thinking is an identifiable component of human intelligence (Gardner 1983); that it is an important predictor of success in college physics courses (Siemankowski and McKnight 1971); and that certain types of abilities linked with spatial thinking may be taught (see, for instance, Brinkmann's (1966) report of a curriculum for teaching visual thinking, or Olson's work in developing an educational toy to help teach very young children the often-problematic concept of diagonality (Olson 1970)). It is our firm belief that — consistent with the folklore — much of mathematical thinking is indeed distinctly visual in nature, and that mathematical education would therefore profit from a greater emphasis on activities that strengthen and exercise visual and spatial reasoning.

That said, however, there are delicate pedagogical questions about how to help students develop such reasoning abilities. It would certainly be possible to create "visual workbooks", or drill-and-practice software systems, focusing perhaps on the types of problems (e.g., mental-rotation tasks) typical of standardized psychological tests of visual thinking. While such efforts may prove effective in raising students' test scores, it is our belief that they would prove equally effective in destroying any sense of enjoyment, creativity, or personal expression that students might feel in their mathematical work. Indeed, as with so many other efforts in skill-training, "visual drill-and-practice" runs the risk of placing the cart of skill acquisition before the horse of motivation: students might well learn to perform visual tasks while growing to detest (or at best tolerate) the context in which the learning is taking place.

In contrast, we believe that it is possible to create educational software environments in support of mathematical activities that are rich in important ideas and content, intensely visual in nature, and respectful of students' powers of self-expression. Over the past five years, we have developed a software application named HyperGami (Eisenberg and Nishioka 1997) which reflects this educational philosophy. HyperGami is a system with which students (and adults) are able to create customized polyhedral models and sculptures in paper. As such, it might be characterized as a "constructionist" (Papert 1991) mathematical application — i.e., one that encourages students to create and design mathematical objects.

This paper is not about HyperGami in its current instantiation. Rather, this paper is devoted to relatively recent work that we have begun with an eye toward augmenting the "basic" HyperGami program with additional tools to assist students in thinking more creatively or productively about the polyhedral forms that they can build in the system. Much of our motivation in this regard has come from observing students (and ourselves) using HyperGami and noting a variety of interesting patterns regarding the ease or difficulty that people have in thinking about polyhedra — in seeing the symmetries inherent in shapes, seeing the relationships between distinct shapes, even seeing the aesthetic or engineering possibilities afforded by particular shapes. The work that we have begun is eventually aimed toward providing useful online "advice", supplied by the HyperGami program itself, and encouraging students to think in potentially new or unexpected ways about polyhedra and the manner in which they may be altered or customized.

The second section of this paper gives a very brief outline of the HyperGami system by way of background. In the third section, we discuss the notion of what it might mean to think creatively or powerfully about polyhedral shapes; and in the fourth section we describe our current work in developing software "advisors" to assist students in developing such thinking skills. The fifth and final section of the paper describes our plans for extending this work in the near future, as well as speculation about where these efforts might lead in the longer term.

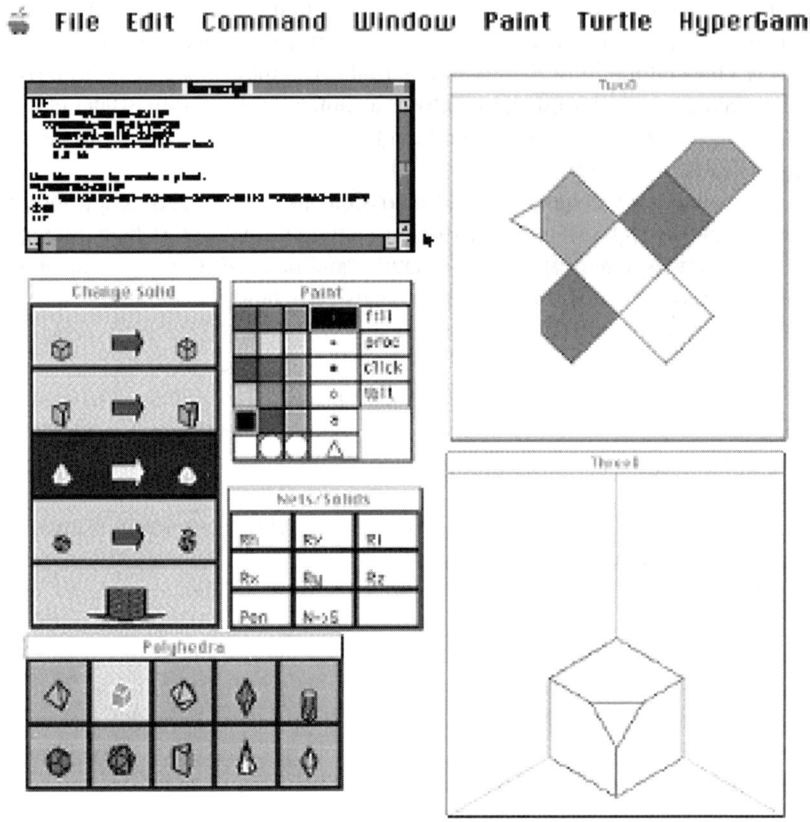

Figure 1. The HyperGami screen in the course of a sample project

HyperGami: A brief overview

HyperGami is a software application written by the authors in the MacScheme dialect of Lisp (S1); it runs on all color Macintosh machines with at least 16M of memory. Figure 1 depicts the HyperGami screen in the course of a sample project (here, creating a cube that has been truncated at one vertex). In the figure, the user has selected (from the Polyhedra palette toward the bottom of the screen) a cube as a starting shape. The user then brings up the "Change Solid" window which includes a variety of iconic representations of operations that may be performed upon solid shapes. Here, the user has selected the "truncate solid at vertex" icon; this selection causes a sample Scheme language expression to appear in the transcript window at the top of the figure. When this expression is evaluated, the user generates a new solid shape; this shape may then be "unfolded" to produce both the solid form shown in the ThreeD window at bottom right, and the folding pattern (also known as a folding net) in the TwoD window at upper right. In the figure, the user has shaded in several faces of the folding net on the screen.

Much more detail about the HyperGami system — and the wealth of polyhedral forms and sculptures that may be created with the program — can be found in Eisenberg and Nishioka (1997). The figure and description above, however, should serve to indicate the basic idea behind the program: namely, that the student may design new three-dimensional shapes on the screen by applying functions (such as the "truncation" function) to pre-existing shapes. Once a new 3D solid has been created, the program will attempt to create a folding net for the shape; this net may now be decorated through a variety of means (including Scheme language expressions), printed out and folded into an attractive tangible model. By way of illustration, Figure 2 shows two examples of polyhedral figures designed with HyperGami (both are relatively complex shapes, constructed from multiple pieces).

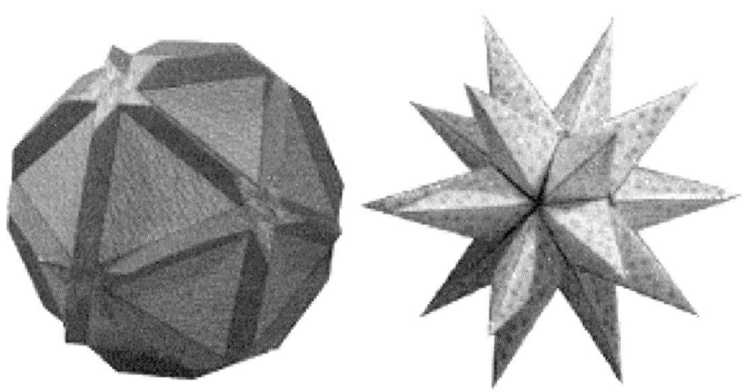

Figure 2. Two HyperGami polyhedra: a variant of the regular icosahedron (left), and a great stellated dodecahedron (right).

How does one come to understand polyhedra?

The previous section summarized the HyperGami application and suggested the (immense) range of polyhedra that can be produced in the system. While these shapes and sculptures have an undeniable appeal, they leave an important question unresolved — namely, that of mathematical content. To put the matter another way: why should these shapes have importance for mathematicians, scientists, and engineers; and what are the important ideas or themes that we as educators should stress in discussing these shapes with our students?

There are several types of answer to these questions. One style of response stresses the occurrence of polyhedral forms in nature: the tetrahedral arrangement of the bonds of carbon, the space-filling forms of crystallography, the geodesic-dome-like shape of certain microorganisms (Cf. Senechal 1988). This style of answer might be called "naturalistic": it emphasizes the surprisingly ubiquitous character of polyhedra in the world and (by implication) would encourage students to develop familiarity with the shapes, as a bird watcher might learn the identities of so many songbirds. A related theme — one that naturally accompanies this urge toward easy familiarity with shapes — is the notion of developing a "taxonomy" of shapes, spotting a family resemblance between distinct polyhedra. This is a theme that one often encounters in mathematical writing on the subject: the classical polyhedra are related to each other by a variety of operations including stellation, vertex and edge truncation, taking the dual of a solid (identifying the faces of one with the vertices of another, and vice versa), "capping" of faces, and so forth. Finding such relationships between shapes is an activity with an ancient pedigree: the fifteenth book of Euclid's Elements (added after Euclid's death) described the inscription of a cube inside an octahedron and vice versa (Coxeter 1973, p. 30); while (according to Senechal (1988)), the 16th-century goldsmith Wenzel Jammitzer wrote a book entitled *Perspectiva Corporum Regularium* in which "each of the five regular solids is presented in exquisite variation." (p. 11) Among contemporary authors, Loeb (1991), for instance, writes in the introduction to his book *Space Structures* that "one aim of the present volume is to present fundamental principles underlying this variety of (polyhedral) structures, to show their family relationships and how they may be transformed into one another..." (p. xix). Similarly, Holden (1971) suggests that by truncating selected features of a solid (e.g., the corners of a cube) "(you) can engage in a useful exercise, which will cultivate your abilities in visualizing spacial relations and in specifying symmetries." (p. 57)

Finding relationships between polyhedra is an indispensable way of knitting together the huge variety of shapes encountered in nature and mathematics.

While the HyperGami system does afford students a medium in which many such relationships may be encountered in principle (i.e., the operations of truncation, capping, stretching and others are available to students), the program currently offers little guidance or advice in helping students think about the types of operations that could be employed to transform one polyhedron into another. The "advisors" to be described in the following section are intended to strengthen in particular the skill of seeing the potential relationships between polyhedra.

As an example of what this type of "seeing" entails — and before we describe our own attempts to represent aspects of this skill in software — it is worth looking at a vivid example of a talented seventeenth-century "visualizer" at work. In Johannes Kepler's book *Harmonices Mundi*, he provides sketches of various polyhedra, some of which suggest the author's remarkable ability to interpret polyhedral forms. Consider, for instance, Kepler's interpretation of the icosahedron. In his sketch, Kepler displays both the entire icosahedron and a "parsing" of the shape into three portions, as suggested by the two parts of Figure 3 below. (For a view of Kepler's original sketch, see Cromwell (1997)). In Kepler's interpretation of the icosahedron, the shape is composed of two pentagonal pyramids joined onto either side of a pentagonal antiprism. By dividing the shape in this manner — by "seeing" the icosahedron as composed of three component shapes — Kepler is able to highlight the relationship between the icosahedron and other, simpler shapes. (At the same time, Kepler's sketch suggests other possible polyhedra that one might wish to construct — e.g., it would be interesting to vary his construction so that it employs a square, as opposed to pentagonal, antiprism with two pyramidal caps.)

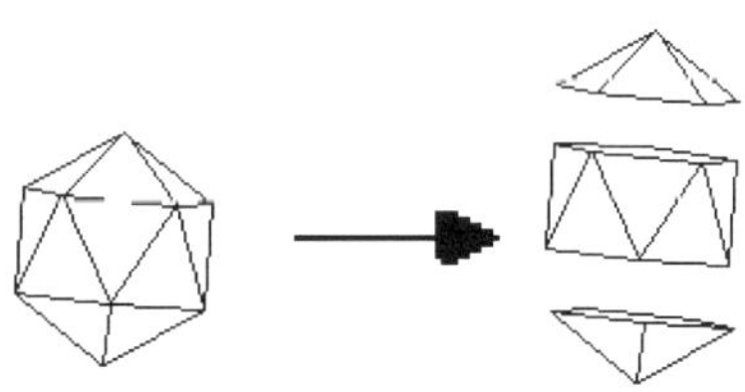

Figure 3. Kepler's "parsing" of the icosahedron (at left) into two pyramidal caps and a central pentagonal antiprism.

Ideally, a suite of online advisors built into HyperGami should help students work toward the type of understanding of polyhedra exhibited by Kepler. One advisor might, e.g., suggest ways in which to "slice" polyhedra — in much the same manner as indicated by Kepler's "slicing" of the icosahedron. Another advisor might suggest likely faces for which a capping operation might be tried, or might suggest an interesting vertex for truncation. (Compare the quote from Holden above.) In the following section we describe our progress toward incorporating advisors of this nature in the HyperGami program.

Several prototype advisors for operations on Polyhedra

To date, we have developed a small suite of advisors that can be used in conjunction with HyperGami (and that will eventually be incorporated into the released system). In structure, a typical advisor is a procedure which may be invoked by the student (eventually from a HyperGami menu or palette), and which displays suggestions about the likely applicability of a given transformation on a solid shape. Figure 4 shows the essential idea at work for one of our operational advisors: at left, a starting shape (a truncated tetrahedron) is shown, and we wish to know whether the operation of "capping parallel edges with an edge" may be employed. We therefore call the appropriate advisor procedure: this procedure takes as its input the starting solid shape, and redisplays the shape at right with some highlighting indicating additional information. Here, one of the hexagonal faces of the original shape has been shown with its three pairs of parallel edges in distinct colors. Thus, the advisor has presented us with a plausible face upon which we can place an "edge cap", as shown in Figure 4.

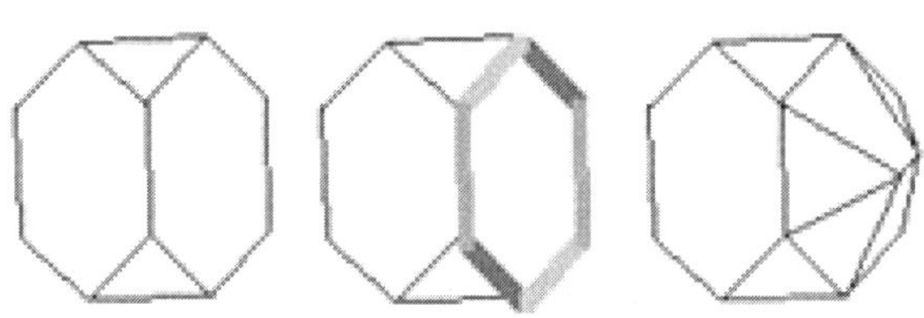

Figure 4. A truncated tetrahedron (left) is redisplayed with one of its hexagonal faces highlighted to show three pairs of parallel edges (at center). At right, a new shape derived from the truncated tetrahedron by adding an "edge cap" on the highlighted face.

In addition to the "parallel edge capping advisor", we have developed similar procedural tools for the following operations:

- Capping a single face with a new vertex
- Truncating a single vertex
- "Exchanging" a pair of adjacent triangular faces (as described below)

– "Slicing" a polyhedron through the plane determined by a set of vertices
– Obtaining the convex hull of the vertices of a (nonconvex) solid

In every instance, the basic idea of the advisor is much as in the example shown above: we invoke the advisor when we would like to see if there is a plausible (or potentially interesting) use of the given operation on a starting shape.

As another example, consider employing our "slicing" advisor on the icosahedron (the same shape so effectively visualized by Kepler). In this instance, there are actually two related advisory procedures that we may call: one which looks for sets of four vertices composing a parallelogram that may be the cross-section of an appropriate slice through the solid, and a second which looks for linked sets of polyhedral edges that compose a planar shape which could be the cross-section of a slice.

In the first instance, our slicing-advisor takes as input the icosahedron and redisplays the shape with a highlighted rectangle as shown in Figure 5. Here, the advisor is providing us with a (arguably non-obvious) rectangle through which we can slice the icosahedron; once that slicing operation is performed, we have the two halves shown toward the right of the figure.

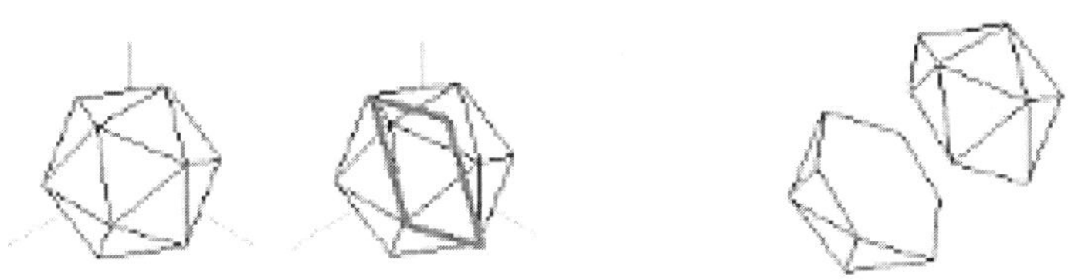

Figure 5. An icosahedron, redisplayed with a "slicing rectangle" at center. Note that the upper right vertex of the highlighted rectangle is one of the hidden vertices in the view at left. At the right, the two resulting halves of the sliced icosahedron.

In the second instance, our slicing-advisor takes the icosahedron as input and redisplays the shape with the highlighted pentagon as shown in Figure 6. Here, the advisor is providing us with a set of vertices, all linked by edges, through which the icosahedron might be sliced. (Note the difference between this piece of advice and that shown in Figure 5: in that case, the four edges of the "slicing rectangle" did not all appear among the edges of the icosahedron.)

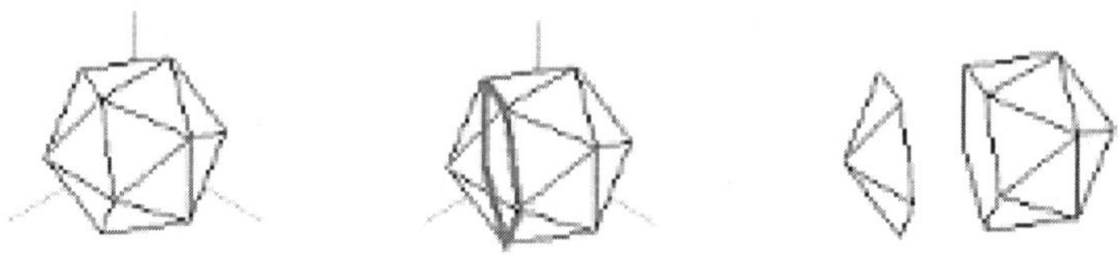

Figure 6. An icosahedron, redisplayed with a set of "slicing edges" (in this case forming a regular pentagon) at center. The resulting slices are shown at right. (Note the similarity to the "slicing" operation used by Kepler as represented earlier in Figure 3).

Two more examples of advisors at work may serve to indicate the general utility of the idea. The "triangle-exchange" advisor simply looks for instances within a starting polyhedron of two triangular faces that share an edge. Once found, these two triangles will be suggested as a possible site for the operation shown graphically in Figure 7. Here, the original edge between the two triangles is removed and replaced by an edge between the (hitherto unconnected) opposite vertices of the two faces. In the figure we see the operation of the "triangle-exchange" advisor as applied to a capped cube. The original shape is given as input to the advisor, which highlights the pair of adjacent triangles shown at center, indicating that these two faces are a possible site for an exchange operation. Once that operation is performed, we obtain the shape depicted at the right of the figure.

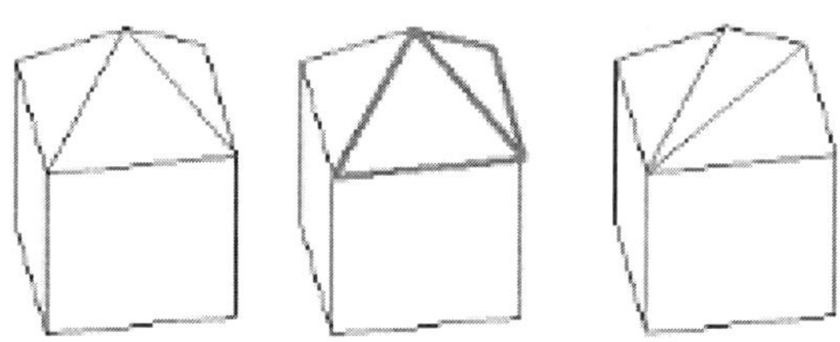

Figure 7. A capped cube (left), redisplayed with two adjacent triangles highlighted (at center). When these two triangles are "exchanged", their adjoining edge is removed and replaced by an edge between the formerly unconnected vertices to form the "notched" shape at right.

Finally, the "truncation advisor" looks for vertices in a solid such that the line connecting the vertex with the "midpoint" of the solid is an axis of rotational symmetry for the solid. As an example, consider once more the capped cube (as shown again in Figure 8). Here, the advisor suggests the topmost "cap" vertex as a likely site for truncation, since the capped cube has fourfold rotational symmetry about the axis joining that vertex and the center of the solid. (In contrast, none of the other vertices of the solid has this property.) Once the truncation operation has been performed, we obtain the shape at the right of the figure.

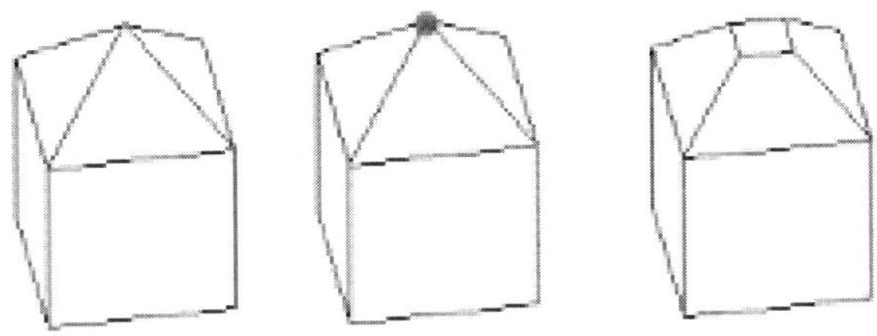

Figure 8. A capped cube (at left) is redisplayed with a highlighted "top" point (at center). After the solid is truncated at the suggested vertex we obtain the shape at right.

Ongoing work and future directions

The already-developed software advisors described above represent only one step toward our eventual goal of building computational advisors for visual and spatial reasoning. Some interesting HyperGami operations (such as "stretching" shapes, or joining two shapes together at a face) have yet to be accompanied by advisors; moreover, some interesting geometric operations (such as stellating polyhedra) are not currently implemented in HyperGami at all. The current set of advisors, while representing an interesting beginning, is still relatively simple: for instance, the "slicing" advisor described in the previous section can suggest only one slicing operation at a time, and hence only one of the two slicing operations implicit in Kepler's parsing of the icosahedron shown in Figure 3 earlier. It would thus be desirable to extend even the current set of advisors so that they could suggest richer variations or combinations of polyhedral operations: just to take one more example, an advisor could suggest multiple vertex truncation operations instead of only one (as in our current implementation of the truncation advisor).

These are short-term goals for improvement of our existing system. Currently we are also at work in devising computational models whose purpose is to provide a meaningful metric of the "visualizability" of solids — the difficulty or ease with which a shape is likely to be imagined by a typical student. As part of this effort, we have conducted psychological experiments to discover the common patterns by which students tend to orient three-dimensional shapes when those shapes are visualized. (A preliminary description of the results of one such experiment may be found in (Eisenberg, Nishioka, and Schreiner 1997)). It is our belief that the "orientability" of certain solids — the presence of cues that people use to suggest a typical or standard orientation for solids — offer important clues as to the difficulty (or ease) of visualization of solids.

In the longer term, our goal is to develop software advisors for more complex spatial ideas. One could imagine, for instance, a "symmetry" advisor to help students identify the various symmetry operations present in a newly-created solid (and to suggest known solids whose symmetry group is the same as that of the newly-created shape). An "embedded shape" advisor might draw the student's attention to the ways in which certain shapes may be incorporated within others (for instance, by choosing eight particular vertices of a dodecahedron, we obtain the corners of an embedded cube (Holden 1971)). Or a "polyhedra database advisor" might examine a student's newly-created polyhedron and compare that shape to others in the same "family" (e.g., when a student first constructs a cube, the database advisor might show a related set of more complex prisms).

Our hope, then, is to develop a collection of educationally effective "spatial heuristics" (in the spirit of Polya's (1957) influential work in mathematics education). Going beyond this, however, we would hope that our preliminary efforts in creating spatial advisors can eventually help us to understand more clearly the fundamental issues in cognitive science with which this paper began. By constructing working computational models of "effective visual thinking" — even tentative and early models such as those described here — we believe that we can make progress toward understanding the essential nature of mathematical visualization.

Acknowledgments

This work is supported in part by the National Science Foundation under awards no. REC-961396 and CDA-9616444, by a Young Investigator award (IRI-9258684), and by the National Science Foundation and the Advanced Research Projects Agency under Cooperative Agreement No. CDA-9408607. The second author is supported by a fellowship from the National Physical Science Consortium.

Notes

1. See also the many fine papers in Sutherland and Mason (1995) around this general theme.
2. More detail may be found by following the HyperGami link from the first author's World Wide Web page: www.cs.colorado.edu/~duck/
3. Again, see (Eisenberg, Nishioka, and Schreiner 1997) for more details.

References

Brinkmann, E. (1966). Programed Instruction as a Technique for Improving Spatial Visualization. *Journal of Applied Psychology*, 50:2, 179–184.

Cooper, N. G. , ed. (1989). *From Cardinals to Chaos*. Cambridge: Cambridge University Press.

Coxeter, H. S. M. (1973) *Regular Polytopes*. New York: Dover.

Cromwell, P. (1997) *Polyhedra*. Cambridge: Cambridge University Press.

Eisenberg, M. and Nishioka, A. (1997). Creating Polyhedral Models by Computer. To appear in *Journal of Computers in Mathematics and Science Teaching*.

Eisenberg, M.; Nishioka, A. and Schreiner, M. E. (1997). Helping Users Think in Three Dimensions: Steps Toward Incorporating Spatial Cognition in User Modelling. *Proceedings of 1997 International Conference on Intelligent Interfaces (IUI 97)*, Orlando, Florida, January 1997, 113–120.

Ferguson, Eugene S. (1992). *Engineering and the Mind's Eye*. Cambridge, MA: MIT.

Fomenko, A. (1994) *Visual Geometry and Topology*. Berlin: Springer-Verlag.

Gardner, H. (1983) *Frames of Mind*. New York: Basic Books.

Hadamard, J. (1949) *The Psychology of Invention in the Mathematical Field*. New York: Dover.

Holden, A. (1971) *Shapes, Space, and Symmetry*. New York: Dover.

Lightman, A. and Brawer, R. (1990) *Origins*. Cambridge, MA: Harvard University Press.

Loeb, A. (1991) *Space Structures*. Boston: Birkhäuser.

Miller, A. (1984) *Visual Imagery in Scientific Thought*. Cambridge, MA: MIT Press.

Olson, D. (1970) *Cognitive Development*. New York: Academic Press.

Papert, S. (1991) Situating Constructionism. In I. Harel and S. Papert (eds.), *Constructionism*. (1–11). Norwood, NJ: Ablex.

Polya, G. (1957) *How to Solve It*. Garden City, NY: Doubleday.

Siemankowski, F. and McKnight, F. (1971) Spatial Cognition: Success Prognosticator in College Science Courses. *Journal of College Science Teaching*, 1:1 , 56–59.

Senechal, M. (1988) A Visit to the Polyhedral Kingdom. In Senechal, M. and Fleck, G. (eds.) *Shaping Space*. Boston: Birkhäuser.

Sutherland, R. and Mason, J., eds. (1995) *Exploiting Mental Imagery with Computers in Mathematics Education*. Berlin: Springer-Verlag.

Software

(S1) LightShip Software. *MacScheme*. Palo Alto, CA.

Using Spatial Semantics to Discover and Verify Diagrammatic Demonstrations of Geometric Propositions

Robert K. Lindsay
University of Michigan

Introduction

The Logic Theorist (LT) of Newell, Shaw & Simon (1957) introduced a computational style, the first employed in artificial intelligence. The program sought proofs to theorems of the sentential calculus, an unquantified formal logic. (An unquantified logic lacks the universal quantifier "for all x" and the existential quantifier "there exists an x" present in a full predicate logic.) Axioms and theorems were represented as uninterpreted "sentences," that is, strings of characters selected from a finite alphabet. The logical rules of inference, also represented as character strings, can be applied to sentences to produce other sentences. A proof is a sequence of rule applications that, when applied to an initial set of sentences (axioms and previously-proved sentences), yields a sentence that is the conclusion of the theorem. To discover this sequence of rule applications, the program determined how the goal and givens differed and found rules that would reduce that difference.

LT represented the mathematical system in a way that mimicked its standard printed structure, namely one-dimensional objects (strings) with an implicit hierarchical phrase-structure imposed by the formation rules (the grammar) of the language. For example, one axiom-sentence is "(p *or* p) *implies* p" in which the connectives "*or*" and "*implies*" could be written as single characters since they have no internal structure, but are here written as English words for clarity. The symbol "p" in this sentence is a variable that stands for any well-formed sentence of the logic. The reader may think of sentences as being either true or false and interpret the logic as showing how the connectives (interpreted as logical operations) can combine true sentences to yield other true sentences. However, LT had no such understanding and merely manipulated sentences according to its rules. Parentheses indicate phrase grouping in the usual way (e.g., "*implies*" connects two subphrases in the axiom above), but again this is our interpretation, not LT's. The rules of the calculus formally define the legal transformations of sentences that result in (i) legal substitutions of sentences for variables, (ii) the replacement of a connective by its definition, and (iii) detachment, i.e., the rule of modus ponens ("p" together with "p *implies* q" allows one to conclude "q"). Logics and other fully formal branches of mathematics use these representations — a linear surface structure with an implicit hierarchical phrase structure — extensively. The rules used by the Logic Theorist maintained the syntactic constraints: they applied only to well-formed sentences and each sentence generated was well-formed by definition.

This logic is said to be uninterpreted because the variables do not refer to real or even abstract objects or sets of objects or any things that are related or interacting. As noted above, as far as LT was concerned they did not even refer to truth values. In the case of uninterpreted sentences such as those of the sentential calculus the computational style of the Logic Theorist seems quite natural and powerful. However, for interpreted systems such as predicate logic, whose sentences are normally meant to refer to sets of objects with various properties and structure, or geometry, where the sentences are intended as descriptions of real objects in space, or most other fields of mathematics that are "about" something, one might also represent these interpretations, i.e., the semantics, and bring those constraints to bear on proof discovery.

Another early system, the Geometry Machine (Gelernter, 1959; Gelernter, Hansen & Loveland, 1960) employed essentially the method of LT, but introduced semantics in a limited way, by employing a heuristic to prune the set of rule-application options to be considered. A "diagram" illustrating the theorem was constructed by the programmer and supplied to the Geometry Machine as a list of points and lines, represented as coordinate pairs and endpoint pairs, respectively. The program could then determine the falsity of certain conjectures, vis-a-vis this supplied interpretation, by examining the diagram. For example, when it conjectured that two triangles were congruent, their perimeters in the diagram were compared in the obvious way, by numerical computation. If the perimeters differed, no attempt was made to prove congruency.

Subsequent to the Geometry Machine, other work has been done in an attempt to incorporate semantic interpretations into geometry theorem proving. The goal of such work has in part been to reduce the space of formal operations and sentences by introducing heuristics to eliminate sterile paths and to focus effort on paths that are more likely to be successful, much as the Geometry Machine did. Most if not all of this work, however, construes the underlying problem as one of finding proofs by computations that maintain the syntactic constraints of a formal (linear-hierarchical) language, albeit aided by semantic heuristics. That is, the diagrams play a secondary role.

The work reported here can best be seen as removing the formal sentences from center stage, and placing the focus on the semantic interpretations. The system does not produce proofs in the literal sense of mathematics, and thus nothing it represents has the status of a mathematical theorem. To do so would require the reconstruction of the notion of proof into entirely diagrammatic terms. Several recent efforts by others have been made to do this but I do not have space here to review that work or describe it in relation to my work. Suffice it to say that they differ in intent and mechanism.

The objects that are represented and manipulated in my system are not sentences, but elements of geometric diagrams. One may argue that any representation of an element of a geometric diagram could be reduced to sentences, much as the "diagrams" in Gelernter's program were so represented. Indeed, one might argue that such a representational style is the only one available to conventional computers. I think such arguments are misguided, although at some level they are correct, and I have made this point repeatedly elsewhere (Lindsay 1963a, 1963b, 1973, 1988, 1989, 1992, 1993, 1996, 1997; Lindsay & Kochen 1987). Here I will merely summarize my analysis. Mathematical domains, such as geometry, have a structure that amounts to a set of constraints on what can be truly stated. In formal theories constraints are introduced by axioms and maintained by the proof procedure, all with computational objects that have linear structure and a hierarchical syntax. Constraints can also be introduced in other types of representations in ways that achieve the same ends. Some familiar examples are default hierarchies and spreadsheets. Although such representations forego the generality of formal language representation, they often exhibit large computational advantages. Furthermore, they often closely mirror human experience and hence human intuition, yielding greater plausibility as psychological models.

ARCHIMEDES is a programming language that can be used to represent geometric objects such as points, line segments, polygons and circles. The representations consist of a rectangular pixel array (defined by numerical coordinates), explicit links defining neighbor relations in eight directions (north, northeast, east, etc.), and frames that identify objects by their type and also record definitional information. The representations are constructed and processed in such a way that the structural properties of space (distance, direction, etc.) are maintained. In addition, other constraints, called situation constraints, may be stated and enforced. Situation constraints are not simply properties of space, but are assertions about a particular diagram, such as that two specific line segments must always be of the same length. The program can be instructed to construct additional elements of the diagram, and can be instructed to manipulate existing features, for example by translating an object in a given direction or rotating an object about a given point. These manipulations are called simulation constructions, and are accomplished by an algorithm that makes incremental changes while maintaining all constraints. Finally, the program can look at what it has constructed and what results from its manipulations and can detect certain newly emerged properties, such as that two objects have become superimposed, or that a new polygon has emerged by the conjoining of previously disconnected line segments.

Thus the primitive operations of this system are not processes that recognize, analyze, and manipulate linear-hierarchical formal sentences while maintaining their grammatical structure, but are perceptual and cognitive (simulated motor) processes that operate on structures that represent and maintain the semantic structure of two-dimensional space.

Given this functionality, it has been possible to "demonstrate" to the program certain propositions of geometry. Many of these were taken from the interesting compendia by Loomis (1940) and Nelsen (1993). Examples may be found in Lindsay (1998).

The result of this work is a system that can understand geometry in a limited sense. It can verify that performing the manipulations while honoring the spatial structure and maintaining the imposed situation constraints results in a representation that establishes the truth of a proposition (such as that the hypotenuse square of a right triangle has area equal to the sum of the areas of the squares on the other two sides). The program's understanding of the generality of such demonstrations is limited since it is based on observation and manipulation of a particular instance of a diagram. That problem is addressed by other computational methods that I will not describe here (see Lindsay 1998).

Discovering demonstrations

Verifying demonstrations in this fashion is a limited form of understanding that avoids the problem of determining the manipulations that underlie the demonstration; that problem is solved by the inventor of the demonstration. The program has been extended so that it can discover demonstrations by finding sequences of manipulations that achieve a particular end. Note that the system still must be given a goal proposition; it has no way to decide what might be an interesting proposition to demonstrate. It must also be given the diagram appropriate to the goal.

Consider Figure 1, taken from Nelsen (1993). An instance of this diagram was "drawn" for the program, which assigned names to the points as indicated and then noticed, and constructed in its memory, structures corresponding to each of the figures that were implicitly created by the construction of the major segments.

The program noticed the following objects.

points (13):	(n m l k j h g f e d c b a)
segments (42):	(fg bg eh dh fm bm en dn bj dj jn hn jm gm km dm cm ln bn cn bf de cl fl al bl ck ek ak dk gj cg ch hj ae ej fj af ad cd bc ab)
triangles (14):	(afb alb bcg bcm blf bnj adk ade cdn cdh cnh cgm dek djm)
rectangles (2):	(cgjh afje)
parallelograms (4):	(bcda bmka alnd cmkd)
quadrilaterals (54):	(jekm flnj dekm djmk cmdn cmjn clfm cnek cndk cgfl cgmk cgjn ckeh cmdh ckdh clnh cmjh cdnl cdjm cdjg cgmd cked alck alne afmk afjd afmd akmd alcd akcd bndm bmcn bgcn bnlf bjnl bmcl bgcl bjnc bnlc bflc bckm bnhc bjhc bcdn bcdj bcdm baln balc bcka bnea bjea bnda bjda bmda)

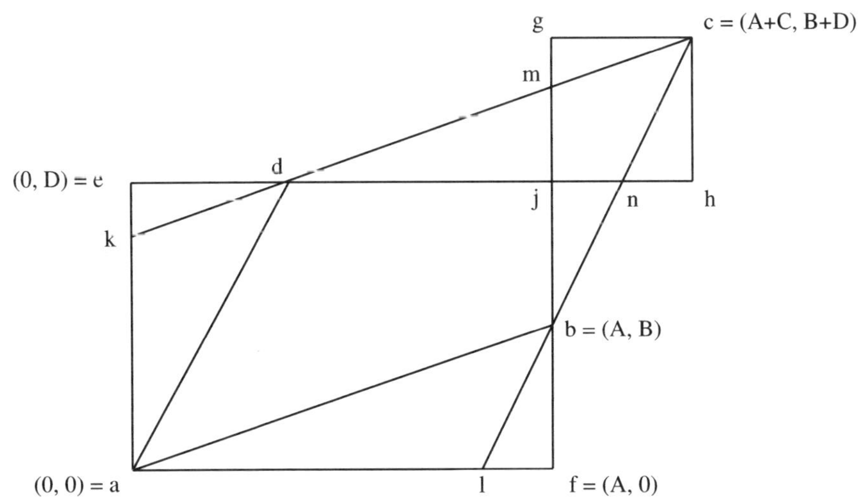

Figure 1. A 2 × 2 Determinant is the Area of a Parallelogram after Nelson (1993: 133)

This may appear to be a large number of objects, particularly of quadrilaterals, in that they do not all leap out at the human observer. However, each object can readily be found from its name and, with great care and good record keeping, one can produce these lists from an examination of the diagram. However, some of the objects listed above are degenerate, such as the "parallelogram cmkd" whose vertices are collinear, that is the "parallelogram" looks like a line segment. Such "objects" are not routinely detected by human perception (or perhaps more correctly are ignored by human cognition). The program does not cull these degenerate cases, though to do so would be straightforward.

Once the diagram has been drawn and the program has noticed this inventory of objects, it is given the target proposition: The area of rectangle afje equals the sum of the areas of rectangle cgjh and parallelogram bcda. That is, the area of the large rectangle is the area of the large parallelogram plus the area of the small rectangle. If one assigns point a to the origin and point b to (A, B), point c to (A+C, B+D) and d to (0, D), then the area of the large rectangle is $A \times D$ and of the small rectangle is $B \times C$. The 2×2 determinant

$$\begin{vmatrix} A & B \\ C & D \end{vmatrix} = AD \quad BC$$

is the difference in the areas of the two rectangles. The proposition as stated by Nelsen is that the value of this determinant equals the area of the large parallelogram. Transforming this statement to eliminate the minus sign yields the target proposition stated above.

Let us call the method now to be described Discover-1. It also works in exactly the same form for other demonstrations that depend upon establishing an area equivalence, including other examples in Lindsay (1998).

Discover-1 first attempts to see if it can verify the target from what it knows already. It does this by consulting a list of known area-equivalences (which initially is empty) and attempting to combine them by substitutions of equivalences and by using the properties of symmetry and transitivity of the equivalence relation. The knowledge of the properties of the equivalence relation and of substitution of equals is built into the program and is not related to its knowledge of space. Without such extra-spatial knowledge none of these "proofs without words" could be understood (or even verified). The geometric axiom system of Euclid includes such properties as axioms of "common notions," and the axiom system of Hilbert explicitly presupposes such properties as well. Thus predicative ("verbal") reasoning is an essential component of understanding these demonstrations. It is also essential for understanding geometry more generally, since predications are required for the statement of general conclusions.

Discover-1 next examines each side of the target proposition equation. Each object mentioned on either side is considered in turn. For each of these objects, every possible decomposition into a set of other objects is detected, such that the set exactly covers the initial object without overlap. For example, triangle ade can be decomposed into triangle adk plus triangle dek.

These computations are not done algebraically, but make use of the pixel representation and its underlying eight neighborhood relations that permit one to find the immediate neighbors of a given pixel. The method is a "color-spreading" iteration; see Ullman (1985). The interior of an object is marked by first labeling the border with one "color", say red. (This merely means that the associated pixels are marked with a "red" tag; when the diagram is displayed on a color monitor they in fact show as red.) Starting with an interior point of the object, that point is colored a different color, say orange, and each neighbor is examined. If a neighbor is border-colored or interior-colored already, it is ignored. Other neighbors are colored the interior-color and added to the list of points whose neighbors remain to be examined. The iteration continues until no more pixels remain on that list. Notice that this procedure works for closed objects of any shape, including non-convex polygons, circles, and any closed curve, such as Figure 2.

It should be pointed out that the discovery of an interior point is an interesting problem itself. This is a problem that human perception appears readily able to solve, provided the object is not too complex. Exactly what makes an object too complex for human perception is a matter for empirical study, but it is easy to find non-trivial examples such as Figure 3. Unlike the simple cases of Figures 1 and 2, where a person can immediately determine if a point is within a given object, examining Figure 3 requires a slower, sequential analysis, perhaps aided by pointing and tracing with a pencil.

Here Discover-1 relies on the fact that its objects are polygons. It discovers interior points by examination of several candidates such as the intersection of diagonals (which always works for non-degenerate convex polygons). The general problem of finding an interior point cannot be solved by Discover-1, and is indeed a subtle perceptual computation in the general case if the representation is a pixel array.

The next step in finding decompositions is to determine which other objects are contained within the putative container object. This is true of a polygon if its vertices are now either the interior-color or the border-color. This is not a sufficient condition for complete containment (consider a non-convex container), but partially overlapping false candidates are eliminated in the following steps. Next, the collection of all subsets of the set of contained objects is enumerated.

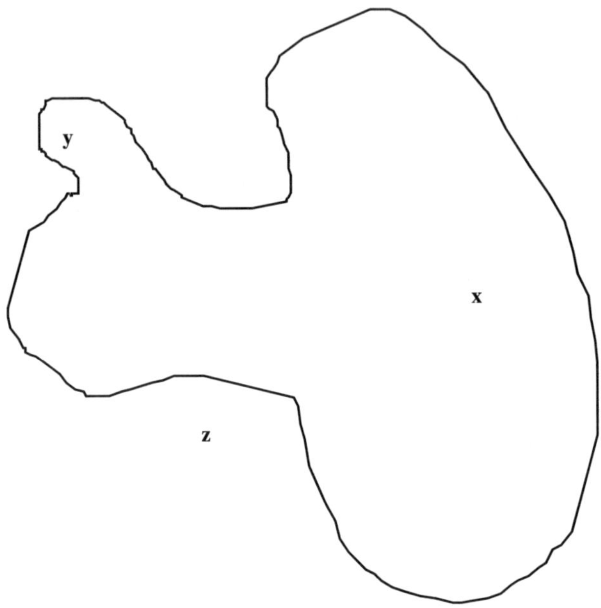

Figure 2. How many closed curves are there, 0, 1, 2, or 3? Which of x, y, and z are within one of them?

For example if there are three objects a, b, and c, there are seven non-null subsets: {a}, {b}, {c}, {a,b}, {a,c}, {b,c}, and {a,b,c}. In general with n objects there are 2^n-1 non-null subsets. Each of these subsets may or may not exactly decompose the initial object. There may be a very large number of such subsets to try. For example, there are nine objects that are at least partly within parallelogram bcda, yielding 511 subsets to examine (excluding the null set). To cull this large number, Discover-1 first considers the nine objects pair-wise and determines which pairs overlap; any two objects that overlap cannot both be part of an exact decomposition. Testing for overlap is done with a color-spreading procedure also. First the interior of one member of the pair is colored a distinct color, say yellow, and then the second interior is colored differently, say green, but coloring stops if yellow is encountered. Culling the 511 subsets mentioned above in this way leaves only 38 to be checked for exact fit.

This last step is done by tracing the boundary of the putative container and then tracing the boundaries of the subset of partially contained objects, halting if

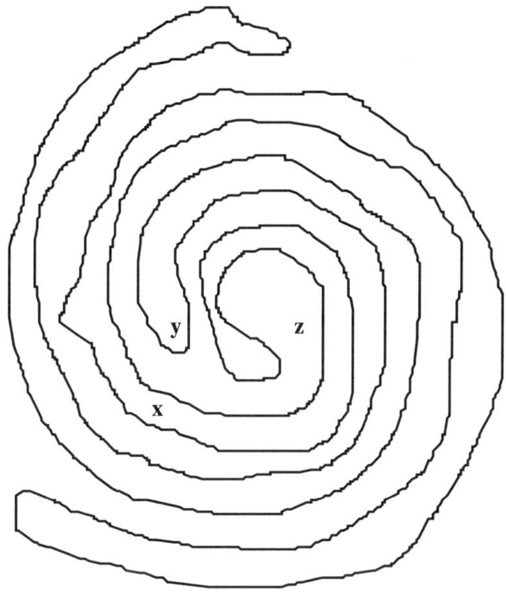

Figure 3. How many closed curves are there, 0, 1, 2, or 3? Which of x, y, and z are within one of them? Inspired by Minsky and Papert (1969).

the number of retracings is inconsistent with exact decomposition. The details are given in Lindsay (1998).

The result of these steps is to produce a set of area equivalences of the form: the area of the container equals the sum of the areas of the contained. With these additions to the list of known area equivalences, a test is again made to see if the target proposition follows from these by substitution, symmetry, and transitivity.

If this fails, as it does in this example, Discover-1 determines all possible congruencies that it sees in the diagram. For example, each pair of triangles is considered in turn. The program determines if one can be rotated and translated onto the other. If so, it generates the program that could demonstrate this by using the simulation construction algorithm. This program could actually be executed to effect the demonstration. However, here it is assumed that the program at this stage of its education knows that two triangles are congruent if they have sides that are equal pair-wise in the same order. (If they are equal but not in the same order they are still in fact congruent but one of them would have to be flipped in three-dimensional space to achieve coincidence, and Discover-1 does not know this because it does not know about three-dimensional space, so it cannot generate a simulation-construction program to do this and fails to detect this form of congruency.)

Every pair of congruent figures yields an area equivalence statement, and these are added to the list of known equivalences. In our example, this yields enough information to verify the target proposition.

Discussion

Discover-1 works both forward and backward, beginning with the goal proposition but then working from all present figures to see what inferences can be made. This proves to be a successful strategy for these demonstrations. However, Discover-1 is tailored to the kinds of operations that are useful in this and related demonstrations, those involving establishing a relation among areas, such as in the determinant problem and the Pythagorean Theorem. It is not a general method for discovering demonstrations.

Different methods, Discover-2, Discover-3, and so forth, will be needed for different classes of problems. What these methods will have in common is that they each will construct sequences of reasoning that reduce to manipulations of a diagram, that is, they work on the semantics of the diagram rather than the syntax of formal propositions. Again, this is not to say that they do not also use predicative reasoning or are not descriptive.

A more subtle question is whether these semantic methods employ predicative reasoning in the diagrammatic manipulations themselves. Here again, the answer is yes, although the predications are related to the semantics of space rather than to the algebra of equivalence relations. I call ARCHIMEDES' reasoning diagrammatic not to allege it is totally non-predicative, but because the structure of space is maintained by representations of diagrams, and this structure is used in substantive ways to make inferences.

Not all mental processes should be characterized as predicative. For example the sophisticated and skilled perceptual-motor processes exhibited by most mammals are more appropriately characterized as temporally continuous processes, albeit processes that on some occasions yield a result that can be stated as a predication. Some manipulations of diagrams may appropriately be described as non-predicative perceptual-like processes. However, *reasoning* refers to a special class of cognitive mental processes that, by definition, employ explicit predications. In most if not all cases these predications include generalizations, certainly so in the case of mathematics. Therefore if one insists that diagrammatic computations be limited to non-predicative processing, *purely diagrammatic reasoning*, *proof without words*, and even *diagrammatic demonstration* become oxymorons. There must be some way for the non-predicative computations to make contact with predications if reasoning is to be done.

In addition to procedural knowledge of two-dimensional space, propositional definitions of several types of geometric objects, and procedural knowledge of the algebra of area-equivalence, the program has built-in knowledge of other kinds. For example, it knows — that is, it behaves as though — translating and rotating rigid objects does not alter their area. (Incidentally, rigidity is a situation constraint, and the program can also manipulate non-rigid objects.) More generally it knows — that is, it behaves as though — area, length, angle measure, and ratios of these are independent of absolute position and orientation. In Lindsay (1997) I elaborated on the kinds of knowledge such a system must possess in order to do human-like geometric reasoning.

Where might this knowledge come from? In humans perhaps some was built into our nervous systems by evolution. Other human knowledge is doubtless induced by interacting with objects in space. Neither ARCHIMEDES nor any other existing program that I know of is able to acquire this knowledge from experience. The alternative chosen here was to build in knowledge as appropriate. This leads to what John Holland has called the unwrapping problem of AI: You put in the knowledge and wrap it up with a lot of code. Then you unwrap it and say "Aha, the system knows this!" This is ultimately unsatisfying, and eventually must be replaced with an account of how new knowledge is acquired. Of course if one is only interested in building intelligent machines rather than understanding human minds it is not logically necessary that the machines be adaptive, although in practice it may in fact be necessary for success. Viewed as a work of psychological theory, building in knowledge is justified insofar as it describes what knowledge is actually sufficient to account for interesting human behavior.

There is no way to establish the *necessity* of any theory in psychology or any other science. All that can be done is to postulate a theory and compare its behavior to the phenomena to be explained. This research has demonstrated the *sufficiency* of a set of operations, described in functional terms, for accomplishing certain tasks, namely discovering and verifying demonstrations of a certain type. One can be far more demanding than the gross description of human performance examined here, and even slightly more stringent demands would soon yield clear differences in behavior between ARCHIMEDES and humans.

The operations found sufficient can be described at many levels of analysis. At the level of function — what answers are given to what questions — they relate to the structure of space and the semantics of diagrams. Described thus, they do such things as find interior points and area decompositions. Each of these functions could be realized with a variety of methods. For example, curves might be described algebraically and locations of points with respect to these curves could be computed numerically or symbolically. In ARCHIMEDES they were implemented by edge-following and color-spreading methods. Color-spreading computations have the virtue that they apply to arbitrary closed curves as readily as to polygons, and that is consonant with human performance even as measured informally by self-observation. Thus color spreading methods bear a certain degree of psychological plausibility that algebraic methods do not, although this in and of itself offers minimal support for psychological claims.

Having selected edge-following and color-spreading as the methods that implement the interior finding and decomposition functions, one may still choose among a variety of computational styles that follow edges and spread colors. In the present work these have been implemented as pixel-array operations on a digital computer using a list processing language. Once an implementation has been made the operations have a certain efficiency profile (i.e., solution-time for each problem). The same function and method (e.g., area-decomposition by color-spreading) could be implemented in different ways on different computer architectures, say an array processor, neural net, or brain. A fully implemented psychological theory would be tested primarily by comparing its efficiency profile with that of humans, using the usual methods of empirical psychology.

For example, it is not clear why finding interiors by color-spreading should be more difficult for complex stimuli than for simple ones (compare Figure 2 and Figure 3), as alluded to above. And yet humans, even when working from a physical display, readily get lost on complex figures and are aided by actual pencil shading or tracing analogous to the calculations of the color spreading method. When working from mental images rather than physical diagrams, humans have much greater difficulty keeping track of what has been examined, and yet are able to do so for at least intermediate levels of complexity. A good psychological model would posit implementations that separate the spreading from the bookkeeping aspects of these methods and show how they respond differentially to memory loads.

Present knowledge from cognitive neuroscience gives little assistance in determining how such algorithms could be embodied in brain. To the extent that the implementations are plausible as putative psychological processes by virtue of a reasonable efficiency profile, they might serve as a guide for neuroscience explorations. Thus it is conceivable, as the methods of cognitive neuroscience develop, that one could seek evidence that the brain does or does not implement these methods in specific ways with specific neural structures and functions.

Acknowledgments

This material is based on work supported by the United States National Science Foundation under Grant No. IRI-9526942.

References

Gelernter, Herbert (1959). Realization of a geometry theorem proving machine. In *International Conference on Information Processing* (273–282). Paris: UNESCO House.

Gelernter, Herbert, James R. Hansen & Donald W. Loveland (1960). Empirical explorations of the geometry theorem proving machine. In *Western Joint Computer Conference,* 17 (143–147). New York: National Joint Computer Committee. (Reprinted in E. A. Feigenbaum & J. Feldman (Eds.) *Computers and Thought*, 1963, New York: McGraw Hill.)

Lindsay, Robert K. (1963a). Inferential memory as the basis of machines which understand natural language. In E. A. Feigenbaum & J. Feldman (Eds.), *Computers and Thought*. (217–233). New York, NY: McGraw-Hill.

Lindsay, Robert K. (1963b). A program for parsing sentences and making inferences about kinship relations. In A. C. Hoggatt & F. E. Balderston (Eds.), *Symposium on Simulation Models: Methodology and Applications to the Behavioral Sciences*. (111–138). Cincinnati, OH: South-Western.

Lindsay, Robert K. (1973). In defense of ad hoc systems. In R. Schank & K. Colby (Eds.), *Computer Models of Thought and Language*. (372–395). San Francisco: W. H. Freeman.

Lindsay, Robert K. (1988). Images and inference. *Cognition*, 29, 229–250. (Reprinted in J. I. Glasgow, N. H. Narayanan, and B. Chandrasekaran (Eds.), *Diagrammatic Reasoning: Computational and cognitive perspectives*. Cambridge, MA: MIT Press, 1995, 111–135).

Lindsay, Robert K. (1989). Qualitative geometric reasoning. In *Proceedings of the Eleventh Annual Conference of the Cognitive Science Society* (Ann Arbor, MI), 1 (418–425). Hillsdale, NJ: Lawrence Erlbaum.

Lindsay, Robert K. (1992). Diagrammatic reasoning by simulation. In *Reasoning with Diagrammatic Representations. Technical Report SS-92–02*. (130–135). Menlo Park, CA: American Association for Artificial Intelligence.

Lindsay, Robert K. (1993). Distinguishing visual imagery and spatial reasoning. *Computational Intelligence*, 9(4), 343–345.

Lindsay, Robert K. (1996). Generalizing from diagrams. In *Cognitive and Computational Models of Spatial Reasoning*. (51–55). Menlo Park, CA: American Association for Artificial Intelligence.

Lindsay, Robert K. (1997). Knowing about diagrams. In M. Anderson (Ed.), *Reasoning with diagrammatic representations II*. (15–22). Menlo Park, CA: AAAI Press.

Lindsay, Robert K. (1998). Using diagrams to understand geometry. *Computational Intelligence*, 14(2), 222–256.

Lindsay, Robert K. & Manfred Kochen (1987). Novelty and redundancy in problem solving. In M. Kochen & H. M. Hastings (Eds.), *Advances in Cognitive Science: Steps Toward Convergence*. (228–240). Boulder, CO: Westview Press.

Loomis, Elisha S. (1940). *Pythagorean Proposition: Its proofs analyzed and classified and bibliography of sources for data of the four kinds of "proofs"* (2nd ed.). Ann Arbor, MI: Edwards Brothers.

Minsky, Marvin & Seymour Papert (1969). *Perceptrons*. Cambridge, MA and London, England: MIT Press.

Nelsen, Roger B. (1993). *Proofs without Words. Exercises in Visual Thinking.* Washington, D. C.: The Mathematical Association of America.

Newell, Allen, J. Clifford Shaw & Herbert A. Simon (1957). Empirical explorations with the Logic Theory Machine. In *Proceedings of the Western Joint Computer Conference,* 15 (218–239). (Reprinted in E. A. Feigenbaum and J. Feldman (Eds.), *Computers and Thought*, 1963, New York: McGraw-Hill, 109–133.)

Ullman, Shimon (1985). Visual routines. In S. Pinker (Ed.), *Visual Cognition*. (97–159). Cambridge, MA: MIT Press. (Reprinted from Cognition: International Journal of Cognitive Psychology, vol. 18, 1–63.)

Formal Specifications of Image Schemata for Interoperability in Geographic Information Systems

Andrew U. Frank and Martin Raubal
Technical University Vienna

Introduction

Exchange of data between GIS and interoperability of different vendors' GIS software are topics of enormous practical interest (Buehler & McKee 1996). Unambiguous definitions are at the core of any effort to achieve the necessary standardization that allows data exchange and cooperation of different GIS.

Standardization of technical terms and the fundamental concepts necessary to make computers interact is mostly achieved or can be achieved with current tools. The abstract behavior of computerized systems can be specified in a formal language and it requires then the checking of the compliance of the target computer system — which is by definition also a formal system — with the abstract formal system. This problem is not particular for GIS but general for all computer system standardization. The difficulties are of a practical nature and related to the lack of formal definition of most current computer languages, commercial interests in maintaining incompatible systems, and the rapid development compounded with legacy systems.

The economically important and scientifically challenging question is to describe the meaning of GIS data in terms of the real world, i.e., the so-called *semantics problem*. What does it mean that "P 271" is a point, "343a" a land parcel, that building "A1" is on parcel "343a", A-town is on the B-river, etc., and how is this meaning communicated between systems. The naive assumption that a "rose is a rose is a rose" (Gertrude Stein) is obviously not correct: the definitions of simple geographic properties differ from country to country, despite corresponding names (Chevallier 1981; Mark 1993; Kuhn 1994).

Image schemata describe high-level, abstract structures of common situations, most of them expressing spatial relations (Johnson 1987). Image schemata (Johnson 1987; Lakoff 1987) are the fundamental experiential elements from which spatial meaning is constructed, but so far image schemata have mostly resisted formal descriptions. This paper shows exemplar formalizations of image schemata important in the geographic context (PATH) and in tabletop space (CONTAINER, SURFACE). This investigation is, therefore, part of the quest for naive or commonsense physics (Hayes 1978, 1985; Hobbs & Moore 1985) and in particular for "Naive Geography" (Egenhofer & Mark 1995).

The next section argues why the formalization of spatial relations in geographic space is crucial for further advances in the standardization and interoperability of GIS. In Section 3 the specification of image schemata is discussed and Section 4 describes methods to formalize image schemata. Section 5 gives a comprehensive method — built upon linguistics — to discover and formally describe image schemata. Section 6 explains exemplar image schemata for geographic and tabletop space (i.e., PATH, CONTAINER, SURFACE) and presents their formalizations. Section 7 presents conclusions, discusses open questions, and suggests directions for further research.

Formalizing spatial meaning

The spatial domain — in which GIS facts are situated — is fundamental for human living and one of the major sources for human experience (Barrow 1992). Human language exploits the communality of spatial experience among people and uses spatial situations metaphorically to structure purely abstract situations in order to communicate them (Lakoff & Johnson 1980; Johnson 1987). The formalization of spatial relations has, therefore, been an active area of research at least since 1989 (Mark et al. 1995).

Topological relations between simply connected regions were treated in (Egenhofer 1989) and extensive work has followed from this (Egenhofer 1994). Metric relations between point-like objects, especially cardinal directions (Frank 1991b; Frank 1991a; Freksa 1991; Hernández 1991) and approximate distances (Frank 1992; 196b; Hernández et al. 1995) were discussed. Other efforts dealt with orderings among configurations of points (Schlieder 1995) and formal descriptions of terrain and relations in terrain (Frank et al. 1986), but formal methods were also used to formally describe the working of administrative systems — e.g., cadastre (Frank 1996a). Linguists have made systematic efforts to clarify the meaning of spatial prepositions (Herskovits 1986, 1997; Lakoff 1987). However, it remains an open question how to combine these interesting results within a uniform system and to apply them systematically to other examples.

The specification of spatial relations is of great practical interest to define spatial relations in spatial query languages unambiguously; the current plethora of proposals for spatial relations to complete database query languages is useless unless the relations are formally specified (which is the case for the standard relations in SQL) (Egenhofer 1992). The formal properties are the base for query optimization. Image schemata are considered good candidates as a foundation for the formal definition of spatial relations. Kuhn has pointed out the importance of image schemata as a tool to build "natural" (i.e., cognitively sound) user interfaces for GIS (Kuhn & Frank 1991; Kuhn 1993).

Specification of image schemata

Johnson (1987) proposes that people use recurring, imaginative patterns — so-called *image schemata* — to comprehend and structure their experiences while moving through and interacting with their environment. Image schemata are supposed to be pervasive, well defined, and full of sufficient internal structure to constrain people's understanding and reasoning. They are more abstract than mental pictures and less abstract than logical structures because they are constantly operating in people's minds while people are experiencing the world (Kuhn & Frank 1991). An image schema can, therefore, be seen as a very generic, maybe universal, and abstract structure that helps people to establish a connection between different experiences that have this same recurring structure in common.

Previous formal description of image schemata

Despite efforts, success in specifying spatial image schemata has been limited. An early paper (Kuhn & Frank 1991) gave algebraic definitions for the CONTAINER ("in") and SURFACE ("on") schemata for a discussion of user interface design. At the level of detail and for the purpose of the paper, the two specifications were isomorphic. A recent effort by Rodríguez and Egenhofer (1997) introduced more operations and differentiated the CONTAINER schema from the SURFACE schema for small-scale space, using operations such as *remove*, *jerk*, and *has_contact*, and compared the application to objects in small-scale and large-scale (geographic) space. Raubal et al. (1997) presented a methodology based on image schemata to structure people's wayfinding tasks.

Image schemata were represented in the form of predicates in which the predicate name referred to the image schema and the argument(s) referred to the object(s) involved in the image schema (see also Raubal 1997).

In a recent paper (Frank 1998) formal descriptions for the small-scale-space-image-schemata CONTAINER, SURFACE, and LINK were given and some of the methodological difficulties reviewed. The large-scale-space-image-schemata LOCATION, PATH, REGION, and BOUNDARY were treated in (Frank & Raubal 1998).

Definition of the concept of an image schema

The concept of image schemata is not well defined in the cognitive and linguistic literature (Lakoff & Johnson 1980; Johnson 1987; Lakoff 1987). Researchers in the past have used a working definition that implied that image schemata describe spatial (and similar physical) relations between objects. Most have concentrated on spatial prepositions like "in", "on", etc., and assumed that these relate directly to the image schemata (Freundschuh & Sharma 1996; Raubal et al. 1997; Raubal 1997).

Image schemata are seen as fundamental and independent of the type of space and spatial experience. But a single schema can appear in multiple, closely related situations. For example, "in" is used for a bowl of fruit ("Der Apfel ist in der Schale." — "The apple is in the fruit bowl."), but also for closed containers ("Das Geld ist im Beutel." — "The money is in the purse."). "Prototype effects" as described by Rosch (1973a,b, 1978) also seem to apply. For example, different levels of detail can be selected to describe the same image schema.

Language dependence of particular image schemata

It is possible that image schemata provide language-independent building blocks for structure and different languages may combine the building blocks differently; the list of image schemata overlaps with Wierzbicka's list of universal language primes (Wierzbicka 1996). The obvious differences between languages are one important point in the cultural difference that hinders the use of GIS (Campari & Frank 1995) and the problem is further aggravated by regional differences within a language.

Methods to formalize image schemata

Predicate calculus

Lakoff (1987) gives a definition of the CONTAINER schema using predicate calculus. In theory, predicate calculus has all the expressive power necessary, but it is practically limited by the frame problem, which makes succinct definition for changes impossible (Hayes 1977; McCarthy 1985). McCarthy (1980, 1986) proposed situation calculus with circumscription as an extension of the logical theory to overcome this limitation.

Relations calculus

The behavior of topological relations (Egenhofer 1994; Papadias & Sellis 1994), but also cardinal directions and approximate distances (Hernández et al. 1995; Freksa 1991; Frank 1992; Frank 1996b) can be analyzed using the relations calculus (Schröder, 1895; Tarski 1941; Maddux 1991). Properties of relations are described as the outcome of the combination (the ";" operator) of two relations. The description abstracts away the individuals related (in comparison to the predicate calculus) and gives a simple algebra over relations. This leads to succinct and easy-to-read tables, as long as the combination of only a few relations is considered.

a (R;S) c = aRb and bSc
for example: North;NorthEast = {North or NorthEast}
meet;inside = {inside, covered, overlap}

Functions

Functions are more appropriate to capture the semantics of image schemata with respect to operations. Relation composition is replaced by function composition (the "." operator). In order to use this notation flexibly, a "curried" form of function writing must be used (Bird & Wadler 1988; Bird & de Moor 1997).

$$f \cdot g\ (x) = f\ (g\ (x)).$$

Function composition can be described by tables as well, but these grow even faster than relation composition tables. Axiomatic descriptions as algebras are more compact but also more difficult to read.

Model based

A model of the scene is constructed and used for reasoning — there is some evidence that this is also one of the methods humans apply (Knauff et al. 1995). A fundamental set of operations to construct any possible state of the model and a sufficient number of "observe" operations to differentiate any of these states are provided. In addition, more complex operations can be constructed using the given operations.

The simplest model is to use the constructors of the scene directly and to represent each scene as the sequence of constructors that created it (Rodríguez 1997). This gives a (possibly executable) model for functional or relation oriented description.

Such models can be ontological — modeling some subset of the existing world — or they can be epistemological — modeling exclusively the human conceptualization of the world. More than one epistemological view can follow from an ontological model.

Tools used

Formal specifications written and checked only by human minds must be regarded with great skepticism: humans are not particularly apt in finding errors in formal descriptions. For effective work, formal (computerized) tools must be used. Two types have been used: Logic-based languages — e.g., Prolog (Clocksin & Mellish 1981) — used for the definition of spatial terminology (Frank et al. 1986) and for spatial relations calculus (Egenhofer 1989). Logic-based systems must use "extralogical" operations when change is considered (*assert* and *retract* in Prolog). Recently, functional languages (Bird & Wadler 1988) have been advocated (Frank 1994; Kuhn & Frank 1997), especially Haskell (Peterson et al. 1997) and Gofer (Jones 1991, 1994). Allegories (a special kind of categories) provide the theoretical structure to unify the two approaches (Bird & de Moor 1997).

A linguistic method to discover and describe image schemata

Mark and Frank (1996) showed how image schemata can be deduced from natural-language expressions describing geographic situations. The image schema that has been in the speaker's mind while making a statement can be inferred from the preposition (e.g., in, on, under) used (Mark 1989). The same approach was also used by Freundschuh & Sharma (1996), Raubal et al., (1997) and Frank (1998). A number of restrictions and assumptions are necessary to make progress with this line of investigation:

Operational definition of image schemata

As an operational definition of image schemata we consider spatial situations as image schemata if they can be used as a source domain for metaphorical transfer to some target domain; this demonstrates that a commonly understood structural content, which is independent of the specific situation, exists.

Assumption of polysemy

A single word may have multiple meanings (e.g., the English word "spring" can be the verb "to jump", a season, a source, etc.). We assume that polysemy helps to initially separate what are potentially different meanings of a word for formalization. If the meanings are the same after formal description is achieved, the assumed polysemy can be dropped.

Exclusion of partial spatial relations

Spatial relations may be partial: a pen may be partially on a sheet of paper, a city partially in one, partially in another state or country (e.g., Niagara Falls is a city both in Canada and the U.S.A.). At the present time such situations are excluded from consideration and their analysis is postponed. Ongoing work by Egenhofer (Rashid et al. 1998) to differentiate situations with the same topology by metric measures characterizing the degree of overlap etc. may answer these questions.

Restriction to a single level of detail and abstraction

The level of abstraction differs depending on the requirements of the situation (Timpf et al. 1992; Voisard & Schweppe 1994, 1997). These multiple levels of detail play an especially important part in geographic space and make the specification of image schemata difficult. Level of detail may be spatial subdivision, may be the consideration of additional rules, or may be the subdivision of categories into subcategories (Jordan et al. 1998; Giunchiglia & Walsh 1992). All these effects are excluded from this investigation.

Different image-schematic details for geographic and tabletop spaces

We assume that image-schematic details for geographic space are separate from image-schematic details for small-scale space (Montello 1993; Couclelis 1992). Some of Johnson's (1987) suggested image schemata use terminology from geographic space (e.g., PATH), others suggest that the same image schema (e.g., SURFACE) is used for different types of spaces. If the same terminology is used, we assume here — for methodological reasons — polysemy.

Concentration on a single language and epistemology

The examples given here are in German (with English translations) as this is the authors' native language; the results can be compared with the English language situation and some differences observed (Herskovits 1986; Montello 1995). The language examples are the driving force here and the concentration is on the epistemology.

Formal specifications of image schemata for large-scale and small-scale space

This section shows examples of image-schematic formalizations for geographic and tabletop space.

Example of formal image-schematic specification for large-scale space

The subset of reality considered here consists of some geographic-space-objects plus the immediate relations between them. Our example focuses on the path schema: A PATH connects locations and consists of a starting point, an endpoint and a connection between them, as defined in (Johnson 1987).

Geographic space is rich in derived spatial relations and only when we consider the movement of persons in the landscape preconditions and changes in the scene — of which the person is part — must be discussed. The relations among geographic objects are static and can, therefore, be formalized with predicate calculus. For each given relation, a converse relation exists. Relations are written in a prefix notation (similar to a predicate). Path (a, b) means there exists a path from a to b. This world is closed in the logical sense (Reiter 1984): everything is known about the scene and what is not known can be assumed to be false. In particular, there are no unknown objects; all objects have different names, and all relations are known or inferred from the image schemata. This is all typically not the case in natural human discourse.

Location and relations between places

A path connects places. We differentiate between the simple "direct path" and the "indirect path", which consists of a sequence of "direct paths." At this level, different types of paths are not differentiated (i.e., no particulars of railways, highways, etc., are considered).

A direct path connects locations directly, without any intervening location (at the level of detail considered). A direct path has a start and an end location (Figure 1a). At this level of detail there is no need to model 'path' as an object, just as a relation between two places (path (a, b)).

Es gibt einen Weg von Wien nach Baden.
There is a path from Vienna to Baden.

For this environment (but not for a city with one-way streets) the path relation is symmetric (Figure 1b):

path (a, b) ⇔ *path (b, a)*

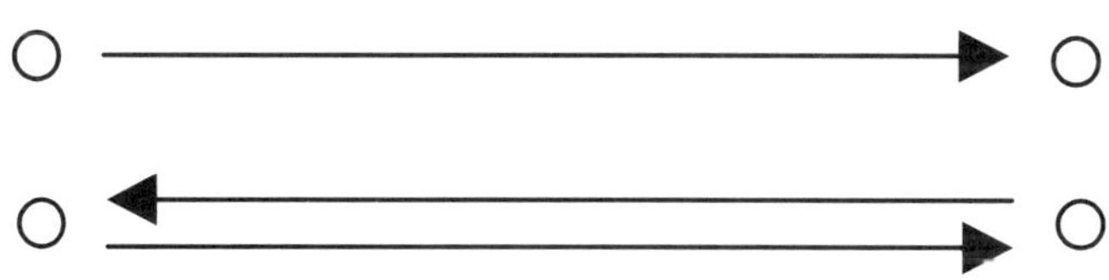

Figure 1a,b. Direct path and symmetry of path relation

Path is its own converse relation:

Du kannst von Baden nach Wien fahren und am Abend wieder zurück.
You can drive from Baden to Vienna, and back in the evening.
conv (path (a, b)) = path (b, a) = path (a, b)

It is derived from a non-redundant base relation as the symmetric completion.

An indirect (transitive) path (ind-path) connects two locations through a sequence of direct-path-relations, such that the end location of one direct path is the start location of the next path (Figure 2).

ind-path (a, b) = [path (a, a1) & path (a1, a2) & path (a2, ...) & ... & path (..., bn) & path (bn, b)]
conv (ind-path) = ind-path

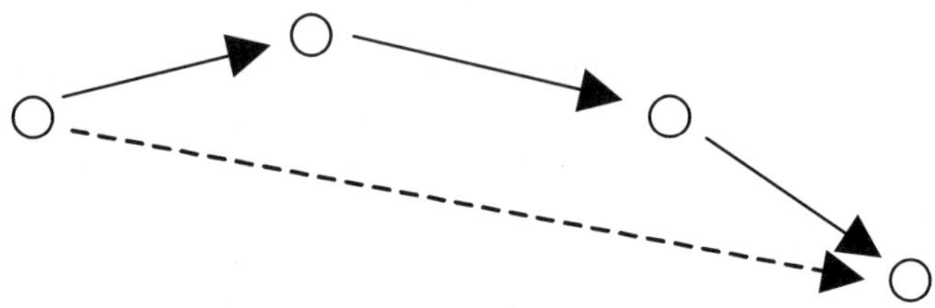

Figure 2. Indirect path

The indirect path is derived using transitive closure. The details of the algorithm are particular to deal with cyclic and bi-directional graphs as formed by path networks and well known as the shortest path algorithm (Dijkstra 1959; Sedgewick 1983).

Persons (and other autonomous and movable objects)
Persons move to places and are then "in" the place, unless they move further:

Er ist nach Györ gefahren; jetzt wartet er dort auf dich.
He went to Györ; now he is waiting there for you.
scene2 = move (place1, scene1) ⇒ isIn (place2, scene2)

If a person is found "in" place p1 at time t1 and place p2 at time t2 one can deduce a move (Figure 3):

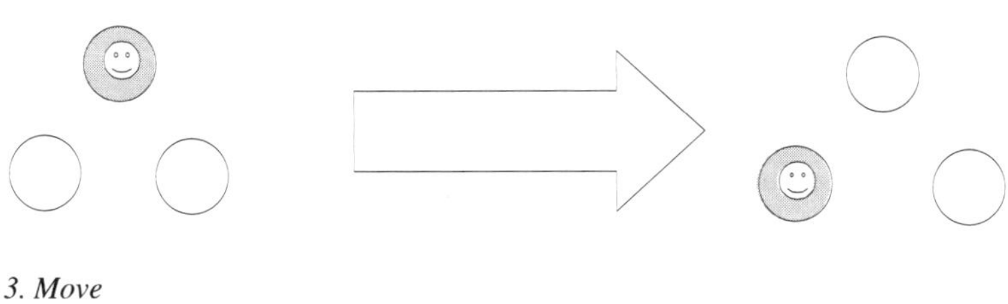

Figure 3. Move

Simon war letzte Woche in der Steiermark; jetzt ist er wieder in Wien.
Ist er am Samstag oder am Sonntag nach Hause gefahren?
Last week Simon was in Styria; now he is back in Vienna.
Did he drive home on Saturday or Sunday? (move inferred in the time in-between)

To move requires for a person some preconditions, unestablishes (retracts) some facts, and establishes new facts:

> *move (p, a, b): in (p, a) & path (a, b)*
> *unestablish (in (p, a)), establish (in (p, b))*

A person cannot move from one place to another unless there is a path:

> *Du kannst von Baden nicht direkt nach Schwechat fahren; du musst über Wien fahren.*
> *You cannot drive directly from Baden to Schwechat; you have to go through Vienna.*

If the person is at an unspecified location within a region, then it is only required that there is a path from every location in this region to the target.

Formal executable model
A formal, executable model for a complete set of relations has been written in a functional programming language. The difficulties of coding have mostly to do with finding consistent conventions to name all the relations. Most rules can be written as equations between relations and relation-transforming functions — i.e., point-free in the categorical sense (Bird & de Moor 1997) — and the formulae are valid for any scene.

Example of formal image-schematic specification for small-scale space

In the second case study — tabletop space — we concentrate on the affordability of movement. Again, for each relation we have a converse *(a (conv Rel) b = b Rel a)*. The spatial relations and their converses are interpreted as Boolean functions *fRel (a, b)* $\rightarrow$ *Bool*, or functions that return for an object the relatum *fRel (a)* $\rightarrow$ *b = a Rel b*. We say that an object *participates* in a spatial relation *Rel* if the corresponding *fRel* returns an object (this is equivalent to $\exists$ *b: a Rel b*).

We consider the following image schemata for small-scale (tabletop) space:

a. CONTAINER: A CONTAINER has an inside, an outside, and a boundary.
b. SURFACE: The SURFACE schema is used to describe the support of objects.

We focus on the common-sense spatial reasoning conclusions from the relations "in" (CONTAINER) and "auf" (SURFACE) between an object and a relatum, and the operations to establish such relations (*moveIn, moveAuf*).

"In" blocks target of movement
An object cannot be moved to a target if this is already in another object (Figure 4). This is justified by situations such as:

x 'in' y (in scene) ⇒ blocked (move z into x (in scene))
Du musst den Beutel zuerst aus der Tasche nehmen, bevor du die Münze hineingeben kannst.
You must take the purse out of the pocket to put the coin in.

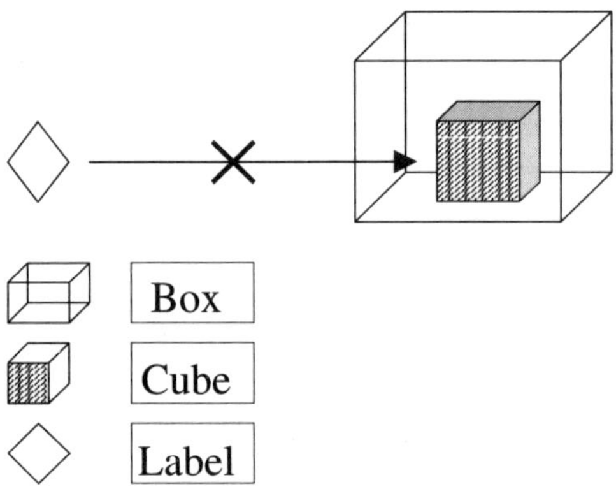

Figure 4. Cube is in box. Not permitted: paste label on cube

Converse of "auf" blocks object of movement
"Auf" blocks the movement of the supporting object (Figure 5). It cannot be moved unless the object "auf" it is removed.

x 'auf' y (in scene) ⇒ blocked (move y in scene)
Teller und Gläser sind auf dem Tisch. Wir müssen den Tisch zuerst abräumen, bevor wir ihn auf die andere Seite des Zimmers bringen können.
Plates and glasses are on the table. We have to remove all objects from the table, before we can move it to the other side of the room.

Formal model
A function composition model can be constructed and the rules listed are directly coded. The central operation "move" for one example given with the arguments: relation type, object, target, scene is shown below;

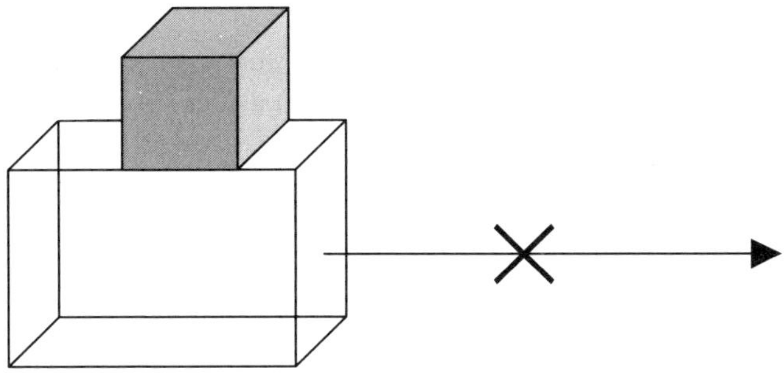

Figure 5. Cube is on (auf) box. Not possible: move box

move i a b s =
if fRel' In b s –rule 7.2 : in blocks target of movement
then error ("in blocked: already in")
move i a b s

Conclusions, open questions and future work

Formal descriptions of spatial relations as encountered in everyday life are very important for GIS. They can be used to formally define query language predicates and to optimize the execution of spatial queries. They are crucial for the specification of spatial data exchange formats and GIS interoperability standards.

Most previous efforts to analyze spatial relations have used relation calculus and have concentrated on spatial relations that are amenable to this treatment. The extension of relation calculus to a function calculus is discussed here, linking two previously unconnected tools. The two tools are not as different and their conceptual merging can be found in category theory (Barr & Wells 1990; Herring et al. 1990; Asperti & Longo 1991; Walters 1991). Function composition tables can be used similarly to relation composition tables; they show patterns that can then be succinctly formulated as rules.

In this paper we applied a linguistic method based on prepositions to describe image schemata. We showed examples for large-scale and small-scale space and presented them in a formal way. With this approach common-sense knowledge about the environment considered is captured in a strong set of implications following from individual relations.

Many open questions still remain and should be considered for further research:

Methodological

The method used here is borrowed from linguistics. For linguistic demonstrations, a single utterance that is acceptable by a native speaker is sufficient to demonstrate the existence of a construct. Is a single commonsense reasoning chain as given here sufficient? It documents that at least one situation exists where the suggested spatial inference is made — thus it demonstrates at least one aspect of a spatial relation in (one human's) cognition. In order to verify the universality of such spatial inference mechanisms, extended human subjects testing among people with different native languages is needed.

Language-independent primitives

Can language-independent primitives be identified — in the sense of Wierzbicka (1996)? Investigation of the same domain by researchers with different mother tongues would be necessary (or at least a collection of the related natural language descriptions). For the domains and examples here, the spatial inferences are also correct in the translations, but the use of spatial prepositions differs between German and English.

Relation between relations and functions

The use of category theory to establish a common theoretical ground for a relation (static) view and a function (dynamic) view is new and must be further explored. A category can be constructed over both functions and relations (Bird & de Moor 1997). It is also possible to map relations into functions (aRb $\rightarrow$ f (a,b) : Bool) and functions into a relation (f (a):: b $\rightarrow$ aRb) as was used here. Certain formalizations seem to be easier in the one, others in the other.

In any case, the formulae must be interpreted with respect to an "environment" of the facts (we used the term "scene"). Functions like "move" change the scene. We currently experiment with monads — a device from category theory — to have the environment implicit in the formulae and, therefore, reduce the complexity of formalization (Wadler 1997; Liang et al. 1995).

Composition and interaction of image schemata

The combination of multiple image schemata and the interaction of image schemata with object's properties must be further explored. For an object to move along a path, it must be of the appropriate kind (only trains run along railway lines, cars cannot follow a footpath, etc., and similar restrictions apply in other cases). Possibly, the current approach of trying to capture image schemata with the definition of spatial prepositions is too limited. Raubal et al. (1997) used prepositions and semantic connotation to investigate superimpositions of image schemata. Another interesting approach is to look at affordances. Affordances seem to be closely related to image schemata because both of these concepts help people to understand a spatial situation in order to know what to do (Gibson 1979). Affordances might be operational building blocks of image schemata but further research in this area is needed (Jordan et al. 1998).

Are image schemata the smallest constituent parts of spatial cognition?

Are image schemata the atoms of spatial cognition or are there smaller semantic units from which image schemata can be composed? It appears as if these were smaller pieces from which the more complex image schemata could be built, but one could also argue that these are the image schemata proper.

Acknowledgments

Numerous discussions with Werner Kuhn, Max Egenhofer, David Mark, and Andrea Rodríguez have contributed to our understanding of image schemata and their importance for GIS. We appreciate the efforts of Roswitha Markwart to edit the manuscript. Damir Medak prepared the environment used here for formalization. Funding from the Oesterreichische Nationalbank and the Chorochronos project supported the base work underlying the formalization presented here.

References

Asperti, Andrea & Guiseppe Longo (1991). Categories, types and structures: An introduction to category theory for the working computer scientist. Cambridge, Mass.: MIT Press.

Barr, Michael & Charles Wells (1990). *Category Theory for Computing Science*. London: Prentice Hall.

Barrow, John D. (1992). *Pi in the Sky: Counting, thinking and being*. Oxford: Clarendon Press.

Bird, Richard & Oege de Moor (1997). *Algebra of Programming*. London: Prentice Hall.

Bird, Richard & Philip Wadler (1988). *Introduction to Functional Programming*. Hemel Hempstead, UK: Prentice Hall International.

Buehler, Kurt & Lance McKee (Eds.) (1996). *The OpenGIS Guide: An Introduction to interoperable geoprocessing*. Wayland, Mass., USA: The OGIS Project Technical Committee of the Open GIS Consortium.

Campari, Irene & Andrew U. Frank (1995). Cultural differences and cultural aspects in GIS. In Nyerges, T., D. Mark, R. Laurini & M. Egenhofer (Eds.), *Cognitive Aspects of Human-Computer Interaction for Geographic Information Systems* (249–266). Dordrecht, The Netherlands: Kluwer.

Chevallier, J. (1981). Land information systems: A global and system theoretic approach. In proceedings of FIG International Federation of Surveyors, Montreux, Switzerland, 3, 301.2.

Clocksin, William F. & Christopher S. Mellish (1981). *Programming in Prolog*. Berlin: Springer-Verlag.

Couclelis, Helen (1992). People manipulate objects (but cultivate fields): Beyond the raster-vector debate in GIS. In Frank, A. U., I. Campari & U. Formentini (Eds.), *Theories and Methods of Spatio-Temporal Reasoning in Geographic Space* [Lecture Notes in Computer Science 639, 65–77]. Berlin: Springer-Verlag.

Dijkstra, Edsger (1959). A note on two problems in connection with graphs. *Numerische Mathematik*, 1, 269–271.

Egenhofer, Max (1989). Spatial query languages. Ph.D. thesis, University of Maine, Orono, USA.

Egenhofer, Max (1992). Why not SQL! *International Journal of Geographical Information Systems*, 6(2), 71–85.

Egenhofer, Max (1994). Deriving the composition of binary topological relations. *Journal of Visual Languages and Computing,* 5(2), 133–149.

Egenhofer, Max & David Mark (1995). Naive geography. In Frank, A. U. & W. Kuhn (Eds.), *Spatial Information Theory: A theoretical basis for GIS. Int. Conference COSIT'95* [Lecture Notes in Computer Science 988, 1–15]. Berlin: Springer-Verlag.

Frank, Andrew U. (1991a) Qualitative spatial reasoning with cardinal directions. In proceedings of 7th Austrian Symposium on Artificial Intelligence, Vienna, Austria, 157–167.

Frank, Andrew U. (1991b). Qualitative spatial reasoning about cardinal directions. In Mark, D. & D. White (Eds.), proceedings of Auto-Carto 10, ACSM-ASPRS, Baltimore. 148–167.

Frank, Andrew U. (1992). Qualitative spatial reasoning about distances and directions in geographic space. *Journal of Visual Languages and Computing*, 1992(3), 343–371.

Frank, Andrew U. (1994). Qualitative temporal reasoning in GIS: Ordered time scales. Technical Report. Dept. of Geoinformation, Technical University Vienna.

Frank, Andrew U. (1996a). An object-oriented, formal approach to the design of cadastral systems. In Kraak, M. & M. Molenaar (Eds.), proceedings of 7th Int. Symposium on Spatial Data Handling, SDH'96, Delft, The Netherlands, 5A.19–5A.35.

Frank, Andrew U. (1996b.) Qualitative spatial reasoning: Cardinal directions as an example. *International Journal of Geographical Information Systems*, 10(3), 269–290.

Frank, Andrew U. (1998). Specifications for interoperability: Formalizing spatial relations "in", "auf" and "an" and the corresponding image schemata "container", "surface" and "link". Internal Report. Dept. of Geoinformation, Technical University Vienna.

Frank, Andrew U. & Martin Raubal (1998) Specifications for interoperability: Formalizing image schemata for geographic space. In proceedings of 8th Int. Symposium on Spatial Data Handling, SDH'98, Vancouver, Canada, 331–348.

Frank, Andrew U., Bruce Palmer & Vincent Robinson (1986). Formal methods for accurate definition of some fundamental terms in physical geography. In Marble, D. (Ed.), proceedings of Second Int. Symposium on Spatial Data Handling, SDH'86, Seattle, Wash., 583–599.

Freksa, Christian (1991). Qualitative spatial reasoning. In Mark, D. & A. U. Frank (Eds.), *Cognitive and Linguistic Aspects of Geographic Space* [NATO ASI Series D: Behavioural and Social Sciences, 361–372]. Dordrecht: Kluwer.

Freundschuh, Scott & M. Sharma (1996). Spatial image schemata, locative terms and geographic spaces in children's narratives: Fostering spatial skills in children. *Cartographica*, Monograph 46, Orienting Ourselves in Space, 32(2), 38–49.

Gibson, James (1979), *The Ecological Approach to Visual Perception*. Hillsdale, NJ: Lawrence Erlbaum.

Giunchiglia, Fausto & Toby Walsh (1992). A theory of abstraction. Technical Report 9001–14. Istituto per la Ricerca Scientifica e Tecnologica, Trento, Italy.

Hayes, Patrick (1977). In defense of logic. In proceedings of International Joint Conference on Artificial Intelligence, Cambridge, Mass., 1, 559–565.

Hayes, Patrick (1978). The naive physics manifesto. In Mitchie, D. (Ed.), *Expert Systems in the Microelectronic Age* (242–270). Edinburgh: Edinburgh University Press.

Hayes, Patrick (1985). The second naive physics manifesto. In Hobbs, J. & R. Moore (Eds.), *Formal Theories of the Commonsense World* (1–36). Norwood, NJ: Ablex.

Hernández, Daniel (1991). Relative representation of spatial knowledge: The 2-D case. In Mark, D. & A. U. Frank (Eds.), *Cognitive and Linguistic Aspects of Geographic Space: An introduction* (373–386). Dordrecht: Kluwer.

Hernández, Daniel, Eliseo Clementini & Paolino Di Felice (1995). Qualitative distances. In Frank, A. U. & W. Kuhn (Eds.), *Spatial Information Theory: A theoretical basis for GIS. Int. Conference COSIT'95* [Lecture Notes in Computer Science 988, 45–57]. Berlin: Springer-Verlag.

Herring, John, Max Egenhofer & Andrew U. Frank (1990). Using category theory to model GIS applications. In Brassel, K. (Ed.), proceedings of 4th Int. Symposium on Spatial Data Handling, SDH'90, Zurich, Switzerland, 820–829.

Herskovits, Annette (1986). *Language and Spatial Cognition: An interdisciplinary study of the propositions in English*. Cambridge, UK: Cambridge University Press.

Herskovits, Annette (1997). Language, spatial cognition, and vision. In Stock, O. (Ed.), *Spatial and Temporal Reasoning* (155–202). Dordrecht: Kluwer.

Hobbs, Jerry R. & Robert C. Moore, Eds. (1985). *Formal Theories of the Commonsense World*. [Ablex Series in Artificial Intelligence]. Norwood, NJ: Ablex.

Johnson, Mark (1987). *The Body in the Mind: The bodily basis of meaning, imagination, and reason*. Chicago: University of Chicago Press.

Jones, Mark (1991). An introduction to Gofer. Technical Report. Yale University, USA.

Jones, Mark (1994) The implementation of the Gofer functional programming system. Technical Report YALEU/DCS/RR-1030. Yale University, USA.

Jordan, Troy, Martin Raubal, Bryce Gartrell & Max Egenhofer (1998). An affordance-based model of place in GIS. In proceedings of 8th Int. Symposium on Spatial Data Handling, SDH'98, Vancouver, Canada. 98–109.

Knauff, Markus, Reinhold Rauh & Christoph Schlieder (1995). Preferred mental models in qualitative spatial reasoning: A cognitive assessment of Allen's calculus. In proceedings of 17th Annual Conference of the Cognitive Science Society, Hillsdale, NJ, 200–205.

Kuhn, Werner (1993). Metaphors create theories for users. In Frank, A. U. & I. Campari (Eds.), *Spatial Information Theory: A theoretical basis for GIS. European Conference COSIT'93* [Lecture Notes in Computer Science 716, 366–376]. Berlin: Springer-Verlag.

Kuhn, Werner (1994). Defining semantics for spatial data transfers. In Waugh, T. & R. Healey (Eds.), proceedings of 6th Int. Symposium on Spatial Data Handling, SDH'94, Edinburgh, U. K., 973–987.

Kuhn, Werner & Andrew U. Frank (1991). A formalization of metaphors and image-schemas in user interfaces. In Mark, D. & A. U. Frank (Eds.), *Cognitive and Linguistic Aspects of Geographic Space* [NATO ASI Series, 419–434]. Dordrecht: Kluwer.

Kuhn, Werner & Andrew U. Frank (1999). The use of functional programming in the specification and testing process. In Goodchild, M., M. Egenhofer, R. Fegeas & C. Kottman (Eds.), *Interoperating Geographic Information Systems* [International Series in Engineering and Computer Science]. Boston: Kluwer.

Lakoff, George (1987). *Women, Fire, and Dangerous Things: What categories reveal about the mind*. Chicago: University of Chicago Press.

Lakoff, George & Mark Johnson (1980). *Metaphors We Live By*. Chicago: University of Chicago Press.

Liang, S., Paul Hudak & A. M. Jones (1995). Monad transformers and modular interpreters. In proceedings of ACM Symposium on Principles of Programming Languages.

Maddux, R. (1991) The origin of relation algebras in the development and axiomatization of the calculus of relations. *Studia Logica*, 50(3–4), 421–455.

Mark, David (1989). Cognitive image-schemata for geographic information: relations to user views and GIS interfaces. In proceedings of GIS/LIS'89, Orlando, Florida, 551–560.

Mark, David (1993). Toward a theoretical framework for geographic entity types. In Frank, A. U. & I. Campari (Eds.), *Spatial Information Theory: A theoretical basis for GIS. European Conference COSIT'93* [Lecture Notes in Computer Science 716, 270–283]. Berlin: Springer-Verlag.

Mark, David, David Comas, Max Egenhofer, Scott Freundschuh, Michael Gould & Joan Nunes (1995). Evaluating and refining computational models of spatial relations through cross-linguistic human-subjects testing. In Frank, A. U. & W. Kuhn (Eds.), *Spatial Information Theory: A theoretical basis for GIS. Int. Conference COSIT'95* [Lecture Notes in Computer Science 988, 553–568]. Berlin: Springer-Verlag.

Mark, David & Andrew U. Frank (1996). Experiential and formal models of geographic space. *Environment and Planning*, Series B, 23, 3–24.

McCarthy, John (1980). Circumscription: A form of non-monotonic reasoning. *Artificial Intelligence*, 13, 27–39.

McCarthy, John (1985). Epistemological problems of artificial intelligence. In Brachman, R. & H. Levesque (Eds.), *Readings in Knowledge Representation* (24–30). Los Altos, Calif.: Morgan Kaufmann.

McCarthy, John (1986). Applications of circumscription to formalizing common sense knowledge. *Artificial Intelligence*, 28, 89–116.

Montello, Daniel R. (1993). Scale and multiple psychologies of space. In Frank, A. U. & I. Campari (Eds.), *Spatial Information Theory: A theoretical basis for GIS. European COSIT'93* [Lecture Notes in Computer Science 716, 312–321]. Berlin: Springer-Verlag.

Montello, Daniel R. (1995). How significant are cultural differences in spatial cognition? In Frank, A. U. & W. Kuhn (Eds.), *Spatial information theory: A theoretical basis for GIS. Int. Conference COSIT'95* [Lecture Notes in Computer Science 988, 485–500]. Berlin: Springer-Verlag.

Papadias, Dimitris & Timos Sellis (1994). A pictorial language for the retrieval of spatial relations from image databases. In proceedings of 6th Int. Symposium on Spatial Data Handling, SDH'94, Edinburgh, U. K.

Peterson, John, Kevin Hammond, Lennart Augustsson, Brian Boutel, W. Burton, J. Fasel, A. Gordon, J. Hughes, P. Hudak, T. Johnsson, M. Jones, E. Meijer, S. Jones, A. Reid & P. Wadler (1997). The Haskell 1.4 Report. Available from: http://haskell.org/report/index.html.

Rashid, A., B. Shariff, Max Egenhofer & David Mark (1998). Natural-language spatial relations between linear and areal objects: The topology and metric of English-language terms. *International Journal of Geographic Information Science*, 12(3), 215–246.

Raubal, Martin (1997). Structuring space with image schemata. Master's Thesis, University of Maine, Orono, USA.

Raubal, Martin, Max Egenhofer, Dieter Pfoser & Nectaria Tryfona (1997). Structuring space with image schemata: Wayfinding in airports as a case study. In Hirtle, S. & A. Frank (Eds.), *Spatial Information Theory: A theoretical basis for GIS. Int. Conference COSIT'97* [Lecture Notes in Computer Science 1329, 85–102]. Berlin: Springer-Verlag.

Reiter, R. (1984). Towards a logical reconstruction of relational database theory. In Brodie, M., M. Mylopolous & L. Schmidt (Eds.), *On Conceptual Modelling,*

Perspectives from Artificial Intelligence, Databases, and Programming Languages (191–233). New York: Springer-Verlag.

Rodríguez, Andrea (1997.) Image-schemata-based spatial inferences: The container-surface algebra for solid objects. Master's Thesis, University of Maine, Orono, USA.

Rodríguez, Andrea & Max Egenhofer (1997). Image-schemata-based spatial inferences: the container-surface algebra. In Hirtle, S. & A. U. Frank (Eds.), *Spatial Information Theory: A theoretical basis for GIS. Int. Conference COSIT'97* [Lecture Notes in Computer Science 1329, 35–52]. Berlin: Springer-Verlag.

Rosch, Eleanor (1973a). Natural categories. *Cognitive Psychology*, 4, 328–350.

Rosch, Eleanor (1973b). On the internal structure of perceptual and semantic categories. In Moore, T. (Ed.), *Cognitive Development and the Acquisition of Language*. New York: Academic Press.

Rosch, Eleanor (1978). Principles of categorization. In Rosch, E. & B. Lloyd (Eds.), *Cognition and categorization*. Hillsdale, NJ: Erlbaum.

Schlieder, Christoph (1995). Reasoning about ordering. In Frank, A.U. & W. Kuhn (Eds.), *Spatial Information Theory: A theoretical basis for GIS. Int. Conference COSIT'95* [Lecture Notes in Computer Science 988, 341–350]. Berlin: Springer-Verlag.

Schröder, Erwin (1890). *Vorlesungen über die Algebra der Logik (Exakte Logik)*. Leipzig: Teubner.

Sedgewick, Robert (1983). *Algorithms*. Reading, Mass.: Addison-Wesley.

Tarski, Alfred (1941). On the calculus of relations. *The Journal of Symbolic Logic*, 6(3), 73–89.

Timpf, Sabine, Gary S. Volta, David W. Pollock & Max Egenhofer (1992). A conceptual model of wayfinding using multiple levels of abstractions. In Frank, A.U., I. Campari & U. Formentini (Eds.), *Theories and Methods of Spatio-Temporal Reasoning in geographic space* [Lecture Notes in Computer Science 639, 348–367]. Berlin: Springer-Verlag.

Voisard, Agnes & Heinz Schweppe (1994). A multilayer approach to the Open GIS design problem. In Pissinou, N. & K. Makki (Eds.), proceedings of 2nd ACM-GIS Workshop, New York.

Voisard, Agnes & Heinz Schweppe (1998). Abstraction and decomposition in interoperable GIS. *International Journal of Geographical Information Science*, 12, 315–333 (special issue).

Wadler, Philip (1997). How to declare an imperative. *ACM Computing Surveys*, 29(3), 240–263.

Walters, Robert F. (1991). *Categories and Computer Science*. Cambridge: Cambridge University Press.

Wierzbicka, Anna (1996). *Semantics: Primes and universals*. Oxford: Oxford University Press.

Using a Spatial Display to Represent the Temporal Structure of Multimedia Documents

Mireille Bétrancourt, Anne Pellegrin and Laurent Tardif
INRIA, Grenoble

Introduction

The research presented in this paper investigates the practical problem of representing the temporal structure of multimedia documents in the light of the research in spatial cognition. This study is the result of a collaboration between researchers in cognitive science and researchers in computer science.

The paper is structured as follows: the first section presents the problems that multimedia documents authoring tools encounter to convey the temporal organization of these documents. In the second section we review research on spatial cognition that is relevant to the design of temporal diagrams. The third section describes the multimedia document authoring tool MADEUS and its solution to visualize the temporal relationships between objects. Finally, the fourth section presents and analyzes the results of the experimentation carried out to evaluate the choices made in MADEUS.

Problems of multimedia document authoring

With the integration of dynamic data like video, sound or object moving on the screen, electronic documents have today a temporal dimension in addition to the spatial, logical and hypertext dimensions. Thus, the documents, so called multimedia documents, are characterized not only by components of various nature — static (text, graph, table, image) or dynamic (sound, video, animation) — but also by the temporal organization of these components. The description of the sequence of objects in time is called temporal scenario.

The current research on multimedia documents focuses mainly on the specification of the temporal scenario since it is the new characteristic to take into account. Because of the dynamic nature of the manipulated objects (such as video and audio), the phases of edition and presentation can not be merged in a single view. The static principle of WYSIWYG ("what you see is what you get"), that is very useful for the edition of a traditional document, cannot be applied to the edition of the temporal scenario of multimedia documents.

In the declarative edition of multimedia documents, the choice of a constraint-based language allows the author to specify constraints between objects (for example a video is presented after a text and at the same time as an audio comment) without having to specify all the temporal information attached to these objects (starting and ending dates). A temporal scenario is defined by a set of objects and temporal constraints (before, during…) between these objects.

The description of the temporal scenario is based on Allen's relations (Allen 1983). They express relations between objects by means of constraints, such as "A before B", "A starts C", "C finishes D"… The authors can introduce flexibility in their document by way of loose relations, such as "before" or "during". Indeed, the relation "A before B" does not specify the duration of the interval between the two objects A and B. This interval will be determined when the document is presented according to the other constraints. Another advantage of the constraint-based language is that the scenario is easier to modify, since the modification of the duration of a delay does not require the author to modify the whole organization. This reorganization will be automatically taken in charge by the system.

Currently, the author specifies the temporal scenario by editing the text of constraints. The solutions of presentation that are consistent with the constraints are automatically computed. The functions of edition are thus limited to those of textual data entries. The authors have to run the presentation to see the results of the textual source, then they have to go back to the textual source to make any modification. Since the textual source is not a direct matching to the presentation, the authors have difficulties in finding which constraints must be modified. A simple way to solve this problem is to offer editing features at the level of the presentation view. However, this solution is not optimal since the execution of the document in the presentation view enables the authors to visualize only one solution. They do not have the possibility to know the whole set of solutions of the scenario. In addition, the authors have in the presentation view only an instantaneous view of the behavior of their scenario: there is no trace of the past, nor possible anticipation.

In order to help the authors in the edition of the temporal scenario, it is necessary to visualize, during the specification, the behavior of the set of possible temporal solutions that are consistent with the scenario. Thus, the visualization should not only offer a graphic equivalent to the textual source, but should also provide the authors with the whole information contained in this textual source.

The next section examines some results of the literature in spatial cognition in order to define which type of graphic representation would help the authors to visualize and manipulate the temporal organization of multimedia documents.

The mental representation of temporal relations

In the spatial domain, it has been demonstrated that humans reason from analogical representations, called mental models, that represent "objects, states of affairs, sequence of events, the way the world is..." (Johnson-Laird 1983, p 397). According to this theoretical framework, providing a diagram that depicts the situation improves subjects' ability to solve spatial problems, since the diagram helps subjects elaborating and processing the mental model of the situation.

It has been argued (Baddeley 1993) that temporal and causal relationships are also coded spatially in working memory. Indeed, Glenberg & Langston (1992) showed that the understanding of a text describing a four-step procedure was improved if a diagram was provided, as evidenced through subjects' performance to inferences on the succession of steps. Moreover, it has been shown that subjects understand better the functioning of engineered or natural systems when a diagram is provided (Mayer 1989; Kieras 1992).

Thus, regarding the multimedia documents editing process, the research on mental model supports the hypothesis that a diagram should facilitate the authors' specification of the temporal structure of a multimedia document. Moreover, the literature provides guidelines concerning how to design a diagram that would be cognitively appropriate. For our purpose, two aspects are worth of interest.

First, the temporal dimension is spontaneously drawn from left to right, following the occidental writing order. Research on the graphic representation of temporal relations by children of three different cultures (English, Hebrew and Arab) showed an effect of the language on the temporal concepts. Children of English language represented the temporal concepts from left to right and children of Arab language represented the temporal concepts from right to left (Tversky, Kugelmass & Winter 1991). Moreover, subjects solved inferences on temporal relations better when the diagram was oriented from left to right than from right to left. In a task of classification, Winn (1982) showed that the subjects who saw the diagram directed from left to right, had better performance than the subjects who saw the diagram in the other direction (from right to left). Winn concluded that people of English language read the diagrams in the same way they read their language, from left to right and from top to bottom. Thus, the diagrams which are not oriented in this way are a source of difficulties in data processing and training.

Second, in order to be effective adjuncts to instructions, diagrams should "support" three cognitive processes involved in learning (Mayer 1989):

- they should guide learners' attention to relevant passages and act as an "external memory";
- they should help the learners organizing ideas within a coherent structure;
- they should facilitate the integration of the new structure with existing knowledge in long-term memory, mainly by way of metaphors and analogies.

Even though the editing process is not a learning process, we regard these three properties as relevant, since the editing process still requires the processing of a mental model in working memory.

Finally, another difficulty we have pointed out in the first section is the difficulty to represent graphically a set of solutions. There are two difficulties from the cognitive point of view.

First, whereas language supports non-determinism, a graphic representation of temporal relations is necessarily determinist : for example, "A before B" does not tell how far before is A from B, but a drawing instances this delay to a fixed value. To our knowledge, no research has ever addressed the issue of integrating a set of solutions in a single diagram. Second, due to our limited working memory capacity, we experience difficulties in mentally representing the simultaneous motion of objects. For example, Hegarty (1992) showed that users did not mentally animate a pulley system as a whole, but in a piecemeal fashion. Similarly, if the objects' position in time was represented statistically, it would be difficult for users to generate mentally all the possible combinations.

The next section describes the diagrammatic solution proposed in MADEUS to represent the temporal relationships. We study to what extent the choices made in MADEUS correspond to the guidelines of the literature. More details on the application MADEUS are available in Jourdan, Layaïda, Sabry-Ismail & Roisin (1997).

The MADEUS solution

Static visualization

In constraint-based systems, there are two types of approaches to display temporal information. The first one uses a graphic representation of the graph of constraints (Yu & Xiang 1997). According to the research previously mentioned, this type of approach is not cognitively satisfactory because it does not reproduce the temporal relations between objects in an analogical way.

A second type of approach tries to combine the semantic information of the temporal relationships with a time-line based representation. For example in ISIS (Kim & Song, 95), the objects and their relations are displayed in a linear graphic way (which strongly suggests a time-line). Nevertheless, the selected graphic metaphors for some relations (meets, starts…) prevent from tracing an absolute temporal axis under their representation. In some cases, this can even bias the representation of the execution of the document that the author elaborates.

The MADEUS solution (Jourdan, Roisin & Tardif 1997) consists in displaying an arrangement of the objects which respects the constraints of the scenario, and allows the author to move objects within the limits enabled by the scenario, in order to examine the whole set of possible solutions. In this version of the application, the flexibility taken into account comes only from the flexibility of the relations and not from the duration of objects. The adopted presentation, called "the temporal view", makes possible the visualization of a solution; the manipulation of the temporal view gives access to the whole set of solutions.

In the temporal view, the basic objects are represented by rectangles which length is proportional to their actual duration. Each type of object (video, sound, text, image) is represented by a discriminating pattern. The objects are placed on horizontal lines which represent temporal axes, the time running from left to right (Figure 1).

The constraints introduce three types of elements into the temporal view:

* The horizontal lines represent the fixed delays (Image1 before (2) Image2).
* The springs represent the flexible delays (Video1 before Image1).
* The vertical features represent the constraint of simultaneity of two moments (Image1 Starts Text2).

The arrangement selected by the system tries to minimize the visualization of false information (no alignment of objects if it is not imposed by the set of

Video 1 *Starts* Text
Video 1 *Equals* Son 1
Video 1 *Before* Image1
Image 1 *Starts* Text 2
Image 1 *Before (2)* Image 2
Text 2 *During* Text 1
Text 2 *Finishes* Image 2

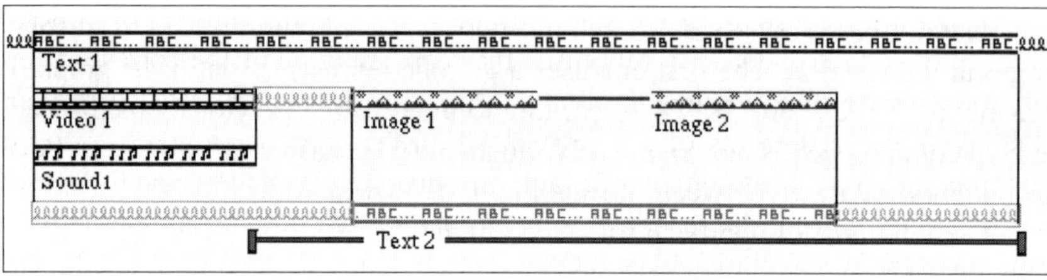

Figure 1. Example of textual source and corresponding Temporal view[1]

constraints) and the superposition of objects or relations in the vertical arrangement of objects. The explicit representation of objects, constraints and duration allows a direct interpretation of the scenario without necessarily requiring the textual source.

Interaction with the user

In order to help the author surveying the whole set of solutions, MADEUS allows the visualization of the interval of displacement so that the author can anticipate the behavior of the selected object (criterion of foreseeability). In the example of Figure 1, the author has selected the object Text2. A red stroke appears under the line where is placed the selected object (Text2), thus indicating its latitude of displacement. On our example, Text2 is limited on its left-hand side by the end of Video1 (Text2 after Video1) and on its right-hand side by the end of Text1 (Text2 during Text1).

The objects which are connected to the selected object by rigid constraints get colored in blue. The rigid constraints do not introduce flexibility (for example *starts*, *finishes*, *meets*). These objects are dependent on the selected object in its moves. The springs which play the part of shock absorber for the selected object get colored in green.

Dynamic visualization

The objective is to allow the author to access to the set of solutions of the scenario by manipulating the objects in the temporal view. Thus, the authors do not have to generate mentally all the combinations of objects moves, which would be difficult because of the limited capacity of mental animation we mentioned before. They can directly manipulate the position of all moving objects and actually generate the whole set of solutions.

When the authors move the selected object in its entire interval of validity, the display system updates, in real time, the representation of the corresponding solution. It is worth noting that the limits of this displacement always correspond to the complete absorption of a flexible delay of the scenario (a green spring in the temporal view). Consequently the authors should easily understand the reason of a blocking. Indeed, the reactions to manipulation provide the authors with an immediate feedback, where static representation and manipulation are coherent.

Thus, the diagrammatic representation proposed in MADEUS is consistent with guidelines deduced from the research. However, is this representation adapted to the specific task of multimedia documents authoring process?

The experiment

This experiment was designed to comply with both ergonomic and cognitive concerns. We focused the analysis on three questions:

- how do people spontaneously represent the temporal relations between objects, especially when they are undetermined? from an ergonomic point of view, does that fit in with the diagrammatic choices made in MADEUS?
- does the diagram facilitate the authors' processing of temporal relations compared to the text of constraints alone?
- does the manipulation enable authors to reason on the set of solutions?

Methods

Participants

11 graduates, 8 male and 3 female, were individually tested. 7 were graduated in computer science, and all were using computers at work. Their age ranged from 27 to 37.

Material

For the first task, we used two scenarios. A text of constraints and a temporal view were derived from each one. The scenario 2 was the scenario 1 in reverse, whose objects were renamed. Half subjects saw the text of constraints of scenario 1 and the temporal view of scenario 2, whereas the other half saw the text of constraints of scenario 2 and the temporal view of scenario 1. Three questions about the text of constraints and three questions about the temporal view were designed. For the second task, we used two different temporal views (different from the temporal view used for the first task) and two set of three different problems for each temporal views (see appendix).

Procedure
The experiment consisted of two successive tasks, designed to be close to the real activity of multimedia document authoring. The participants were briefly presented with the objectives of a multimedia document authoring tool. Then the constraints language was explained.

In the first task, the participants were presented with the text of constraints from one of the scenario and were asked to describe the corresponding presentation in a written text. They were told they could make a drawing if they wanted. Then, they were asked three inference questions about temporal relationships, whose answers were not explicitly indicated in the constraints. Secondly, the temporal view from the other scenario was presented to the participants and the representation options (springs, vertical lines) were briefly explained. As for the text of constraints, participants were asked to describe the corresponding presentation and to answer three questions. The order in which the two scenarios were presented was counterbalanced across subjects.

The second task aimed to evaluate whether subjects were able to infer the set of solutions from the diagram, and to explore it by manipulation. From a temporal view presented on the screen, the subjects were asked to solve three problems about the attainability of temporal situations. They were told to answer first without manipulating, and then, to verify the accuracy of their answer by manipulating the temporal view. A second temporal view was then presented on the screen, on which subjects were similarly asked to solve three problems.

Time spent on each task and performance were recorded by the experimenter. Moreover, the subjects evaluated on a scale the task difficulty and their certitude regarding their answer.

Results

Task 1: Reasoning from the textual source or from the temporal view

Description of the presentation
Subjects were significantly faster to describe the presentation from the temporal

view (m = 256 s.) than from the list of constraints (m = 526 s.), ($F(1,10) = 11.66$, $p < .01$). Moreover, 36% of subjects (4) made an accurate description of the presentation from the constraints, whereas 82% of subjects (9) did so from the temporal view.

Questions on temporal relations
As three questions were asked for the text of constraints and for the temporal view, performance ranged from 0 (no correct answer) to three (all three questions correctly answered). A repeated measures analysis of variance was computed on the number of correct answers and on the response times.

As presented in Table 1, when the subjects answered from the temporal view, they were significantly more accurate than when they answered from the list of constraints ($F(1,10) = 7.64$, $p < .05$). Moreover, they were faster to answer with the temporal view than with the constraints but the difference was not significant ($F(1,10) = 3.2$, *NS*).

Table 1 Number of questions correctly answered and response times (in seconds) in the first task (m = mean and SD = standard deviation)

	Accuracy	Response time
Temporal view	m = 2.73 *SD* = .47	m = 32.81 *SD* = 23.29
Text of constraints	m = 1.91 *SD* = .83	m = 66.27 *SD* = 56.89

Describing the presentation and answering the questions were judged significantly more difficult to perform from the text of constraints than from the temporal view ($F(1,10) = 13.4$, $p < .005$, without interaction).

Qualitative analysis of the drawings
Even though the production of a drawing was only suggested, 10 subjects out of 11 made a drawing when they described the presentation from the constraints, and none from the temporal view.

Out of the 10 subjects who made a drawing, 8 subjects oriented time in their drawing from left to right and the remaining 2 subjects oriented time from top to bottom. These 2 subjects depicted the succession of events, represented as dots on the time line, whereas the 8 other subjects represented the objects as lines or bars which length represented approximately the duration. For these 8 subjects, the objects were drawn on several lines. 2 subjects affected one object per line, whereas the other 6 put on the same line objects that could not overlap.

Another question was how subjects graphically conveyed the flexibility introduced by the constraints. 4 subjects used a graphic representation of the flexibility: 2 subjects used dotted lines to indicate the interval in which the object can be located, one subject represented the flexible delays as spaces, another filled those spaces with dotted lines. Two subjects represented starting and ending constraints between objects with vertical lines.

Qualitative analysis of the descriptions
5 subjects did not account explicitly for the flexibility of the relations, neither from the constraints, nor from the temporal view. Produced descriptions were unspecified, insofar as a great number of verbal expressions for temporal relations are naturally unspecified ("during", "before", "afterwards"...). Those are used jointly with other deterministic expressions for the strong relations ("at the same time", "immediately afterwards"). Out of the 6 subjects which accounted for flexibility, 3 did it for the temporal view only, 2 for the constraints only and one for both the constraints and the temporal view. The markers of flexibility used were: "delay" or "pause", "not necessarily immediately", "a few moments later", "one does not know exactly when", "without precision of the time", "an indefinite time later".

Task 2: Problem solving and manipulation of the temporal view

In this task, subjects had to solve 6 problems (see appendix), 4 of which required one or two moves only (simple manipulation) and 2 of which required the manipulation of two distinct objects in addition to the object mentioned in the question (complex manipulation). Subjects were first asked whether the manipulation was possible (without manipulating) and then to perform it.

For the simple manipulation problems, only five errors were made (11%), usually due to the misunderstanding of vertical lines (inflexible constraints).

The two complex manipulation problems were attainable. For the first problem (question 3 in appendix), without manipulation, 8 subjects out of 11 got the correct answer. In order to achieve the goal, the manipulation required to move first another object (Image 1), due to the "before" constraint between Video1 and Image1 and to the "starting" constraint between Text1 and Video1 (Figure 1). With manipulation, only 3 subjects succeeded in achieving the goal. The other subjects did not get the idea of moving Image1. For the second complex manipulation problem, only one subject did not get the correct answer with and without manipulation. However, 4 subjects were not sure that "the spring was long enough". This is quite inconsistent with the concept of spring in the temporal view, which means a flexible delay with no intrinsic duration.

Discussion and conclusion

The multimedia document authoring tool MADEUS proposes to convey the temporal organization of the document by using a spatial representation. An experimentation was carried out to evaluate the cognitive relevance of this representation.

With regards to the diagrammatic representation proposed in MADEUS, the results showed that the diagram improved significantly the performance (speed and accuracy) to questions on temporal relationships, compared to the list of constraints. This result is consistent with the literature : providing an analogical device supports the reasoning on temporal relations (Glenberg & Langston 1992). This is mainly because relations have to be inferred from the text (or from a list of propositions), whereas they are directly perceptible on a diagram (Larkin & Simon 1987). When asked to graphically represent temporal relations, the subjects drew spontaneously temporal relations from left to right which is consistent with findings of the literature (Tversky, B., Kugelmass, S. & Winter, A. 1991). Moreover, the successive objects were drawn on the same line and overlapping objects on different lines. Only 44,4% of subjects' drawing conveyed the flexibility by using dotted lines or spaces. This way of spatially organizing the objects is consistent with the chosen representation in MADEUS.

The problem of representing a set of solutions in a single diagram has not been extensively studied yet. In the representation chosen in MADEUS (the temporal view), the authors have access to the set of solutions by manipulation. In order to assess the cognitive relevance of this representation, subjects were provided with a temporal view and were asked to state whether some objects could be in given temporal positions. For simple manipulation problems, only 3 subjects made errors without manipulation but they all succeeded in the manipulation. Overall the two complex manipulation problems (where more than two moves were necessary), the error rate was 10 % without manipulation but raised to 45 % with manipulation. This was due to some problems in the interface where the objects intervals of moving were not easily recognizable.

These results showed that the spring's metaphor to represent flexible delays was easily understood by the subjects. However, some subjects imagined that the springs had a limited duration, which is the result of a too direct transposition of the physical spring concept. This problem of the use of metaphors was already observed in many other fields (Brown 1989).

The whole results presented in this article must however be considered within the framework of a development tool. Indeed the research that we carried out here was dependent on the actual development of the MADEUS tool which was still a prototype. For example, we could not choose the example of temporal views used in the experimentation, they were imposed by the state of progress of MADEUS at the time of the research. Moreover the choices for the interface were still in discussion (design of objects, framing and so forth).

In the context of multimedia document authoring tasks, many issues related to spatial cognition are still to investigate like the visualization of the hierarchical organization of scenes in the document and the integration of the spatial and temporal dimensions.

This study illustrates how research and application can gain from each other. On one hand, the research on spatial cognition suggested guidelines for the design of a diagrammatic representation in a real environment. On the other hand, the observation of subjects interacting with the diagram provided useful hints on the further research to be carried out on spatial cognition.

Appendix

Example of problems presented to subjects for the second task

These problems concern the temporal view presented in Figure 1.

1. Is it possible for Text 2 to begin before the end of Sound 1?
2. Is it possible for Image 2 to finish at the same time as Text 1?
3. Is it possible for Text 1 to start at 12*?

* This number refers to the time scale displayed on the screen but not represented here. 12 is about in the middle of the view.

Acknowledgments

We are grateful to André Bisseret, Gilles Bisson, Muriel Jourdan and Cécile Roisin for their useful comments on earlier drafts, and to Claude Castelluccia for proofreading this manuscript.

Notes

1. The patterns used here to distinguish the types of components — video, text, image, sound — have not been tested yet.

References

Allen, J. F. (1983). Maintaining knowledge about temporal intervals. *CACM*, 26 (11), 832–843.

Baddeley, A. (1990). *Human Memory. Theory and practice.* East Sussex: Lawrence Erlbaum Associates, 547 p.

Brown, A. (1989). Analogical learning and transfer: What develops? In S. Vosniadou, A. Ortony (eds.) *Similarity and Analogical Reasoning*. Cambridge: Cambridge University Press.

Glenberg, A. M. & Langston, W. E. (1992). Comprehension of illustrated text: Pictures help to build mental models. *Journal of Memory and Language*, 31,129–151.

Hegarty, M. (1992). Mental animation: Inferring motion from static displays of mechanical systems. *Journal of Eperimental Psychology: Learning, Memory and Cognition,* 18, 5, 1084–1102.

Johnson-Laird, P. N. (1983). *Mental Models: Toward a cognitive science of language, inference and consciousness*. Cambridge: Cambridge University Press.

Jourdan, M., Layaïda, N., Sabry-Ismail. L. & Roisin. C. (1997). An integrated authoring and presentation environment for interactive multimedia documents. *Proceedings of the 44th Conference on Multimedia Modelling*, World Scientific Publishing, Singapore, 18–19 November 1997.

Jourdan, M., Roisin, C. & Tardif, L. (1997). User Interface of a new generation of authoring environment of multimedia documents. *Proceeding of the Third ERCIM Workshop on User Interfaces for All*, Strasbourg (France), 3–4 November 1997.

Kieras, D. (1992). Diagrammatic displays for engineered system: Effects on human performance in interacting with malfunctioning systems. *International Journal of Man-Machines Studies,* 36, 861–895.

Kim, M. Y. & Song, J. (1995). Multimedia documents with elastic time, *Proceedings of the 3rd ACM Conference on Multimedia* (pp. 143–154), San Francisco, November 1995.

Larkin, J. H. & Simon, H. A. (1987), Why a diagram is (sometimes) worth ten thousand words. *Cognitive Science,* 11, 65–99.

Mayer, R. E. (1989). Models for understanding, *Review of Educational Research*, 59 (1), 43–64.

Tversky, B., Kugelmass, S. & Winter, A. (1991). Cross-cultural and developmental trends in graphic productions. *Cognitive Psychology* 23, 515–557.

Winn, W. (1982) The role of diagrammatic representation in learning sequences, identification and classification as a function of verbal and spatial ability. *Journal of Research in Science Teaching,* 19 (1), 79–89.

Yu, J. & Xiang, Y. (1997). Hypermedia presentation and authoring system. *Proceedings of the 6th Web Conference,* Santa Clara.

Part III

Language and Space

A Computational Multi-layered Model for the Interpretation of Locative Expressions

Luca Anibaldi and Seán Ó Nualláin
Dublin City University and Nous Research

Problems with spatial language

It seems at first sight that the task of formalising the use of spatial language sufficiently to simulate people's real use of it is an intractable one.

For example, consider the use of "put" in the following sentences:

1. Put the book on the table.
2. Put the water in the bottle.
3. Put the thread through the eye of the needle.

Similarly, let's attend to the spatial preposition "on" in the following:

1. Stack the book on the pile of books.
2. Place the book on the table.
3. Float the rubber duck on the water.

We now come to our first generalisation. People will often use general purpose verbs (e.g. "put") and prepositions ("on", etc.) when the context is sufficiently clear to disambiguate them. The context can be derived from physical properties of objects (for example, a pile of books requires the action be the *stacking* instance of *put*) or, in absence of such naïve physics evidence, from the preposition employed. For example, specifying the object must go through the eye of the needle obviates the need to use *thread* as a verb instead of *put*; *Put the thread through the eye* rather than *thread the needle*.

Approaches to analysis of spatial expressions

Studies of the meaning of locative prepositions can be classified as *simple relation models* versus *multiple relations models*, as proposed in (Herskovits 1986). The first class includes theories coming both from linguistics (Bennett 1975) and from the computational paradigm (Miller & Johnson-Laird 1976, Waltz 1980).

Presumably the approach of (Jackendoff 1983, 1990), one of the most discussed recent positions, also falls in this class. From this point of view, language draws on spatial cognition so that we can manage to talk what we perceive and it thereby provides a window on the nature of spatial cognition, that is a Spatial Representation. Jackendoff suggests a level of mental representation devoted to encoding the geometric properties of objects and the relationships among them in space, in order to express our spatial experience in talking about objects (encoding of object shapes) and talking about spatial relations (locations of objects). According to (Marr 1982), Spatial Representation is the 3D model level, the format in which objects are encoded independent of viewer's perspective. The primitives for 3D object description follow these principles:

1. describing "generalized cones" in terms of axis and a cross section;
2. elaborating a main axis with a subsidiary axis of a particular size and orientation relative to the main axis, so objects are composed by parts applying recursively.

Moreover, Jackendoff claims that the notion of place — or location — and path — or trajectory — plays a basic role in the lexical-semantic representation, that is the Conceptual Structure. For example, in locative sentences such as *the book is lying on the table* or *the arrow flew through the air past my head*, the constituents Place and Path are shared between Conceptual Structure and Spatial Representation. The notion of physical motion is also central to Conceptual Structure, and it must be represented in spatial cognition so that we can track moving objects. The following could be one possible schema of the different modules related to a lexical entry for a physical object word, including a 3D model representation in addition to its phonological, syntactical and conceptual structures (Figure 1).

So, the meaning goes beyond the features and functions available in Conceptual Structures, in particular allowing shape information in a lexical Spatial Representation. We will examine this schema later much in detail, trying to extend it to a multilevel model.

The theory seen above is based on a single geometric relation for all spatial

Phonological & Syntactical Structures	Linguistic Representations (conceptual structures)	Spatial Representations (3D model)	Visual representations (2½ D sketsch haptic representations representations for auditory localization
		motor representations	

Figure 1. Phonology & Syntax + Conceptual Structure & Spatial Representation

uses of a given preposition. This position is seen to fail in the attempt to apply the approach to cases where the use of a preposition diverges from the standard geometric relation: tolerance and sense-shift phenomena.

Hence, accounting for the flexibility and adaptability in the use of spatial relations, the class exemplified by (Lakoff 1987) and (Herskovits 1986) claims that each preposition identifies a *central* or *ideal* meaning from which the others can be obtained via transformations, "categorizing relationships of schematicity" (Langacker 1988).

In particular, the representation of the meaning of locative prepositions viewed as the result of a schematization, namely *a process that involves the systematic selection of certain aspects of a referent scene to represent the whole, disregarding the remaining aspects* (Talmy 1983), should enable the disambiguation of the preposition. Hence to select, idealize, approximate and conceptualize a given meaning, we reduce its indeterminacy by specializing the real physical scene to a sketchy semantic content.

That reduction can not solve the disambiguation problem without detailed information about the abstract spatial relation applied to geometric objects — as points, lines, surfaces and ribbons — and the objects involved in the scene. Here the claim is that there is a strict interaction between the spatial properties of the entities involved in the description and the general world knowledge encoded in the ontology of the system. In addition, we suggest that such information should be part of the conceptual representation of events and physical objects. Thus, the fact that an action spatially identifies a flat region of space, either as a region conceptualized as a container or a cognitively salient surface, must be available to the process of interpretation.

In spatial locative expressions, where the location of an object is described via a reference to the known location of another object, the literature presents several different terms: we follow Herskovits' definition and we use respectively the terms *Figure Object* (or *Figure* for short) and *Reference Object*. For example, in the sentence *put the book on the stack*, we describe that locative action as a spatial relation between *the book* (Figure) and *the stack* (Reference Object).

Herskovits has presented in (Herskovits 1986) one of the most complete approaches to formalization of the use of English locative expressions. The main goal was to give a *lexical semantics* of spatial prepositions to determine the entries in a mental ontology, and the way they are combined with other spatial objects entries, in order to obtain interpretations of spatial propositions. In particular, Herskovits distinguishes two kinds of entries corresponding to two different levels of abstraction: "I suggest two levels of abstraction: ideal meaning and use type. The ideal meaning abstraction is not sufficient to build truth-conditions, but it is a necessary anchor that organizes the overall set of uses of the preposition. The use type abstraction, with several use types derived from the same ideal meaning, is much richer and provides material that brings us much closer to a definition of truth conditions." (Herskovits 1986: 18)

The two concepts *ideal meaning* and *use type* are embedded in a relatively complex model, which includes additional constructions for mapping ideal meanings, use types, and the actual uses. This model can be summarised by the following claim:

> The meaning of a preposition in an expression like NP + PP [prep + NP] is a relation Ri (x, y), where x is the Figure and y the Reference Object, belonging to the family of senses defined by the preposition (use types); the choice of a relation Ri depends on the nature of the objects x and y.

The prepositional category as a whole is organized around a focal relation, the ideal meaning. The whole set of uses of a preposition can then be subcategorized into use types (corresponding roughly to different senses), each such subclass manifesting the ideal meaning, but usually after some transformations.
A level of geometric conceptualization mediates between our naive representations of the physical world and the application of locative terms; prepositional meaning applies in effect to schematic images (geometric descriptions) mapped onto objects. "A number of contextual factors bear on the choice and interpretation of a locative expression: relevance, salience, tolerance, and typicality. There are pragmatic principles relating to these that explain many characteristics of the situation of use." (Herskovits 1986: 343)

There is actually no unique concept of a certain locative preposition, and correspondingly no unique entry in the lexicon, but only a set of interrelated concepts, use types as they are called, which show family resemblance. The ideal meanings form the second-level abstraction of the set of use type concepts associated with one locative preposition: "The ideal meaning of a preposition is a geometrical idea, from which all uses of that preposition derive by means of various adaptations and shifts. An ideal meaning is generally a relation between two or three ideal geometric objects (e.g., points, lines, surfaces, volumes, vectors) — in fact, ideal meanings are usually those simple relations that most linguists and workers in artificial intelligence have proposed as meanings of the prepositions. These relations play indeed an important role, but as something akin to prototypes, not as truth-conditional meanings.“ (Herskovits 1986: 39)

Coincidence of points, inclusion of a point in a line or in an area, and contiguity of two surfaces are some examples of relations considered by Herskovits as ideal meanings. They are directly reflected by language so that idealizations, approximations and conceptualizations mediate between a canonical view of the world and language.

An important issue can be outlined on that study of spatial prepositions. It concerns the proposal by (Landau & Jackendoff 1993) about the "what" and the "where" systems, performing separately object identification and object localization. This hypothesis states that preposition use and noun use access only the encoding produced by the distinct neural systems, see (Ungerleider & Miskin 1982). Thus, when naming objects, we use detailed geometric properties of them. But, when locating them, we use rough representations as points and lines. On the contrary, we may need fine information about shape of objects and locations for applying the appropriate preposition, even if its relative selectional restrictions specify no shapes of Figure and Reference Object. The position adopted seems to fail to distinguish the selectional restrictions from the knowledge of object shape, so we follow Herskovits in rejecting their hypothesis.

Moreover, further evidence shows the boundedness of computational models ignoring schematization and its relationship with the perceptual, conceptual and spatial cognitive analysis.

A multilayered model for pragmatic interpretation

Spatial relations are facets of the schematization of spatial language, which involves geometric idealization, abstracting features of the real scene so they match simple geometric objects as points, lines, ribbons and so on. In other words, a mismatch between the real features and the categories in which they are fitted causes the idealization to abstract features.

As suggested later in (Herskovits 1998), the applicable schematization is the result of composing several elementary functions used in mapping real objects onto their schematic representation. In such application, the selectional restrictions for one sense of the given preposition must be satisfied. Here is a list of essential geometric description functions (for a more detailed description see Herskovits 1986, 1997).

Idealization to a:
1. Point
2. Line
3. Surface
4. Plane
5. Ribbon

Gestalt processes:
1. Linear grouping (2- or 3-D linear object)
2. Complex grouping (area or volume)
3. Enclosure
4. Normalized shape

Selection of axes and directions:
1. Model axis
2. Reference axis
3. Frame of reference
4. Direction of motion
5. Direction of texture
6. Direction of maximum slope of surface

Projections:
1. On layout plane
2. On plane of view

Salient part selections :
1. 3-D part
2. Oriented three top surface
3. Base

In this spatial framework, the information needed to identify a spatial relation will refer the geometric description returned by the *Place* function as well as those ones returned by the functions illustrated above. Given a physical object, the former provides the region of space it occupies; instead the other functions provide alternative conceptualizations of that object.

A NL interface might use such information, hence spatial relations are represented in the system knowledge base — the naïve ontology — in the ways that are described later. In addition, this approach also concerns mapping syntactic arguments onto thematic roles as part of verb meaning representation.

According to their most salient senses, we can put forward a rough classification of prepositions, sorted into two different groups:

Table 1

Location	*Motion*
At/on/in	Across
Upon	Along
Against	To/from
Inside/outside	Around
Within/without	Away from
Near/far from	Toward
Next	Up/down (to)
Beside	Into/(out of)
By	Onto/off
Between	Out
Beyond	Through
Opposite	Via
Above/below	About
Under/over	Ahead of
On (the) top of/bottom of	Past
Behind	
In front of/back of	
Left/right (side) of	
East/north/south/west of	

Contrary to a common belief, not all prepositions treat Figure and Reference Object as simple geometric objects, but the region occupied should be known to determine whether a preposition applies. In fact a closer investigation reveals that the following assumption is unfounded: "If the prepositional predicate applies to objects of any shape, then its truth in particular cases can be assessed without referring to the object's shape". For example, in motion prepositions, such a predicate is approximated to the motion of the *centroid* — centre of gravity — of the object, ignoring rotations and translations around it.

The transformations result in different idealizations of the spatial objects: when an object is described as being *at* some reference object, both objects are idealized as points. To that purpose, a set of geometric description functions was collected by Herskovits (Herskovits 1986: Chapter 5). Usually, several coercions have to be applied in sequence until the appropriate conceptualization is found. The schematization of the spatial objects depends on functional part-whole relations, but also sometimes on certain aspects of the referent scene, such as the distance between Figure and Reference Object for the *projective* prepositions (to the right, above, behind, etc.).

Hence our research on spatial expressions goes toward the design of a multilevel system, taking into account different modules of analysis:

Table 2

Conceptual Level Naïve Semantics: a hierarchy describing relations between conceptual entities — objects and events — by means of prototype theory and other salient properties.
Semantic Level Lexical Semantics: a cognitive representation that refers directly to the linguistic locative expressions. Reference Semantics: a basic spatial representation establishing the connection between the ideal meaning of spatial relations and the spatial entities: a structural description — proximity, surrounding, alignment, etc. — to obtain a local frame of reference for various configurations of objects.
Pragmatic Level Spatial Configuration: a geometric description of objects' location specifying the location and orientation of objects with respect to the local axes by appropriate topological — metric information (measures of angles and distances).

From this point of view, the schematization described above (Herskovits 1998) and conceptual structures (Jackendoff 1990, 1995) play a central role in our model, in conjunction as related modules of the Semantic Level. Both these modules refer directly to locative expressions, so they concern the linguistic part and they are independent of the context-specific information. Hence world knowledge, which is requested for appropriate handling of specific situations, is included in the latter level for processing locative actions in terms of topological-metric knowledge on angles and distances in the given context.

On one hand, such a modularization allows abstraction from the concrete scene; on the other, it also permits the interaction between semantic and pragmatic representation.

Pragmatic interpretation of lexical meanings

Let's assume that each lexical item in the sentence specifies how its conceptual arguments are linked to syntactic positions in the heading phrase. Now a *thematic role* or *θ-role* is a term for an argument position in the conceptual structure, so for locative actions Agent and Theme are particular structural positions as well.

Thus the first fundamental assumption asserts that every content-bearing major phrasal constituent of a sentence (S, NP, AP, PP) corresponds to a conceptual constituent of some major conceptual category. The basic machinery under this approach is that the specification of conceptual structure within arguments of the verb can be regarded as in large part orthogonal to the positions of indices on arguments — the way the verb links its arguments to the syntactic structure. The following rules use this lexical information to integrate the readings of syntactic complements and subjects with indexed argument positions in the conceptual structure of the head:

1. for each indexed constituent in the conceptual structure of a lexical item, substitute the conceptual structure of that phrase, say YP, that satisfies the co-indexed position in the subcategorization feature of that lexical item, if its conceptual category matches that of the constituent;
2. if the lexical item is a verb, substitute the conceptual structure of the constituent indexed in the conceptual structure of that lexical item, if its conceptual category matches that of the constituent.

To express alternations, the subcategorization feature stipulates merely an optional post-verbal phrase of arbitrary major phrasal category. This is possible because of the selectional restrictions of the verb: only specific NPs or PPs can correspond to a conceptual constituent of the proper category, and Objects must always be expressed by NPs as well as Paths are expressed by PPs — in the unmarked case.

Going further, the interpretation of a small class of Path-nouns as in "getting down by climbing *this route*" behaves semantically like a PP, even though its syntax is clearly that of a NP. The reason is that the NP expresses a Path, hence it must fuse with the realization of the Path-constituent or map into Paths instead of Objects.

Moreover, selectional restrictions could restrict the range of spatial region occupied by objects assuming the Destination role, that is enabling a geometrical conceptualization for individual or collective (physical) objects in the sense of Herskovits's analysis. From this point of view, the spatial relations expressed by locative prepositions rule the correspondence between Conceptual Structures and possible spatial relations in the relative spatial representation.

At the end, adopting a fine-grained framework — the conceptual structure — seems necessary to outline the relations among multiple structures of lexical entries and to account for syntactic alternations without loss of generality.

With respect of conceptual structure, the basic organization is based on some realizations in which each conceptual category is decomposed into a *function-argument structure* and each argument is in turn a *conceptual constituent* of some major category.

Basic Function-Argument Structures for Events of Location and Motion
[conceptual_constituent] → [Funct_Argmnt_structure]

[PLACE] → [Place-function ()] ~ mapping into a geometric spatial representation
[{IN, AT, ON} ([Object X])]

[PATH] → [Path-function ()] ~ mapping into a geometric spatial schematization
[Path {TO, FROM, TOWARD, AWAY_FROM, VIA, ALONG}
({[Object X, Place Y]})]

[EVENT] → [Event-function ()]
[Event CAUSE ({[Object X], [Event Y]}), [Event Z])] ~ causative event

[STATE] → [State-function ()]
[State CONF ([Object X])] ~ one-place function of configuration
[State DESC ({[Object X1], [Object X2]})] ~ n-place function of description

Now let's introduce a new term referring to "telic events". Telic is a Greek word and it reflects simply our conceptual vision: going straight for one's goal.

[EVENT] → [TELIC_ACTION ([Object X], [Path Y])] ~ telic event of location/motion
[GO ([Object X], [Path TO ([Place Y])])]

On the other hand, many English verbs — such as *point*, *surround*, *stay*, *cover*–alternate between a State reading and an "paratelic" (or *inchoative*) event reading: an Event whose termination is the State reading. In other words, the resulting configuration feature is filled by the final state, instead of the goal.

[EVENT] → [BE (State-function ()] ~ paratelic event of location/motion
[PARATELIC ([BE [Object X], [Place Y]])]

Following is a summary describing the Telic / Paratelic characteristics, as proposed in the *reversal theory* by the work of Michael Apter (Apter 1989).

The theory is concerned with the experience of one's own motivation. However, the way motivation is experienced is clearly structured.

Underlying subjective experiences are certain structures and patterns. The telic and paratelic states together constitute but one of these underlying constructions. Others are postulated in the theory, hence Apter calls his theory a structural phenomenological theory of human action (Table 3).

Table 3

	Telic	*Paratelic*
Means-ends dimension	Essential goals Imposed goals Unavoidable goals Reactive Goal-oriented End-oriented Attempts to complete activity	No essential goals Freely-chosen goals Avoidable goals Proactive Behaviour-oriented Process-oriented Attempts to prolong activity
Time dimension	Future-oriented Planned	Present-oriented Spontaneous
Intensity dimension	Low intensity preferred Synergies avoided	High intensity preferred Synergies sought

The process of interpretation is incremental, thus the semantic representation is composed as soon as the linguistic expression is parsed. This multilevel model takes into account the specific scene in which the locative expression occurs with the Pragmatic Level, and it performs the contextualization of ideal meanings retrieving a more specific geometrical description in the multimedia context.
Individual and collective physical objects are related to the region of space they typically identify. That region is approximated to a mono-, bi- or tridimensional geometric entity and characterized by some topological features, as *bounded* or *fuzzy* area. Such information is associated with the role *Spatially_Identifies*, but alternative idealizations are specified by the role *Geometric_Description* applying the geometric description functions described above. The schematization forcing an alternative reading is applied when the PP is processed and its result is used in attempting to satisfy the selectional restriction imposed by the preposition.
As a standard example of a locative action realization that subcategorizes an obligatory PP, let's focus on the verb "put". It appears that its argument must express either a Place or else a Path whose function is TO. On the other hand, expession of Source, Direction and Route are impossible. In the following realization, the verb meaning is "cause to go to a place", but it does not show in the syntax the disjunctive expression of the PP as Path and as Place:

Np_i put __NP_j PP_k
[CAUSE ([Object]i, [Event TELIC_ACTION ([Object]j, [Path TO [Place]{k})]{k})])]

Binding a conceptual constituent consisting of a variable — direct or indirect object — to another conceptual constituent must follow a list of conditions. This mechanism has to prevent two syntactic positions from bearing the same index and hence being mapped into the very same thematic role. Thus, phrases that refer to participants in the scene should be arranged into clauses, each of which has three primary positions for verb phrases (subject, direct object and indirect object) and optional places for any number of prepositional phrases. Grammar should provide a systematic way to carry out this mapping so the interpretation process will know which object plays which role and what kind of event-scene is intended.

For example, the superficial marker of the Destination case may be the (logical) indirect object of a *subcategorization frame* headed by some locative prepositions, associating PP and Destination when one of the syntactic-semantic links is selected, that is the correspondence between indirect object and Destination role.

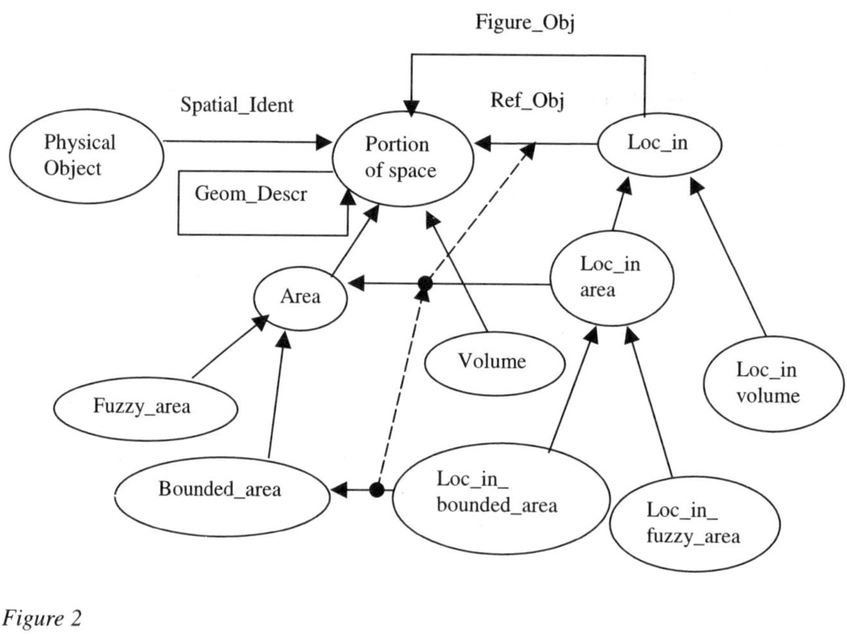

Figure 2

In respect of prepositions, the lexical entry refers to sets of semantic relations in the spatial representation, each one corresponding to a different ideal meaning of a preposition. For example, the preposition *in* deals with the following relations: "located in" (*loc_in* for short) and "destination inward a Reference Object" (*dest_in*). This spatial relation is further specialized when it is associated with the geometric description of the Reference Object, that is the Destination of the action; for example, a spatial relation of location in area may be restricted to *loc_in_fuzzy_area* or *loc_in_bounded_area*.

Referring back to the theories of (Herskovits 1986), such locative actions are discriminated upon the region of space, in terms of geometric description, identified by the spatial relation between Figure and Reference Object.

As result here are the following conceptual entities for verb lexical entries in English and Italian:

Area Location Action

Contact

PUT ON [ordinary solid objects]
[CAUSE ([Object], [Event TELIC ([Object], [Path TO [Place ON ([Object])])])])]

Support
HANG ON appendere [+ by means of]
HEAP UP ammucchiare

STACK accatastare [+ resulting state]

Distribution
NPi COVER/HIDE *coprire*, *nascondere* __NPj <[PP with NPk]>
[CAUSE ([Object]i, [Event PARATELIC ([State BE ([Object]k,
[Place ON ([Object]j)])])])]
SPRAWL *spargere* / SCATTER *disseminare*
STREW *stendere* [flexible solid objects]

Adherence
SPRAY, SPREAD *spruzzare*, *cospargere* [loose solid substances] _NPj <[PP with NPk]>
[CAUSE ([Object]i, [Event PARATELIC ([State BE ([Object]k,
[Place ON ([Object]j)])])])]
WATER *innaffiare* [liquids]

NoContact

PUT OVER, HANG
[CAUSE ([Object], [Event TELIC ([Object], [Path TO ([Place OVER ([Object])])])])]

Volume Location Action

PUT IN , ENTER *mettere in, introdurre* <NPj>
[CAUSE ([Object], [Event TELIC ([Object]i, [Path TO ([Place IN ([Object]j)])])]

Impact (motion culminating in contact with)

NPi INSERT / *DRIVE IN, THRUST IN inserire, ficcare* [± intensive] __NPj
[CAUSE ([Object]i, [Event TELIC ([Object], [Place IN ([Object]j)])])]

Distribution
NPi FILL *riempire, mettere dentro*__NPj <[PP with NPk]>
[CAUSE ([ ]i, [Event PARATELIC ([State BE ([ ]k, [Place IN ([ ]j)])])])]

BOX *inscatolare*
[CAUSE ([ ]i, [Event PARATELIC ([State BE ([ ]k, [Place IN ([BOX]j)])])])]
BOTTLE *imbottigliare* [liquids]
[CAUSE ([ ]i, [Event TELIC ([Object]j, [Path TO [Place IN ([BOTTLE])]])])]
PUT IN SACKS insaccare [commestibles]

Adherence
POUR, SHED / MIX, ADD *versare / mescolare, mischiare* [loose solid substances]

PUT ROUND-ABOUT

Distribution

NPi SURROUND *circondare* __NPj
[State DESC ([Object]i, [Path AROUND ([Object]j)])]

Adherence
WRAP avvolgere
PLUG, *STOP UP* ostruire, bloccare

Line Location Action

PUT ALONG
[CAUSE ([Object], [Event TELIC ([Object], [Path ALONG [Place ON ([Object])])])]

Contiguity
ALIGN, *SET IN ROWS allineare*

Adherence
TWIST, RING *attorcigliare*

Point Location Action
PUT AT

[CAUSE ([Object], [Event TELIC ([Object], [Path TO ([Place AT ([Object])])])])]

Contact
NPi touch/contact NPj
[State BE ([Object]i, [Place AT ([Object]j)])]

Impact
NPi hit/strike NPj
[Event PARATELIC ([State BE ([Object]i, [Place AT ([Object]j)])])]

Moving Contact
NPi stroke/scratch NPj
[Event TELIC ([Object]i, [Path VIA [Place AT ([Object]j])]

Attachment
NPi attach/fasten/glue NPj to NPk
[Event CAUSE ([Object]i, [Event PARATELIC ([State BE ([Object]j, [Place AT ([Object]k)])])]
[Event CAUSE ([Object]i, [Event TELIC ([Object]j, [Path TO ([Place AT ([Object]k)])])])]
NAIL / PIN attaccare, inchiodare / appuntare

Adherence
NPi stick/adhere NPj
[State BE ([Object]i, [Place AT ([Object]j)])

Detachment
NPi detach NPj from NPk
[Event CAUSE ([Object]i, [Event (PARATELIC [State BE ([Object]j, [Place AT-END-OF
[Path FROM [Place AT ([Object]k]]])])])]

Finally, in the our approach, lexical semantics plays a central role indicating the relationship between grammatical relations of sentences and thematic cases of the action described. The fundamental difference of this proposal conceives the appropriate layer of lexical knowledge representation and the use of them in a NL interface.

Moreover, although the model used here derives all linguistic knowledge (pragmatic, semantic and syntactic) from a cognition-action system, so both pragmatic and semantic structures are made of similar cognitive material, they still constitute separate functional processes at different moments in generating natural language sentences. The user can simply use a pragmatic procedure to generate a communicative act, or he can take his own pragmatic procedure as the object or content of a higher conceptualization: he has shifted cognitive levels.

Austin (1962) notes that "To say something is to do something", that is semantics is derived from efforts to do things with words, performing locative actions in the virtual or real world.

Testbed: the SONAS system

We at the IME (Interaction with Modelled Environments) group at Nous are currently implementing the SONAS system, a successor to Spoken Image, which can provide a testbed for our theories on the pragmatic interpretation of spatial language. Each spatial verb and preposition can be implemented in a object-oriented manner by specializing parameters.

For example, the generic function *move* can be specialized by parameters indicating that the movement is single and discrete. The result is *put*. Similarly, the preposition *on* can be modified by the parameter *telic* to become *across*.

One goal of the SONAS system is visual interpretation in VRML (Virtual Reality Modelling Language) or OPEN GL of such spatial expressions. When creating the objects, only coarse-grain predicate like *supports* are attached to objects. The remaining data required for the interpretation are calculated from the several lagers we have postulated, in a way that does justice to the complexity of the task involved.

The system has recently been extended to allow multiple users, and will thus have to cater for viewer-dependent perspective (to take a trivial example, my "left" may be your "right"). We expect our theoretical framework to be rigorously tested by this real world application. The addition of gesture, which we have implemented, will bring the task even closer to situated cognition in the real world (see (Ó Nualláin 1995) for the general cognitive model being proposed).

References

Apter, MJ. (1989). Reversal theory: *Motivation, Emotion and Personality*. London: Routledge.

Austin, J. L. (1962) *How to do things with Words*. New York: Oxford University Press 1962.

Bennett, D. C. (1975). *Spatial and Temporal Uses of English Prepositions: An essay in stratificational semantics*. London: Longman.

Herskovits, A. (1986). *Language and Spatial Cognition*. Cambridge, England: Cambridge University Press.

Herskovits, A. (1997). Language, spatial cognition and vision. In O. Stock (Ed.), *Temporal and Spatial Reasoning*. Boston: Kluwer.

Herskovits, A. (1998). Schematization. In P. Oliver & K.P. Gapp (Ed.), *Representation and Processing of Spatial Expressions*. Mahwah, NJ: Lawrence Erlbaum Associates Inc.

Jackendoff, R. (1983). *Semantics and Cognition*. Cambridge, England: Cambridge University Press.

Jackendoff, R. (1990). *Semantic Structures*. Cambridge, MA: MIT Press.

Jackendoff, R. (1995). *Languages of the Mind*. Cambridge, MA: MIT Press.

Johnson-Laird, P.N. (1983). *Mental Models*. Cambridge, England: Cambridge University Press.

Lakoff, G. (1987). *Women, Fire and Dangerous Things. What categories reveal about the mind*. Chicago: Chicago University Press.

Landau B. & Jackendoff, R. (1993). "What" and "where" in spatial language and spatial cognition. *Behavioral and Brain Sciences,* 16, 217–265.

Langacker, R.W. (1988). A view of linguistic semantics. In B. Rudza-Ostyn (Ed.), *Topics in Cognitive Linguistics* (pp. 49–90). Amsterdam and Philadelphia: John Benjamins.

Marr, D. (1982). *Vision*. San Francisco: Freeman.

Miller, G.A. & Johson-Laird, P.N. (1976). *Language and Perception*. Cambridge, MA: Harvard University Press.

Ó Nualláin, S. & Smith, A. (1994). An investigation into the common semantics of language and vision. AAAI Spring Symposium, Stanford CA. In Mc Kevitt (Ed.), *Integration of Natural Language and Vision Processing*. Dordrecht: Kluwer, 1, 21–31.

Ó Nualláin, S. (1995). *The Search for Mind: A new foundation for Cognitive Science*. Norwood: Ablex/Intellect. Second edition 2000. Bristol: Intellect.

Talmy, L. (1985). Lexicalization patterns: Semantic structures in lexical forms. In T. Shopen (Ed.), *Language Typology and Syntactic Description: Vol.3. Grammatical categories and the lexicon* (pp.57–149). Cambridge University Press.

Ungerleider, L.G. & Miskin, M. (1982). "Two Cortical Visual System". In Ingle, D.J., Goodale, M.A. , and Mansfield R.J.W. eds., *Analysis of Visual Behaviour*, 549–586. Cambridge, Mass.: MIT Press.

Waltz, D.L. (1980). Generating and understanding scene descriptions. In A. Joshi et al. (Eds.), *Elements of Discourse Understanding* (pp. 266–282). Cambridge, England: Cambridge University Press.

The Composition of Conceptual Structure for Spatial Motion Imperatives

John Gurney and Elizabeth Klipple
Army Research Laboratory

1. Introduction

We are concerned with how the full interpretation of language about space and motion is computed from the words in the sentence, the grammatical structures, and the context of utterance. We have implemented a system which simulates this act of interpretation in some detail: a natural language interface to a virtual reality, geographic information system (the NLVR system). Our goal is to provide an expressively powerful human/machine interface by simulating human understanding of natural language imperatives. Examples of the sentences we will discuss include: *turn around*, *drop down to the ground*, *zoom northward*, and *veer off thirty six degrees to your right*. These are the kinds of sentence that a viewer can utter in order to navigate through our virtual environment. Utterances such as these raise two problems for a theory of meaning:

> The problem of computing lexical, phrasal, and full sentence meaning of sentences uttered within an extra-linguistic context; how does the context constrain meaning?
> The problem of composition of meaning; how is the meaning of a sentence composed from the meanings of its parts?

On our view these two problems are linked. In Sections 4 and 5 we motivate and present our theory which (a) captures lexical meaning in terms of conceptual structures of conceptual primitives; and (b) explains how these conceptual structures can be composed into full sentence meanings. We believe that it is important to work out details of this composition of meaning in order to advance and constrain hypotheses about the human conception of space and motion that supports intelligent speech. The ancillary benefit from this work will be a more useful and expressively powerful natural language interface to a VR system.

We begin with a description of the NLVR system in Section 2 followed by a discussion of the situation of the viewer in the virtual environment in Section 3.

2. The virtual environment

The authors have created a fully operational speech and natural language interface to a real-time 3D virtual reality environment. The interface supports navigation in a 3D landscape and is an interesting testbed for detailed semantic interpretation of spatial and motional language.

The virtual environment software runs on a Silicon Graphics Octane computer. We use both a wide screen desktop display (12 inches high by 19 inches wide) and a back-projected glass wall display (5 feet high by 6 and 1/2 feet wide) to show the virtual environment. A snapshot of a typical scene appears in Figure 1. This is a view of the National Training Center in central California. The terrain in this scene is modeled and displayed in real time (about 16 frames per second) using the Virtual Graphic Information System (VGIS) (Koller et al. 1995). The terrain models are derived from elevation and imagery data.

The Spoken Language Navigation Task requires a user (who we call the viewer) to navigate through this environment using only spoken natural language. In this application navigation consists in moving your point of view about in any of six degrees of freedom: at various linear and angular speeds, in various directions, for various distances, or to various locations. It is possible to create complex motions and trajectories in this way. An interesting outcome of this project has been the realization of the importance of perception of spatial motion and how this can be interpreted and controlled through natural language — a point we will return to below.

The theory of lexical meaning as conceptual structure and the composition of these structures into sentence meaning that we present in this paper was implemented in the Interpreter portion of the Navigation Expert Module. We will not take space in this paper to discuss the other modules of the overall computational system, the architecture of which is discussed in (Gurney et al. 1998).

Figure 1. Virtual scene from the viewer's point of view

3. The viewer, the scene, and the environment

To use the NLVR system, a viewer faces the VGIS screen, wearing a microphone headset, and utters commands which are interpreted by the system causing actions in the VGIS system. One utterance will cause changes in the scene to which the viewer may respond with a new utterance in a continuous processing loop. Users quickly learn how utterances affect their movement through the scene. Normal use of this system depends on what the viewer perceives along with other knowledge brought to the task (e.g., notions of compass points) and knowledge inferred. The viewer's utterances and expectations of their effects will depend on his beliefs or conceptions about these and other factors. We will call all of this the viewer's conception of the state of the environment.

We define the actual state of the environment as all of the information about the virtual environment required for fully adequate computation of the meanings

Figure 2. Scene close to a mountain

of the viewer's utterances. There is a well-defined and precise state of the virtual environment that held true at the time of the snapshot in Figure 2. This picture is probably confusing to the reader of this paper. However, the scene at the time this snapshot was captured was not confusing to the viewer because the viewer perceives and represents scenes dynamically and this is essential to the viewer's conception of even stationary objects and (in our case) the terrain. Figure 2 is what the mountain looked like after the viewer had flown straight south from the viewpoint in Figure 1 right up to the side of the mountain. Over this time period the viewer spoke the following utterances into his microphone headset:

stop
crawl straight ahead
look to the southeast
look slowly down thirty degrees
roll

After observing the dynamic effects (motions and turnings) of his utterances the viewer knew what he was perceiving in Figure 2. We will explain how the interpretation of these utterances was computed in Sections 4 and 5. For now we want to use this example of viewpoint navigation to say a few things about system state in our environment. At Figure 2 we have the following values for some of the state variables (where vp is the viewer's viewpoint):

> vp roll = +30.0 degrees from horizontal,
> vp pitch = –30.0 degrees from horizontal,
> vp yaw = 109.0 degrees = southeast bearing,
> vp linear motion vector = 3.75 meters per second and 180.0 degrees bearing,
> vp altitude = +866.0 meters from sea level along vp z axis,
> local ground elevation = +721.9 meters from sea level where vp z axis intersects terrain,
> vp latitude = 35:16:31 N,
> vp longitude = 116:36:46 W.

The representation of these aspects of the state can be accomplished with three coordinate systems that share their origins at the viewer's viewpoint.[1] A gaze coordinate system aligns one axis (its x axis) with the direction of gaze. A local global coordinate system aligns its three axes with the vertical, with North, and with East. The third gravitational coordinate system keeps a vertical axis (shared with the local global system). There are, of course, other collections of coordinate systems that could be employed to represent the same state (Jackendoff 1996 and Tversky 1996). The coordinate systems we use were chosen as natural for the task of computing meanings of the sentences used in this environment, as we will illustrate in the following sections.

As stated above, there are important differences between the state of the environment and the viewer's conception of that state. The former is fully specified or determinate (just as it would be in an actual physical environment where speeds, elevations, bearings, and so on are precisely whatever they are). The viewer's conception abstracts from this. For example, he may conceive of his current speed as fast or slow but not 53 meters per second. Two interesting and pressing questions that arise from this are:

> What is the inventory of spatial entities and structures of the viewer's conceptual state?
> How does this conception correspond to and co-vary with the state of the virtual environment?

Our work in natural language understanding, lexical conceptual structure, and composition of sentence-level meaning offers partial answers to these questions. In the next section we discuss a selection of typical NLVR utterances in this light. And in Section 5 we will discuss our theory of meaning and lexical conceptual structure more formally.

4. Spatial language used for the navigation task

Our purpose in this section is to discuss the problem of computing lexical, phrasal, and full sentence meaning of sentences uttered within the extra-linguistic context, the problem of composition of meaning, and the link between the two.

4.1 *Referring to coordinate systems with verbs*

Interpretation of a sentence like (1) requires that lexical information be combined with contextual information. In our application, the relevant contextual information will be available as state information.

(1) turn the chopper all the way around

The noun phrase *the chopper* in (1) refers to a helicopter. The use of noun phrases to refer to entities has been the most studied aspect of the influence of context on meaning in this century (Russell 1905; Kripke 1972; and Heim 1982). But the meaning of (1) also depends on other aspects of context that are more relevant to our NLVR application and our notion of state discussed above. We are interested here in the verb *turn* and the particle *around* both of which also refer to entities, namely, coordinate systems, vectors, and other items of the state of the environment.

The interpretation of the verb *turn* depends on: choosing a coordinate system; and choosing an axis in that system. The coordinate system must be one that is embedded in the object that bears the thematic role "theme", in this case the helicopter. The axis for turning (the axis about which the rotation occurs) is some salient axis of the gaze system (in this case) of the helicopter. We assume that, by default, this is normally a vertical axis and that, by necessity, this axis must be a canonical axis of the object. For a helicopter, one canonical axis would normally be the one aligned with the shaft of the main propeller.

The particle *around* modifies the verb *turn*. It does so by referring to the same axis in the same system as did the verb. If this reference failed the sentence would be uninterpretable. Thus the sentence:

(2) sell the chopper all the way around

could not have a meaning along the lines of (1) because *sell* does not refer to a spatial coordinate system. There may be another constructible meaning; if so, that would employ a different, though perhaps related meaning of *around* as well (see, for example, (Gruber 1965) on semantic fields and (Lakoff 1987)).

Here we have a sketch both of how the meanings of words depend on state and how the meaning of a sentence is composed. We might say that in (1) the verb and the particle invoke hidden references to geometric entities that are available from the state of the environment. Note, finally, that these meanings depend only on selected aspects of state. The compass bearing of the helicopter, for example, is irrelevant to (1).

4.2 *Referring to axes with particles*

In contrast to (1), most of our utterances in the Spoken Language Navigation Task are imperatives with no direct object as in (3) and (4). These are examples of intransitive, unaccusative verb phrases (Levin and Rappaport Hovav 1995).

(3) turn around
(4) turn over

The missing or unexpressed object here is the addressee. This object is actually represented in the syntactic form of the sentence as a pro subject, as shown in Figure 3. This tree is a simplified form of the output from our parser REAP (Garman, *ms*). REAP implements a Principles and Parameters syntax (Chomsky 1981, 1986) which inserts the pro node in the parse tree and marks that node as the theme. The theme of the verb is, by definition, either the moving object or the object affected by the verb. This is the object that supplies its axis for the turning motion. So the coordinate system invoked by the verb *turn* can be read off the parse tree for (3).

The difference between (3) and (4) is in the particles; *around* refers to a vertical axis and *over* refers to a horizontal axis, both of which must be in a coordinate system referred to by the verb. Evidence for these claims comes from considering the sentences as they would be uttered in different contexts. Thus, if (3) were directed at a person who is standing up a rotation about his major longitudinal axis is normally meant. And if (4) were directed at a person who is lying down rotation around the same longitudinal axis in the same coordinate system is meant. This time that axis happens to be horizontal as required by the adverb *over*. But (3) directed at the person who is lying down is somewhat unnatural or puzzling. This follows from the fact that *turn* prefers the major longitudinal axis (which is now horizontal) while *around* requires a vertical axis. There is a caveat: these effects can be overridden by pragmatic factors. We will not analyze pragmatics in this paper; see (Levinson 1983). We note, however, that pragmatics is somewhat ubiquitous, even in our virtual environment. For example, whether *around* calls for a rotation of 180 degrees, 360 degrees, or some other angular distance is a matter for pragmatics. In our application we

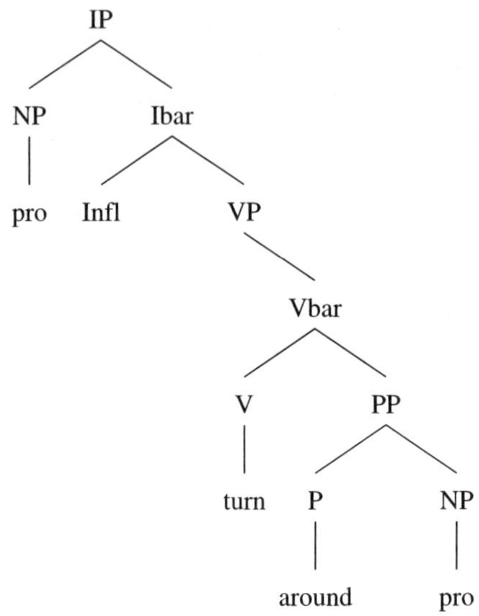

Figure 3. Parse tree for (3)

short-circuit this bit of reasoning by writing 180 degrees into the meaning of *around* (see Section 5). Our plan for the NLVR project includes a more principled and adequate treatment of pragmatics in the future along the lines of (Gurney et al. 1997).

4.3 *Referring to vectors with adverbs and particles*

Imperatives to alter a scalar property of an event, such as speed, as in (5), depend on some current speed for satisfaction. There is also a presupposition of some current speed in (5). Both the existence of speed and the existence of motion are normally perceptible by the viewer, though their determinate values are not normally perceptible. So in (5) the viewer is referring to a speed he can see although he need not know its magnitude.

(5) fly faster
(6) fly up

The verb *fly* in (5) refers to some action and its vector that is in a coordinate system of the theme. Given this, the adverb *faster* refers to the magnitude of that vector, leaving any other properties alone. To capture this we propose that the conceptual structure of the action includes a vector in a coordinate system. Thus a meaning for (5) can be constructed because the adverb refers to the same vector as the verb. How much *faster* increases the speed referred to is a matter for pragmatics or beliefs about normal speeds.[2]

Example (6) differs from (5) by using a particle instead of an adverb. In this case *up* refers to the vector of the linear motion action as did *faster* in (5), but it modifies the direction rather than the magnitude of the vector. In our application *up* simply redirects the motion vector in its coordinate system, leaving all else untouched.

Before moving on to a completely different type of verb modification we should mention an important variation on (6).

(7) fly up the hill
(8) go up the hill

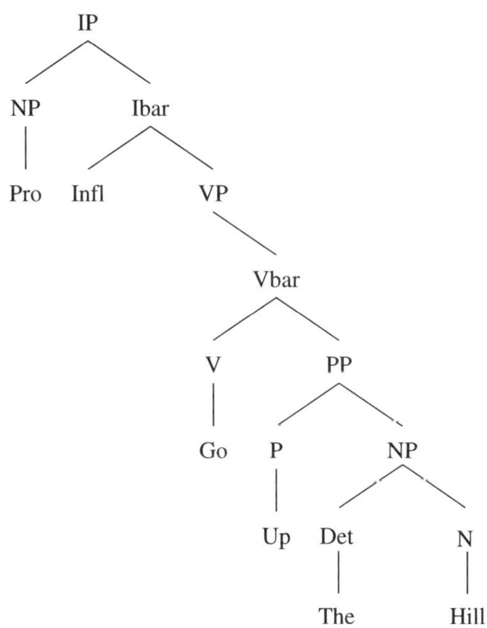

Figure 4. Parse tree for (8)

Here we have replaced the particle *up* with the prepositional phrase *up the hill*. The parse tree for (8) appears in Figure 4. As before, the word *up* refers to an axis in a coordinate system, as well as the positive direction. The coordinate system is still embedded in the object referred to by pro, that is, its origin is in the object. But the vector referred to by *up* must be aligned with the intrinsic coordinate system of the object of the preposition, the hill. The question is which coordinate system of the hill does *up* refer to? Unlike the viewer's viewpoint, a hill has spatial size and structure. For this reason, none of the three coordinate systems (gaze, gravitational, global) may suffice for what is meant by *up the hill*. Elsewhere (Klipple and Gurney 1997) we proposed a family of curvilinear coordinate systems that conforms to the outer surface of the hill. After referring to one of these coordinate systems, *up* aligns its vector with the appropriate z-axis within. Our current NLVR application does not implement cases like these, mainly because we have no computations yet that can recognize or extract proper hills or other such emergent terrain objects in our environment.

4.4 *Creating goals for actions with prepositional phrases*

Sentences like (9), which refer to a goal of an action, have been at the center of research in lexical semantics (Gruber 1965; Jackendoff 1983; Levin and Rappaport Hovav 1996; Tenny 1987).

(9) drop down to the ground
(10) drop down

Example (9) requests a completed action. (10) requests an action that has no definite end; any amount of dropping down would do.[3] In a sense, these two actions are of different kinds. The verb *drop* in (9) refers to the viewer's local gravitational coordinate system. It also refers to an axis in that coordinate system (namely, the vertical axis) as well as a motion vector, pointing down, aligned with that axis. In this way, the verb *drop* incorporates meaning that is typically expressed by verb modifiers (like the particle *down*). In our implementation, the particle *down* in (9) is redundant; explaining why it looks natural for it to appear in (9) is beyond our current interest. Since it is redundant, its meaning composes nicely with the meaning of *drop*; it also refers to the vertical axis and a vector along it pointing down. On the other hand (11):

(11) drop up

would be uninterpretable. The verb and the particle refer to the same coordinate system and axis but they also refer to opposite (therefore, incompatible) vectors.

The prepositional phrase *to the ground* creates a goal in (9). This result arises out of composition of meaning — as it must. The noun phrase *the ground* refers to a piece of the terrain. The preposition *to* operates on this terrain to refer to a location in the coordinate system referred to by the verb *drop*. This location is the goal. So the original unbounded, atelic motion action becomes part of a more complex telic action. Our views on the transformation of atelic to telic spatial motion actions follow the lines originally proposed by (Pustejovsky 1992) (which fails to account for spatial geometry, however). An adequate cognitive theory of telicity for spatial motion actions has not been developed at this time. For the NLVR implementation, we simply distinguish two versions for each action — one atelic and one telic.

4.5 *Other examples*

There are several other ways that the meanings of words access conceptions of the state of the environment. Examples of a few other kinds of sentence that fall into this group are: *start dropping a lot faster*, *veer off thirty six degrees to your right*, *look straight down*, *back up three klicks*.

We have said little about the mood of our sentences. All of the examples we have discussed are in the imperative mood. The declarative mood of (12) and the interrogative mood of (13) have rather different effects in our application, of course.

(12) he turned around
(13) did he turn around

Meanings of words and phrases are the same no matter what the mood of the sentences. Mood, however, takes scope over a sentence. It ranges over the conceptual structure that was composed for a sentence and determines how a sentence is to be understood and responded to.

5. The composition of meaning in the navigation expert module

Our natural language interpreter composes meanings for sentences that have been parsed by REAP and translated into logical forms by the Logical Form (LF) Module. The logical forms for some of the sentences we have discussed include:

LF for (3): *[pro:X1, [turn:E:X1, [around:E:X2, pro:X2]]]*
LF for (5): *[pro:X1, [fly:E:X1, faster:E]]*
LF for (9): *[pro:X1, [drop:E:X1, [down:E:X2, pro:X2], [to:E:X3, [the:X3, ground:X3]]]*
LF: *[pro:X1, [veer:E:X1, [off:E:X2, pro:X2], [measure:E:X3, [number:thirty-six:X3, degree:X3], [to:E:X4, [your:X4, right:X4]]]]*

In these logical forms of natural language sentences, *E* is the event referred to by the verb (Davidson 1966) and the *Xs* are the various participants in the event. Thus, *turn:E:X1* means that *E* is a turning event with *X1* as its theme.[4] The process of interpretation in the Navigation Expert Module works by traversing the LF structure recursively while accessing lexical entries for words (which have become predicates in the LF). The composition of meaning occurs during this process by accessing the sub-lexical elements not visible in the LF (see next subsection) and applying compositional functions over them.

5.1 *The lexicon*

Lexical entries for verbs, adverbs, particles, prepositions, nouns, and so on, must specify structures of the appropriate state elements. These are the lexical conceptual structures, LCSs.[5] Thus, words decompose into structures of non-linguistic primitives. Fully adequate LCSs for the lexicon of a natural language such as English is a goal of ongoing research (Levin 1993; Pustejovsky 1993; Klipple 1997). For our purposes, we have built an inventory of LCSs that aims to be adequate for the NLVR navigation task.

Here in schematic form are a few of our lexical entries. An explanation of terminology follows below. Some verbs:

vm(turn, rotate-act:E:TH).
vm(turn, rotateto-act:E, TH).
vm(rotate, rotate-act:E:TH).
vm(rotate, rotateto-act:E:TH).

In the lexical entries for *turn* and *rotate* — which we do not distinguish in our current system — *E* is the event (Davidson 1966) and *TH* is the theme (moving object).[6] Both words refer to the same basic (i.e., conceptual) action, *rotate-act*. As mentioned above, we divide all basic motion acts into telic and atelic versions, for example, *rotate-act* and *rotateto-act*.

The verb *zoom* can mean either an axial act like *rotate-act* or a linear act like *translate-act*. This verb incorporates not only a reference to the act but also one of the properties of a basic act, namely, *speed*, as shown in the following lexical entries.

*vm(zoom, [A, speed(A:E:TH, FS)]) :- typeact(A, axial), canon(A, TH, speed, S), FS is 4.0 * S.*
*vm(zoom, [A, speed(A:E:TH, FS)]) :- typeact(A, linear), canon(A, TH, speed, S), FS is 4.0 * S.*

In the first entry for *zoom*, *A* is the basic motion act (it could be *rotate-act)*, and *FS* is the required speed, which is (perhaps arbitrarily) fixed at four times some canonical speed for the object *TH* undergoing the act *A*.

The particle *around* is represented as:

partm(around, A:E:X, [coordsystem(E, CS), axis(Z, CS), embed(CS, X), goal(E, 180.0)]) :- typeact(A, axial), typeact(A, telic).

In this lexical entry for *around*, *E* is the event and *X* is some entity referred to by the pro object of the particle in the parse tree. As we can see, the word *around* refers to several properties of a basic action: *coordsystem*, *axis*, and *goal.* Furthermore, this meaning for *around* can only apply to acts of type *axial.*[7]

In general, these words refer to actions, geometrical and other entities, or their properties. There is a finite number of these conceptual items and there are various restrictions on their types and application. Furthermore, the members of this relatively small group of conceptual items are constituents of a relatively large number of word meanings.

5.2 *Conceptual primitives: Basic actions and properties*

The basic actions, entities, and their properties that we employ in building the lexicon are the types of things that also become the components for the state of the virtual environment discussed in Section 3. Many of them are observable by the viewer or can be easily brought into the viewer's conception of the state. Below we list a few examples of these conceptual primitives.

Basic actions occur in a taxonomy, a portion of which we display here. *rotate-act* is a motion that is axial. *translate-act* is a motion that is linear.

motion(E) :- axial(E)
motion(E) :- linear(E).
axial(E) :- rotation act(E).
linear(E) :- translate-act(E).

The basic actions have structure, examples of which are specified by the following two formulae. *rotate-act* has an axis *A* in a coordinate system *C* that is embedded in some object *X*. *E* is a variable that will be bound to any particular instance of a *rotate-act* event.

rotate-act(E, X) :- axis(E, A), coordsystem(A, C), embed(C, X).
translate-act(E, X) :- vector(E, V), coordsystem(V, C), embeddedin(C, X).

As illustrated in the lexical and basic action examples above, the basic actions have various associated properties. In addition to *axis*, *vector*, etc., others are: *direction(E, D)* which is the positive or negative direction of an axial act, *gaze(C)* which is a type of coordinate system, and *zaxis(A)* which singles out an axis in a coordinate system. In addition, there are: linear measure, angular measure, coordinate points, and rates of change of quantities, among others.

5.3 *Other actions*

Properties and quantities get fixed by value-setting and value-getting actions. For example, for the imperative (3) (*turn around*) the following value-setting action would be performed before executing the main action:

> *set(goal, E, 180.0).*

And for the imperative (7) (*drop down to the ground*) there are two preliminary value-setting actions and one preliminary value-getting action:

> *set(direction, E, negative),*
> *get(elevation(H, terrain)),*
> *set(goal, E, H).*

Value-getting actions corresponding to the state variables include:

> *get(E, speed, S),*
> *get(X, pitch, P),*
> *rotating(X, YN).*

The formula *rotating(X, yes)* means that *X* is currently rotating.

6. Conclusion

The lexical semantic constituents of the words we have been discussing refer to pieces of the viewer's conception of the state of the environment. For language about space and motion, these include coordinate systems, axes, motion vectors, direction vectors, the terrain and other objects, including the viewer. These types of entities should be added to the ontology already assumed for LCSs. This is necessary for two reasons: first, for an adequate treatment of the semantics; and second, for grounding interpretation in real or artificial non-linguistic contexts. Vagueness and other kinds of uncertainty must be accounted for by pragmatics and inference from world knowledge, and values determined in this way must be input to the algorithm that composes meaning. Meanings of phrases and sentences are found by coherently composing the items referred to by the words, in an algorithmic and predictable manner.

Acknowledgments

The authors are indebted to: Joseph Garman of the University of Maryland for the Generative Grammar parser REAP; Timothy Gregory of the Army Research Laboratory (ARL) for the Navigation Application Program Interface to the VGIS system; and Michael Salonish and others for the ARL version of VGIS.

Notes

1. (Jackendoff 1996) talks about coordinate systems as "frames of reference". The same notion (or a closely related one) is called "perspective" in (Levelt 1996; Tversky 1996).
2. If we were to extend normal Tarskian denotational semantics to this case we would say that the verb denotes a set of vectors and the adverb denotes a subset of this set. See (Chierchia and McConnell-Ginet 1990) for an example of Tarskian formal semantics applied to natural language and see (Larson and Segal 1995) for a non-set-theoretic and, to our thinking, more interesting version of formal semantics.
3. The lexical semantics of *drop* has to be compatible with telic (bounded) and atelic (unbounded) meanings. This is not trivial, but we will not discuss it here. See (Dowty 1979; Tenny 1987; Dorr and Olsen 1997).
4. The notation here and throughout Section 5 is Prolog.
5. Our theory of LCS is not identical to that of (Jackendoff 1983) or (Levin and M. Rappaport Hovav 1995, 1996) but it is in the same spirit. We would envision that the theory of LCS be supplemented by our proposals.
6. The verbs *turn* and *rotate* actually have significant but only partially overlapping distributions in English.
7. This kind of restriction achieves for verb meaning what (Pustejovsky 1993) calls co-composition.

References

Chomsky, Noam (1981). *Lectures on Government and Binding*. Dordrecht: Foris.

Chomsky, Noam (1986). *Knowledge of Language*. New York: Praeger.

Davidson, Donald (1966). The Logical Form of Action Sentences. In D. Davidson, *Essays on Actions and Events* (105–121). Oxford: Clarendon Press, 1980.

Dorr, Bonnie and Mari Olsen (1996). Multilingual Generation: the Role of Telicity in Lexical Choice and Syntactic Realization. *Machine Translation*, 11, 37–74.

Dowty, David (1979). *Word Meaning and Montague Grammar*. Dordrecht: Reidel.

Emonds, Joseph (1985). *A Unified Theory of Syntactic Categories*. Dordrecht: Foris.

Garman, Joseph (*ms.*). REAP: A Right-Edge Adjunction Parser. University of Maryland.

Gruber, Jeffrey (1965). *Studies in Lexical Relations*. Ph.D. dissertation, MIT.

Gurney, John, Elizabeth Klipple, and Timothy Gregory, (1998). The Spoken Language Navigation Task, In *Proceedings of the American Association for Artificial Intelligence Workshop on Representations for Multi-Modal Human-Computer Interaction*, Madison, Wisconsin.

Gurney, John, Donald Perlis, and Khemdut Purang, (1997). Interpreting Presuppositions Using Active Logic: From Contexts to Utterances. *Computational Intelligence*, 13, 391–413.

Gurney, John, Elizabeth Klipple and Clare Voss (1996). Talking about What We Think We See: Natural Language Processing for a Real-Time Virtual Environment. In *Proceedings of the IEEE International Joint Symposia on Intelligence and Systems*, Washington, DC.

Heim, Irene (1982). *The Semantics of Definite and Indefinite Noun Phrases*. PhD. dissertation, University of Massachusetts.

Jackendoff, Ray (1983). *Semantics and Cognition*. Cambridge, MA: MIT.

Jackendoff, Ray (1996). The Architecture of the Linguistic-Spatial Interface. In P. Bloom et al. (Eds.), *Language and Space* (1–30). Cambridge, MA: MIT.

Kamp, Hans (1981). A Theory of Truth and Discourse Representation. In J. Groenendijk and T. Janssen and M. Stokof (Eds.), *Formal Methods in the Study of Language*. Amsterdam: Mathematical Centre.

Klipple, Elizabeth (1997). Prepositions and Variation. In A. M. Di Sciullo, ed.,
Projections and Interface Conditions: Essays on Modularity (74–108). Oxford University Press.

Klipple, Elizabeth and John Gurney (1997). A Theory of Spatial Structure for Motion-Verb Phrases: From Lexical Syntax to Meaning Representation. International Conference on Computational Semantics, Tilburg, Netherlands.

Koller, David, Peter Lindstrom, William Ribarsky, Larry F. Hodges, Nick Faust, and Gregory Turner (1995). Virtual GIS: A Real-Time 3D Geographic Information System. Abstract. *In Proceedings of Visualization 95.*

Kripke, Saul (1972). *Naming and Necessity*. Cambridge, MA: Harvard University.

Lakoff, George (1987). *Women, Fire, and Dangerous Things*. Chicago: University of Chicago.

Larson, Richard and Gabriel Segal (1995). *Knowledge of Meaning*. Cambridge, MA: MIT.

Levelt, Willem (1996). Perspective Taking and Ellipsis in Spatial Description. In P. Bloom et al. (Eds.), *Language and Space* (77–108). Cambridge, MA: MIT.

Levin, Beth (1993). *English Verb Classes and Alternations*. Chicago: University of Chicago.

Levin, Beth and Malka Rappaport Hovav (1995). *Unaccusativity: At the Syntax-Lexical Semantics Interface*. Cambridge, MA: MIT.

Levin, Beth and Malka Rappaport Hovav (1996). Lexical Semantics and Syntactic Structure. In S. Lappin (Ed.), *Handbook of Contemporary Semantic Theory* (487–508). Oxford: Blackwell.

Levinson, Stephen (1983). *Pragmatics*. Cambridge, MA: Cambridge University.

Pustejovsky, James (1991). The Generative Lexicon. In *Computational Linguistics*.

Pustejovsky, James (1992). The Syntax of Event Structure. In B. Levin and S. Pinker (Eds.), *Lexical and Conceptual Semantics* (47–82). Oxford: Blackwell.

Russell, Bertrand (1905). On Denoting. In *Mind*.

Tenny, Carol (1987). *Grammaticalizing Aspect and Affectedness*. PhD. dissertation, MIT.

Tversky, Barbara (1996). Spatial Perspective in Descriptions. In P. Bloom et al. (Eds.), *Language and Space* (463–492). Cambridge, MA: MIT.

Modelling Spatial Inferences in Text Understanding

Ute Schmid, Sylvia Wiebrock and Fritz Wysotzki
Technical University of Berlin

1. Introduction

When reading a text describing the arrangement of objects, humans construct a *mental model* (Garnham 1981; Glenberg and Langston 1992) representing the situation. This mental model is "structurally identical" (Johnson-Laird 1983) to the described situation in the sense that the relations holding in the situation can be inferred from the model. In our approach, the mental model is represented by a graph. The nodes correspond to the objects, while the arcs are labelled with the relations.

A sample text describing spatial configurations — similar to the texts used in experiments by Franklin and Tversky (1990) and Hörnig et al. (1996) — is:[1]

(1) Torsten is standing in the kitchen.
(2) The refrigerator is standing on the left of Torsten.
(3) The bowl is standing on the refrigerator
Sentences for the other three basic directions
(4) Torsten turns left.
...

In this paper, we will deal with inferences in the static situation described by (1)–(3) only, and not with those involving motions (e.g. (4)).

To handle texts like the one above, we want to be able (a) to distinguish *deictic* and *intrinsic* uses of spatial propositions, (b) to allow for a reorientation and/or movement of objects, and (c) to infer spatial relations after reorientation of the protagonist. Therefore, objects are supplied with a coordinate system. The x-axis corresponds to the left/right axis, the y-axis to the front/back axis and the

z-axis to the above/below axis of the body. The orientation of these axes is arbitrary for objects without intrinsic axes. To describe relations, we follow an approach that is used in robotics (Ambler and Popplestone 1975). A relation between two objects A and B is described by the 4 × 4 matrix corresponding to the rotation and translation needed to map the coordinate system of A onto that of B. For the restricted case where only rotations around the vertical (z) axis are allowed, this matrix has the form:

$$T = \begin{pmatrix} & & & \Delta_x^{(A,B)} \\ & R & & \Delta_y^{(A,B)} \\ & & & \Delta_z^{(A,B)} \\ 0 & 0 & 0 & 1 \end{pmatrix} \quad \text{with} \quad R = \begin{pmatrix} \cos\theta & -\sin\theta & 0 \\ \sin\theta & \cos\theta & 0 \\ 0 & 0 & 1 \end{pmatrix}$$

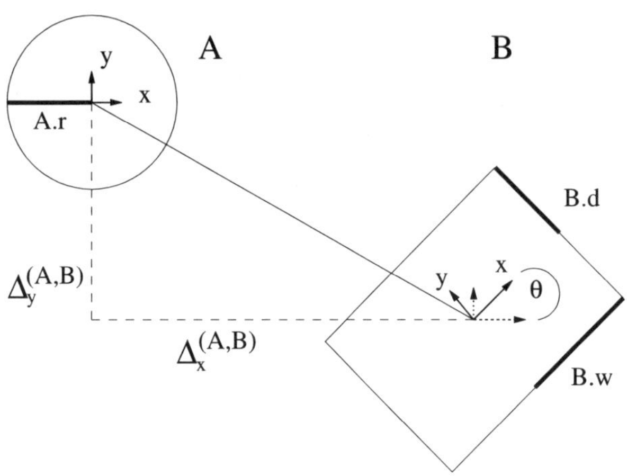

Figure 1. Relatum A and localized object B

In Figure 1, the meaning of the parameters of the transformation matrix is shown. We use extended objects. At present, two forms are possible: cuboids with dimensions *w*idth for the x-axis, *d*epth for the y-axis, and *h*eight for the z-axis, and cylinders with dimensions *r*adius for the x- and y-axes and *h*eight for the z-axis. We don't have default objects, i.e. in general there may be bounds on the extension of an object, but we don't know the exact size. The origin of the coordinate system is positioned at the geometric center of the object. The dimensions are always measured from the origin of the coordinate system along the corresponding axis. That means that the parameters denote half the size of the object. Note that even in a situation where all objects are standing on the ground, the $\Delta_z^{(A,B)}$ values will be non-null whenever objects have different heights.

Spatial relations like *right_of* are defined by constraints on the parameters of the transformation matrix. To find psychologically valid definitions for spatial relations is an open problem.

Though Franklin, Henkel, and Zangas (1995) and Vorwerg and Rickheit (1998) report overlapping, non-symmetric regions of different sizes for the four basic directions, we are not sure whether these results are applicable to text understanding. For a discussion of the influence of relative size and orientation on the so-called "acceptance areas" see, e.g. Hernández (1994), Gapp (1994) or Gapp (1995). In our model, we usually know neither the exact sizes, nor the exact distances and angles of objects. Therefore it is hard to include these results in our definitions. Other results from Zimmer et al. (1998) support the theory that the four base relations are nearly exclusively used for the prototypical positions (only along the axes). Thus, at present we simplify the definitions and use the relations shown in Figure 2. B is *right_of* A if and only if the smallest bounding box containing B (shown with dotted lines in the picture) is completely included in the *right* region of A. Such simplifications are common in artificial intelligence solutions. We plan to include more realistic definitions in the future, but concentrate on other aspects of the model at the moment. For the sample texts considered so far, these definitions are sufficient.

Intrinsic spatial relations are defined by a set of (in)equations using the parameters of the matrix and the dimensions of the two objects. As any movement (and rotation) can be described by a transformation matrix, the relation between two objects can easily be updated. It is also possible to introduce a third parameter (the current reference frame, see Claus et al. (1998) for a discussion) and compute the relation between A and B for a given perspective V in case of a deictic interpretation of the relation. Currently, we always assume that an intrinsic reading is intended. In contrast to qualitative spatial reasoning (e.g. Hernández 1993), where it is not possible to compute the relation between B and A, given only the *intrinsic* relation between A and B, we only need to invert the matrix to compute the transformation. As can be seen in Figure 2, this transformation need not correspond to a defined relation. In the example, we cannot label the arc from C to A with the name of a relation. This means, the arcs in

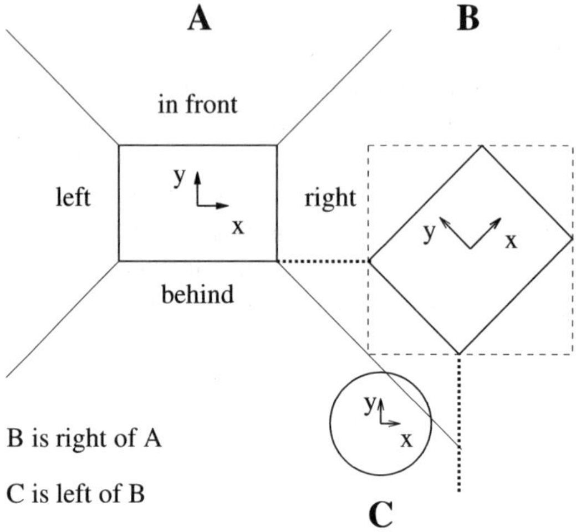

Figure 2. A possible set of relations

our graphs will always be labelled with a transformation matrix and may also be labelled with the name(s) of one or more defined relations.

In the following, we will use the example text to explain the algorithm we have implemented. The psychological motivation for our program, and the unsolved questions with respect to the construction of and the access to a mental model are discussed in Claus et al. (1998). Recent results can also be found in Hörnig et al. (1999).

2. Description of the Program

When started, the program reads the definition of objects and predefined relations from two files.An object description contains the name of an object class (e.g. *person*), the form (*cylinder*), the names of the dimensions (r and h) and optionally upper and lower bounds on the possible extensions. The graph is initialized with a subgraph representing a *room* object[2] (see Figure 3). When sentence (1) is read, a node for Torsten is created and an arc from *Torsten* to the *room* node is introduced which is labelled with *is_in_room* and the generic transformation matrix. The constraints for the *is_in_room* relation are stored in the constraint table. The transformation matrix $T^{(room,To)}$ describes the rotation of the axes and the translation of the origin of the *room* coordinate system necessary to identify both coordinate systems. When this matrix is multiplied with a vector representing a location of an object A (respectively its origin) in *Torsten's* coordinate system, the result is the location of A with respect to the *room* coordinate system. Therefore the arc is pointed from *Torsten* to the *room* node. In Figure 3 the default graph for a *room* node and the default layout of a room is shown. Neither the *room* object nor any of its sub-objects have intrinsic front or right sides. The coordinate system of *room* is positioned parallel to its walls. The coordinate systems of the walls are positioned in such a way that the relation *is_in_room* corresponds to a negative $\Delta_x^{(Wall,A)}$ value for any object A and any wall.

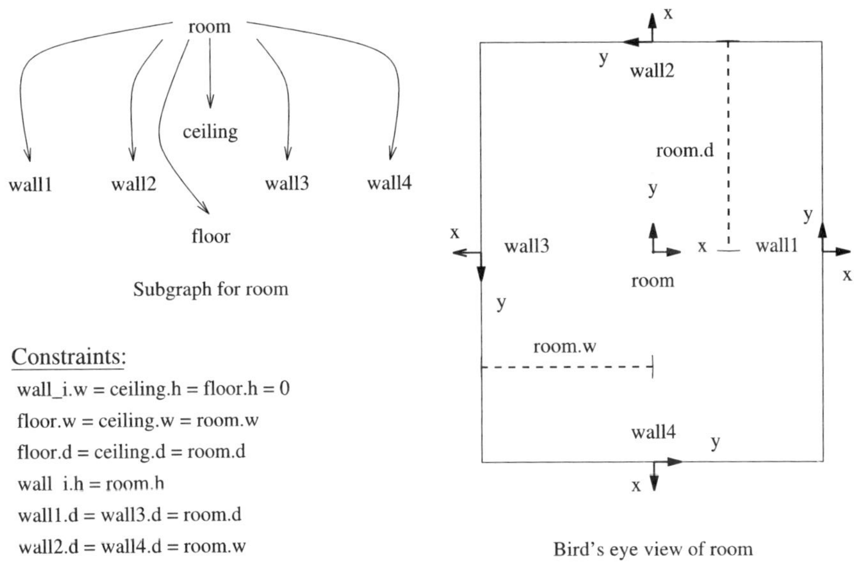

Figure 3. Default constellation for room object(s)

When sentence (2) is read, a node for the *refrigerator* is created, the arc for the mentioned relation *left_of (Torsten, refrigerator)* is introduced, and the arc for the relation *is_in_room* (*refrigerator*) is introduced (as part of our background knowledge). The transformation matrix and constraints for the *is_in_room* (*refrigerator*) arc are computed by multiplying the matrices for $T^{(room,To)}$ and $T^{(To,re)}$ and propagating the constraints. In addition, the generic constraints for the is_in_room relation are stored (they only state that an object must be com-

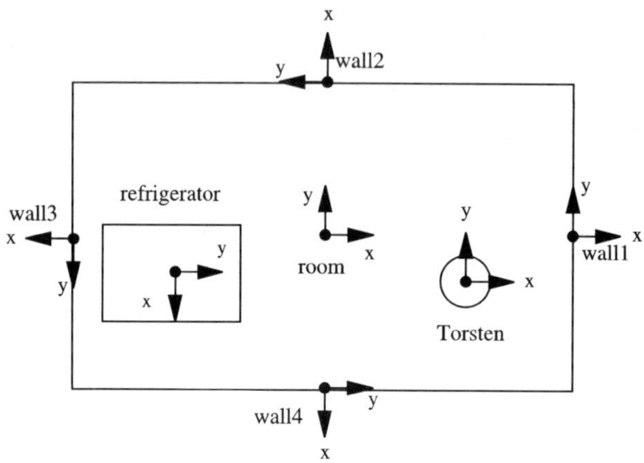

Figure 4. Possible situation for sentences (1) and (2)

pletely inside the room). A possible situation for these two sentences is shown in Figure 4. As the walls are not distinguished, we have chosen to orient *Torsten* so that his coordinate system is parallel to the *room* coordinate system. This corresponds to the transformation matrix

$$T^{(room,\,To)} = \begin{pmatrix} 1 & 0 & 0 & \Delta_x^{(\text{room},\text{To})} \\ 0 & 1 & 0 & \Delta_y^{(\text{room},\text{To})} \\ 0 & 0 & 1 & \text{To.h} - \text{room.h} \\ 0 & 0 & 0 & 1 \end{pmatrix}$$

with the constraints for the *is_in_room* relation

$$-(\text{room.w} - \text{To.r}) \leq \Delta_x^{(\text{room},\text{To})} \leq \text{room.w} - \text{To.r} \qquad \text{and}$$

$$-(\text{room.d} - \text{To.r}) \leq \Delta_y^{(\text{room},\text{To})} \leq \text{room.d} - \text{To.r}$$

The refrigerator has an intrinsic front (presumably where the door is) and is oriented with its back side against the wall. The transformation matrices for *left_of* (*Torsten, refrigerator*) and *is_in_room* (*refrigerator*) are

$$T^{(To,\,re)} = \begin{pmatrix} 0 & 1 & 0 & \Delta_x^{(\mathrm{To,re})} \\ -1 & 0 & 0 & \Delta_y^{(\mathrm{To,re})} \\ 0 & 0 & 1 & \mathrm{re.h} - \mathrm{To.h} \\ 0 & 0 & 0 & 1 \end{pmatrix}$$

with the constraints

$$\Delta_x^{(\mathrm{To,re})} \le -(\mathrm{To.r} + \mathrm{re.d})$$

$$-\Big[\Big(\big|\Delta_x^{(\mathrm{To,re})}\big| - \mathrm{To.r} - \mathrm{re.d}\Big) + (\mathrm{To.r} - \mathrm{re.w})\Big] =$$

$$-\Big(-\Delta_x^{(\mathrm{To,re})} - \mathrm{re.d} - \mathrm{re.w}\Big) \le \Delta_y^{(\mathrm{To,re})} \le \Big(-\Delta_x^{(\mathrm{To,re})} - \mathrm{re.d} - \mathrm{re.w}\Big)$$

and $$T^{(room,\,re)} = \begin{pmatrix} 0 & 1 & 0 & \Delta_x^{(\mathrm{room,re})} \\ -1 & 0 & 0 & \Delta_y^{(\mathrm{room,re})} \\ 0 & 0 & 1 & \mathrm{re.h} - \mathrm{room.h} \\ 0 & 0 & 0 & 1 \end{pmatrix}$$

with the constraints

$$\Delta_x^{(room,re)} = \Delta_x^{(room,To)} + \Delta_x^{(To,re)}$$

$$-(\mathrm{room.w} - \mathrm{re.d}) \le \Delta_x^{(room,re)} \le \mathrm{room.w} - 2\mathrm{To.r} - \mathrm{re.d}$$

$$\Delta_y^{(room,re)} = \Delta_y^{(room,To)} + \Delta_y^{(To,re)}$$

$$-(\mathrm{room.d} - \mathrm{re.w}) \le \Delta_y^{(room,re)} \le \mathrm{room.d} - \mathrm{re.w}$$

To get these (in)equations, we use the fact that $T^{(room,re)} = T^{(room,To)}$ x $T^{(To,re)}$. Thus we get the generic constraints for the *is_in_room* relation updated with the upper bound on $\Delta_x^{(To,re)}$ plus the equations for $\Delta_x^{(room,To)}$ and $\Delta_y^{(room,To)}$. The constraints on $\Delta_y^{(To,re)}$ contain the variable $\Delta_x^{(To,re)}$ and are not used to build further constraints for $\Delta_y^{(room,re)}$.

This strategy of immediately updating the *is_in_room* arcs corresponds to the selection of the *room* coordinate system as a global reference frame. Though we retain all arcs given by the propositions, we always compute the position relative to the *room*. To use the coordinate system of the protagonist (e.g. *Torsten*) would be cognitively more plausible, but as yet we have no conclusive results about the building and updating of mental models and have opted for the most efficient (from a computer science point of view) strategy.

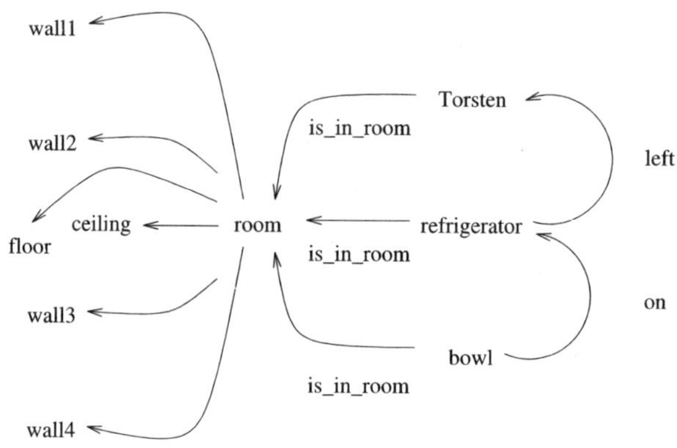

Figure 5. The graph after three sentences

Suppose that after sentence (3), we have the graph in Figure 5. In this graph all and only the relations given in the text plus the implicit *is_in_room* arcs are represented. Suppose further that we were asked the relationship between *Torsten* and the *bowl*. To infer the relation between *Torsten* and *bowl*, we have to find a directed path from *bowl* to *Torsten*. In the figure there is exactly one such path, but — as stated above — we can easily compute the inverse relation, i.e. invert the arc, by computing the inverse matrix. These inverted arcs are not introduced into the graph, because we want to keep the number of arcs as small as possible, but can be used for the inference. Now we get four possible paths: *bowl – refrigerator – Torsten*, *bowl – room – Torsten*$^{-1}$, *bowl – refrigerator room – Torsten*$^{-1}$, and *bowl – room – refrigerator*$^{-1}$ *– Torsten*, where the raised $^{-1}$ denotes inverting the preceding arc. The default relation is_in_room introduced for every object ensures that the graph is always connected. Therefore we will always find at least one path. Which path is chosen for the inference depends on the search strategy. From a computational point of view, we might prefer to omit the search altogether and take the path via the *room* node which is always a shortest path. This is the default strategy we have implemented at present.[3] If we have found a path, we can multiply the transformation matrices at the arcs. For the default path via the room node, we get the equation

$$T^{(\text{Torsten,bowl})} = T^{(\text{room,Torsten})^{-1}} \times T^{(\text{room,bowl})}$$

If we substitute the known matrices on the right side, we get

$$\begin{pmatrix} 1 & 0 & 0 & -\Delta_x^{(\text{room,To})} \\ 0 & 1 & 0 & -\Delta_y^{(\text{room,To})} \\ 0 & 0 & 1 & -(\text{To.h} - \text{room.h}) \\ 0 & 0 & 0 & 1 \end{pmatrix}$$

$$\times \begin{pmatrix} 0 & 1 & 0 & \Delta_x^{(\text{room,bowl})} \\ -1 & 0 & 0 & \Delta_y^{(\text{room,bowl})} \\ 0 & 0 & 1 & \text{2re.h+bowl.h} - \text{room.h} \\ 0 & 0 & 0 & 1 \end{pmatrix}$$

$$= \begin{pmatrix} 0 & 1 & 0 & \Delta_x^{(\text{room,bowl})} - \Delta_x^{(\text{room,To})} \\ -1 & 0 & 0 & \Delta_y^{(\text{room,bowl})} - \Delta_y^{(\text{room,To})} \\ 0 & 0 & 1 & \text{2re.h+bowl.h} - \text{room.h} - (\text{To.h} - \text{room.h}) \\ 0 & 0 & 0 & 1 \end{pmatrix}$$

After simplifying the expressions as far as possible and propagating the constraints for the parameters in the matrix, we have to match the constraints for the transformation matrix against the definitions of *all* pre-defined relations. For the example above, it can easily be proved that *left_of* (*Torsten, bowl*) holds (and none of the other relations, if we only provide the set shown in Figure 2 and *on*). For the natural path *bowl* – *refrigerator* – *Torsten*, the computations would be even simpler.

In general, this task is by no means trivial, because we can get nonlinear equations involving trigonometric expressions. As shown above, a possible simplification of the problem is the use of defaults. Currently, we restrict the orientations of objects to multiples of 90° around the *z*-axis. This means that the coordinate systems of all objects become parallel or orthogonal. This makes the inferences easier without too much loss of expressive power. We are at present working on the problem of finding heuristics to prove trigonometric (in)equations for arbitrary rotations around the z-axis. We are also investigating the application of machine learning algorithms for constraint solving (see Geibel et al. 1998).

3. Related Work

We have described above a quantitative approach to spatial reasoning. Typically, this approach is used when both the size and the positions of the objects are known. In applications, as for example the virtual office environment of Jörding and Wachsmuth (1996), where a robot can move objects to support computer aided design tasks, the use of quantitative methods is mandatory. While our focus is on the inference of spatial relations, in their scenario the emphasis is on changing perspective (involving such inferences) and on the interpretation of spatial expressions. The early work from Waltz and Boggess (1979) is also similar to our approach, but relies heavily on defaults, which greatly simplifies the inference process. Compared to these works we face two additional problems: (a) our (in)equations are not strictly numerical, but contain variables for object extensions and distances. This means we often have incomparable expressions in constraints on the same variable which makes constraint propagation and constraint solving more difficult, and (b) in the general case those (in)equations will also contain trigonometric functions.

Most papers on spatial reasoning favour qualitative calculi. Mukerjee and Mittal (1995) argue that spatial information is usually non-quantitative and under determined. Therefore, a coarser qualitative calculus may often suffice for the task at hand. In their work, they compare different calculi for qualitative homogeneous coordinate transformations, i.e. all matrix entries are elements of $\{-1, 0, 1\}$. Though they additionally make use of topological information, the composition of relations yields a high degree of uncertainty in the general case. There are only nine possible sectors for objects in two dimensions, and the extension of objects (non-overlapping) cannot be formulated. On the other hand, the inference process is very efficient and Mukerjee and Mittal suggest the use of such calculi in restricted domains or in hybrid reasoning systems.

More typical for qualitative spatial reasoning is the work of Hernández (Hernández 1994; 1993). In his calculus, a relation between two objects is determined by an orientation (e.g. front-right), topological information (e.g. touching) and the current frame of reference. His 2-D model allows the specification of different levels of granularity for the orientation.

Despite the computational advantages of qualitative reasoning, we feel the lack of expressive power — (relative) size of objects, and distances cannot be expressed — justifies to investigate the more involved quantitative methods described above.

4. Discussion and outlook

In this paper we have focussed on the program and have largely ignored the psychological questions concerning the mental model. These questions are discussed in Claus et al. (1998). The model as presented above is implemented as a prototype SPACE/0 (Wiebrock et al. 2000). In this prototype, we only consider intrinsic uses of spatial expressions. The graph we build contains the explicitly given relations plus the implicit *is_in_room* arcs. After inference (including constraint propagation) these arcs contain all available information about an object's position in the room. Therefore the most efficient inference strategy is to use the path via the room node. This corresponds to a mixed strategy of localizing all objects with respect to the global reference frame of the room and still retaining the arcs for the explicitly given relations. As this example shows, our (implemented) mental model is not equivalent to a single perspective but allows to compute different perspectives, if necessary. For the sample text above, another plausible strategy would be to assume a protagonist's perspective and use the protagonist's coordinate system as global reference frame. We have preferred the room reference frame because a reorientation of the protagonist would necessitate the recomputation of all adjacent arcs. Therefore we tried to keep the number of those arcs as small as possible.

In the example above we never had to consider more than one mental model. When using relation definitions with disjunctions (i.e. for the relation beside), we may be forced to construct several pairwise incompatible models. Another case is discussed in Wysotzki et al. (1997). In this paper, disjoint models have to be constructed for the sentence "The oven stands at the wall." As there are four possible walls, the sentence is ambiguous. At encoding time it cannot be decided which wall is meant. The situation is disambiguated with the next sentence of the text, and three of the models can then be discarded.

In the future we plan to parameterize the model so that different strategies both for the introduction of arcs — at encoding time — and the inferences at access time can be modelled.

Acknowledgments

This research was supported by the Deutsche Forschungsgemeinschaft (DFG) in the project "Modellierung von Inferenzen in Mentalen Modellen" (Wy 20/2–1) within the priority program on spatial cognition ("Raumkognition").

Notes

1. We omit introduction, filler sentences and object descriptions. In our experiments (Hörnig et al. 1996), we are using german texts.
2. At present, *room* objects are the only structured objects we consider.
3. Recent results described in Hörnig et al. (1999) suggest that the initial position of the protagonist, e.g. Torsten may serve as global reference frame. This would correspond to another organization of the graph.

References

Ambler, A. P. and R. J. Popplestone (1975). Inferring the Positions of Bodies from Specified Spatial Relationships. *Artificial Intelligence 6*, 157–174.

Claus, B., K. Eyferth, C. Gips, R. Hörnig, U. Schmid, S. Wiebrock, and F. Wysotzki (1998). Reference Frames for Spatial Inferences in Text Comprehension. In C. Freksa, C. Habel, and K. F. Wender (Hrsg.), *Spatial Cognition — An Interdisciplinary Approach to Representing and Processing Spatial Knowledge*, LNAI 1404. Springer Verlag. http://ki.cs.tu- berlin.de/~sppraum/Papers/Trier97/trier.ps.

Franklin, N., L. A. Henkel, and T. Zangas (1995). Parsing surrounding space into regions. *Memory and Cognition 23* (4), 397–407.

Franklin, N. and B. Tversky (1990). Searching imagined environments. *Journal of Experimental Psychology: General 119*, 63–76.

Gapp, K.-P. (1994). Basic Meanings of Spatial Relations: Computation and Evaluation in 3D Space. In *Proceedings of the 12th National Conference on Articial Intelligence (AAAI-94), Seattle, Washington, USA*, S. 1393–1398. Also published as SFB 314 (VITRA), Bericht Nr. 101, April 1994.

Gapp, K.-P. (1995). An Empirically Validated Model for Computing Spatial Relations. In *Proceedings of the 19th German Conference on Articial Intelligence (KI-95)*, Bielefeld, Germany, September 1995. Also published as SFB 314 (VITRA), Bericht Nr. 118, Juli 1995.

Garnham, A. (1981). Mental Models as Representation of Text. *Memory and Cognition 9*, 560–565.

Geibel, P., C. Gips, S. Wiebrock, and F. Wysotzki (1998). Learning Spatial Relations with CAL5 and TRITOP. Technical Report Fachberichte des Fachbereichs Informatik,

Report No. 98–7, TU Berlin. http://ki.cs.tu-berlin.de/~sppraum/Papers/CAL5-Report/paper.ps.gz.

Glenberg, A. M. and W. E. Langston (1992). Comprehension of Illustrated Text: Pictures Help To Build mental Models. *Journal of Memory and Language 31*, 129–151.

Hernández, D. (1993). Maintaining Qualitative Spatial Knowledge. In A. U. Frank and I. Campari (Hrsg.), *Spatial Information Theory. A Theoretical Basis for GIS. European Conference, COSIT'93.*

Hernández, D. (1994). *Qualitative Representation of Spatial Knowledge*. LNAI 804. Springer.

Hörnig, R., B. Claus, D. Durstewitz, E. Fricke, U. Schmid, and K. Eyferth (1996). Object access in mental models under different perspectives induced by linguistic expressions. Technical Report KIT-Report 126, KIT Research Group, Technische Universität Berlin.

Hörnig, R., B. Claus, and K. Eyferth (1999). In Search for an Overall Organizing Principle in Spatial Mental Models: A Question of Inference. This volume.

Johnson-Laird, P. N. (1983). *Mental Models: Towards a Cognitive Science of Language, Inference and Consciousness*. Cambridge: Cambridge University Press.

Jörding, T. and I. Wachsmuth (1996). An Antropomorphic Agent for the Use of Spatial Language. In Proceedings of *ECAI'96-Workshop on Representation and Processing of Spatial Expressions*, S. 41–53.

Mukerjee, A. and N. Mittal (1995). A qualitative representation of frame-transformation motions in 3-dimensional space. In *Proceedings of the IEEE Conference on Robotics & Automation*.

Vorwerg, C. and G. Rickheit (1998). Typicality effects in the Categorization of Spatial Relations. In C. Freksa, C. Habel, and K. F. Wender (Hrsg.), *Spatial Cognition — An Interdisciplinary Approach to Representation and Processing of Spatial Knowledge*, LNAI 1404, S. 203–222. Springer Verlag.

Waltz, D. and L. Boggess (1979). Visual analog representations for natural language understanding. In *Proc. of the 6th IJCAI*, S. 926–934.

Wiebrock, S., C. Gips, U. Schmid, and F. Wysotzki (2000). SPACE/0–Documentation of a Program for Spatial Inference. In preparation.

Wysotzki, F., U. Schmid, and E. Heymann (1997). Modellierung räumlicher Inferenzen durch Graphen mit symbolischen und numerischen Constraints. In C. Umbach, M. Grabski, and R. Hörnig (Hrsg.), *Perspektive in Sprache und Raum*. Deutscher Universitätsverlag, Wiesbaden.

Zimmer, H., H. Speiser, J. Braus, A. Blocher, and E. Stopp (1998). The Use of Locative Expressions in Dependence of the Spatial Relation between Target and Reference Object in Two Dimensional Layouts. In C. Freksa, C. Habel, and K. F. Wender (Hrsg.), *Spatial Cognition — An Interdisciplinary Approach to Representing and Processing Spatial Knowledge*, LNAI 1404, S. 223–240. Springer Verlag.

Linguistic and Graphical Representations and the Characterisation of Individual Differences

Keith Stenning and Padraic Monaghan
Edinburgh University

1. Introduction

Differences between linguistic and graphical representations play an important role in determining the differences between peoples' information processing. There has been broad agreement about this proposition, as a pre-theoretical observation, for the last century. However, agreement about how to conceptualise the differences has been hard to come by. There have been major disagreements about what the differences between the kinds of representations are; about what the differences between people are with respect to their representational behaviour; and about the origins of these differences.

The purpose of the present paper is to try to conceptually connect up computational insights into the nature of linguistic and graphical representations with recent approaches to individual differences between people's information processing. Any contribution will be conceptual, but a clearer conceptual framework might prove a useful foundation for empirical work.

The next section outlines the foundations of a computational characterisation of the differences between linguistic and graphical representations with a view to relating them to psychological work on individual differences. It concentrates on issues of expressiveness, and on the contrast between reasoning *about* interpretations, and reasoning *within* interpretations. The third section outlines recent approaches to individual differences which contrast cognitive *styles* with cognitive *capacities*, and debates over whether behaviours result from *representational* or *strategic* differences. The fourth section explores relations between the computational concepts and the psychological directions. It concludes by proposing the need for connections to be established to sociological theories and to theories of communication.

2. Computational background

On the computational side, the functionally important difference between graphical and linguistic representations can be seen in terms of their *expressiveness* (in a technical sense), and between the availability of meta-information about their expressiveness to users with different amounts of background knowledge about their interpretation (see, for example, Levesque 1988; Stenning, Inder & Neilson 1995; Stenning & Lemon, in press). Casting the essential informational difference in terms of expressiveness gives direct access to the breadth of computational theory to express essential concepts such as strategy use, and access to interpretations — concepts which are at the centre of the problematic psychological issues raised by individual differences.

Computational theory also provides the tools necessary to understand the equivalences and differences between representation systems. Much of the controversy in the field has stemmed from the fact that representation systems which have very distinct 'surfaces' actually turn out, on careful analysis, to be computationally indistinguishable. Stenning & Yule (1997) have shown that, despite the controversies in the field of syllogistic reasoning between models proposed to contrast in the 'propositional' or model-based, graphical nature of their representations, in fact all the extant psychological models (e.g. mental models, Euler's Circles, sentential 'conversion theories') are implementations of the same abstract algorithm.

But computational theory does not just provide checks on the functional distinguishability of different representations. It also provides suggestions about how theories might be distinguished. Despite the indistinguishability of reasoning *internal* to the variant models described by Stenning & Yule, the systems are highly distinct in terms of the possibilities they afford for *external* reasoning about their meta-properties. So, for example, the Euler system's *self-consistency* is derivable from properties of the plane which are plausibly psychologically available to inexpert reasoners, whereas deriving self-consistency results for the equivalent 'mental-models', or for the sentential systems requires some logical sophistication which is plausibly unavailable to naive reasoners. This aspect of computational conceptualisations of the differences between representations points to the fact that reasoning *about* interpretations should be an important focus of cognitive models of information processing, but almost all attention within cognitive science has so far been focussed on reasoning *within* interpretations (whether logic, grammars, expert systems or whatever).

3. Visual and verbal thinking

On the psychological side, recently there has been a growing interest in a 'cognitive styles' approach to individual differences (e.g., Messick 1984; Kirby 1988). Cognitive styles are intended to contrast with more traditional psychometric approaches in terms of cognitive capacities in several ways. Styles are taken to be manifestations of *preferences* for modes of processing (Jonassen & Grabowski 1993), rather than an ability to process *within* a mode. It is a moot point to what degree styles are based on capacities, i.e., whether the availability or lack of resources determines cognitive style, but at least the door is left open to the operation of other factors. The shift in interest in styles is exemplified in the work of Sternberg, whose analyses of individual differences in complex task performance have altered from considerations of capacity and ability (Sternberg & Weil 1980; Sternberg 1980) to considerations of cognitive style (Wagner & Sternberg 1987).

Along with this basis in preference, styles are deemed to be non-evaluative categories. Whereas having a greater mental capacity *ipso facto* makes us better at doing something (even if only performing better on a test of the capacity), contrasting styles are deemed to be equally 'good' things. So a test of style may place people at one extreme or the other, but it is a criterion of being a style dimension that either extreme should be neutral, or perhaps be laudable or lamentable by turns, across a range of contexts. There may be advantages for one task or context in one stylistic approach, but if so, then there are deemed to be countervailing advantages of the contrasting style in other contexts.

Of course this diagnostic of style vs. capacity is empirically fraught, hinging mainly on whether the characteristic of having a low score on the test in question has a name, and whether performance on the test is thought to be negatively correlated with some other ability. For example, 'field independence' can be measured by an ability to pick out embedded geometrical figures from a complex ground (Witkin, Oltman, Raskin & Karp 1971). 'Field dependent' students score low on this test. If one believes that there is some advantage (over their field independent peers) that people who are field dependent might have in performing some other task (measured by some other possible test), then one might describe this as a style dimension. If not, then it is an ability dimension. Messick and

Kogan (1963) have derived bipolar cognitive styles by contrasting scores on tests designed to measure abilities at the two poles, they term this methodology 'constructed contrasts'.

This idea that styles have a 'balance of advantage' across tasks leads to their third characteristic: they are taken to be *pervasive* rather than *focussed*, affecting what people do across a wide variety of situations rather than in a single situation. To continue with our previous example, if field independence were only the capacity to perform extractions of geometrical figures from complex grounds, then it would be a poor candidate for a style. Field independence is of interest because this apparently 'low level' perceptual ability correlates with abilities on superficially quite different tasks.

The contrast between 'visual' and 'verbal' thinking bears most of the hallmarks of a cognitive style dimension. These are modes of processing which certainly manifest in terms of strong personal preferences. For a wide range of tasks there are choices between doing them in different ways which might at least loosely be called visual or verbal. They are not obviously societally evaluative abilities. To say of someone that they are not intelligent is negative: to say they aren't visual or aren't verbal is more neutral, bearing the implication that they have a profile of abilities at specific tasks where this style will advantage some and disadvantage others.

Along with this growth in thinking about individual differences in terms of styles rather than capacities, there has continued a not unrelated controversy about whether visual or verbal ability ought to be conceived in terms of differential ability to *represent* information in one or other modality, as opposed to different *strategies* for choosing and reasoning with representations.

There are many different 'visual' abilities — at least many different tests of plausibly 'visual' tasks which yield less than totally correlated scores — mental rotation, paper folding, embedded figures, Raven's matrices, the GRE analytical reasoning (analytical) subscale, etc. Setting aside for the moment the issue of how to individuate these abilities, perhaps the most obvious explanation of individual differences associated with visual/verbal tasks is in terms of capacity to summon up, or maintain mental representations in the two modalities. However, Lohman and Kyllonen (1983) have suggested that 'high spatial' subjects are to be characterised in terms of their *flexible choice of strategies* for reasoning, rather than representational capacity *per se*.

Lohman & Kyllonen studied performance on the paper-folding test, and found that there were various strategies students adopted in the solution of the task. Those students that scored highest on the test adapted their strategy from a 'spatial representation' for the easier problems, to a more 'analytic' method for harder problems. This analytic method relied on observations of symmetry or asymmetry in the folding, and deduced the correct answer by cancelling possibilities: it can be loosely classified as a 'verbal representation' in contrast to the spatial strategy. Hence the students scoring high on a 'spatial ability' test actually showed more flexibility in selecting 'verbal' strategies when these were more efficient. Roberts, Gilmore and Wood (1998) assessed strategy use in a 'compass direction' task, where journeys are described as sequences of movements in given directions (north, south, east, west), and the task is to state the relative position of the final destination with respect to the starting point. In a more difficult version, the subject must describe the relative position of two moving objects. High spatial subjects (measured by the Saville and Holdsworth Advanced Test Battery Spatial Reasoning test (Saville & Holdsworth Ltd., 1979)) were good at adopting the optimal (but 'verbal') strategy which is to 'cancel' opposed pairs of instructions on the easier version of the task, but used a spatial method on the more difficult task. Note that 'cancellation' is more effortful than a spatial strategy on the harder task.

Our own studies of diagrammatic and sentential logic teaching with *Hyperproof* (Barwise & Etchemendy 1994) reveal large aptitude by treatment interactions (ATIs) between students' pre-course GRE Analytical reasoning scores, and the modality of teaching (diagrammatic + sentential vs. just sentential) (Stenning, Cox & Oberlander 1995). We should note that this study, in contrast to those previously cited, used *external* representations distinguished by their modality rather than hypothetically contrasting *internal* ones. Of course, the great advantage of studying external representation use is that it is possible to directly observe which are selected and how they are used. Equally clearly, the downside is that inferences from these results to conclusions about their relation to studies of internal representations is indirect.

Analysis of these ATIs (Oberlander, Cox, Monaghan, Stenning & Tobin 1996) shows that they are not based on preferences for one modality or the other. In fact, paradoxically, the students who fail to gain from diagrammatic teaching are distinguished by their *preference* for translation of information into diagrammatic form. The students who gain most from diagrammatic teaching are ones who are strategically adept at choosing whether to translate information into or out of the diagrams.

A related study of the same students' spontaneous use of diagrams in performing the GRE Analytical pre- and post-tests (Cox, Stenning & Oberlander 1995) showed that the students who benefited from diagrammatic teaching were distinguishable on their spontaneous graphical representational behaviour from those that didn't. The former were better at making optimal selections of diagrammatic representation. But interestingly, their problem solving performance was much more susceptible to the rarer instances when they selected the wrong kind of representation. The latter students were less adept at selecting representations, but also less susceptible to their commoner incorrect choices. These results again suggest that strategy of representational choice is an important component of 'spatial ability'.

More recently, Monaghan and Stenning (1998) have analysed on-line teaching/learning in the simpler domain of categorial syllogisms. Here, because learning can be achieved in a single session, and because both graphical and sentential methods for these simple problems can be mapped onto isomorphic 'single pass' sequences of algorithmic steps, it is possible to relate psychometric measures to the learning of particular reasoning stages in the two graphical and linguistic modalities. This study shows that even though the sentential and the graphical-plus-sentential teaching methods are equally good overall, students show reliably divergent responses to them, both in terms of their number of reasoning errors made, and in the number of tutor interventions. Furthermore the psychometric measures correlate with errors and interventions at different stages of the algorithm. Paper-folding test (PFT) scores predict ability to translate out of the graphical formalism, whereas GRE analytical and serialist/holist learning styles predict ability at manipulation within the graphical formalism.

This is a teaching study in which students have no choice as to whether they learn the graphical or the sentential algorithm, and because of the algorithm's organisation in stages, there is not the same scope for choosing alternative directions of translation between sentence and diagram as there is in the Hyperproof study. However, it does cast some light on the relation between psychometric test abilities and the processes of learning to reason. The PFT is apparently a test of spatial operations, yet it relates not to the graphical operations stage of the Euler algorithm, but to the stage of translating from the finished diagram back into the sentential conclusion. This should alert us to the possibility of verbal components in the solution processes. The GRE analytical subscale test is apparently a test of verbal reasoning which sets verbal questions and demands verbal answers. However, its problems are problems which are strongly aided by diagram construction. Scores on the GRE relate to graphical manipulations in the Euler method. The serial/holist learning style is characterised by differences in learning *strategies*, yet its distinction relates again to the graphical manipulation stage of the Euler task. Plainly, this is yet further evidence to add to that reviewed above that the computations underlying psychometric test performances are not to be taken at face value.

A further observation in this study is that, watching the tutoring sessions, one cannot escape strong intuitions that there can be a separation of 'operative skill' with an algorithm, from 'insight' into why the algorithm is sound. The graphically inclined students often spontaneously explain, in a non-technical vocabulary, why the algorithm is as it is and how it maps on to the logical model-theory for the domain. This might, for example, be couched as an observation about how the algorithm ensures that 'all cases are searched'. In contrast, the graphically disinclined may have perfectly mastered the operation of the 'graphical calculator', but in debriefing, it remains for them merely a graphical rigmarole. Asked why some aspect of the graphical procedure is as it is, the stereotypically graphically disinclined reasoner might reply: 'Search me guv, that's how you said to do it!'

Conceiving of individual differences as styles, and attributing visual/verbal differences to strategic adoption and deployment of methods are movements in similar theoretical directions. It might be objected that moving to studies of external representation use more or less guarantees that the data will be dominated by strategic differences rather than pure capacity to hold representations. Perhaps the right rhetorical stance is to accept this truth, but to adopt a research program which asks to what extent we can explain the phenomena of representation use (both internal and external) in terms of strategic differences. The computational studies of the last half century have provided us with a rich conceptual vocabulary and considerable understanding of the importance of strategy in reasoning, and how strategies interact with representations. Psychometric approaches have always suffered from their lack of process accounts of the mental goings on which they measure. Applying computational concepts to issues of individual difference would appear a promising program.

4. Connecting individual differences to computational concepts

Roberts (1998) responds to the studies that reveal that individual differences are replete with strategic influences by proposing there is a consistent progression of development of strategies as subjects gain expertise with a task. This progression starts out with adoption of spatial strategies but develops in the direction of their progressive optimisation by the intercalation of verbal 'short cuts' which increase the efficiency of reasoning. The 'cancellation' of reciprocal spatial operations in the compass directions task is a paradigm example of this kind of efficiency gain. Spatial, or visual, subjects are the ones who are more adept at making these modifications of strategies in the course of practice with a task.

At one level, our logic teaching observations reviewed above, the Hyperproof results, the GRE workscratchings study, and the Euler Circles ones, are all consistent with Roberts' line of reasoning. Explanations of these findings in terms of differences in subjects' strategies, or their learning of strategies, are more consistent with the data than explanations in terms of some fundamental ability to represent.

However, at another level, the computational explanation is at least superficially opposite. Our approach to the issue of when graphical representation is useful is predicated on the fact that graphical representations are weakly expressive and therefore tractable to reason with as long as the reasoning task can be solved within the expressiveness of resources offered. So graphical reasoning is efficient relative to reasoning in general expressive languages which suffer from providing too many avenues of reasoning for computational tractability. By the same token, graphical reasoning systems are also specialised. They may well constrain reasoning in a way that means that some class of answers lies completely outside their range of expression. A reasoner operating within some graphical system who was set such a problem would have to switch out of the system, either into a more general linguistic one, or perhaps to an alternative graphical system specialised for a range of problems which included the new one.

So there is a definite tension between Roberts' idea that linguistic methods arise by the optimisation of graphical ones, and our idea that graphical systems are efficient because they are special purpose. What is the resolution of this conflict? There is plenty of scope for resolution within a computational conceptualisation, if only because so little is specified, in general terms, about the psychological tasks which crop up in this literature. Notably, what 'verbal' systems of representation are in play in these tasks is rather unclear. Although languages of the kind whose computational properties are much explored are highly expressive, there are of course other 'verbal systems of representation' which are highly restricted in their expressiveness. Particularly relevant to one of our graphical examples above, categorial syllogistic logic is an extremely restricted language which is exactly equivalent in expressive power to Euler's graphical system. The great difficulty that arises in understanding language use in reasoning is exactly the question of what language is 'in play' at any given point. The syllogism is a very tiny fragment of a natural language such as English. When someone 'does syllogisms' verbally, are we to think of them as 'doing them in English' or 'doing them in the syllogistic fragment of English'?

These are deep questions, but ones which are important for further development of our understanding of human representational behaviour. This is an area where understandings from AI and computer science may provide some help with questions about how to conceptualise mental processes. Whereas an interpreted language is a representation system, *reasoning* over the language requires both a 'proof theory' (roughly an apparatus defining valid *immediate inferential relations between sentences*), and a theorem prover. The latter is some extra-logical mechanism which is not a part of the representation system, but which steers reasoning along extended inferential paths to target conclusions.

In the introductory examples from AI text books, theorem provers are rather simple devices, typically working over sentential representations which are exactly designed to make the theorem provers rather simple. But it has been known since the earliest work of Newell and Simon (1972) that the domain-general strategies of reasoning which result are too weak for modelling most human reasoning. When deeper reasoning is modelled, the theorem prover itself becomes a complex device which has its own representations which it uses to reason about which inferential paths to follow in the object language. These representations themselves may be graphical, but they are representations of a proof-space — not representations of domain objects.

Theorem provers are specialised for proving target theorems of a certain class. Their specialisation may actually determine that they cannot 'reach' all parts of the language over which they operate. A trivial example would be a sentential theorem prover working over the syllogistic fragment of English (e.g. the one in Stenning & Yule 1997). This theorem prover could be implemented in a way in which it only ever reached the sentences of the syllogism. It is then a moot point whether the theorem prover works over English, or over the syllogistic fragment of English. In the simpler computer simulated cases, there would be little reason to even consider the first option — the machine need have no representation of any of the language outside the syllogism. On the other hand, in more interesting simulations, or in the human case, the 'reasoner' does have a representation of the general language which can be brought into play as the reasoner shifts tasks (and presumably theorem provers) to reason in other domains, and over other fragments.

In the picture of inference that emerges, the general language defines a larger landscape, but episodes of reasoning about a restricted class of problems are controlled by theorem provers which restrict the available space to small sub-regions of this general landscape. Much of the burden of understanding human reasoning behaviour comes down to explaining how people get from one sub-region of the space to another by changing the mechanisms which control their inference patterns. General languages like English define a larger landscape, and in so doing they define certain invariant meanings of terms which crop up in many sub-spaces. The reasoner knows what *all* and *some* mean across the whole language, and the theorem provers which they employ within language fragments must respect these general meanings, but in order to be efficient, they must exploit limitations of the particular fragments at hand in the ways they exert their extra-logical control of reasoning processes.

This is the kind of picture of inference we get from AI and computer science. From this perspective, graphical reasoning systems can be seen as bundling together language and theorem provers in ways that makes their separation a great deal less clean than it is in the linguistic case. This is the reason why graphical systems are by their nature specialised and local and do not include anything corresponding to the general languages so prominent in the sentential systems. The jumps from graphical system to graphical system are much more idiosyncratic (think of the change from Hyperproof's blocks-world diagrams to Euler's Circles). Indeed, to invent an account of the space in which these transitions take place we would be forced back onto thinking in terms of some general logical language.

So coming from a logical/computational direction it is natural to think of graphical systems as the specialisation of reasoning within localities of a space defined by some general language. Roberts, in contrast, is thinking of subjects who start their reasoning from some specification of a task which is often naturally represented graphically (e.g. the compass directions tasks mentioned above). Within such restricted systems, it is nevertheless often possible to impose *further* restrictions which then allow yet simpler representations for reasoning. So, for example, the cancellation strategy only works in a fragment of the graphical system of compass directions if the task is restricted to unit distances or the task is limited to computing the outcome direction of travel.

A rather richer and more interesting set of relationships between graphical and sentential methods occur with syllogisms. Here it is possible to illustrate how one can start with a graphical system of reasoning and transform it into the equivalent of a sentential system by introducing optimisations which start out as *strategies for selecting* graphical representations. In the 'primitive' interpretation of Euler's Circles, which is uniformly the one people initially adopt, one circle diagram depicts one model of the syllogism. This leads to a combinatorial explosion of diagrams if one solves syllogisms by drawing diagrams of all possible models of a pair of premisses, and then searching to see whether some statement holds of all such models (and is therefore a valid conclusion). This is the crux of Johnson-Laird's argument for rejecting Euler as the basis for syllogistic reasoning, which prompted the invention of mental models notation.

This approach is hopelessly inefficient, but equally easy to improve on by improving the strategy of diagram selection. Instead of exploring all possible diagrams, the constraints of the domain allow the reasoner to adopt the 'weakest case' diagram for each premiss, and to combine them into the 'weakest case' graphical unification. Adopting this strategy requires corresponding limitations to be placed on drawing inferences from the final diagram, but with a suitable strategy for conclusion drawing, the method becomes extremely efficient — every problem can be solved by constructing a single diagram according to general principles. Finally, the strategies of representational choice can be reflected explicitly in the graphics by a simple notation given a systematic semantics (for a fuller explanation see Stenning & Oberlander 1995). Graphical representation system plus reasoning strategy leads to a far more efficient modified graphical system by the incorporation of a theorem prover into a primitive graphical system. This amounts to an example of Roberts' honing of a representational system to gain reasoning efficiency, but takes place by graphical modifications rather than linguistic ones. The incorporation of strategy into representation must be a common method of increasing efficiency. It is in fact not uncommon for subjects to invent something like this 'cross notation' to augment Euler. We have seen our subjects do it, and Ford (1995) reports data which include similar cases.

But the story about relations between graphical and linguistic systems doesn't end there. It turns out that the augmented Euler system is functionally equivalent to a simple propositional sentential system (see Stenning & Yule 1997). What all these methods abstractly share is that they construct specifications of *critical individuals* which are minimal models of the premisses and which specify the drawing of valid conclusions. The graphical method specifies them in terms of sub-regions in the plane defined by closed curves representing properties: the sentential method constructs conjunctions of propositions representing the same properties. The sentential method lends itself to an optimisation which saves working memory by only representing the single critical individual, though in doing this it incurs some extra overhead of a more complex theorem prover. The graphical method more naturally represents all possible types of individual, though focusing on a single one by the cross notation. Again it is the focusing of a parallel strategy of reasoning onto a single serially constructed case which transforms a graphical method into something in step-by-step correspondence with a linguistic method. This more obviously accords with Roberts' notion of honing graphical methods towards linguistic ones.

These examples give us a clue that strategy and representation may not be quite as cleanly separable as our original discussion suggested. True, within a reasoning system at a particular point in its development, what is strategy and what is representation may be crisply distinguishable. But when we think of systems of reasoning evolving during learning and optimisation of a new task, we see that what is strategy at one point may become representation at another. And we must think of these evolutions if we are to understand human reasoning. Human reasoning is as much about developing new systems of reasoning as about operating them.

This returns us to our observation of the independence of graphical 'operative skill' and understanding of the rationale behind it. The same gulf may well exist for linguistic operation and understanding, but we have just seen some reasons why such a gulf may be somewhat less crisply evident. The very nature of linguistic rule systems is that their subsystems are less neatly demarcated and therefore less susceptible to meta-logical demonstration. Be that as it may, the graphical case suffices to illustrate an important point.

Even when systems of reasoning by graphical and sentential methods can be shown to be internally identical, the properties of their representations may give very different opportunities for meta-reasoning about their properties. The Euler system is obviously *self-consistent* to any reasoner who understands intuitively the basic plane geometry of closed convex curves. Proving the self-consistency of the equivalent sentential system requires some sophistication. It is also less likely to occur to a naive reasoner as a property of the system, if only because the neighbouring fragments of the language do not have this property. If, as we have argued throughout, we must understand much of human reasoning as reasoning about systems as much as reasoning within them, then the accessibility of their properties from the externals of the systems becomes critically important. This points to the need for further understanding about how users of linguistic systems structure their understandings of the various fragments which make up the whole patchwork. Because the borders between one fragment and the next are less clear, it is also less clear what knowledge is required to derive a theorem prover to exploit constraints to solve a new task in a new domain.

Characterising cognitive styles computationally requires a better understanding of how reasoners learn to get around in the spaces we have been discussing. Getting around consists of preferring some strategies and representations for reasoning to others. Perhaps even more, it consists in different approaches to *learning* how to develop efficient ways of reasoning in new domains under new sets of constraints. The trajectories from naivety to expertise within the space of possibilities for a new domain and task may be more coherent than the particular patterns of reasoning at any point along the trajectory. Styles are preferences for systems of reasoning either more or less applicable across a wide ranges of tasks. Styles will, of their nature, be more successful in some domains and for some tasks than others.

It is customary to think of individual differences in terms of individuals performing solitary information processing tasks, but styles of information processing play a central role in how people configure and distribute themselves in social groups, and how groups solve problems. Where does the theory of the computational properties of alternative methods of information processing contact the social dimensions that constitute human social groupings?

Some sociologists, philosophers and anthropologists have already offered answers to this question. Bloor (1981), following the anthropologist Douglas (1978) and the philosopher Lakatos (1976), proposes that societies can be taxonomised on the basis of their responses to demands to categorise newly encountered aberrant cases. Here is a claim about the origin of conceptual schemes which might begin to be connectable to computational conceptualisations of style. It is intriguing that sociologists should appeal to the processes of classifying people as 'belonging' or 'strange' which define communities, in the same terms as can be applied to categorisation of any other objects in whatever conceptual domain. Bloor (1981) reports one historical study of an episode in the history of mathematics which hinged on a shift in representational style from geometric to algebraic methods. He documents the social attitudes to the sources of authority in professional, political and religious practice which accompanied the intellectual battles centred on the two representational styles. Authority for patterns of reasoning can be seen as group internal, or group external. A theory which could link the computational properties of representations, the individual differences between people, and the ways in which they interact in communities — now that really would be a theory worth having?

References

Barwise, J. & J. Etchemendy (1994). *Hyperproof.* Stanford: CSLI Publications.

Bloor, D. (1981). Hamilton and Peacock on the essence of algebra. In H. Mehrtens, H. Bos & I. Schneider (Eds.), *Social History of Nineteenth Century Mathematics.* Basel: Birkhauser.

Douglas, M. (1978). *Purity and Danger: An Analysis of Concepts of Pollution and Taboo.* London: Routledge & Kegan Paul.

Ford, M. (1995). Two models of mental representation and problem solution in syllogistic reasoning. *Cognition, 54*, 1–71.

Jonassen, D. H. & B. L. Grabowski (1993). *Handbook of Individual Differences, Learning, and Instruction.* Hillsdale: Lawrence Erlbaum Associates.

Kirby, J. R. (1988). Style, strategy, and skill in reading. In R. R. Schmeck (Ed.), *Learning Strategies and Learning Styles.* New York: Plenum Press.

Lakatos, I. (1976). *Proofs and Refutations: The Logic of Mathematical Discovery.* J. Worrall & E. Zahar (Eds.). Cambridge: Cambridge University Press.

Levesque, H. (1988). Logic and the complexity of reasoning. *Journal of Philosophical Logic*, *17*, 355–389.

Lohman, D.F. & P.C. Kyllonen (1983). Individual differences in solution strategy on spatial tasks. In R.F. Dillon & R.R. Schmeck (Eds.), *Individual Differences in Cognition*, Volume 1. New York: Academic Press.

Messick, S. (1984). The nature of cognitive styles: problems and promise in educational practice. *Educational Psychologist*, *19*, 59–74.

Messick, S. & N. Kogan (1963). Differentiation and compartmentalization in object-sorting measures of categorizing style. *Perceptual and Motor Skills*, *16*, 47–51.

Monaghan, P. & K. Stenning (1998). Effects of representational modality and thinking style on learning to solve reasoning problems. *Proceedings of the 20th annual conference of the Cognitive Science Society of America* (716–721). Madison: Lawrence Erlbaum Associates.

Newell, A. & H. Simon (1972). *Human Problem Solving*. N.Y.: Prentice Hall.

Oberlander, J., R. Cox, P. Monaghan, K. Stenning & R. Tobin (1996). Individual differences in proof structures following multimodal logic teaching. G.W. Cottrell (Ed.). *Proceedings of the 18th annual conference of the Cognitive Science Society of America* (201–206). La Holla: Lawrence Erlbaum Associates.

Roberts, M.J. (1998). Individual differences in reasoning strategies: a problem to solve or an opportunity to seize? In G. d'Ydewalle, W. Schaeken, A. Vandierendonck & G. De Vooght (Eds.), *Deductive Reasoning and Strategies*. Mahwah: Lawrence Erlbaum Associates.

Roberts, M.J., D.J. Gilmore & D.J. Wood (1997). Individual differences and strategy selection in reasoning. *British Journal of Psychology*, *88*, 473–492.

Saville and Holdsworth Ltd. (1979). *Advanced Test Battery: Manual and User's Guide*. Surrey: Thames Ditton.

Stenning, K., R. Cox & J. Oberlander (1995). Contrasting the cognitive effects of graphical and sentential logic teaching: reasoning, representation and individual differences. *Language and Cognitive Processes*, *10*, 333–354.

Stenning, K., R. Inder & I. Neilson (1995). Applying semantic concepts to the media assignment problem in multi-media communication. In B. Chandrasekaran & J. Glasgow (Eds.), *Diagrammatic Reasoning: Computational and Cognitive Perspectives on Problem Solving with Diagrams* (303–338). Cambridge: MIT Press.

Stenning, K. & O. Lemon (in press). Aligning logical and psychological perspectives on diagrammatic reasoning. *AI Review*.

Stenning, K. & J. Oberlander (1995). A cognitive theory of graphical and linguistic reasoning: logic and implementation. *Cognitive Science*, *19*, 97–140.

Stenning, K. & P. Yule (1997). Image and language in human reasoning: a syllogistic illustration. *Cognitive Psychology*, *34*, 109–159.

Sternberg, R.J. (1980). Representation and process in linear syllogistic reasoning. *Journal of Experimental Psychology: General*, *109*, 119–159.

Sternberg, R. J. & E. M. Weil (1980). An aptitude x strategy interaction in linear syllogistic reasoning. *Journal of Educational Psychology*, *72*, 226–239.

Wagner, R. K. & R. J. Sternberg (1987). Alternative conceptions of intelligence and their implications for education. *Review of Educational Research*, *54*, 179–223.

Witkin, H., P. Oltman, E. Raskin & S. Karp (1971). *A Manual for the Embedded Figures Test*. Palo Alto: Consulting Psychologists Press.

Part IV

Memory, Consciousness and Space

Given-New Versus New-Given?

An analysis of reading times for spatial descriptions

Thom Baguley
Loughborough University

Stephen J. Payne
Cardiff University

Background

How do people understand simple spatial descriptions such as *The supermarket is behind the bank*? One view is that comprehension of these descriptions relies on preserving the propositional form of the language used in the description (e.g. behind[supermarket,bank]). An alternative view is that comprehension requires going beyond the propositional form and constructing some representation of the described situation which is independent of the describing language. Both views have a long history in philosophy and in psychology (Johnson-Laird 1983; Kintsch & Van Dijk 1978; Pylyshyn 1984). This paper will focus on the latter view and explore some of the consequences of going beyond propositions and constructing a spatial *mental model*; a representation of the spatial structure of the described situation (Bower & Morrow 1990; Bransford, Barclay & Franks 1972; Johnson-Laird 1980; Tversky 1991).

Going beyond the propositional form of a description requires constructing a new representation which embodies the aspects of the situation that a reader or listener is interested in (e.g. the spatial structure of the situation). Constructing a mental model therefore involves additional processing time and effort (Glenberg, Meyer & Lindberg 1987; Johnson-Laird 1983; Tardieu, Ehrlich & Gyselinck 1992; Zwaan & van Oostendorp 1993). The additional cognitive demands of constructing a mental model do, however, have potential pay-offs when people later use the model to make inferences or to act in the world (Thorndyke & Hayes-Roth 1982; Tversky 1991; Wilson, Rinck, McNamara, Bower & Morrow 1993). Costs and benefits associated with mental model construction also form one of the most important sources of empirical evidence in their favour.

One substantial cost associated with constructing a mental model is that of *premise integration* (Evans, Newstead & Byrne 1993). The idea behind this is quite simple: a representation of the described situation has to integrate information across two or more propositions in order to build an appropriate model. The origin of this idea appears to date back at least as far as William James (1890), but was articulated as a process theory by Hunter (1957). Hunter suggested that people manipulate the premises of three-term series problems in order to place them in a suitable form with which to reach a conclusion.[1] He proposed that problems of the form

Anna is happier than Barbara
Chris is sadder than Barbara

require *conversion*. In this case readers convert the sentence *Chris is sadder than Barbara* into *Barbara is happier than Chris*. This means that the conclusion *Anna is happier than Chris* can be reached without considering the middle term *Barbara* (James termed this method the "axiom of skipped intermediaries"). Similarly, problems of the form

Barbara is sadder than Anna
Chris is sadder than Barbara

require re-ordering. If we consider *Chris is sadder than Barbara* before *Barbara is sadder than Anna,* the axiom of skipped intermediaries gives us *Chris is sadder than Anna* as the conclusion. There is only one problem with the simple and elegant theory that Hunter proposed; it makes the wrong pattern of predictions of accuracy and reading time for three-term series problems. To take just one example, Huttenlocher (1968), Clark (1969) and Sternberg (1980) all found that problems like

A is better than B
B is better than C

took longer to answer than problems such as

A is better than B
C is worse than B

This goes against Hunter's theory because the latter, but not the former, supposedly require conversion (for a comprehensive review of the evidence see Evans et al. 1993). Nevertheless, the evidence that premise integration occurs is considered rather strong. For example, Mayberry, Bain and Halford (1986) showed that pairs of sentences which permit integration (those with a shared term) take longer to read than control sentences (sentences with no shared term).

The resolution of this apparent discrepancy is that Hunter was right to propose that people go beyond a simple propositional representation of the premises, but wrong in the nature of the principle which guides their thinking. The operations required to reach a conclusion appear to be those required to support the construction of a mental model. This becomes clearer if we consider a computer simulation of spatial mental model construction first described by Johnson-Laird (1983) and later re-implemented by Payne (1993). Payne (1993) proposed that memory for a spatial description incorporates an *episodic construction trace*. The *episodic construction trace* consists of a set of propositions each of which records an operation in the process of constructing a mental model. In the present paper the episodic construction trace is used to illustrate the operations used to construct a spatial mental model. Thus the episodic construction trace will be used to clarify the predictions made by the mental models theory (Johnson-Laird 1983) about the cost of constructing a spatial mental model. Consider the following description

(1) The A is to the left of the B
(2) The B is the left of the C
(3) The D is below the A

On reading sentence (1) the first step in constructing a spatial mental model is to set two tokens (*A* and *B*) in the appropriate relationship

A B

resulting in the following episodic construction trace proposition being recorded

[start [A B left]]

The term *start* here denotes the fact that two tokens are added to the model. A key principle of the construction process is that new tokens are added to a model relative to old tokens. In sentence (2) a new token *C* has to be added to the model. In the resulting operation *C* is placed to the right of *B*

A B C

This operation is recorded in the episodic construction trace proposition

[C B right]*

The asterisk here denotes that the sentence has to be *converted*. A crucial observation is that, according to Hunter (1957), sentence (2) does not require conversion; the theories make different predictions about when conversion occurs. Sentence (3) illustrates that the model view generalizes to two-dimensional situations not found in traditional three-term series problems

A B C
D

The final proposition in the trace shows that conversion is not required when a sentence describes new tokens in relation to old tokens

[D A below]

The construction processes described here carry with them the implication that introducing old, given information before new information in a sentence imposes a greater cost during premise integration. This prediction appears to contravene the "given-new contract" proposed by psycholinguists (Haviland & Clark 1974). The mental model account also suggests two other situations where construction costs are increased. The first, and least interesting, is that the initial sentence of the description should carry an increased processing burden because two tokens are being added to the model (indicated by the term *start*). This prediction is analogous to that of Gernsbacher and colleagues who argue that laying a foundation for a mental structure increases reading times (Gernsbacher 1990; Gernsbacher & Hargreaves 1988). The second additional prediction is that when a description becomes indeterminate, processing should become more difficult. For example, consider a fourth sentence

(4) B is to the left of E

In this case the position of *E* is indeterminate with respect to *C* and is indicated in the episodic construction trace like so

[E B right [clash [E C]]]*

What happens after a *clash* proposition is recorded depends on how a reader responds. If, as suggested by Mani and Johnson-Laird (1982), readers abandon model construction post-clash processing load may decrease. Some readers may however attempt to resolve the indeterminacy by constructing one, or possibly both, of the possible models entailed by the description (Brédart 1987; Johnson-Laird 1983).

Evidence in the literature on spatial descriptions for increased processing cost associated with old-relative-to-new sentences is mixed. It may be worth noting that in Hunter's own experiment 11-year olds found problems requiring conversion (by his account) easier than those of the form given by sentence (1) and (2) above (predicted to require conversion by the mental model account). Ehrlich and Johnson-Laird (1982) concluded that there was little evidence to suggest a difference in reading times (or accuracy) in favour of either the new-old or old-new sentence forms in the three experiments they reported. There are several reasons why such a difference might be hard to find; low statistical power, materials effects, and differences in tasks. Reading times are a more sensitive measure of difficulty than is accuracy, but are potentially influenced by many different factors which need to be controlled for (e.g. word length, orthography, frequency or concreteness). Tasks such as three-term series problems are not the most powerful test of the model view outlined above and two-dimensional spatial problems are considered more decisive (Byrne & Johnson-Laird 1989). For example, the operations described by Hunter (1957) are a viable strategy for three-term-series problems (particularly when both premises are presented simultaneously), and may be used by some participants some of the time. Three-term series problems with spatial or non-spatial adjectives are probably also heavily influenced by markedness as suggested by Clark (1969). The unmarked, positive form of adjectives like "taller" or "better" seem to be encoded in a simpler, more accessible form than their marked counterparts "shorter" or "worse" (Clark 1969, 1973). However, the role of markedness in encoding spatial prepositions (such as those used in the experiments reported here) is less clear; it is not obvious that "right" and "left" can be categorized as marked and unmarked prepositional pairs. For instance, the marked form "worse" implies both relative and absolute badness, whereas neither "to the left of" nor "below" necessarily imply absolute location in physical space (though this does not extend to metaphorical usage such as in politics).

This paper analyses a large data set of reading times for spatial descriptions. The chief focus is on predictions which follow from the computational model described by Johnson-Laird (1983). The main prediction is that when mental model construction entails the conversion of a sentence in order to enter a new token in an existing model, reading times will increase. A secondary prediction is that when a description is rendered indeterminate (i.e. when a *clash* occurs) reading times will increase. Last, the account also predicts that reading times for the initial sentence will be greater than for subsequent sentences (because two tokens have to be added to the model).

Data set

The reading time data were pooled across 118 participants from three different experiments. The participants were recruited at Cardiff University and were paid or given course credit for taking part. All three experiments were carried out in two phases. In the first phase participants were presented with a series of spatial descriptions to read. Each description consisted of four sentences and was presented by computer, one line at a time. Immediately after each description participants had to try and remember the description by using the mouse to place items in an empty grid on the computer screen. Each participant read 8 different descriptions (4 determinate and 4 indeterminate). Of the 4 indeterminate descriptions half became indeterminate in the third sentence (indeterminate-at-S3) while the remaining descriptions became indeterminate in the last sentence (indeterminate-at-S4). For the determinate descriptions exactly half the relevant sentences from the determinate descriptions contained sentences of the new-old form (and therefore not predicted to require conversion). For the indeterminate descriptions 5 out 12 of the relevant sentences had sentences of the new-old form. Each participant read the eight descriptions in a random order (new random orders were generated in turn for each participant prior to the experiment). In phase 2, participants in the experiments carried out a surprise recognition test (not necessarily the same test in each experiment). The analyses presented here focus solely on the initial reading times of participants in phase 1.

Table 1

Determinate description:	*Corresponding EC Trace:*
D1. The blouse is in front of the kilt	[start [blouse kilt front]]
D2. The vest is in front of the blouse	[vest blouse front]
D3. The shawl is to the left of the blouse	[shawl blouse right]
D4. The overcoat is behind the shawl	[overcoat shawl behind]
Indeterminate description:	*Corresponding EC Trace:*
I1. The coke is in front of the lemonade	[start [coke lemonade front]]
I2. The lemonade is to the right of the vodka	[vodka lemonade left]*
I3. The lemonade is to the right of the scotch	[scotch lemonade left [clash [scotch vodka]]]*
I4. The vodka is behind the brandy	[brandy vodka front]*

Note: Sentences D2, D3 and D4 are examples of the new-old sentence form. I2, I3 and I4 are examples of the old-new sentence form.

The three experiments were identical in phase 1 except for minor differences in the wording of the descriptions (the basic form of the descriptions remained unchanged). The same basic structure was used for the eight descriptions in each experiment. The eight descriptions used objects from eight different categories (animals, birds, clothing, drinks, fruit, instruments, gems and vegetables). In each experiment participants were randomly assigned to one of several different sets of materials (different sets were used for each experiment). For each set every description was randomly allocated to a category and the objects within that description randomly selected from the five members of the allocated category. Category members were approximately matched for Kucera-Francis frequency, imagery and concreteness (Kucera & Francis 1967; Quinlan 1992). Table 1 gives sample materials typical of those used in phase 1 of all three experiments.

Analyses

Mean reading times per syllable were calculated for those descriptions which were correctly recalled during phase 1. (Reading times for incorrectly recalled descriptions were not included in the analysis, but followed a similar overall pattern, as did the reading times uncorrected for sentence length in syllables). Two analyses were conducted. In the first analysis a 3×4 repeated measures ANOVA was performed on reading times per syllable with determinacy (determinate, indeterminate-at-S3, or indeterminate-at-S4) and sentence order (S1, S2, S3 or S4) as the factors.

Figure 1 shows a graph of the means for each combination of determinacy and sentence order for the 70 participants who contributed to the analysis (participants with missing cells could not be included in the factorial design). The interaction between determinacy and sentence order was significant, $F_{(6,420)} = 8.09$, $MSE = 0.286$, $p < .0002$.

Three planned comparisons were made (these analyses were carried using paired t tests on the whole data set, not just those included in the factorial ANOVA). The first comparison tested the prediction that the initial sentences would take longer to read than later sentences; this was tested by comparing the mean reading times for the first and second sentences (this excludes consideration of determinacy from the analysis, as all descriptions are determinate prior to sentence 3). As predicted, reading times for sentence 1 were longer than for sentence 2, $t_{(112)} = 2.51$, $SE = 0.051$, two-sided $p = .014$. The remaining two planned comparisons compared reading times for sentence 3 of the indeterminate-at-S3 descriptions and sentence 4 for the indeterminate-at-S4 descriptions with a control sentence (the corresponding sentence 3 or 4 of the determinate descriptions). It took participants longer to read sentences which introduced an

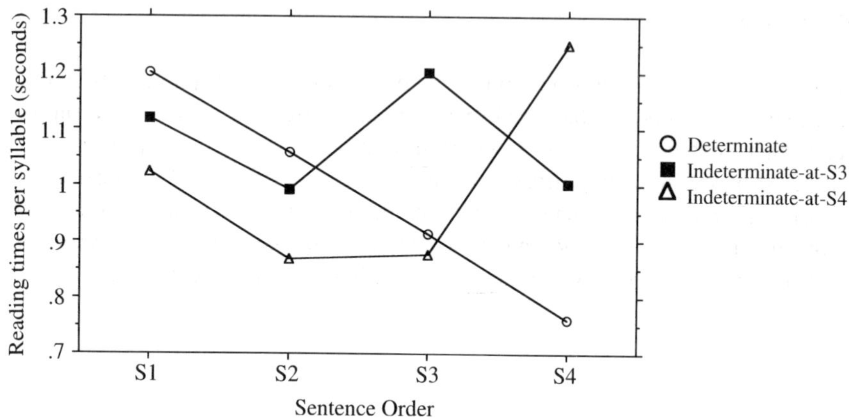

Figure 1. Reading times per syllable by determinacy and sentence order

indeterminacy (i.e. sentences with a *clash*) for both the indeterminate-at-S3, $t_{(83)}=5.07$, $SE=0.056$, two-sided $p<.000003$, and the indeterminate-at-S4 conditions, $t_{(83)}=3.27$, $SE=0.066$, two-sided $p<.0016$.

The second analysis focused on the predictions regarding conversion in relation to new-old and old-new sentences. A 2x2 repeated measures ANOVA was carried out on reading times per syllable with sentence form (new-old or old-new) and determinacy (determinate or indeterminate) as factors. Figure 2 shows the mean reading times per syllable by sentence form and determinacy for the 95 participants who contributed to the analysis. There were significant main effects of both determinacy, $F_{(1,94)}=5.59$, $MSE=0.315$, $p=.020$, and sentence form, $F_{(1,94)}=5.23$ $MSE=0.499$, $p=.025$. The main effect of sentence form matches the predicted advantage of new-old sentences over old-new sentences, while the main effect of determinacy confirms the earlier finding that reading times increase when an indeterminacy is detected. The interaction between determinacy and sentence form did not reach significance, $F_{(1,94)}=2.49$ $MSE=0.322$, $p=.12$, though there was a trend towards a reduced effect of sentence form for the determinate descriptions (which would be expected if some participants abandoned model construction on encountering an indeterminacy).

@@Please supply new electronic file for figure 2

Discussion

Reading times follow the pattern predicted by the operations required to construct a spatial mental model. The initial sentence takes longer to process than comparable later sentences. Sentences which introduce an indeterminacy result in a sudden increase in reading times. Last, but not least, sentences of the form new-old are easier to process than sentences of the form old-new. This is consistent with the view that old-new sentences, but not new-old sentences, need to be converted in order to integrate the new token into a spatial mental model.

Conclusions

These findings provide strong support for the three predictions derived from theory of mental models (Johnson-Laird 1983). In this paper we have used the episodic construction trace to clarify the predictions about increased processing cost during premise integration. These predictions follow from the idea that people construct and manipulate mental models during reasoning and language comprehension. All three predictions were confirmed in an analysis of reading times, and therefore support the view that spatial mental models are constructed when people read and understand spatial descriptions.

The findings reported here go against a simple interpretation of the given-new strategy proposed in psycholinguistics. In at least one domain it appears that people find the order new-given easier to read and understand. While this may seem counterintuitive (particularly in the light of alternative accounts such as that proposed by Hunter), it makes more sense if you consider the way common spatial language terms are used. In general, people introduce new spatial locations relative to known landmarks. Thus people seem to use spatial language in a way which eliminates an unnecessary conversion cost on readers and listeners. Natural conversation is much less constrained than the sentence structures we have used in our experiment, and speakers are readily able to separate the given-new status of information from the demands it makes on model construction. For instance, a speaker might introduce a new token as a potential topic prior to providing the information necessary to add the token to a spatial mental model ("That new shop I told you about is behind the library" rather than "The library is in front of that new shop I told you about"). From a given-new perspective the given information is that there is a new shop (which had previously been mentioned). The new information is that the shop is behind the library. From a mental models perspective the new token in the model is the shop and the old token is the library. This kind of separation between the given-new contract and the demands of mental model construction requires writers and speakers to draw on a rich well of general and individual knowledge about their intended audience (e.g. what they might be interested in, what landmarks they are familiar with and so on). One promising line of research in this area is to consider language as "processing instructions" for constructing an appropriate mental model (e.g. Gernsbacher 1990).

Acknowledgments

The authors wish to thank Keith Stenning and two anonymous reviewers for constructive comments on earlier versions of this work. Preparation of this research was supported by the United Kingdom Economic and Social Research Council (project grant number R000235641) and the Faculty of Science, Loughborough University. Correspondence concerning this paper should be addressed to Thom Baguley at the Department of Human Sciences, Loughborough University, Loughborough, Leicestershire, LE11 3TU, United Kingdom (email: T.S.Baguley@lboro.ac.uk).

Notes

1. In a strict sense the theory proposed by Hunter might still be viewed as propositional because it involves operations applied to the premises rather than to a mental model. In practice his operational account can be considered a half-way house between propositional theories and later image or model accounts.

References

Bower, G.H. & Morrow, D.G. (1990). Mental models in narrative comprehension. *Science, 247*, 44–48.

Bransford, J.D., Barclay, J.R. & Franks, J.J. (1972). Sentence memory: a constructive versus interpretive approach. *Cognitive Psychology, 3*, 193–209.

Brédart, S. (1987). Two ways of coping with indeterminate spatial discourse. *Psychologica Belgica, XXVII-2*, 143–151.

Byrne, R.M.J. & Johnson-Laird, P.N. (1989). Spatial reasoning. *Journal of Memory and Language, 28*, 564–575.

Clark, H.H. (1969). Linguistic processes in deductive reasoning. *Psychological Review, 76*, 387–404.

Clark, H.H. (1973). Space, time, semantics and the child. In T.E. Moore (Ed.), *Cognitive Development and the Acquisition of Language* (pp. 27–63). New York: Academic Press.

Ehrlich, K. & Johnson-Laird, P. N. (1982). Spatial descriptions and referential continuity. *Journal of Verbal Learning and Verbal Behaviour, 21*, 296–306.

Evans, J. S. B. T., Newstead, S. E. & Byrne, R. M. J. (1993). *Human Reasoning: The psychology of deduction*. Hove: Lawrence Erlbaum Associates.

Gernsbacher, M. A. (1990). *Language Comprehension as Structure Building*. Hillsdale, N. J.: Lawrence Erlbaum Associates.

Gernsbacher, M. A. & Hargreaves, D. J. (1988). Accessing sentence participants: The advantage of first mention. *Journal of Memory and Language, 27*, 699–717.

Glenberg, A. M., Meyer, M. & Lindberg, K. (1987). Mental models contribute to foregrounding during text comprehension. *Journal of Memory and Language, 26*, 69–83.

Haviland, S. E. & Clark, H. H. (1974). What's new? Acquiring new information as a process in comprehension. *Journal of Verbal Learning and Verbal Behaviour, 13*, 512–521.

Hunter, I. M. L. (1957). The solving of three term series problems. *British Journal of Psychology, 48*, 286–296.

Huttenlocher, J. (1968). Constructing spatial images: A strategy in reasoning. *Psychological Review, 75*, 550–560.

James, W. (1890). *Principles of psychology*. New York: Holt.

Johnson-Laird, P. N. (1980). Mental models in cognitive science. *Cognitive Science, 4*, 71–115.

Johnson-Laird, P. N. (1983). *Mental Models: Towards a cognitive science of language, inference and consciousness*. Cambridge: Cambridge University Press.

Kintsch, W. & Van Dijk, T. A. (1978). Toward a model of text comprehension and production. *Psychological Review, 85*, 363–394.

Kucera, H. & Francis, W. N. (1967). *Computational Analysis of Present-Day American English*. Providence: Brown University Press.

Mani, K. & Johnson-Laird, P. N. (1982). The mental representation of spatial descriptions. *Memory and Cognition, 10*, 181–187.

Payne, S. J. (1993). Memory for mental models of spatial descriptions: an episodic construction trace account. *Memory and Cognition, 21*, 591–603.

Pylyshyn, Z. W. (1984). *Computation and Cognition: Towards a foundation for cognitive science*. Cambridge, MA: MIT Press.

Quinlan, P. T. (1992). The Oxford psycholinguistic database. Oxford: Oxford University Press.

Sternberg, R. J. (1980). Representation and process in linear syllogistic reasoning. *Journal of Experimental Psychology: General, 109*, 119–159.

Tardieu, H., Ehrlich, M.-F. & Gyselinck, V. (1992). Levels of representation and domain-specific knowledge in comprehension of scientific texts. *Language and Cognitive Processes, 7*, 335–351.

Thorndyke, P. W. & Hayes-Roth, B. (1982). Differences in spatial knowledge acquired from maps and navigation. *Cognitive Psychology, 14*, 560–589.

Tversky, B. (1991). Spatial mental models. In G. H. Bower (Ed.), *The Psychology of Learning and Motivation: Advances in research and theory* (Vol. 27, pp. 109–145). San Diego: Academic Press.

Wilson, S. G., Rinck, M., McNamara, T. P., Bower, G. H. & Morrow, D. G. (1993). Mental models and narrative comprehension: some qualifications. *Journal of Memory and Language, 32*, 141–154.

Zwaan, R. A. & van Oostendorp, H. (1993). Do readers construct spatial representations in naturalistic story comprehension? *Discourse Processes, 16*, 125–143.

A Connectionist Model of the Processes Involved in Generating and Exploring Visual Mental Images

Mathias Bollaert
LIMSI-CNRS, Université de Paris-Sud

This work was undertaken to construct a connectionist model of the mental processes involved when people generate and explore mental images (Bollaert et al. 1996). We assumed that most of the cognitive resources used in imagery overlap with those used in visual perception, as indicated by several psychological and neuropsychological studies (Farah 1985; Kosslyn et al. 1993; Roland & Gulyas 1994). Our model therefore attempts to reflect the functional and the modular structure of the known cortical centers of vision, the ventral and the dorsal systems. There are constraints to the generation and exploration of a mental image, as shown by the work of Kosslyn on the mental drawing of letters (Kosslyn et al. 1988), that of McNamara et al. (1984) on the mental exploration of road maps and the experiments by Wagener and Wagener-Wender (1985 1990) on the spatial inferences derived from visual representations constructed from verbal descriptions of spatial configurations (Figure 1). In a priming situation (detailed methodology will be explained later as we used the same method; see below), they showed that response times were longer for items whose relative positions were not explicitly stated in the description. They also found that response times were shorter for inferences concerning short distances than for inferences involving long distances. This confirms the scanning effect for spatial relations inferred from verbal descriptions. Some subjects reported that the path defined by the verbal description affected the way they explored the mental image during the first stages of learning. We therefore set out to investigate the influence of the path on the generation and exploration of mental images. We expected the influence of the path to decay as learning proceeded, and the internal representation to lose the features which depended on the structure of the description.

The glass is in front of the salt.

Left to the salt is the cup.

Behind the cup is the pot.

Right to the pot is the plate.

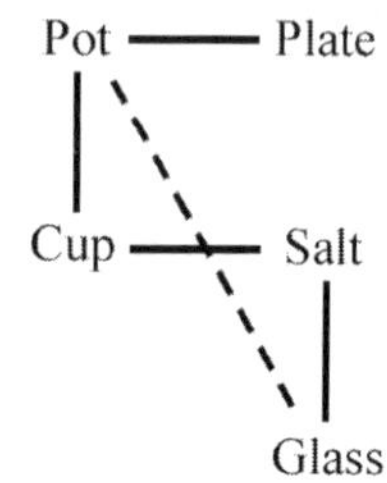

The paprika is in front of the cucumber.

Left to the the cucumber is the potato.

In front of the potato is the onion.

In front of the onion is the tomato.

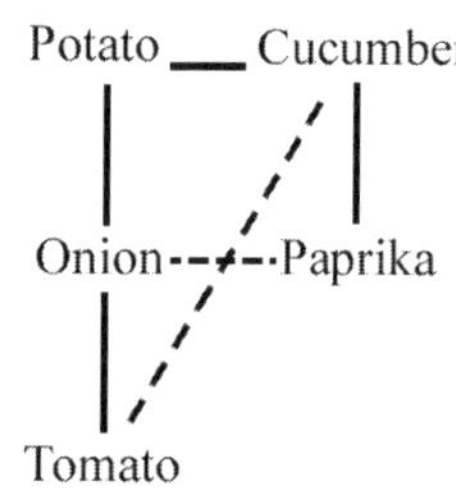

Figure 1. The materials used by Wagener and Wender (1985)

1. The experiment

We designed an experiment to investigate the effect of the modality of presentation on the generation and exploration of mental images, that is on the structure of the internal representation, and to assess how this representation develops during learning. In the *visual condition*, subjects learned the configuration which was visually presented to them. In the *verbal condition*, the subjects learned from sentences describing the relative positions of objects. In this condition, two types of description were used, the S-like path and the loop-like path (Figure 2). We expected the verbal condition to reflect the effect of the description path, with longer response times when the path between two objects was longer. Also, the spatial relations between pairs of objects which were explicitly stated in the description should result in shorter response times than those which had to be inferred. We also expected this path effect to disappear as learning proceeds, so that the two kinds of internal representations became more and more similar.

Thus in both conditions the material was presented three times consecutively, defining three stages of learning, to study the evolution of internal representations during learning.

Visual Presentation

Verbal description

At the upper left, there is the brush.
Below the brush, there is the teapot.
To the right of the teapot, there is the candle.
Above the candle, there is the envelope.
To the right of the envelope, there is the knife.
Below the knife, there is the clock.

At the upper left, there are the scissors.
Below the scissors, there is the bottle.
To the right of the bottle, there is the pen.
To the right of the pen, there is the hammer.
Above the hammer, there is the cigar.
To the left of the cigar, there is the bulb.

Loop path *S path*

Figure 2. Materials

In the *visual condition*, the subjects learned two configurations. During the test, they heard a first word and then had to mentally reconstruct the configuration in which the corresponding object was present, as fast as possible, and focus their attention on this object. Then they pressed a key, which provided a generation time. A second word was given, and subjects had to decide whether or not the corresponding object belonged to the same configuration as the first object, by pressing the « Yes » or « No » key. This provided an exploration time. Subjects were not explicitly required to scan the mental image. Thus, the term « exploration » refers not only to the scanning of a mental image, but to any sub-process involving the visuo-spatial internal representations which may provide the decision. The *verbal condition* differed only in the way in which the configurations were presented, that is, sentences describing the relative positions of pairs of objects. After the three stages of learning in one condition, the subjects went through the experiment again with the other condition, which involved new sets of objects (half of the subjects started with each condition). At the end, they were asked to answer a follow-up questionnaire.

2. Results

Learning had a significant effect on the generation and exploration times, under both conditions, with the longest response times occurring at the first stage of learning, and the shortest ones during the last stage (Figure 3). The percentage of correct responses also increased during the three stages, from 78%, to 87%, to 90%. Both generation and exploration times were shorter when the information was presented visually, but the effect was not significant (Figure 4). For the generation times, the difference was obvious for the first and the second stages, and almost disappeared in the third stage. This may indicate that the processes responsible for generating the internal representations from long term memory became similar for the two conditions. The differences in response times between conditions were smaller for the exploration times.

2.1 *Generation*

In the *visual condition*, the site of the object had a significant effect on generation times, with site B having significantly shorter generation times than site C (Figure 5). Closer examination revealed that the objects in the center of the configuration resulted in shorter generation times. The patterns of learning during the three stages also differed significantly. For the objects in the corners,

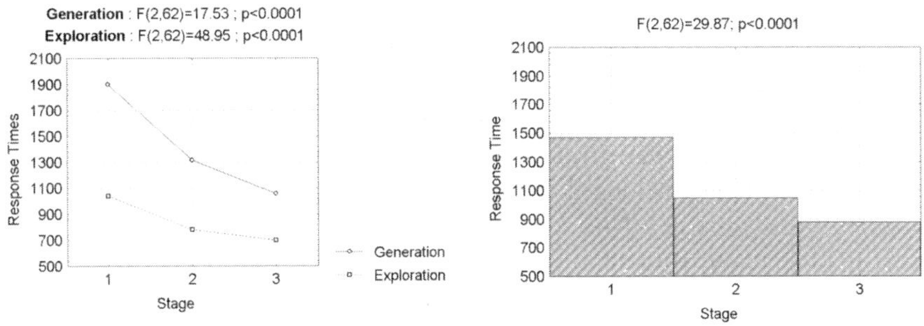

Figure 3. Learning

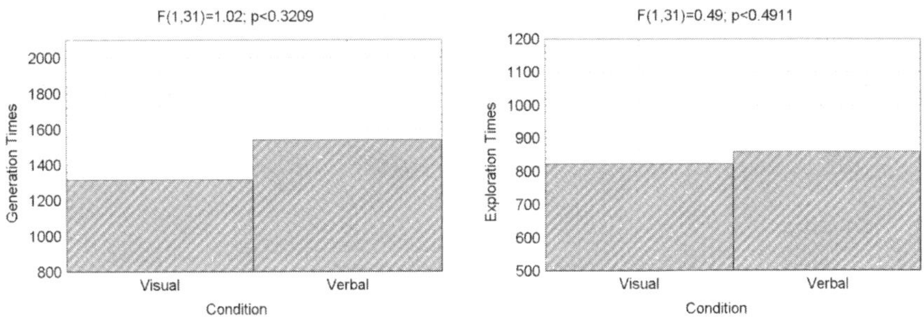

Figure 4. Conditions

learning seemed to be completed at the second stage, as response times no longer decreased. On the contrary, the response times for the objects in the center of the configuration continued to decrease.

In the *verbal condition*, the description path influenced the generation times for the S-like path, as showed by longer response times for longer distances on the path, except for site F (Figure 6). The generation time for site C was also significantly longer than for site A.

This effect was less obvious for the loop-like path (Figure 7). However, there was a significant effect of learning between sites A and B, with site B showing shorter response times during the first and second stages, and longer response times during the third stage. This is compatible with the fact that this path was reported to be hard to learn, so that subjects learned the special case of site B with special attention, which resulted in shorter response times at the beginning. Indeed, at the third stage, the response times for sites were in about the same order as the position of the sites on the loop-like path.

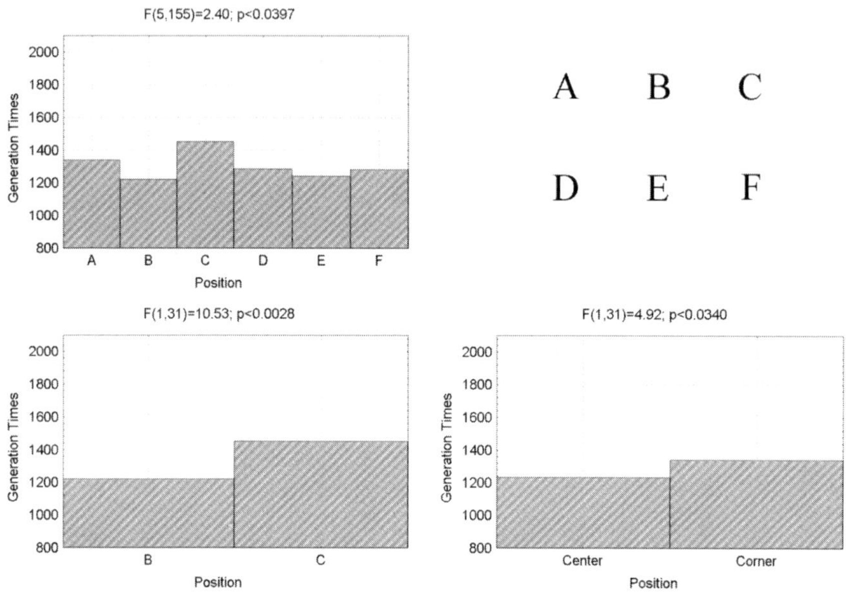

Figure 5. Generation: Visual condition

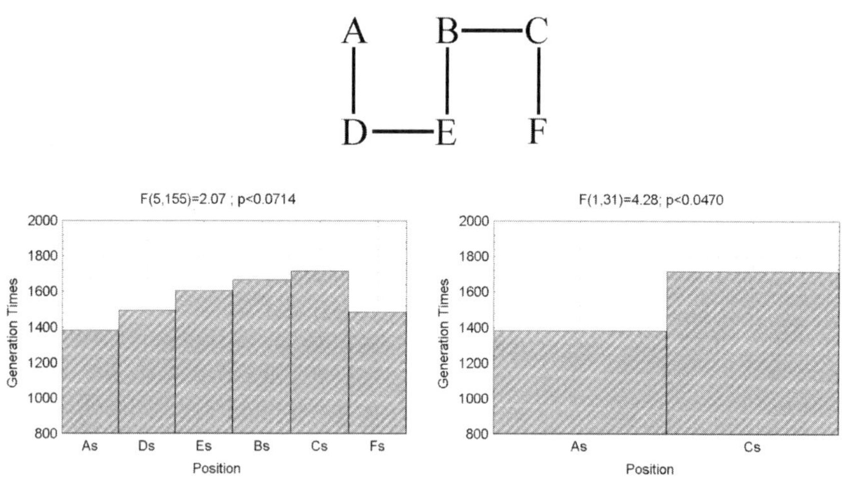

Figure 6. Generation: Verbal condition (S-like path)

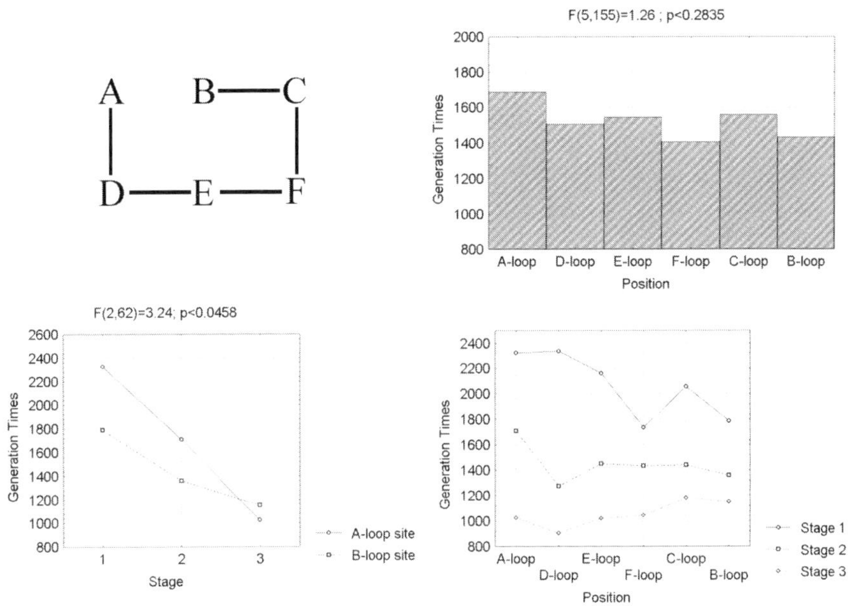

Figure 7. Generation: Verbal condition (loop-like path)

2.2 *Exploration*

The main results for exploration times were quite surprising, as there was a significant reversed mental scanning effect: the response times were shorter for distant objects than for close ones. For visually-presented information, the reverse scanning effect was significant for the second and third stages of trials, and for the whole set of data (Figure 8). For verbally-presented information, the effect was significant for all stages and for the whole set of data. However, in this experiment, the material was not specifically designed for studying the already well known scanning effect, and the distant pairs were only between the sites D and F.

As expected, we found an effect of the description path (Figure 9). The time taken to answer the AB pair was longer with the loop-like path than with the S- like path, although the difference was not significant (about 125 ms). When we grouped together the AB and EF inferred pairs (in the S-like path) instead of only the AB pairs, the effect was still present and remained non-significant (about 50 ms less for the small inferences). Also, the pairs explicitly

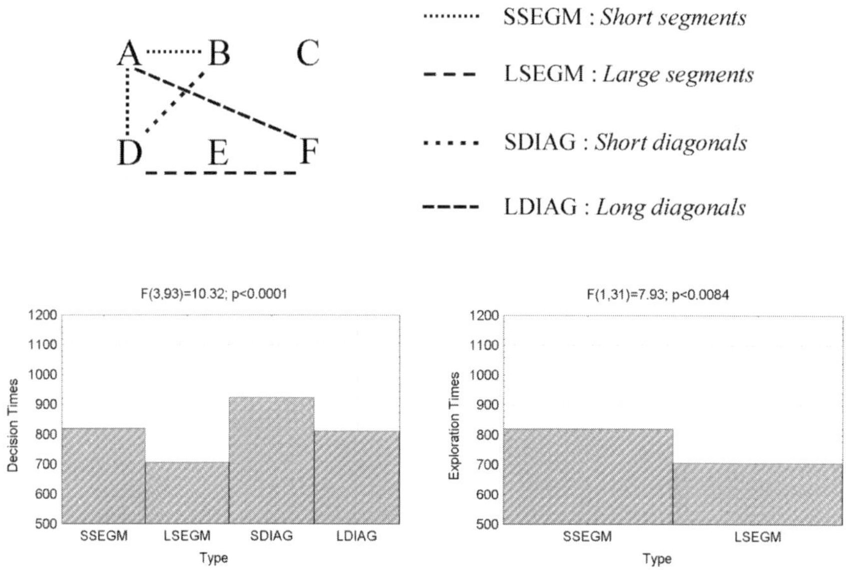

Figure 8. Exploration: Visual condition

stated in the description resulted in the shortest response times. It has to be noticed that this global pattern was only true for the second and third stages. Thus, the path effect did not appear during the first steps of learning, as we initially assumed. Again, this may indicate that the processes responsible for exploration became dissimilar when learning was pursued.

2.3 *Other results*

We have also investigated other effects which may explain the obtained results. Here we present the clearest ones only. We studied how each site influences the memorization of the item located at its position. Concerning exploration, response times for the EF pair were significantly shorter than for the DE pair and response times for the ED pair were also significantly shorter than for the FE pair. Moreover, response times obtained for the site D or F as a target were similar, independently of the distance between the two items. So what we called the reverse scanning effect can be explained in terms of higher accessibility of sites D and F. We also studied if some directions were privileged during mental exploration. For both conditions, the response times were shorter when the

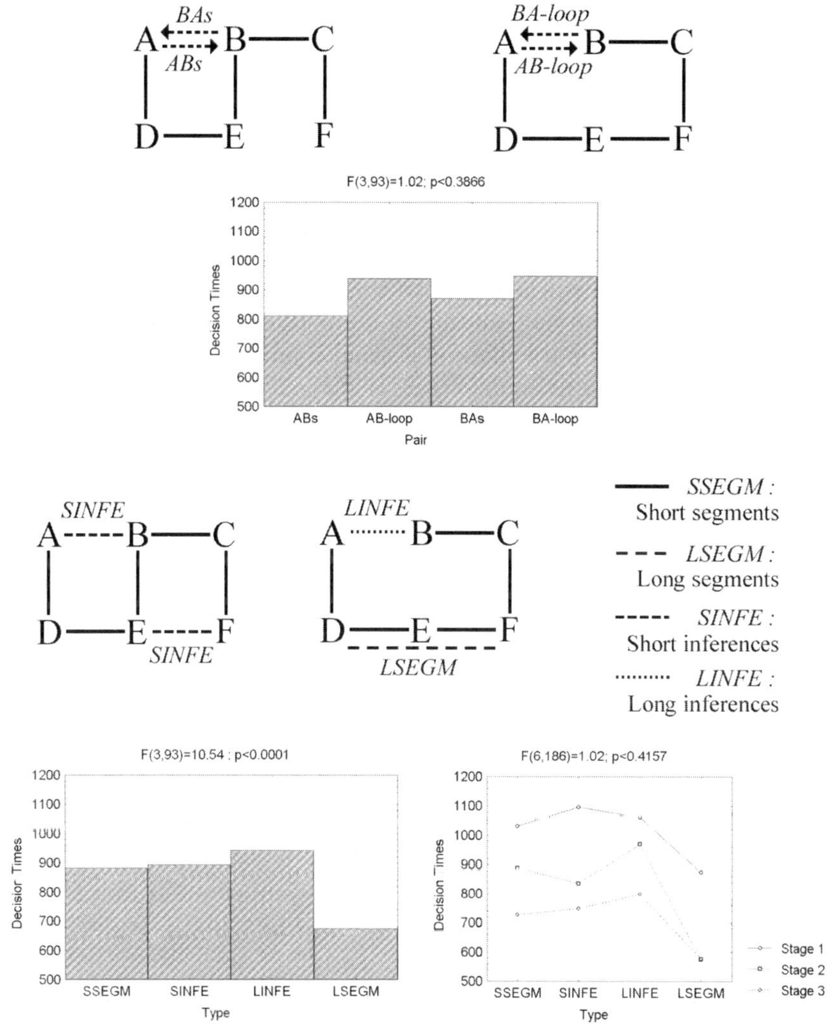

Figure 9. Exploration: Verbal condition

second item was to the right of the first one than when it was to its left. Moreover, we found that response times were significantly shorter when the second item was below the first one than when it was above. This may be partly responsible for better accessibility for sites D and F than for sites A and C.

3. Discussion

The conditions had an effect on both generation and exploration times. Thus, the internal representations constructed from verbal descriptions seem at first glance to differ from those constructed from visual presentation. But the path effect during generation was probably due to the fact that subject re-scanned the image after generating it, following the path in the verbal condition (cf. Kosslyn 1994). So the internal representations generated under both conditions might become similar while the processes applied during exploration become more dissimilar, resulting in response times that differed with the condition of presentation during exploration as well as for the generation of the visuo-spatial internal representation. The unexpected position effect on generation times may be due to the fact that subjects focused more on the center of the image when it was presented visually, and thus better memorized the objects in the center. We referred above to the high accessibility of sites D and F, independently of the distance from the source item. This better accessibility during exploration seems to be due to the conjunction of better accessibility of the objects in the corners and of better learning of the target's relative position when it is below the source. This may indicate that two different subsystems are used for the memorization of the spatial information: one storing the absolute position of the target, responsible for better accessibility of objects in the corners, and the other one storing the relative position between objects, being responsible for the path effect and better accessibility when the target is below the source. The same idea of two subsystems for shifting visual attention has been developed by Kosslyn, with one subsystem for the categorical properties, more involved in the visual tasks related to language, and one for the coordinate properties (Kosslyn 1994; Kosslyn & Koenig 1992).

4. The psychological model

The results described here and those of earlier studies were used to build a psychological model of the processes used by people to explore a mental image (Figure 10). The model describes the various abstraction levels in the ventral system, with three modules: the *Object memory* for higher visual areas (like STPa), which is independent of the size of objects; the *Feature memory* for intermediate visual areas, like CIT or AIT, which is size dependent; and the *Shape memory* for retinotopically organized areas, which is equivalent to the visual buffer in Kosslyn's model. The internal representations in these three modules slowly decay with time. The *Attention shifting system* is used to shift the visual attention between the different parts of the *Shape memory*, and contains two subsystems: a between-objects association for categorical spatial relations, and an object-position association for coordinate spatial relations. The results of both subsystems are summed. There is no competition algorithm between subsystems as they are cooperative rather than competitive. However, there is a competition after the summation, in the *Attention zone*, accounting for response times proportional to the activation of the selected unit. Once the position of the target is found in the *Attention zone*, the contrast of this region of the *Shape memory* is increased, which permits the features of the item under examination to be extracted in the *Feature memory*. As for the *Shape memory*, the *Attention zone* increases the contrast and selects the part of the *Feature memory* to be identified in the *Object memory*. The structure of the *Feature memory* is such that it can be used as a visual store, without activating the *Shape memory*, allowing less visual strategies. The *Spatial schema* is a module used to extract spatial information, or, more precisely, the positions of the different parts of the scene, from the scene represented in the *Shape memory*. This module uses the spatial information to generate the exploration paths used when scanning a mental image, for instance from left to right, line by line. In the *verbal condition*, the *Spatial schema* learns the description path, and uses it during the generation of the visuo-spatial internal representations. We also assume that other associations are learned: Position — Item associations between the *Attention zone* and the *Object memory*. These associations allow subjects to use different strategies for achieving the tasks, such as a purely spatial strategy.

Concerning the learning processes, we assume that the internal spatial representations constructed during the learning period in the visual condition are more activated than those constructed in the verbal condition. But the main difference between conditions is that the spatial information is extracted and identified from lower to higher areas during learning in the *visual condition*, while the categorical spatial information is directly generated from the verbal system to the visuo-spatial system in the *verbal condition*, and only the coordinate spatial relations are identified from the *Attention zone*, as they are not explicitly stated in the verbal description. We also assume that the categorical spatial information extracted from the visual areas in the *visual condition* is more activated when scanning from top to bottom, due to environmental factors. This leads us to infer that activation of the categorical spatial information should be greater for this direction of exploration in the *visual condition*, and thus should result in shorter response times. Indeed, this is the case in the experiment: response times in the *visual condition* are significantly shorter when scanning

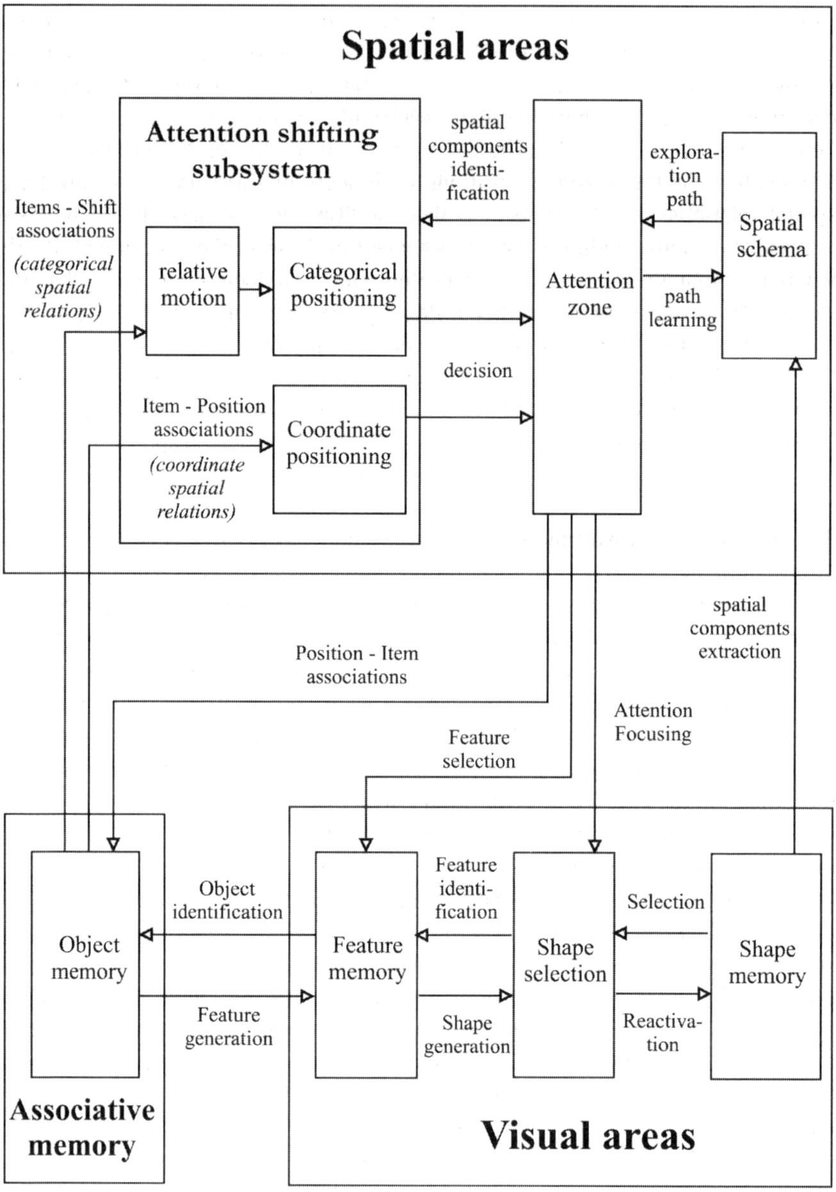

Figure 10. Psychological model

from up to bottom than when scanning from bottom to top; the same tendency can be found in the *verbal condition*, but it is not significant. Regarding the coordinate spatial relations, we assume that they are more activated when computed for objects in the corners, especially in the lower corners, and then better memorized. Thus, the absolute positions of objects in the corners are more accessible than the absolute positions of objects in the center. As coordinate spatial relations are identified in both conditions, the corners should be more accessible in both condition. This was indeed the case in the experiment. Lastly, we assume that the internal spatial representation also decays with time. The time to scan from one item to another following the description path in the *verbal condition* is longer when the relative position of the two items has to be inferred than when it is explicitly stated in the description. Therefore, the spatial internal representation is less activated for inferred spatial relations, which results in poorer memorization of the associations and then in longer response times.

5. The connectionist model

The units of the *Shape memory* are spatially organized (Figure 11). Reactivation in the *Shape memory* is performed with recurrent connections from the *Shape selection* to the *Shape memory*. The *Attention zone* is also spatially organized. The *Feature memory* has two subsystems, a local subsystem which first identifies the features in each region of the *Shape memory*, and a global subsystem, in which is copied the activation of the local *Feature memory* for the region where the attention focuses. As for the *Shape memory*, the signal is reactivated via recurrent connections linking the global to the local *Feature memory*. The features are used to identify the item in the *Object memory*. The *Object memory* has a second layer, a temporal buffer, identical to the first one, and the content of the first layer is moved into the second layer at each step of propagation, to simulate the progressive deactivation of the internal representation. During the *generation*, the *Spatial schema* activates sequentially the units of the *Attention zone*, following the description path in the *verbal condition*, and predefined paths in the *visual condition*. The object associated with the current position is found by the Item — Position associations. The features of this object are generated in the *global Feature memory*, and then in the *local Feature memory*. During the *exploration*, the spatial information associated with the items represented in the *Object memory* is activated in the coordinate and the categorical attention shifting subsystems. The categorical subsystem involves another module, which computes the position of the target, given the position of the prime and the relative motion to be made to join the position of the target. The implementation of this module uses a temporal buffer of the *Attention window*, too. The responses of both subsystems are filtered and then added to the *Attention zone*. We assume that the visual system has little influence on this task, as it is more spatial than visual. Thus, the activation level in the *Attention zone* is assumed to be mostly responsible for the response times and is used as the result of the simulations.

Learning occurs as follows: The dashed links are learned with a Hebbian algorithm. The object identification and feature generation processes are learned, in order to implement an exemplar memory system and to simulate the presentation of the items during the experiment. The learning patterns are constructed as indicated in the psychological model: in the *visual condition*, we assume that subjects scan their mental image using the *Spatial schema*; in the *verbal condition*, the visuo-spatial internal representations are generated from higher to lower modules. Learning proceeds in three stages, as in the experiment. All the other links represent the prior knowledge of the subjects. They are learned with a backpropagation learning algorithm, except for the competition in the *Attention zone* and the simpler sub-processes like deactivation, reactivation or copy from one module to another, for which the weights were calculated. All the modules were fully implemented except the Spatial schema. The specifications of this module were used to produce the patterns for the dependent processes. These patterns were some predefined exploration paths (in the visual condition) and the description paths memorized during the learning period (in the verbal condition). We do not assume that visual imagery involves retinotopical visual areas, which is still the subject of debate. The execution of the task relies more on spatial ability than on visual capacity (via the *Attention zone*). The model accounts for less visual strategies with the Position — Item associations and the *Feature memory*. Thus, it is possible to manipulate rather rich visuo-spatial internal representations to perform the task, without activating the retinotopical visual areas.

6. Results of the simulations

The simulations shown here are for a fully spatial strategy used during exploration. This strategy was chosen because 52% of the subjects in the visual condition and 68% in the verbal condition declared in the follow-up questionnaire that they did not really « see » the objects in the visual condition, but rather used a spatial internal representation. In this spatial strategy, activation of the position of the target in the *Attention zone* allowed the system to answer the question correctly, using the Position — Item associations (only the positive answers were simulated).

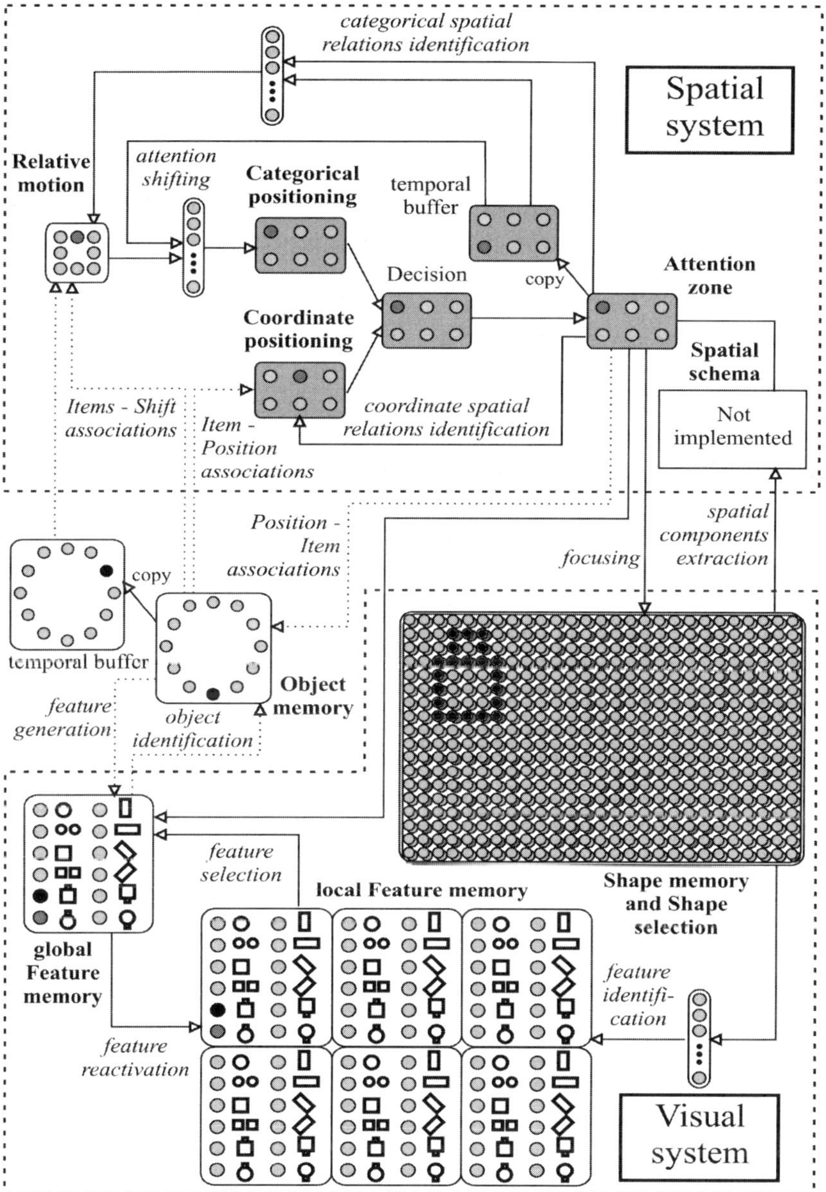

Figure 11. Connectionist model

Other simulations were also used to reproduce the generation in the *Feature memory*. They reproduced some of the results found in the experiments, notably better identification of the features of an object in the visual condition than in the verbal condition, which results in shorter response times in the visual condition. The linear trend in the *verbal condition* was also reproduced, due to the sequential generation of the items. The model also effectively generates, stores, identifies and reactivates visual internal representations in the *Feature memory*, but a strong visual similarity effect makes the results difficult to compare with those from the experiment. The strength of this similarity effect seems to be partly due to the few features used during the simulation (12) and to the low resolution of the visual representation of the items, drawn on a 7×7 grid. But the fact that our network shows a similarity effect is a clue to its validity, as this effect is also found in human data (see e.g., Logie 1995).

All the following data are levels of activation in the *Attention zone*. According to the competition in this module, the response time is shorter when activation is greater. The competition is not performed here, as it mostly depends on arbitrary parameters, and only excites the single activated unit. Thus, the competition provide no new information on the simulation. The mean levels of activation during exploration were 0.570 for the first stage of learning, 0.729 for the second and 0.854 for the third, corresponding to decreasing response times during learning. The difference was bigger between the first and second stages than between the second and third, as in the experimental results. The activation was greater for the visual condition (0.589, 0.766, 0.890) than for the verbal condition (0.560, 0.710, 0.837), resulting in shorter response times for the visual condition. The levels of activation were as expected from the results of the experiment: in the *visual condition*, the mean activation of the unit selected in the *Attention window* was lower for close objects (0.736) than for distant objects (0.821); in the *verbal condition*, the mean activation for the large segments (LSEGM) was greater (0.791) than the mean activation for the small segments (SSEGM), the small inferences (SINFE) and the large inferences (LINFE), which were 0.699, 0.665 and 0.629 respectively. In the *visual condition*, sites D (0.803) and F (0.817) were more accessible than the other sites (all under 0.712). This holds true for the *verbal condition* (sites D and F: 0.755 and 0.739; other sites all under 0.699). Finally, we reproduced the effect of the direction of scanning, particularly with better accessibility to the target object when it was below the source (visual condition: 0.844; verbal condition: 0.722) than when the source was below the target (visual condition: 0.679; verbal condition: 0.704).

7. Conclusion

The results of our experiment and data on the structure of the cortical areas of vision were used to construct a modular network that gives patterns of results that are compatible with the experimental results. The model is able to generate, reactivate, store and identify visual internal representations. Although some numerical results were obtained with the generation, complete simulations were not done because of a strong similarity effect. We will extend the number of features and the resolution of the image to reduce this effect. Concerning the exploration, the results obtained with the model were very similar to those obtained in the experiment. We successfully reproduced the effect of learning, the effect of the condition, and all the main effects observed in exploration, under both conditions. Hence this modular network provides a valid model of the sub-processes involved in learning, generating and exploring visual mental images.

References

Bollaert, M., Denis, M. & Memmi, D. (1996). Une modélisation connexionniste de la génération d'images mentales à partir de descriptions spatiales. *Paper read at the XXVIth International Congress of Psychology*, Montreal, 16–21 August 1996.

Farah, M. J. (1985). Psychophysical evidence for a shared representational medium for mental images and percepts. *Journal of Experimental Psychology: General, 114*, 91–103.

Kosslyn, S. M. (1994). *Image and Brain: The resolution of the imagery debate*. Cambridge MA, The MIT Press.

Kosslyn, S. M., Alpert, N. M., Thompson, W. L., Maljkovic, V., Weise, S. B., Chabris, C. F., Hamilton, S. E., Rauch, S. L. & Buonanno, F. S. (1993). Visual mental imagery activates topographically organized visual cortex: PET investigations. *Journal of Cognitive Neuroscience, 5*, 263–287.

Kosslyn, S. M., Cave, C. B., Provost, D. A. & von Gierke, S. M. (1988). Sequential processes in image generation. *Cognitive Psychology, 20*, 319–343.

Kosslyn, S. M. & Koenig, O. (1992). *Wet mind: The new cognitive neuroscience*. New York: Free Press.

Logie, R. H. (1995). Visuo-spatial working memory. *Essays in Cognitive Psychology*, Hove: Lawrence Erlbaum Associates.

McNamara, T. P., Ratcliff, R. & McKoon, G. (1984). The mental representation of knowledge acquired from maps. *Journal of Experimental Psychology: Learning, Memory and Cognition, 10*, 723–732.

Roland, P.E. et Gulyas, B. (1994). Visual representations of scenes and objects: Retinotopical or non-retinotopical? *Trends in Neurosciences, 17*, 294–297.

Wagener, M. & Wender, K.F. (1985). Spatial representations and inference processes in memory for text. In G. Rickheit & H. Strohner (Eds.), *Inferences in Text Processing* (pp. 115–136). Amsterdam: North-Holland.

Wagener-Wender, M. & Wender, K.F. (1990). Expectations, mental representations, and spatial inferences. In A.C. Graesser & G.H. Bower (Eds.), *The Psychology of Learning and Motivation* (Vol. 25) (pp. 137–157). New York: Academic Press.

Working Memory and Mental Synthesis

A dual-task approach

David G. Pearson and Robert H. Logie
University of Aberdeen

Introduction

This chapter reviews a series of studies which have examined the role that verbal and visuo-spatial working memory may play during the performance of mental synthesis, in which visual imagery is used to manipulate and combine separate components into new configurations. Mental synthesis has been shown to be involved during a wide variety of different creative tasks, including the visualisation and development of scientific models (Miller 1984), architectural design (Reed 1993), and many aspects of everyday problem-solving (Kaufmann 1988; Finke 1990). Also, anecdotal reports from highly creative individuals such as Einstein (1949), Watson (1968), Mozart or Poincare (reported in Vernon 1970) suggest that mental imagery can aid not only the conceptualisation of a problem, but also the discovery of creative and original solutions. For example, mental synthesis has been proposed as a useful reasoning technique in theoretical physics (Finke 1990). Einstein advocated 'combinatory play' as a key feature of his own scientific thinking, during which he mentally reproduced and combined images so as to discover new insights and relationships between the constituent parts (Gardner 1993). Mental synthesis has also been claimed to play a fundamental role during the concept phase of creative design (Purcell & Gero 1998; Verstijnen et al. 1998). Suwa and Tversky (1996) collected protocols of design sessions from student and expert architectural designers and found that both groups used sketches based on the results of mental synthesis while designing, although the expert designers were better at considering perceptual and functional features and relations within potential designs. On a more general level, the mental recombining of images has been implicated during everyday reasoning problems, such as deciding how to re-arrange furniture in a room (Kosslyn 1994; Finke, Ward & Smith 1992).

Although previous research has demonstrated that imagery can support both the production and invention of novel forms through the mental combination of separate parts (i.e., Cooper 1990; Finke & Slayton 1988), the exact nature of the cognitive processes that underlie such synthesis remains unclear. Other research has indicated that there are some circumstances in which imagery may be insufficient to support mental synthesis, and may even constrain creative discovery. Reed and Johnsen (1975) demonstrated that participants were extremely poor at discovering hidden figures within imagined patterns compared with when the patterns were visually present, suggesting a difficulty in reanalysing an image in order to discover new information. Further evidence for this was presented by Chambers and Reisberg (1985), who found that participants had great difficulty in reinterpreting images of ambiguous figures (e.g., duck/rabbit figure; Necker cube), even though perceptual reversals of actual drawings were comparatively easy. Findings such as these suggest that the imagery system has a limited capacity to hold information and successfully transform this information in a meaningful way, and that such resource limitations can place constraints on what can be accomplished with synthesis based on imagery alone.

A theoretical model which can be usefully applied to the study of resource limitations is that of working memory (Baddeley & Hitch 1974; Baddeley 1986), which details a model of short-term working memory comprising multiple components. The first component comprises an executive controlling mechanism that has been implicated in reasoning, problem-solving, and in the coordination of specialist slave systems. One of these specialist components, the phonological loop, is thought to be involved in the storage of verbal material via a rehearsal mechanism linked to the speech system. A second component, the visuo-spatial sketchpad, deals with the rehearsal of visuo-spatial material, and has also been implicated in the generation and manipulation of visuo-spatial images (see Logie 1995, for a review). As there are limited visuo-spatial resources available during any cognitive task, this will place a limit on the complexity of the visuo-spatial transformations that can be carried out (Kosslyn et al. 1988; Roskos-Ewoldsen 1993).

Spatial manipulation and mental synthesis

The issues raised above will be addressed within the theoretical framework of a revised model of the visuo-spatial component of working memory (Logie 1995; Pearson, Logie & Green 1996; Logie & Pearson 1997; Pearson, Logie & Gilhooly, 1999). In this model the temporary storage of visual material is achieved by a passive memory system, referred to as a 'visual cache', and the contents of this cache are refreshed by means of a spatially based rehearsal mechanism, acting as a form of 'inner scribe'. The contents of the cache are not 'mental images', however, as the visual cache is considered a separate component from the visual buffer in which conscious mental images are represented. The passive visual cache is closely linked with the visual perceptual system, while the spatial rehearsal mechanism is linked with the planning and cognitive control of movement. Although spatial locations can be stored within the cache in the form of a static visual representation (Smyth & Pendleton 1989), the storage of *sequential* locations or movements requires the operation of the inner scribe. The scribe also extracts information from the visual cache to allow for targeted movement, and hence any concurrent movement to discrete spatial locations can result in a disruption of the visuo-spatial rehearsal mechanism (Baddeley, Grant, Wight & Thomson 1975; Quinn & Ralston 1986).

In addition to rehearsing material held within the visuo-spatial sketchpad, the inner scribe is also proposed as a means to support the manipulation and transformation of visuo-spatial images. Logie and Salway (1990) have reported that concurrent spatial tapping significantly disrupts participants accuracy during the mental rotation of abstract shapes. In addition, concurrent tapping has been shown to disrupt both the encoding and mental comparison of objects' relative size (Engelkamp, Mohr & Logie 1995).

Successful performance of mental synthesis is known to normally require a complex number of spatial transformations to be carried out, including manipulations of position, size, and orientation (Finke & Slayton 1988; Neblett et al. 1989 (reported in Finke 1990); Anderson & Helstrup 1993). The majority of these studies have used the Finke and Slayton 'creative synthesis' task (Finke & Slayton 1988), which has been widely used in the literature as an experimental test of mental synthesis. During the task participants are verbally presented with the names of overlearned symbols, which they are then asked to visualise, such as a circle, a capital letter D, and a square. They must then mentally manipulate and synthesise the symbols to form a nameable image, which is then assigned a verbal label and then drawn onto a sheet of paper (Figure 1). In so doing the participants are free to alter the size and orientation of the symbols, but cannot distort them in any other way. The correspondence between the verbal label and completed drawing is later rated by a panel of independent judges.

A study conducted by Pearson, Logie and Gilhooly (1999) found that concurrent spatial tapping during the construction phase of the creative synthesis task significantly reduced the number of legitimate patterns that participants produced using the presented shapes. This was in contrast to only a marginal effect of tapping on the number of trials on which participants correctly recalled all of the presented shapes, and no effect of tapping at all on the rated correspondence between the patterns and their corresponding verbal descriptions.

Figure 1. Example of response sheet for the creative synthesis task (presented shapes were circle, D, square, d, eight). Data taken from Pearson, Logie and Gilhooly (1999)

These results are consistent with the hypothesis that the inner scribe component of visuo-spatial working memory is utilised during the spatial manipulation of imaged shapes. Such manipulation is necessary in order to produce legitimate patterns during mental synthesis, and concurrent tapping appears to interfere with this process, resulting in the pattern of disruption observed. In contrast, the scribe would seem to have a much less significant role in the retention of the presented parts themselves.

There is little evidence that the degree of correspondence between the verbal labels and the drawings of the synthesised patterns is affected by concurrent tapping. This suggests that the locus of the interference is during the actual combination of the imaged parts, and that once synthesis is successfully achieved there is no further disruption of concurrent tapping on participants' ability to assign a verbal label to the completed pattern. This result is consistent with a task analysis model of creative synthesis reported by Helstrup and Anderson (1991), who divide mental synthesis into two phases; a construction phase, in which the presented shapes are mentally assembled into a pattern, and a verbal interpretation phase, in which the synthesised pattern is then given an appropriate verbal description. The results of Pearson et al. suggest that the main involvement of the inner scribe is during the construction phase of the synthesis task.

Passive visual storage and mental synthesis

As discussed in the introduction, the revised model of the visuo-spatial sketchpad consists of two inter-related components; an active spatial rehearsal mechanism, and a passive visual cache that acts as a temporary store for visual material. Recent research in this area has investigated the involvement of this cache during mental imagery using visual interference paradigms. This was first demonstrated by Logie (1986), who showed that concurrently presented line drawings could significantly reduce participants' memory for material learned using a visual imagery-based mnemonic. This effect occurred even when participants were instructed to attempt to ignore the irrelevant drawings, and has therefore been likened to the irrelevant speech effect that has been reported in the literature on verbal working memory (Salame & Baddeley 1982, 1987, 1989).

Recently, methodological developments have replaced line drawings with dynamic visual noise as a means of inducing visual interference effects within visuo-spatial working memory. Quinn and McConnell (1996a, b; McConnell & Quinn 1996) have claimed that such dynamic displays gain direct access to the visual cache component of working memory and thereby disrupt the storage of any visual material being held there. However, much of the empirical evidence for this is based upon the use of imagery-based mnemonics such as the pegword strategy, and it is less clear how such visual noise may affect the kind of imagery processing that occurs during mental synthesis. Pearson et al. (1999) examined the effect of a concurrent dynamic visual noise display on participants' performance of the Finke and Slayton creative synthesis task. They found no significant effect of concurrent visual noise either on the number of legitimate patterns produced, the memory for the shapes themselves, or on the degree of rated correspondence between the verbal labels and their associated drawings. There is therefore no evidence from this study to support a role for the passive visual cache in the temporary storage of visual material during mental synthesis.

These results do not appear consistent with the claim that the visual cache component of working memory is involved during the generation and manipulation of visual images, or that visual images are maintained within the visual cache (i.e., Baddeley 1986, 1988; Quinn & McConnell 1996a, b). However, the revised model of the visuo-spatial sketchpad discussed previously disputes this interpretation of the relationship between visual imagery and visuo-spatial working memory, and argues instead that the maintenance of conscious visual images within a visual buffer is primarily the function of the *central executive system* rather than the specialised visuo-spatial component (Logie 1995; Pearson, Logie & Green 1996; see also Pearson, De Beni & Cornoldi, in press). This conclusion is based upon a number of empirical findings which have shown that visual imagery can be highly demanding upon general-purpose attentional resources (i.e., Salway & Logie 1990; Logie & Salway 1995) and suggest that the generation and maintenance of visual images within a visual buffer is best viewed as a function of the central executive rather than the visual cache. Instead, the cache operates primarily as a *storage* mechanism, which provides temporary storage of visual material during imagery tasks if required. Crucially, however, any material stored in the cache is deemed *functionally separate* from material maintained via the central executive within the visual buffer. Hence, there is a clear distinction in this revised model between the maintenance of visual images by the operation of the central executive, and the rehearsal of visual material within the visual cache by the operation of the inner scribe. Such a separation is not without precedent, as a comparable distinction has been made in the literature between auditory imagery and verbal rehearsal within the phonological store component of verbal working memory (Baddeley & Logie 1992; Reisberg et al. 1991). In addition, the involvement of attentional resources during the generation and maintenance of visual images is also a feature of many current cognitive models of mental imagery (e.g., Kosslyn 1980, 1994).

Verbal representations and mental synthesis

Although mental imagery tasks have been traditionally assumed to draw primarily upon visuo-spatial cognitive systems, a growing number of empirical studies have demonstrated the important role that verbal encoding and rehearsal can play during creative discoveries based on imagery. Brandimonte and colleagues (Brandimonte, Hitch & Bishop 1992; Brandimonte & Gerbino 1993) have reported that concurrent articulatory suppression can significantly improve participants' performance on image subtraction and reinterpretation tasks, but only for those items which can be easily verbally encoded. In addition, Intons-Peterson (1996) has shown that performance of image subtraction declines when linguistic processing is encouraged, and increases when the visual aspects of the task are emphasised. These results have been interpreted as demonstrating that verbal representations can significantly impair the ability to make novel discoveries on the basis of visual imagery alone, and that concurrent articulatory suppression can remove this effect by preventing the use of verbal labelling during imagery. However, this interpretation of the effect of articulatory suppression is contentious, as it implies that suppression operates on a much deeper level of verbal processing than has previously been assumed (Logie 1995; Reisberg 1996).

In terms of the task analysis model of mental synthesis proposed by Helstrup and Anderson (1991), articulatory suppression could potentially interfere with participants' performance by disrupting the verbal interpretation phase of the process. However, an alternative prediction is that articulatory suppression will instead disrupt the verbal rehearsal of the presented shapes themselves, and thereby lower performance through memory interference rather than at the verbal labelling stage of the synthesis task. Pearson et al. (1999) addressed these issues by examining the effect of concurrent articulatory suppression on performance of the creative synthesis task. If the focus of any interference was in terms of verbal rehearsal of the presented parts, then disruption should have been evident for the number of trials in which all parts were correctly recalled, but absent in terms of the degree of rated correspondence between the verbal label and associated drawing. The results of the study supported the hypothesis that the phonological loop component of working memory is involved during the rehearsal of verbal representations during performance of the creative synthesis task. Concurrent articulatory suppression not only significantly lowered the number of legitimate patterns that participants produced, but also significantly lowered the number of trials on which they were able to successfully recall all of the presented shapes.

As there was a specific effect of suppression on participants' memory for the shapes themselves, this suggests they were continuing to rehearse the verbal labels during the construction phase of the synthesis task. There was also a significant increase in the variance of responses for articulatory suppression when it was performed concurrently with creative synthesis, and this is also indicative of mutual interference occurring between the two cognitive tasks. Finally, the fact that there was no significant effect of suppression upon degree of rated correspondence between verbal labels and associated drawings suggests that the cause of the interference was based upon the verbal rehearsal of the labels for the shapes, rather than during the verbal interpretation phase of the synthesis task, in which a verbal label was assigned to the synthesised pattern.

Conclusions

Figure 2 represents how the specialist components of working memory are involved during mental synthesis based upon the findings of the studies discussed previously. As the shapes are verbally presented to participants via their verbal labels, initially they should gain direct access to the phonological store component of working memory and be maintained there via the operation of the articulatory loop (Baddeley & Lewis 1981; Baddeley 1986). It is then argued that participants generate conscious images of the shapes using the verbal representations, but continue to maintain the representations within the loop so as to provide a memory backup for the shapes that is separate from the use of visual imagery. Such a strategy represents a much more effective means of spreading the cognitive load of the task across the whole of the working memory system.

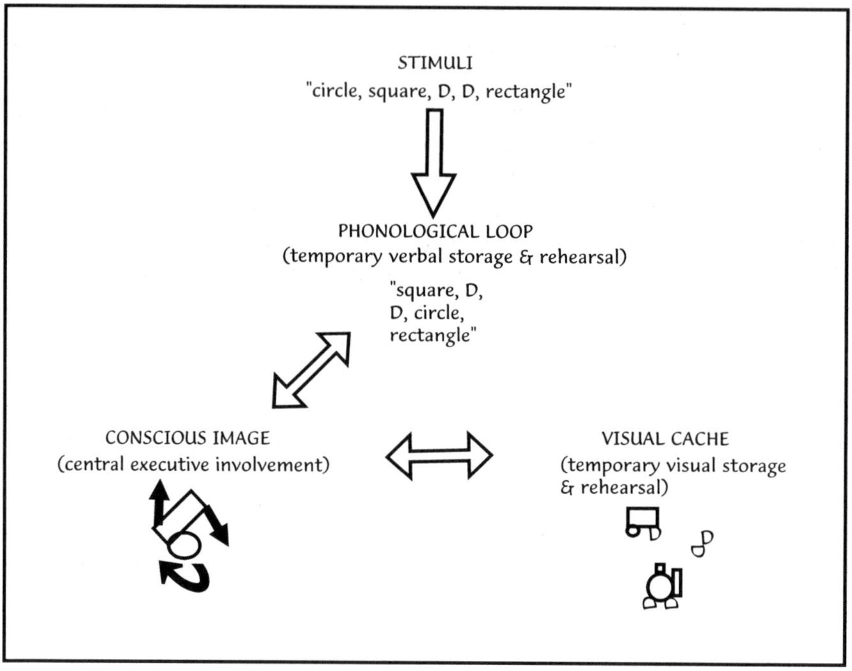

Figure 2. Diagram of relationship between phonological loop/visual cache components and conscious imagery during mental synthesis (from Pearson, Logie & Gilhooly, 1999)

Maintaining the presented shapes as verbal representations would considerably reduce the load on the visuo-spatial sketchpad and central executive components, as they would not be required to maintain the shapes to be combined purely in a visual form.

Pearson et al. (1999) asked participants to give written protocols of what they were consciously aware of experiencing while completing the creative synthesis task. Many of the responses given indicate that, for most of the construction phase of the task, participants do not experience maintaining a conscious image of all five of the presented shapes simultaneously; e.g.,

(1) "took the most geometrically interesting shape (i.e., 'J' being very interesting, also 'X' and to a lesser extent 'T' and 'C') and tried to use it's shape alone or combined with a few other letters to form a shape, then just worked the other parts in."

(2) "I tried combining three of the shapes, then fitting the others to the result."

Concurrent articulatory suppression interferes with the verbal rehearsal of the presented shapes, placing a greater load on the other components of the working memory system. This disruption of the maintenance of verbal representations significantly reduces the number of legitimate patterns that participants can produce, because they are no longer able to accurately recall the correct shapes to add to their developing patterns.

During the construction phase of the task the spatial manipulation of the shapes requires the operation of the inner scribe component of the visuo-spatial sketchpad, but the control of these manipulations and the continued maintenance and inspection of the conscious image is primarily dependent upon the resources of the central executive system. This interpretation of synthesis performance would therefore predict substantial dual-task interference if creative synthesis was performed concurrently with an executively-demanding secondary task. Recent work carried out by the authors (Pearson, Logie & Gilhooly 1998) has demonstrated this using oral random generation as a secondary task, for which significant disruption was evident for both three and five part synthesis trials (Figure 3).

Although the generation and maintenance of conscious imagery requires a substantial involvement of the central executive system, any spatial manipulations

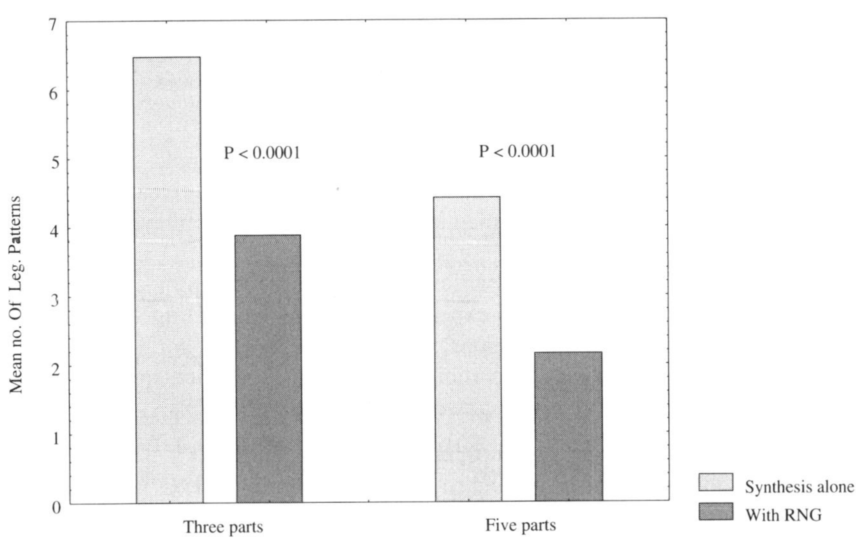

Figure 3. Effect of concurrent oral random number generation (RNG) on mean number of legitimate patterns produced for three and five part trials (from Pearson, Logie & Gilhooly, 1998)

of images (such as changes in size or orientation) are assumed to also require the operation of the inner scribe component. Concurrent spatial tasks have been shown to interfere with mental rotation (Logie & Salway 1990), mental comparisons (Engelkamp, Mohr & Logie 1989), and mental animation (Sims & Hegarty 1997). Such a role for the inner scribe in manipulating imagery is also supported by the finding discussed previously that concurrent spatial tapping results in significantly fewer legitimate patterns being produced during mental synthesis (Pearson et al., 1999).

The model depicted in Figure 2 also allows for the visual cache to store material during synthesis as a back-up store for imagery, in a fashion analogous to the way in which the phonological loop is used to maintain the identity of the shapes being manipulated via mental imagery. However, as no studies have so far demonstrated any significant interference from concurrent visual noise, this means currently any involvement of the visual cache during mental synthesis must remain speculative.

In conclusion, the research findings reviewed in this chapter have demonstrated the involvement of spatial working memory during the spatial manipulation of material during mental synthesis, and have also demonstrated the importance of verbal representations during what may initially appear to be primarily a visuo-spatial task. Specifically, mental synthesis appears to occupy the resources of the working memory system as a whole, rather than relying solely on the operation of the visuo-spatial sketchpad component.

References

Anderson, R. E. & Helstrup, T. (1993a). Multiple perspectives on discovery and creativity in mind and on paper. In B. Roskos-Ewoldsen, M. J. Intons-Peterson & R. Anderson (Eds.), *Imagery, Creativity and Discovery: A cognitive perspective*. Amsterdam: North-Holland.

Anderson, R. E. & Helstrup, T. (1993b). Visual discovery In mind and on paper. *Memory and Cognition, 21,* 283–293.

Baddeley, A. D. (1986). *Working Memory*. Oxford: Oxford University Press.

Baddeley, A. D. (1988). Imagery and working memory. In M. Denis, J. Engelkamp, and J. T. E. Richardson (Eds.), *Cognitive and neuropsychological approaches to mental imagery*, pp. 169–180, Martinus Nijhoff Publishers.

Baddeley, A. D., Grant, W., Wight, E. & Thomson, N. (1975). Imagery and visual working memory. In P. M. A. Rabbit & S. Dornic (Eds.), *Attention and Performance V,* pp. 205–217, London: Academic Press.

Baddeley, A. D. & Hitch, G. J. (1974). Working memory. In G. Bower (Ed.), *The Psychology of Learning and Motivation, Vol. VIII*, pp. 47–90, New York: Academic Press.

Baddeley, A. D. & Lewis, V. J. (1981). Inner active processes in reading: The inner voice, the inner ear and the inner eye. In A. M. Lesgold & C. A. Perfetti (Eds.), *Interactive Processes in Reading*, pp. 107–129. Hillsdale, NJ: LEA.

Baddeley, A. D. & Logie, R. H. (1992). Auditory imagery and working memory. In D. Reisberg (Ed.), *Auditory imagery*. Hillsdale, NJ: Lawrence Erlbaum Associates Inc.

Brandimonte, M. & Gerbino, W. (1993). Mental image reversal and verbal recoding: When ducks become rabbits. *Memory and Cognition, 21,* 23–33.

Brandimonte, M., Hitch, G. J. & Bishop, D. (1992). Verbal recoding of visual stimuli impairs mental image transformations. *Memory and Cognition, 20,* 449–455.

Chambers, D. & Reisberg, D. (1985). Can mental images be ambiguous? *Journal of Experimental Psychology: Human Perception and Performance, 11,* 317–328.

Cooper, L. A. (1990). Mental representation of three-dimensional objects in visual problem solving and recognition. *Journal of Experimental Psychology: Learning, Memory, and Cognition, **16***, 1097–1106.

Einstein, A. (1949). Autobiographical notes. In P. A. Schlipp (Ed.), *Albert Einstein: Philosopher-scientist*. Evanston, III.: Library of Living Philosophers.

Engelkamp, J., Mohr, G. & Logie, R. H. (1995). Memory for size relations and selective interference. *European Journal of Cognitive Psychology, 7(3),* 239–260.

Finke, R. (1990). *Creative Imagery: Discoveries and inventions in visualization.* Hillsdale, NJ: Lawrence Erlbaum.

Finke, R. & Slayton, K. (1988). Explorations of creative visual synthesis in mental imagery. *Memory and Cognition, 16,* 252–257.

Finke, R., Ward, T. B. & Smith, S. M. (1992). *Creative Cognition: Theory, research, and applications.* Cambridge, Mass.: M. I. T. Press.

Gardner, H. (1993). *Creating Minds.* NY: BasicBooks.

Helstrup, T. & Anderson, R. E. (1991). Imagery in mental construction and decomposition tasks. In R. H. Logie & M. Denis (Eds.), *Mental Images in Human Cognition.* Amsterdam: North-Holland.

Intons-Peterson, M. J. (1996). Linguistic effects in a visual manipulation task. *Psychologische Beitrage, 38(3/4),* 251–278.

Kauffman, G. (1988). Mental imagery and problem solving. In M. Denis, J. Engelkamp & J. T. E. Richardson (Eds.), *Cognitive and Neuropsychological Approaches to Mental Imagery.* Dordrecht: Martinus Nijhoff Publishers.

Kosslyn, S. M. (1980). *Image and Mind.* Cambridge, MA: Harvard University Press.

Kosslyn, S. M. (1994). *Image and Brain: The resolution of the imagery debate.* Cambridge, MA: MIT Press.

Kosslyn, S. M., Cave, C. B., Provost, D. & Von Gierke, S. (1988). Sequential processes in image generation. *Cognitive Psychology, 20,* 319–343.

Logie, R. H. (1986). Visuo-spatial processing in working memory. *Quarterly Journal of Experimental Psychology, 38A,* 229–247.

Logie, R. H. (1995). *Visuo-Spatial Working Memory*. Hove: LEA.

Logie, R. H. & Pearson, D. G. (1997). The inner eye and the inner scribe of visuo-spatial working memory: Evidence from developmental fractionation. *European Journal of Cognitive Psychology, 9(3),* 241–257.

Logie, R. H. & Salway, A. F. S. (1990). Working memory and modes of thinking: A secondary task approach. In K. Gilhooly, M. Keane, R. Logie & G. Erdos (Eds.), *Lines of Thinking: Reflections on the psychology of thought, Vol. 2,* pp. 99–113. Chichester: Wiley.

McConnell, J. & Quinn, J. G. (1996). Interference at the encoding and maintenance of visual information. *Psychologische Beitrage, 38(3/4),* 343–354.

Miller, A. I. (1984). *Imagery in Scientific Thought: Creating 20th century physics.* Boston: Birkhauser.

Neblett, D. R., Finke, R. A. & Ginsburg, H. (1989). Creative visual discoveries in physical and mental synthesis. Unpublished manuscript.

Pearson, D. G., De Beni, R. & Cornoldi, C. (in press). The generation, maintenance, and transformation of visuo-spatial mental images. In M. Denis, C. Cornoldi, R. H. Logie, M. de Vega & J. Engelkamp (Eds.), *Imagery, Language, and Visuo-Spatial Thinking*. Hove: The Psychology Press.

Pearson, D. G. & Logie, R. H. & Gilhooly, K. (1999). Verbal representations and spatial manipulation during mental synthesis. *European Journal of Cognitive Psychology 11,* 295–314.

Pearson, D. G., Logie, R. H. & Gilhooly, K. (1998). Creative synthesis and executive resources: The impact of computer-based stimulus support. Paper presented at the *15th Annual BPS Cognitive Section Conference,* Bristol.

Pearson, D. G., Logie, R. H. & Green, C. (1996). Mental manipulation, visual working memory, and executive processes. *Psychologische Beitrage*, 38(3/4), 324-342.

Purcell, A. T. & Gero, J. S. (1998). Drawings and the design process. *Design Studies, 19(4),* 389–430.

Quinn, J. G. & McConnell, J. (1996a). Irrelevant pictures in visual working memory. *Quarterly Journal of Experimental Psychology: Human Experimental Psychology, 49A(1),* 200–215.

Quinn, J. G. & McConnell, J. (1996b). Exploring the passive visual store. *Psychologische Beitrage*, 38(3/4), 355–367.

Quinn, J. G. & Ralston, G. E. (1986). Movement and attention in visual working memory. *Quarterly Journal of Experimental Psychology, 38(A),* 689–703.

Reed, S. K. (1993). Imagery and Discovery. In B. Roskos-Ewoldsen, M. J. Intons-Peterson & R. Anderson (Eds.), *Imagery, Creativity and Discovery: A cognitive perspective.* Amsterdam: North-Holland.

Reed, S. K. & Johnsen, J. A. (1975). Detection of parts in patterns and images. *Memory & Cognition, 3,* 569–575.

Reisberg, D. (1996). The nonambiguity of mental images. In C. Cornoldi, R. H. Logie, M. A. Brandimonte, G. Kaufmann, and D. Reisberg (Ed.), *Stretching the Imagination:*

Representation and transformation in mental imagery. New York: Oxford University Press.

Reisberg, D., Wilson, M. & Smith, J. D. (1991). Auditory imagery and inner speech. In R. H. Logie & M. Denis (Eds.), *Mental Images in Human Cognition.* Amsterdam: North-Holland.

Roskos-Ewoldsen, B. (1993). Discovering emergent properties of images. In B. Roskos-Ewoldsen, M. J. Intons-Peterson & R. Anderson (Eds.), *Imagery, Creativity and Discovery: A cognitive perspective.* Amsterdam: North-Holland.

Salame, P. & Baddeley, A. D. (1982). Disruption of short-term memory by unattended speech: Implications for the structure of working memory. *Journal of Verbal Learning and Verbal Behaviour, 21,* 150–64.

Salame, P. & Baddeley, A. D. (1987). Noise, unattended speech and short-term memory. *Ergonomics, 30,* 1185–1193.

Salame, P. & Baddeley, A. D. (1989). Effects of background music on phonological short-term memory. *Quarterly Journal of Experimental Psychology, 41(A),* 107–122.

Salway, A. F. S. & Logie, R. H. (1995). Visuo-spatial working memory, movement control, and executive demands. *British Journal of Psychology, 86,* 253–269.

Sims, V. K. & Hegarty, M. (1997). Mental animation in the visuospatial sketchpad: Evidence from dual-task studies. *Memory and Cognition, 25(3),* 321–332.

Smyth, M. M. & Pelky, P. L. (1992). Short-term retention of spatial information. *British Journal of Psychology, 83,* 359–374.

Smyth, M. M. & Pendleton, L. R. (1989). Working memory for movements. *Quarterly Journal of Experimental Psychology, 41(A),* 235–250.

Suwa, M. & Tversky, B. (1996). What architects see in their sketches: Implications for design tools. *CHI 96 Companion.* Vancouver, B. C., Canada.

Vernon, P. E. (Ed., 1970). *Creativity.* Suffolk: Penguin Books Ltd.

Verstijnen, I. M., van Leeuwen, C., Goldschmidt, G., Hamel, R. & Hennessey, J. M. (1998). Creative discovery in imagery and perception: Combining is relatively easy, restructuring takes a sketch. *Acta Psychologica, 99,* 177–200.

Watson, J. D. (1968). *The Double Helix.* New York: New American Library.

Subject Index

A
Aesopworld xii, 164
affordances x, 24, 25, 27, 30, 227
agent 150, 153, 164, 174, 177, 182-184, 257, 297
Archimedes xiii, 201, 208-210

B
Baddeley, A. 7, 17, 235, 245, 348, 349, 351-353, 356, 357, 359
Barwise, J. xiii, 303, 311
Bloomsday xiv
Boltzmann, L. 185
Bourdieu, P. 137, 141-145

C
central executive system 351, 355
Chameleon vi, xii, 149, 150, 152-156, 159, 162-165, 169
Chomsky, N. 273, 281
cognitive architecture 19, 21, 22, 29
cognitive map xi, xiv, 66, 105, 114, 125, 126
cognitive style 301, 302
cognitive vector system 49
Cohn, A. 83, 84, 86, 87, 103, 104
configurational knowledge 105-107, 110-112, 122-124
coupled architectures 23, 24
creative synthesis 349-351, 353-355, 358

D
Davidson, D. 278, 281
deictic reference 70, 152, 153, 159
deixis 73, 129, 169
describer 35-40, 42
diagrammatic reasoning vi, x, xii, 147, 209, 211, 312
dispositif 142, 143
Dowty, D. 281

E
educational software 185, 187
egocentric cognition x
Einstein, A. xii, 185, 347, 357
episodic construction trace xv, 319, 320, 325, 327
Etchemendy, J. 303, 311
Evans, G. 5, 8, 18, 33, 35, 42, 43, 318, 327
explorer 35-40, 42

F
Feldman, J. 163, 166, 211, 212
figure object 179, 251
Foucault, M. 141-145
frame of reference 4, 16, 33, 45, 254, 256, 294
Franklin, N. xi, 48, 49, 65, 71, 74, 75, 80, 81, 285, 287, 296

G
Gapp, K-P 265, 287, 296
Gardner, H. 186, 197, 347, 357
gender differences ix, 3-19, 122
Geometry Machine 200, 201
Gibson, J.J. 24, 30, 47, 66, 123, 124, 227, 229
GIS (Geographical Information Systems) vi, x, xii, xiii, 17, 83, 147, 213-216, 225, 227-232, 282, 297
Gulyas, B. 329, 346

H
habitus 141, 142
Hayes-Roth, B. 45, 67, 317, 327
HCI (Human-Computer interaction) 128, 173, 181
Herman, J. 106, 124
Herskovits, A. xiv, 136, 162, 166, 178, 179, 181, 184, 214, 220, 229, 250, 251, 252-257, 261, 264, 265
hippocampal place cells 106
hippocampus xi, 125
Hypergami xii, 187-192, 195, 197

I
image schema 215, 216, 218, 220
intelligent multimedia ix, x, 165, 166, 175
intellimedia x, xii, 149-153, 164, 165, 167
intersubjective cognition x
invariants xv, 21

J
Jackendoff, R. xiv, 250, 253, 256, 265, 271, 276, 281, 282
Johnson, M. xiii,, 214-216, 220, 230
Johnson-Laird, P. 30, 70, 81, 230, 235, 245, 250, 265, 285, 297, 308, 317, 319, 320, 321, 325-327

K
Kamp, H. 282
Kant, I. 131
Kosslyn, S. 65, 66, 149, 167, 329, 338, 345, 348, 352, 357

L
landmarks 3, 21, 28, 29, 33, 34, 41, 43, 45, 46, 49-53, 55-59, 61-65, 105, 124, 325, 326
large-scale space 45-47, 58, 220
Lemon, O. 300, 312
locomotion 19, 23, 29, 124
Logic Theorist 199, 200
LTM (long term memory) x, 332

M
map reading 4-6, 11, 16-18
Marr, D. 250, 265
mass media ix
Mcluhan, M. 144, 145
Mcnamara, T. 47, 58, 66, 317, 328, 329, 345
mental imagery xiii, 18, 168, 186, 197, 345, 347, 351, 352, 356, 357, 359
mental models v, xi, xv, 30, 69, 71, 73-75, 78-81, 173, 230, 235, 245, 265, 292, 296, 297, 300, 308, 319, 325-328
metric relations 214
Mozart, W. 347
multimedia documents vi, xiii, 233-235, 239, 245
multimodal vi, x, xii, 150, 156, 163, 164, 167, 168, 171, 172, 181, 312
multiple relations model 178

N
navigation ix, 4, 17, 18, 43, 45, 46, 67, 106, 123-126, 130, 141, 268, 270, 272, 273, 277, 278, 281, 282, 327
Nous Research ix, 171, 249

O
O'Keefe, J. xi, 45, 66, 106, 107, 125
object-to-object v, 45-47, 49-51, 53, 61, 65
OpenGL xii, 174, 175, 182

P
Pentland, A. 149, 168
Poincare, H. 347
Polanyi, M. 132, 136
pragmatics xiv, 273-275, 280, 283
premise integration 318, 320, 325
principles and parameters syntax xiv, 273

R
reference object xiv, 162, 175, 177, 251-253, 255, 256, 261, 297
route knowledge 105
route map 34, 38

S
Schneiderman, B. 173
self-reference v, xi, 45, 48-50, 52, 61, 65
sex differences x, 18
Shephard, R. xiii
shortcuts 34, 35, 37, 39-42
Sonas vi, x, xi, xii, 171, 174, 175, 178, 179, 181-183, 264
spatial cognition 1, i, iii, v, vi, ix, 3, 4, 17, 19, 33, 34, 43, 66, 79, 80, 107, 124-127, 136, 149, 166, 184, 197, 227, 229, 231, 233, 235, 244, 250, 264, 265, 296, 297
spatial heuristics 196
spatial inferences vi, xv, 29, 80, 81, 226, 232, 285, 296, 329, 346
spatial language 163, 175, 249, 253, 264, 265, 272, 297, 325
spatial memory v, 45, 46, 58, 66, 124-126
spatial mental models v, 69, 74, 80, 81, 297, 325, 328
spatial metaphor 140
spatial prepositions xiv, 168, 183, 214, 216, 226, 227, 252, 253, 321
spatial reasoning xv, 83, 84, 130, 186, 195, 211, 223, 228-230, 264, 287, 294, 303, 326
spatial relation xv, 69, 71, 162, 163, 175, 177, 178, 223, 226, 251, 254, 261, 297
spatial representation xiv, 14, 35, 36, 41, 42, 45, 83, 104, 116, 123, 243, 250, 251, 250, 256-258, 260, 302, 341
spatial semantics vi, xiii, 199
Spoken Image 128, 174, 175, 184, 264
STM (Short Term Memory) ix, x, xv
survey map 34, 35, 38

T
Talmy, L. 251, 265
temporal scenario 233, 234
Tensors xv
tent-maze v, 105, 107, 108, 111, 120, 122, 123
territory 28, 142
theme ix, x, xi, 138, 177, 179, 186, 190, 197, 257, 272-274, 278
topological relations 103, 104, 214, 217, 228
topology v, ix, 83, 84, 86, 88, 93, 103, 104, 185, 197, 219, 231
transformation matrix 69, 286-290, 293
Tversky, B xi, 14, 18, 34, 35, 38, 43, 46, 48, 65, 67, 71, 74, 75, 80, 81, 235, 243, 245, 271, 281, 283, 285, 296, 317, 328, 347, 359

V

verbal condition 330, 332-335, 337-339, 341, 342, 344
virtual reality ix, 138, 264, 267, 268
visual condition 330, 332, 334, 336, 339, 341, 342, 344
visual storage 351
Vitra xii, 163, 296

W

working memory vii, x, 7, 8, 11, 16-18, 47, 235, 236, 309, 345, 347, 348, 350-353, 355-359
WYSIWYG 234

Z

zoom and filter 173

In the series ADVANCES IN CONSCIOUSNESS RESEARCH (AiCR) the following titles have been published thus far or are scheduled for publication:

1. GLOBUS, Gordon G.: *The Postmodern Brain.* 1995.
2. ELLIS, Ralph D.: *Questioning Consciousness. The interplay of imagery, cognition, and emotion in the human brain.* 1995.
3. JIBU, Mari and Kunio YASUE: *Quantum Brain Dynamics and Consciousness. An introduction.* 1995.
4. HARDCASTLE, Valerie Gray: *Locating Consciousness.* 1995.
5. STUBENBERG, Leopold: *Consciousness and Qualia.* 1998.
6. GENNARO, Rocco J.: *Consciousness and Self-Consciousness. A defense of the higher-order thought theory of consciousness.* 1996.
7. MAC CORMAC, Earl and Maxim I. STAMENOV (eds): *Fractals of Brain, Fractals of Mind. In search of a symmetry bond.* 1996.
8. GROSSENBACHER, Peter G. (ed.): *Finding Consciousness in the Brain. A neuro-cognitive approach.* n.y.p.
9. Ó NUALLÁIN, Seán, Paul MC KEVITT and Eoghan MAC AOGÁIN (eds): *Two Sciences of Mind. Readings in cognitive science and consciousness.* 1997.
10. NEWTON, Natika: *Foundations of Understanding.* 1996.
11. PYLKKÖ, Pauli: *The Aconceptual Mind. Heideggerian themes in holistic naturalism.* 1998.
12. STAMENOV, Maxim I. (ed.): *Language Structure, Discourse and the Access to Consciousness.* 1997.
13. VELMANS, Max (ed.): *Investigating Phenomenal Consciousness. Methodologies and Maps.* 2000.
14. SHEETS-JOHNSTONE, Maxine: *The Primacy of Movement.* 1999.
15. CHALLIS, Bradford H. and Boris M. VELICHKOVSKY (eds.): *Stratification in Cognition and Consciousness.* 1999.
16. ELLIS, Ralph D. and Natika NEWTON (eds.): *The Caldron of Consciousness. Motivation, affect and self-organization – An anthology.* 2000.
17. HUTTO, Daniel D.: *The Presence of Mind.* 1999.
18. PALMER, Gary B. and Debra J. OCCHI (eds.): *Languages of Sentiment. Cultural constructions of emotional substrates.* 1999.
19. DAUTENHAHN, Kerstin (ed.): *Human Cognition and Social Agent Technology.* 2000.
20. KUNZENDORF, Robert G. and Benjamin WALLACE (eds.): *Individual Differences in Conscious Experience.* 2000.
21. HUTTO, Daniel D.: *Beyond Physicalism.* 2000.
22. ROSSETTI, Yves and Antti REVONSUO (eds.): *Beyond Dissociation. Interaction between dissociated implicit and explicit processing.* 2000.
23. ZAHAVI, Dan (ed.): *Exploring the Self. Philosophical and psychopathological perspectives on self-experience.* 2000.
24. ROVEE-COLLIER, Carolyn, Harlene HAYNE and Michael COLOMBO: *The Development of Implicit and Explicit Memory.* 2000.
25. BACHMANN, Talis: *Microgenetic Approach to the Conscious Mind.* n.y.p.
26. Ó NUALLÁIN, Seán (ed.): *Spatial Cognition. Selected papers from Mind III, Annual Conference of the Cognitive Science Society of Ireland, 1998.* 2000.

27. McMILLAN, John and Grant R. GILLETT: *Consciousness and Intentionality.* n.y.p.
28. ZACHAR, Peter: *Psychological Concepts and Biological Psychiatry. A philosophical analysis.* n.y.p.
29. VAN LOOCKE, Philip (ed.): *The Physical Nature of Consciousness.* n.y.p.
30. BROOK, Andrew and Richard C. DeVIDI (eds.): *Self-awareness and Self-reference.* n.y.p.
31. RAKOVER, Sam S. and Baruch CAHLON: *Face Recognition. Cognitive and computational processes.* n.y.p.